Apache Maven 2
Effective Implementation

Build and manage applications with Maven, Continuum, and Archiva

Maria Odea Ching

Brett Porter

BIRMINGHAM - MUMBAI

Apache Maven 2 Effective Implementation
Build and manage applications with Maven, Continuum, and Archiva

First published: September 2009

Production Reference: 1080909

Published by Packt Publishing Ltd.
32 Lincoln Road
Olton
Birmingham, B27 6PA, UK.

ISBN 978-1-847194-54-1

www.packtpub.com

Cover Image by Vinayak Chittar (vinayak.chittar@gmail.com)

Credits

Authors

Maria Odea Ching

Brett Porter

Reviewers

Wendy Smoak

Emmanuel Venisse

Carsten Ziegeler

Acquisition Editor

Sarah Cullington

Development Editor

Dhiraj Chandiramani

Technical Editors

Neha Damle

John Antony

Indexer

Monica Ajmera

Rekha Nair

Editorial Team Leader

Gagandeep Singh

Project Team Leader

Priya Mukherji

Project Coordinator

Leena Purkait

Drawing Coordinator

Nilesh Mohite

Proofreader

Lesley Harrison

Production Coordinator

Shantanu Zagade

Cover Work

Shantanu Zagade

About the Authors

Maria Odea Ching grew up in Daet, a small town in the Philippines, then moved to the country's capital, Manila, when she went to college. She took up Computer Studies at De La Salle University, and graduated in 2004. She started using open source tools from her first job after graduating. From then on, she got interested in the open source philosophy. She was introduced to Apache Maven, Apache Continuum, and Apache Archiva early on in her career. She became a committer and a Project Management Committee member of Apache Maven. Eventually, she was elected as PMC Chair of Apache Archiva. She is also a member of the Apache Software Foundation.

Deng is currently a Senior Software Engineer and serves as the development lead for the Maestro project.

First, I'd like to thank Brett for the whirlwind endeavor which is this book. I'd also like to thank all our reviewers—Wendy, Emmanuel, Carsten and the Packt team, for taking the time to review and go through each chapter. You guys rock! And of course without the communities of Maven, Continuum, and Archiva, we wouldn't have anything to write about. So I'd like to thank each and everyone (committers/developers, contributors, buggers) in these respective communities. I'd also like to give special thanks to our Exist/G2iX family for their continuous support.

And last but definitely not the least, I'd like to thank my family and my boyfriend, Mike, for their unfaltering love and support and for being so patient and understanding when I have to run off to work on the book.

Brett Porter is a software developer from Sydney, Australia with a passion for development tooling and automation. Seeking a more standardized and reproducible solution to organize, build, and deploy a number of software projects across teams, he discovered an early beta of Maven 1.0 in 2003, and has been heavily involved in the development of the project since. He is a member of the Apache Maven Project Management Committee, and has conducted presentations and training on Maven and related tooling at several conferences and events. He founded the Archiva project in 2005. Brett is also a Director and Member of the Apache Software Foundation.

Brett is currently VP, Product Development at G2iX, in charge of the MaestroDev division. He and his team seek to make developers more efficient by offering support and services for development and automation tools including Apache Maven, Apache Continuum, Apache Archiva, and Selenium.

Brett was co-author of the book *Better Builds with Maven*, the first book to be written about the Maven 2.0 release in 2005, and has been involved in reviewing *Maven: A Developer's Notebook* and *Java Power Tools*.

I'd first like to thank my co-author and friend Deng for agreeing to participate in this book and lending her experience with Archiva and Continuum. I am grateful to all of the reviewers that volunteered their time to help make this the best that it can be. My great thanks go to all the members of the open source community that participate in these projects — the developers, as well as those that contribute patches, detailed bug reports, or answer questions on the user lists — not only do we build great software together, but I get the chance to work with truly remarkable individuals.

Finally, my love and thanks go to my wife Laura for sparing some more of our precious time so that I could complete this book, and for supporting me in everything I do.

About the Reviewers

Wendy Smoak is a member of The Apache Software Foundation and a committer on several open source projects, where she focuses on user support, documentation, and infrastructure. By day she is a Solutions Architect with G2iX, where her work centers around enterprise adoption of Apache Maven and related technologies.

Emmanuel Venisse has been developing and architecting J2EE applications for eleven years for bank, government, and holiday company projects. For the past three years, he's been working for Mergere/Devzuz with some other Maven contributors, like Brett and Deng, around a packaged Maven/Continuum/ Archiva product—Maestro. He has been working freelance for five years. For the last six years, he's been working, in his spare time, on Maven, Continuum, and Archiva projects as a core developer, and he's the Continuum project chair. He has contributed too to *Maven: A Developer's Notebook* (O'Reilly) and *Better build with Maven* (Exist). He lives in Versailles, France, with his wife Florence and two children.

I would first like to thank my wife, Florence, without whose love and support, my work on Apache projects and this book wouldn't have been possible. I'd also like to thank my children who have to see their dad working on his laptop instead of playing with them. Finally, I'd like to thank Brett and Deng for letting me help them on this book.

Carsten Ziegeler is senior developer and software architect for JEE and portal applications at Day Software. He is a member of the Apache Software Foundation and has been participating in several open source projects for more than fifteen years. Carsten is a member of several Apache communities and project management committees such as Cocoon, Felix, Sling, Excalibur, and Portals. In addition to this, Carsten frequently writes artcles, reviews books, and can be found presenting at various conferences.

Table of Contents

Preface

This book offers a comprehensive look at using Maven on a project, covering not only the build system itself, but how it is best used in concert with other development infrastructures such as source control, continuous integration and build servers, and an artifact repository. We cover this territory using Subversion, Apache Continuum, and Apache Archiva, respectively, though the concepts learned should apply to other comparable systems.

In many ways, this is the book we've always wanted to write about Maven, and it takes a different approach to the existing Maven titles. Rather than being a reference or documentation for the software, it takes the approach of walking through a single example application and associated infrastructure in the same way that you would develop your own projects. For this purpose, we have crafted the example application Centrepoint—a simple but functional web application composed of several modules that itself interacts with Maven, Continuum, and Archiva.

We believe this book will not only show you how to use Maven, but how to use it *effectively*, covering concepts and best practices that should endure beyond the current versions of Maven and apply to your development infrastructure and teams in general.

What this book covers

Chapter 1: Maven in a Nutshell is a quick overview of the fundamentals of Maven—from creating a simple Maven project to basic plugin configuration to generating sites and reports. These are demonstrated in an easy to follow step-by-step process. By the end of the chapter, you should be able to apply and use the skills that you have learned to your own project.

Chapter 2: Staying in Control with Archiva introduces you to Archiva and its role in building software. You will learn the basics of installing and configuring it for internal use. It also shows you how Archiva complements Maven and how they can be used together efficiently.

Chapter 3: Building an Application Using Maven delves into the details on how to accurately set up and build an application using Maven. The Centrepoint project is introduced in this chapter. This is the sample application that will be used for the hands-on demonstrations throughout the book. You will see how Maven enforces convention over configuration while building the Centrepoint project.

Chapter 4: Application Testing with Maven goes through the various types of automated tests that can be executed from Maven. This includes unit testing, integration testing, and testing web applications using Selenium to name a few. Instrumenting tests, implementing test coverage, and reporting of test results are also covered.

Chapter 5: Reporting and Checks shows how to configure Maven to generate project reports and incorporate them in the generated site. This chapter also tackles the basics on enforcing certain rules or checks on your code such as conforming to code styles and standards, and finding common bugs in the code while building your application.

Chapter 6: Useful Maven Plugins discusses some of the Maven plugins, both from Apache Maven and from the Codehaus Mojo project, that may be of great help in your Maven builds. The functionality of these plugins range from keeping track of the source revision number for the build to executing external applications as part of the build. You will learn to identify when to use each plugin and how to configure them properly to address your need.

Chapter 7: Maven Best Practices illustrates the effective usage of Maven. You will learn tips and tricks for setting up your development environment to managing your project dependencies to making your builds portable and reproducible. By the end of this chapter, you should be able to apply what you've learned to your next project, or even to your current one.

Chapter 8: Continuum: Ensuring the health of your source code highlights the importance of continuous integration in software development through Continuum. It covers basic installation and set up, adding projects to Continuum, and effective configuration and build scheduling, at the same time demonstrating how it works in accordance with Maven and also with Archiva.

Chapter 9: Continuum in Depth deals with releasing projects using both Maven and Continuum. The different phases involved in the release process will be covered along with a bit of troubleshooting on the side. You will also learn about building multiple projects simultaneously in Continuum through parallel and distributed builds.

Chapter 10: Archiva in a Team gives you the more advanced features of Archiva and demonstrates how to configure it for use in a team. You will learn how to control access to a repository, how to take advantage of repository groups, how to make use of its reporting feature, and how to maintain your Archiva repositories.

Chapter 11: Archetypes covers Maven archetypes. It discusses some of the archetypes available—what their purpose is and what the generated project from each archetype looks like. You will also create a custom archetype specifically for the Centrepoint application, which will be used in the last chapter.

Chapter 12: Maven, Archiva, and Continuum in the Enterprise shows how to configure Archiva and Continuum effectively for use in the corporate environment. Tips on how to set up projects and repositories across multiple projects with respect to controlling who and what can be accessed by different teams covers the first half of the chapter. The second part demonstrates the web services feature of both applications by creating plugins for the Centrepoint application and using them to get information from Archiva and Continuum.

Appendix A: Troubleshooting Maven provides techniques for troubleshooting Maven. Incorrect POM or settings configuration, and dependency and download problems are a few of the usual suspects that will be covered here.

Appendix B: Recent Maven Features discusses the new features in Maven 2.1 and above. These features include password encryption, reactor project selection, and parallel downloads of dependencies.

Appendix C: Migrating Archiva and Continuum Data illustrates how to migrate data in Archiva and Continuum when upgrading to a higher version. How to switch to a different database from the built-in one is also discussed.

What you need for this book

You need to have the following software installed:

- Java 5 or above
- Subversion 1.4
- An outgoing mail server for some examples

We will be installing the following applications throughout the book:

- Apache Maven 2.2
- Apache Archiva 1.2
- Apache Continuum 1.3

Who this book is for

This book is for Java developers who want to get started with Apache Maven. If you are tasked with build automation in your company, this book will help you to quickly and easily get started with Maven in order to improve the efficiency of your builds.

Conventions

In this book, you will find a number of styles of text that distinguish between different kinds of information. Here are some examples of these styles, and an explanation of their meaning.

Code words in text are shown as follows: "We can include other contexts through the use of the `include` directive."

A block of code is set as follows:

```
<dependencies>
  <dependency>
    <groupId>${project.groupId}</groupId>
    <artifactId>model</artifactId>
    <version>${project.version}</version>
  </dependency>
</dependencies>
```

When we wish to draw your attention to a particular part of a code block, the relevant lines or items are set in bold:

```
<plugin>
  <groupId>org.apache.maven.plugins</groupId>
  <artifactId>maven-surefire-plugin</artifactId>
  <configuration>
    <forkMode>never</forkMode>
  </configuration>
</plugin>
```

Any command-line input or output is written as follows:

```
distribution$ mvn integration-test
```

New terms and **important words** are shown in bold. Words that you see on the screen, in menus or dialog boxes for example, appear in the text like this: "clicking the **Next** button moves you to the next screen".

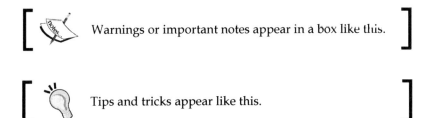

Warnings or important notes appear in a box like this.

Tips and tricks appear like this.

Reader feedback

Feedback from our readers is always welcome. Let us know what you think about this book — what you liked or may have disliked. Reader feedback is important for us to develop titles that you really get the most out of.

To send us general feedback, simply send an email to feedback@packtpub.com, and mention the book title via the subject of your message.

If there is a book that you need and would like to see us publish, please send us a note in the **SUGGEST A TITLE** form on www.packtpub.com or email suggest@packtpub.com.

If there is a topic that you have expertise in and you are interested in either writing or contributing to a book on, see our author guide on www.packtpub.com/authors.

Customer support

Now that you are the proud owner of a Packt book, we have a number of things to help you to get the most from your purchase.

Downloading the example code for the book

Visit http://www.packtpub.com/files/code/4541_Code.zip to directly download the example code.

The downloadable files contain instructions on how to use them.

Errata

Although we have taken every care to ensure the accuracy of our content, mistakes do happen. If you find a mistake in one of our books — maybe a mistake in the text or the code — we would be grateful if you would report this to us. By doing so, you can save other readers from frustration, and help us to improve subsequent versions of this book. If you find any errata, please report them by visiting http://www.packtpub.com/support, selecting your book, clicking on the **let us know** link, and entering the details of your errata. Once your errata are verified, your submission will be accepted and the errata added to any list of existing errata. Any existing errata can be viewed by selecting your title from http://www.packtpub.com/support.

Piracy

Piracy of copyright material on the Internet is an ongoing problem across all media. At Packt, we take the protection of our copyright and licenses very seriously. If you come across any illegal copies of our works, in any form, on the Internet, please provide us with the location address or web site name immediately so that we can pursue a remedy.

Please contact us at copyright@packtpub.com with a link to the suspected pirated material.

We appreciate your help in protecting our authors, and our ability to bring you valuable content.

Questions

You can contact us at questions@packtpub.com if you are having a problem with any aspect of the book, and we will do our best to address it.

1
Maven in a Nutshell

In this chapter, we will take a comprehensive look at the fundamentals of Maven, by example. Moreover, we will also look at the associated terminology that we will be using in this book. If you are already a frequent Maven user, you may only need to skim through this chapter to refresh yourself on some of the basic principles.

For those who are new to Maven; other books and the Maven documentation have covered some of this content in more detail already—so this is the only review we will spend on the basics of Maven. Beyond this chapter, we will assume that you are confident in updating the Maven project without step-by-step instructions so that we can quickly get into more interesting examples.

A whirlwind tour

The best way to get to know Maven is by seeing it in action. In this section, we will create a simple project and explore the different ways in which you can use Maven in it.

Installing Maven

Of course, first we will need to install Maven. If you haven't done this already, you can download and install the latest version by following the instructions from `http://maven.apache.org/download.html`. The samples in this book have been checked against Maven 2.2.1.

Luckily, this is a very simple process. It has only two steps, which any user should be familiar with:

1. Unzip the Maven distribution to the location you would like to install it, such as `/usr/local` or `C:\Program Files`. The distribution stores everything under a subdirectory, for example `apache-maven-2.2.1`. We will refer to this location as `M2_HOME`, so for example this would be `/usr/local/apache-maven-2.2.1`.

2. Add the `bin` subdirectory of `M2_HOME` to your `PATH` variable.

You should verify the installation by running the following command:

```
$ mvn --version
```

A successful result will look similar to the following results from my machine:

```
Maven version: 2.2.1

Java version: 1.5.0_13

Default locale: en_AU, platform encoding: MacRoman

OS name: "mac os x" version: "10.5.4" arch: "i386" family: "unix"
```

Maven is now ready to use.

 There is one situation where you will need to go through an additional configuration step. As Maven downloads much of its functionality from the Internet, and stores it locally, you will need a direct Internet connection. If you would prefer to set up a permanent, shared storage area in your own network (or on your machine) up front, look at how to install a **repository manager** in Chapter 2, *Staying in Control with Archiva*. Once populated, this can allow you to work without an Internet connection whenever necessary.

If you are behind a firewall and need to use an HTTP proxy, you will need to edit the `<M2_HOME>/conf/settings.xml` file, following the template for instructions on how to add the HTTP proxy configuration. This file can also be copied to your home directory, under `<USER_HOME>/.m2/settings.xml`, if you would prefer the settings to be used when you install a different version of Maven.

Troubleshooting
If you have any further problems with Maven failing as it attempts to download these components as you work through this chapter, check out the Appendix A, *Troubleshooting Maven* later in this book.

Creating a new project from an archetype

Maven makes it very simple to start a new project with **archetypes**. An archetype is a template project for a particular type of module, which ranges from a simple JAR or WAR module to a more complete template application for many popular frameworks. Archetypes extend the Maven concept of building on conventions by allowing them to be shared in reusable chunks. In Chapter 11, *Archetypes*, we will discuss how you can create and publish your own archetypes to establish reusable conventions for starting modules and projects in your own organization.

In this chapter, we will create a simple Java web application from an archetype to learn how to apply Maven's functionality to a sample project.

To start your sample project, run the following command from an empty directory to invoke Maven's archetype plugin:

```
$ mvn archetype:generate
```

 You may have seen a command similar to `archetype:create` used in examples elsewhere. This is an older, now deprecated, form of the archetype goal which can be replaced by a corresponding `archetype:generate` goal.

If this is the first time you have run the archetype plugin, you will notice that Maven spends some time downloading the archetype functionality as well as the other Java libraries that it uses. These files are stored in your **local repository** for re-use in the future.

The local repository consists of both a local cache of downloaded libraries and a place to store your own projects as they are built, before they are published for other users. By default, the local repository is stored in the `.m2/repository` subdirectory of your home directory, which can be deleted at any time if necessary.

The local repository acts as an *intermediary* between your builds and a Maven **remote repository**, which is a canonical shared storage area for builds that is commonly hosted on an HTTP server, but can also be accessed using a local filesystem—FTP, SSH, and more.

One particular remote repository that is of note is the Maven **central repository**. Included by default in all Maven builds, and it contains not only Maven's plugins and their required dependencies but also a large host of releases of other open source projects.

On your machine, there is only one single local repository. You can connect to any number of remote repositories for a single build if needed. It is important in all Maven projects to carefully select the remote repositories to be used and to manage your own remote repositories for sharing artifacts among projects. This will be discussed more in detail in Chapter 7, *Maven Best Practices*.

Once the downloads finish from the earlier `archetype` command, you will be prompted (with a long list!) to select an archetype to generate the project from. A similar but abbreviated list is shown below:

```
Choose archetype:

1: internal -> appfuse-basic-jsf (AppFuse archetype for creating a web
application with Hibernate, Spring and JSF)

[...]

15: internal -> maven-archetype-quickstart ()

16: internal -> maven-archetype-site-simple (A simple site generation
project)

17: internal -> maven-archetype-site (A more complex site project)

18: internal -> maven-archetype-webapp (A simple Java web application)

[...]

Choose a number:  (1/2/3/4/5/6/7/8/9/10/11/12/13/14/15/16/17/18/19/20/21/
22/23/24/25/26/27/28/29/30/31/32/33/34/35/36/37/38/39/40/41/42/43/44) 15:
```

Among the many choices, the default is the *quick start* archetype that is used in Maven's getting started guide. This is a good choice for a minimal Maven project or an archetype from which new modules can be built (particularly for JAR projects).

However, in this example, we will be using the simple Java web application. So go ahead and enter the number corresponding to that archetype (at the time of writing it was **18**) and press *Enter*.

A number of projects take advantage of Maven's archetype mechanism to deliver a template project for their framework. A sample of these can be seen at http://docs.codehaus.org/ display/MAVENUSER/Archetypes+List. One in particular to note is **Appfuse** (http://appfuse.org/), which assembles ready-to-use stacks of popular combinations of open source web application frameworks, and is based on Maven's archetype technology. More information on these can be found in Chapter 11, *Archetypes*.

Each Maven project needs some coordinates to allow it to be identified by other Maven projects. These are called the **group ID, artifact ID**, and **version** (sometimes referred to as the **GAV**).

- **Group ID**: An identifier for a collection of related modules. This is usually a hierarchy that starts with the organization that produced the modules, and then possibly moves into the increasingly more specialized project or sub-projects that the artifacts are a part of. This can also be thought of as a *namespace*, and is structured much like the Java package system.

- **Artifact ID**: The Artifact ID is a unique identifier for a given module within a group.

- **Version**: The version is used to identify the release or build number of the project.

The archetype plugin prompts you for these coordinates to add to the project after you have chosen the type of archetype to use. We can use the following values for our sample web application:

```
Define value for groupId: : com.effectivemaven.chapter01

Define value for artifactId: : simple-webapp

Define value for version: 1.0-SNAPSHOT: : 1.0-SNAPSHOT

Define value for package: : com.effectivemaven.chapter01
```

The final prompt for a *package* is the Java package that will be used for source code, as this is a sample Java web application. It is not the *packaging* type that you want the project to take as that is provided by the archetype itself.

> You may have noticed that the version is referred to as a **snapshot**. In Maven, there are two types of versions: **releases** and **snapshots** (those that end in -SNAPSHOT). A snapshot should always be used by your projects during development as it has a special meaning to Maven to indicate that development is still occurring and that the project may change. A release is assumed never to change, so release versions (such as 1.1, 2.0, or 3.0-beta-5) should only be used for a single state of the project when it is released, and then updated to the next snapshot.

After entering the values above, you will be asked to confirm that the values are as you intended, and then the project will be created. If you see this highly desirable banner, then congratulations—you've created a Maven project!

```
[INFO] ------------------------------------------------------------
[INFO] BUILD SUCCESSFUL
[INFO] ------------------------------------------------------------
```

The created project will be stored in the `simple-webapp` subdirectory and should look as shown next:

```
`-- simple-webapp
    |-- pom.xml
    `-- src
        `-- main
            |-- resources
            `-- webapp
                |-- WEB-INF
                |   `-- web.xml
                `-- index.jsp
```

As far as web applications go, that is as simple as it gets. The `src/main/webapp` directory contains the basic web application, while `pom.xml` specifies the information Maven needs to know. This directory structure has followed the Maven convention for web applications, which means that only a minimal amount of configuration will be needed to construct a functional build. If you open `pom.xml`, you will see the following:

```xml
<project xmlns="http://maven.apache.org/POM/4.0.0" xmlns:xsi="http://
www.w3.org/2001/XMLSchema-instance"
  xsi:schemaLocation="http://maven.apache.org/POM/4.0.0 http://maven.
apache.org/maven-v4_0_0.xsd">
 <modelVersion>4.0.0</modelVersion>
 <groupId>com.effectivemaven.chapter01</groupId>
 <artifactId>simple-webapp</artifactId>
 <packaging>war</packaging>
 <version>1.0-SNAPSHOT</version>
 <name>simple-webapp Maven Webapp</name>
 <build>
  <finalName>simple-webapp</finalName>
 </build>
</project>
```

As you can see, the archetype has substituted in the coordinates that it prompted for earlier. It has also added the `war` packaging type to indicate that the build structure for the project is a web application. A default name has been added, which you would typically change to something which describes the project better.

This project file is sufficient to perform a large number of operations. For example, it can be used to assemble the web application archive or run the web application on a development server. Later, when we add some Java source code to the project, the shown configuration is enough for Maven to compile and include it in the web application, and even produce a source cross reference and Javadoc, if requested.

This is possible because Maven's declarative project model defines a number of well-known properties that the whole build can reuse for a number of different purposes. For this reason, the project file is referred to as the **POM**, which stands for **Project Object Model**.

The POM contains important pieces of information about the project, which include:

- The Maven coordinate of the project for reuse by other Maven projects
- The project name, description and license
- Project resource information such as the location of source control, issue tracking, and continuous integration
- The developers, contributors and organizations participating in the project

The POM will also include information about how the project should be built, such as:

- The source directory layout
- Dependencies on other projects
- Build requirements (by means of Maven plugins) and configuration

Maven projects use the concept of **inheritance**. This means that repetition can be avoided by sharing information in a common ancestor of a project. Such parents of the project are POMs themselves.

Nevertheless, let's take one step back—what does Maven mean by "a project"? In software development, the term **project** is very ambiguous—it could mean just one part of a larger application, a plan for one release of a particular subset of an application, or it could be the entire application itself.

In Maven, the term project refers to a **unit of work**. That is, it takes one particular set of sources and produces a build **artifact** identified by the project's coordinate. While a conventional project has a single build artifact, it is possible to attach more artifacts that are alternate derivatives of the same sources in some limited ways. It is also worth noting that a POM can be both an artifact in itself, and a piece of metadata associated with a particular artifact file.

While there are a number of fields in the project file that can be used to describe your project, or change defaults such as the location of source code, Maven defines a number of conventions that reduce the amount of configuration needed to get a standard project up and running. For example, this section is inherited into every Maven project as the default build paths:

```
<build>
 <directory>${project.basedir}/target</directory>
 <outputDirectory>
  ${project.build.directory}/classes
 </outputDirectory>
 <finalName>
  ${project.artifactId}-${project.version}
 </finalName>
 <testOutputDirectory>
  ${project.build.directory}/test-classes
 </testOutputDirectory>
 <sourceDirectory>
  ${project.basedir}/src/main/java
 </sourceDirectory>
 <scriptSourceDirectory>
  src/main/scripts
 </scriptSourceDirectory>
 <testSourceDirectory>
  ${project.basedir}/src/test/java
 </testSourceDirectory>
 <resources>
  <resource>
   <directory>
    ${project.basedir}/src/main/resources
   </directory>
  </resource>
 </resources>
 <testResources>
  <testResource>
   <directory>
    ${project.basedir}/src/test/resources
   </directory>
  </testResource>
 </testResources>
```

Various other settings are also pre-configured, including additional paths needed for certain packaging types such as the web application source directory we saw previously. Together these form the base of Maven's project conventions.

While each setting can be easily customized in an individual Maven project, the strength of following the conventions is that the build remains simpler and more familiar to someone new to a specific project.

For more information on what is available in the POM, refer to the **POM Reference** documentation at `http://maven.apache.org/pom.html`. We will also revisit the recommended practices for what information to include in the POM in Chapter 7, *Maven Best Practices*.

Building the project

The vast majority of the time that Maven is run, it is to build a project. So let's see how to do that for the simple web application we have created.

In Maven, the build is run using a predefined, ordered set of steps called the **build lifecycle**. The individual steps are called **phases**, and the same phases are run for every Maven build using the default lifecycle, no matter what it will produce. The build tasks that will be performed during each phase are determined by the configuration in the project file, and in particular the selected packaging.

Some of the most commonly used lifecycle phases in the default lifecycle are:

- `validate`—checks build prerequisites
- `compile`—compiles the source code identified for the build
- `test`—runs unit tests for the compiled code
- `package`—assembles the compiled code into a binary build result
- `install`—shares the build with other projects on the same machine
- `deploy`—publishes the build into a remote repository for other projects to use

The following is a complete list of phases available in Maven 2.2:

`validate, generate-sources, process-sources, generate-resources, process-resources, compile, process-classes, generate-test-sources, process-test-sources, generate-test-resources, process-test-resources, test-compile, test, prepare-package, package, integration-test, verify, install, deploy.`

The phases are designed to be run in sequence so that they can depend on the results of the previous phases. For example, choosing to run the `test` phase will first run `validate`, `compile`, and the other intermediate phases to ensure that the compiled code is up-to-date before running the tests.

To see the build lifecycle in action, run the following command from the directory that contains pom.xml:

```
simple-webapp$ mvn package
```

Again, if this is the first time you have built this project, Maven may download a few more JAR files to the local repository. A few seconds later, it should complete successfully, with an output that looks similar to the following:

```
[INFO] Scanning for projects...
[INFO] ------------------------------------------------------------
[INFO] Building simple-webapp Maven Webapp
[INFO]    task-segment: [package]
[INFO] ------------------------------------------------------------
[INFO] [resources:resources]
[INFO] Using default encoding to copy filtered resources.
[INFO] [compiler:compile]
[INFO] No sources to compile
[INFO] [resources:testResources]
[INFO] Using default encoding to copy filtered resources.
[INFO] [compiler:testCompile]
[INFO] No sources to compile
[INFO] [surefire:test]
[INFO] No tests to run.
[INFO] [war:war]
[INFO] Packaging webapp
[INFO] Assembling webapp[simple-webapp] in [/Users/brett/code/01/simple-
webapp/target/simple-webapp]
[INFO] Processing war project
[INFO] Copying webapp resources[/Users/brett/code/01/simple-webapp/src/
main/webapp]
[INFO] Webapp assembled in[78 msecs]
[INFO] Building war: /Users/brett/code/01/simple-webapp/target/simple-
webapp.war
[INFO] ------------------------------------------------------------
[INFO] BUILD SUCCESSFUL
[INFO] ------------------------------------------------------------
[INFO] Total time: 4 seconds
[INFO] Finished at: Sat Aug 30 22:20:59 EST 2008
[INFO] Final Memory: 7M/14M
[INFO] ------------------------------------------------------------
```

As you can see, the build has gone through a number of tasks, such as **[compiler: compile]**, **[war:war]**, and so on. These tasks are known as **goals**, and they are attached to the build lifecycle to give the build substance. Behind the scenes, Maven knows when to run all of these different goals in the build lifecycle based on the project type. In the case of a web application, it may have resources to include, Java source code to compile, and tests to compile and execute before finally being packaged. Even though the project doesn't currently contain all of these elements, Maven runs through the goals so that they are able to check their own input and process them if they are found.

In the last step of the build above, the **war:war** goal is run to package up the web application, including the resulting output from the earlier goals, as well as the content in the default location of `src/main/webapp`. The web application archive is produced in the `target` directory, which is Maven's default working directory. There you will find both the `target/simple-webapp` subdirectory that contains the *exploded*, or unpacked, web application contents ready to be packaged, and the `target/simple-webapp.war` file that contains those files after the packaging process.

> Notice that the filename `simple-webapp.war` omits the version number. As a best practice, Maven appends the version number to the archive by default, but in this case the project file specified a `finalName` that did not include the version number. This is handy for web applications as it is common to use the filename as the context path when it is dropped into a servlet container.

By laying out a standard pattern for builds through the build lifecycle, Maven is able to achieve a number of objectives. They are as follows:

- Developers do not need to re-learn a new process each time they move to a new project, as the phases are the same across Maven projects.
- It is easy to incorporate new tools into the lifecycle by binding them to certain phases, without any knowledge of which other tools and plugins have already been incorporated.

The separation of the build order from the selection of goals is important in incorporating new tools without repeating configuration or having to introduce new variables. Take source generation for example—the Compiler plugin knows that it can take a list of source directories from the project model and compile them into the work directory. However, it cannot know all of the various source generation mechanisms that it might need to run first to ensure that the sources are available to compile. Instead, we bind any source generation goals to the `generate-sources` phase of the lifecycle, which is guaranteed to occur before the `compile` phase, and insert any created sources into the project model for compilation.

In addition to the default build lifecycle we have seen above, it is worth noting that Maven has two other lifecycles built-in:

- **Clean lifecycle**: The command `mvn clean` is often used to remove Maven's work directory `target`. However, as some plugins can generate information that does not reside in the work area, it is possible for them to bind to the clean lifecycle to clean up after themselves as well. To help with ordering, the complete list of phases in the lifecycle is `pre-clean`, `clean`, and `post-clean`.

- **Site lifecycle**: While much of the site generation is coordinated by Maven's reporting mechanism, it is also possible to bind plugins to be executed as part of the site generation lifecycle. The phases available are `pre-site`, `site`, `post-site`, and `site-deploy`.

Reusing builds

Previously, we ran the command `mvn package`. If you just needed to produce a web application to test manually, this would be sufficient. However, what if you need to include it in a Java EAR file, or to build a self-contained distribution that includes the web application along with a servlet container? More commonly, what if you were building a JAR project instead that needed to be used by another Java project?

In Maven, instead of passing relative links to other projects and files in the build, projects share their build products in the form of build artifacts, with the mechanism for sharing these artifacts being the Maven repositories that we touched on earlier. We have already seen that Maven downloads remote dependencies to the **local repository**, and we can see here that this is also where Maven places artifacts to share with other builds that you run yourself from the same machine. Note that the local repository is not intended for sharing among multiple users, however, when it comes to publishing a build for other developers or projects to use, a **remote repository** is used instead.

To install the web application we have created already into the local repository, run the command in the folder that contains the `pom.xml` file:

```
simple-webapp$ mvn install
```

 This is the command (or perhaps `mvn clean install`) that you will run in almost all cases while building Maven projects.

First, notice that thanks to the build lifecycle this runs everything that
mvn package did first—it is not necessary to run both. However, this time,
it runs an additional step:

```
[INFO] [install:install]
[INFO] Writing transformed POM using encoding: UTF-8
[INFO] Installing /Users/brett/code/01/simple-webapp/target/simple-
webapp.war to /Users/brett/.m2/repository/com/effectivemaven/chapter01/
simple-webapp/1.0-SNAPSHOT/simple-webapp-1.0-SNAPSHOT.war
```

As you can see, the web application has been copied into the local repository. This
file is now available as a dependency to other projects.

> You might notice that the filename now includes a version again—this is
> always the case for files in the local repository as it follows a predefined
> format to allow Maven to access the files again later. The format starts
> with the group ID split into paths, followed by the artifact ID and version
> as separate paths, and finishing with the filename consisting of the
> artifact ID, version, and extension for the given packaging. Therefore, the
> finalName configuration we used earlier is only suited for manipulation
> of a file within that project's build.

It is worth noting that Maven has one step beyond install, called deploy. This does
lead to some confusion, as it does not refer to deployment of an application into a
development or production server, but rather uploading the build product into a
remote repository. While this can be used as a location to deploy your applications
into a server from, that is not the direct purpose of Maven's deploy step.

We will look at remote repository deployment later in the book. For now, let's focus
on improving the project we have been constructing.

Adding dependencies

In any non-trivial project, it is unlikely (and unwise!) for the programmer to
write every single piece of code that it will use and bundle it all up in one large
all-or-nothing build. This is particularly true for a web application where generally
only the web-based functionality is part of the project, with business logic contained
in separate libraries. For this reason, one of the first features of Maven you will find
yourself using is the **dependency mechanism**.

A dependency is simply a way of expressing that the current project requires another project in order to build or run in some way, using the Maven coordinates to locate it. The dependency may be another project you are building at the same time, another project you have already built on the current machine (shared from the local repository), or a project built by another team member or a third party (downloaded from a remote repository).

Let's see how this works with a simple example using Java source code. For this example, create a source file called src/main/java/com/effectivemaven/ chapter01/ExampleAction.java with the following content:

```
package com.effectivemaven.chapter01;

import org.slf4j.*;

public class ExampleAction {
    final Logger logger =
        LoggerFactory.getLogger(ExampleAction.class);
    public boolean execute() {
        logger.info( "Example action executed" );
        return true;
    }
}
```

This is a very trivial example, but you will notice that the third party library **SLF4J** (http://slf4j.org) is used. With this code added, we will try compiling the project. In this case, we just run until the compile step, which includes the same steps as in the earlier calls to package and install, but stops once the sources are compiled.

simple-webapp$ mvn compile

However, you will notice that this time, the build fails with an error:

```
[INFO] [compiler:compile]
[INFO] Compiling 1 source file to /Users/brett/code/01/simple-webapp/
target/classes
[INFO] ------------------------------------------------------------
[ERROR] BUILD FAILURE
[INFO] ------------------------------------------------------------
[INFO] Compilation failure

/Users/brett/code/01/simple-webapp/src/main/java/com/effectivemaven/
chapter01/ExampleAction.java:[3,0] package org.slf4j does not exist

/Users/brett/code/01/simple-webapp/src/main/java/com/effectivemaven/
chapter01/ExampleAction.java:[6,10] cannot find symbol
symbol   : class Logger
location: class com.effectivemaven.chapter01.ExampleAction
```

```
/Users/brett/code/01/simple-webapp/src/main/java/com/effectivemaven/
chapter01/ExampleAction.java:[7,8] cannot find symbol
symbol   : variable LoggerFactory
location: class com.effectivemaven.chapter01.ExampleAction
```

Here, compilation has failed because the SLF4J library has not been added to the build. Maven makes including this very easy, by adding the dependency to the project file `pom.xml`:

```
[...]
<dependencies>
 [...]
 <dependency>
  <groupId>org.slf4j</groupId>
  <artifactId>slf4j-api</artifactId>
  <version>1.5.0</version>
 </dependency>
</dependencies>
```

Its Maven coordinates identify the dependency — the group ID `org.slf4j`, the artifact ID `slf4j-api`, and the version `1.5.0`. Due to its Java heritage, Maven defaults to looking for JAR files, so the type does not need to be given (though for other types it can be). This is enough to retrieve and utilize the SLF4J library, and as we will see, much more.

What if I don't know the Maven coordinates?

The above case may seem simple, but it might be hard to guess the values to use if you didn't know them! While occasionally libraries will publish the Maven coordinates to use in their documentation and examples, often you will need to find out what they are yourself. In Chapter 2, *Staying in Control with Archiva*, we will learn how to use Archiva to search for the right library based on free text, a missing Java class, or a particular JAR file that you already have.

With the dependency in place, let's try to compile the project again:

```
simple-webapp$ mvn compile
```

If all things have gone well, SLF4J will be downloaded and the build will succeed. The generated class files will be produced in the `target/classes` subdirectory.

This is very useful, but adding the dependency has done more than just let us compile the project. Try packaging the artifact again:

```
simple-webapp$ mvn package
```

This process will follow the same steps as it did before, but with the addition of the new class file and the dependency to the resulting web application. Firstly, the compiled sources are placed in `target/simple-webapp/WEB-INF/classes` (in addition to the main `target/classes` area). Secondly, the dependency added has been copied to `target/simple-webapp/WEB-INF/lib`. This is because the Maven WAR plugin now knows that it will be required to run the web application by reading the project's dependencies. Of course, these files are also packaged into the resulting WAR file.

We will see more examples of how the dependency definition is reused by other plugins throughout this chapter.

It is also worth noting that while this pattern is the most common way to express dependencies, Maven has a number of sophisticated ways to manage which dependencies are used, how they are used, and what version should be used. The SLF4J dependency we used is very simple, but other dependencies will have dependencies of their own. When you use such dependencies in the future, you will notice that Maven resolves these **transitive dependencies** as well.

Some of these concepts will be covered in the dependency management section of Chapter 7, *Maven Best Practices*.

Adding functionality through plugins

The basic model presented above will construct a functional project for a number of different built-in packaging types. However, most projects use a variety of technologies that require additional steps at build time. In addition, there are a vast array of development specific tools that have been integrated with Maven using its **plugin** mechanism.

We saw how plugins are used several times throughout the introductory walkthrough. In some cases, they are explicitly declared in the POM, sometimes they are implied through the default build for a given packaging type, or, in the case of the archetype plugin they are called directly from the command line without a corresponding project.

A plugin is a self-contained piece of reusable functionality for incorporating into the lifecycle of one or more Maven projects. There are two main types of plugin in Maven: **build plugins**, used for all tasks related to the build process of the project; and **reporting plugins**, used for obtaining a visual representation of the state of the project.

Plugins are typically written in Java, but it is possible to write them in a number of interpreted languages, or other languages that will run on the JVM. Through external execution, it has even been possible to write plugins in other languages such as C#.

Maven obtains plugins in the same way as it retrieves other project dependencies; by downloading their artifact and associated dependencies from a remote repository.

The first time you may encounter this is if your code targets Java 5. In another of its conventions, Maven's Java compilation defaults to producing code that is compatible with running on older versions of Java. This means that if you use source code that uses the new features such as generics, you will get compilation failures.

 The Maven developers are currently discussing upgrading the default source and target versions to Java 5, so in a future version of Maven the following example may work without the additional configuration.

You can try this for yourself by adding a line to the `ExampleAction.java` class created in the previous example:

```
private java.util.List<String> values;
```

If you compile this source code, the following error will appear:

```
/Users/brett/code/01/simple-webapp/src/main/java/com/effectivemaven/
chapter01/ExampleAction.java:[9,26] generics are not supported in -source
1.3
(try -source 1.5 to enable generics)
    private java.util.List<String> values;
```

Therefore, it is necessary to pass the `-source` and `-target` parameters to the Java compiler. The goal that was running when the error occurred was `compiler:compile`, so we know that the plugin we are concerned with is the `compiler` plugin, and could look up its configuration page online (this particular plugin is listed at `http://maven.apache.org/plugins/maven-compiler-plugin/`). There you will find a reference for available configuration options for the `compiler:compile` goal, as well as examples for this specific example and others.

Let's add the compiler plugin within the `build` section of `pom.xml` as suggested on that page:

```
<build>
 <finalName>simple-webapp</finalName>
 <plugins>
  <plugin>
   <groupId>org.apache.maven.plugins</groupId>
   <artifactId>maven-compiler-plugin</artifactId>
```

```
    <version>2.0.2</version>
    <configuration>
     <source>1.5</source>
     <target>1.5</target>
    </configuration>
   </plugin>
  </plugins>
```

As you can see, a plugin declaration is much like a dependency declaration — the Maven coordinates of the plugin are used. In fact, the plugins are retrieved in an identical way to any dependencies you use, including being stored in your local repository.

Specifying plugin versions

Even though you will see many examples where this is not the case, it is *always* a good idea to specify the version of the plugin you are using to ensure the build will be reproducible later! Without a version number, Maven will look for the latest available version, and should the plugin's behavior change then your build might change unexpectedly too.

The addition of the plugin achieves the following in a Maven build:

- Makes all the goals in the plugin available to run from the command line for the project. However, note that some plugins that are designed to run standalone, such as the archetype plugin we used earlier, can be run without needing to be added to a project.

- Makes any new packaging and dependency types for the project available (this requires that you declare the project with the `<extensions>true</extensions>` tag as well).

- Allows the definition of additional goals to run in the default build.

- Allows the configuration of the goals within the plugin.

It is this last feature that we have taken advantage of with the compiler plugin. The specified source and target will be used by the `compiler:compile` goal in the plugin, and passed on to the Java compiler that is executed.

With the configuration declared in the way that it has been, it will actually be passed on to all goals that are used from that plugin — for example, the `compiler:testCompile` goal that is automatically used to compile Java test source code will take the same parameters. For this reason, you will notice that we don't encounter the same compiler error we received earlier when Java 5 annotations are used in the next section on running unit tests.

Being able to configure plugins that are already used opens up a number of variations on how the project can be built, but what about adding entirely new pieces of functionality to the default build?

This is achieved with the `executions` section of a plugin definition. This allows the addition of a goal or goals with a given configuration to a particular stage of the build.

As an example, let's look at how to add a rule enforcement to the build. Let's say that because we chose to use SLF4J already, we want to make sure that none of the dependencies added in the future add the Commons Logging implementation into the web application via their transitive dependencies.

To do this, we must add the `enforcer` plugin into the `plugins` section of `pom.xml`:

```
<plugin>
 <groupId>org.apache.maven.plugins</groupId>
 <artifactId>maven-enforcer-plugin</artifactId>
 <version>1.0-beta-1</version>
 <executions>
  <execution>
   <id>enforce-dependencies</id>
   <goals>
    <goal>enforce</goal>
   </goals>
   <configuration>
    <rules>
      <bannedDependencies>
       <excludes>
        <exclude>
          commons-logging:commons-logging
        </exclude>
       </excludes>
      </bannedDependencies>
     </rules>
   </configuration>
  </execution>
 </executions>
</plugin>
```

Here, there are three parts of the execution to note. Firstly, there is an identifier `id` given. This is not mandatory when there is only one execution (it will use the `default` identifier in this case), but it is always recommended. It is used to give a visual clue to the execution that is running when multiple executions for a single plugin are provided. It also acts as a key for Maven's inheritance mechanism if a subproject wants to modify the configuration of the execution.

Secondly, a list of goals is given. In this case, we only have one goal to add — `enforce`. However, it is possible to list multiple goals from the same plugin if applicable.

Finally, we have the configuration for the goals. In case of the `enforcer` plugin, this is a list of rules to execute. In the above example, we have a single rule, called `bannedDependencies`, which as the name suggests takes a list of dependencies to ensure never occur within the project's dependency tree. The configuration given will be applied to all goals in this execution, and will be combined with the configuration that applies to the whole plugin, as shown in the previous section. This allows you to configure just a subset of goals, or all uses of a particular setting, as appropriate.

It is only possible to declare a plugin once in a given project file. If you need to run a goal a number of times, with or without different configuration, you must include multiple executions within the same plugin definition. This will also allow you to place multiple executions of a goal in different phases of the build lifecycle if necessary.

You may have noticed that in the configuration, the library is referred to as `commons-logging:commons-logging`. It is common to refer to dependencies using the format `groupId:artifactId` or even `groupId:artifactId:version` when you are only able to use a single string. We will use this convention throughout the rest of this book to simplify the text.

If we now proceed to build the project, the following line will appear towards the start of the build thanks to the `enforcer` plugin:

```
[INFO] [enforcer:enforce {execution: enforce-dependencies}]
```

Because we are not using Commons Logging, there will be no error and the build will continue as before. However, if you'd like to test that the plugin works correctly, try adding `commons-logging:commons-logging:1.1.1` as a dependency and build the project again.

At this point, you might be wondering how Maven decided to run the goal at the beginning, as the plugin didn't specify anything about *when* to run the goal. As it turns out, running in the `validate` phase (at the beginning of the build) is the default in the `enforce` goal, as it usually makes sense to enforce rules before wasting any time processing the rest of the build. Not all goals specify a default, however, and regardless you may wish to modify when the goal runs. If that is the case, you would add the `phase` parameter to the execution, and all goals in that execution would then be run in that stage of the build instead of the default.

For example, to check the dependencies only after packaging, you could add the following:

```
<execution>
 <id>enforce-dependencies</id>
 <phase>package</phase>
 . . .
```

The order that executions appear in the POM is retained, as the execution of the goal will occur after any goals already in the package phase, including those earlier in the current project file, inherited from a parent project, or declared in the default lifecycle for the current packaging type.

It's worth stating here that there was no intent to pick on Commons Logging with the previous example! Though it may have had a past reputation for being hard to handle in many class loading scenarios in the past, recent versions seem to have improved that situation. Nonetheless, our example simply points out that multiple logging frameworks are often not what you have intended for a single web application, and the enforcer plugin is a useful way to ensure this remains the case.

One additional note: if this particular example were to be used in a real project, should a library you introduce require Commons Logging and you choose to exclude it in favor of SLF4J, you will need to include the jcl-over-slf4j dependency from SLF4J instead.

Adding resources

In addition to source code, Maven uses the concept of resources. A **resource** is a file that will be accessed by the code at runtime but is not required for compilation, and is typically packaged in the artifact that is built. Common examples are static configuration files and localization resources.

The standard build lifecycle for a web application already includes the **[resources: resources]** command to copy any present resources from the default location of src/main/resources into the final web application. Let's try that with the sample application by creating src/main/resources/Application.properties as follows:

```
first.greeting=Hello, World!
```

Now, run the build again:

```
simple-webapp$ mvn package
```

We will now see that the properties file is present in both `target/classes` and `target/simple-webapp/WEB-INF/classes`. How the resource is packaged depends on the type of packaging. In Java, a resource will always be accessible from the root of the class loader at runtime. As such, it will be packaged in the root of a JAR file, or in the `WEB-INF/classes` directory of a web application.

Other types of content resources, such as web application content, are specified by different resource paths in an individual plugin's configuration, rather than using the resources within the build section of the POM.

Resources can also be **filtered** by substituting values into the files under specific build conditions. This can be useful for centralizing the specification of certain values but comes with a similar number of pitfalls and common misuses that will be discussed in Chapter 7, *Maven Best Practices*.

Running tests

You may have noticed as builds have run that Maven tried to execute the goal `surefire:test` and found no tests to run. Unit testing is a fundamental concept of Maven, built-in to the default lifecycle for all code project types, and run on the majority of builds to encourage the practice of not only writing unit tests, but writing *fast* unit tests.

There are two steps needed to add unit tests to this project:

1. Add a dependency for the test library you have chosen to use.
2. Add the test source code to your project in the `src/test/java` subdirectory.

Let's add a simple test case to illustrate this. Firstly, we will add the dependency on the test library. You may see many Maven projects (and particularly those created from basic archetypes) using JUnit 3.8.1 — undoubtedly, the most widely used testing framework today (even in comparison to newer versions of JUnit!). However, in this book, we will be using **TestNG** (`http://testng.org`) as the test library. The dependency declaration for TestNG looks like this:

```
<dependency>
  <groupId>org.testng</groupId>
  <artifactId>testng</artifactId>
  <version>5.8</version>
  <classifier>jdk15</classifier>
  <scope>test</scope>
</dependency>
```

You must have noticed the two new entries in this declaration. At the end was the **scope** of the dependency, which was set to test. This is an important value to set as a hint to the Maven dependency mechanism for a few reasons. The scope is used to control which dependencies are passed to each plugin so that they get the most appropriate set for the function they are performing. You will notice if you rebuild the application that TestNG does not end up in the web application like SLF4J did, because the WAR plugin does not bundle testing dependencies. Likewise, if you try to use TestNG in your main application source code, it will fail. This is because the compiler plugin does not use testing dependencies to build the compilation classpath.

 Not all IDEs support this level of separation between testing dependencies and build dependencies, even when configured with Maven integration. If you find a build is succeeding in your IDE and failing in Maven due to a missing library, you may need to review the scopes.

You may have noticed earlier that the scope wasn't specified for SLF4J as the default is compile, which makes the dependency available to all plugins. If that naming seems confusing, think of the primary scopes (compile, runtime, and test) as a funnel: you will need all the dependencies you compile with to run the application, and all the dependencies you run with to test the application, but the reverse is not true.

The other new entry was a **classifier**. While a single Maven project is designed to handle one set of source files and to produce one output, it can be necessary to produce multiple files that are closely related to the same project. In the case of TestNG, different versions that are suitable for JDK 1.4 projects and JDK 5+ projects are made available, but they are based on the same source project (that is, testng-5.8.pom is the Maven project downloaded in either case).

Now, with the dependency in place, let's add a simple test case in src/test/java/com/effectivemaven/chapter01/ExampleActionTest.java:

```java
package com.effectivemaven.chapter01;

import org.testng.annotations.*;

public class ExampleActionTest {
  private ExampleAction action = new ExampleAction();

  @Test
  public void executionSucceeds() {
    assert !action.execute();
  }
}
```

We have again taken advantage of Maven conventions here—by naming the class with `Test` suffix the Maven testing plugin (called **Surefire**) will use it to run test cases instead of considering it as just a test support class. Of course, these can all be configured using configuration for the given plugin as demonstrated in the previous section.

Let's try running this test:

```
simple-webapp$ mvn test
```

This will run the whole build including the testing stage.

Unfortunately, the build will fail rather spectacularly with an error in the middle, similar to this:

```
-------------------------------------------------------
 T E S T S
-------------------------------------------------------
Running TestSuite
SLF4J: Failed to load class "org.slf4j.impl.StaticLoggerBinder".
SLF4J: See http://www.slf4j.org/codes.html#StaticLoggerBinder for further
details.
```

We didn't think far enough ahead here—we chose to compile against `slf4j-api`, which was a good choice, but we didn't add a required SLF4J logging implementation to use when the code is executed. What we have seen here is the SLF4J library complaining about not being provided with an implementation to use.

To avoid this error, add the `org.slf4j:slf4j-simple:1.5.0` dependency, with a scope of `runtime` to the Maven project file.

Logging libraries

Here, we chose to add the logging implementation with a scope of `runtime`, which will mean that it is bundled in the web application of this sample application as well as being available for the tests. This may or may not be what you desire, as some servlet containers will provide logging libraries for web applications already.

Additionally, in the case of logging for an application library that will be reused by others, the `runtime` scope will pass on your choice of implementation and so again should be used with care.

For examples such as this, and particularly logging libraries, take care with the scope you select. If you would like to defer the decision on which implementation to use, just use the `test` scope to provide that implementation to the test cases without passing it on to the final build product or other projects that depend on the current project.

With the new dependency in place, we will try running the tests again. You should still get a failure, but this time, a little more like you might have expected:

```
------------------------------------------------------------
 T E S T S
------------------------------------------------------------
Running TestSuite
221 [main] INFO com.effectivemaven.chapter01.ExampleAction - Example
action executed
Tests run: 1, Failures: 1, Errors: 0, Skipped: 0, Time elapsed: 0.5 sec
<<< FAILURE!

Results :

Failed tests:
   executionSucceeds(com.effectivemaven.chapter01.ExampleActionTest)

Tests run: 1, Failures: 1, Errors: 0, Skipped: 0
```

Here we see that the test (which was written to fail) has triggered TestNG to fail the Maven build. However, this output doesn't say exactly where or what the failure was. For this, you would look in the `target/surefire-reports` directory. Among other files, TestNG will have generated both—`TestSuite.txt` (a text representation of the test results) and `index.html` (a browsable version that may be easier to navigate, especially if there are a large number of tests or errors).

 Other test frameworks will store their results in the same directory, but possibly in different filename formats. For example, JUnit 3.8.1 will generate text files for each test class, example `com.effectivemaven.chapter01.ExampleActionTest.txt`.

The result file should point out the failure, which in this case is that the condition on the assertion should be reversed:

```
public void executionSucceeds() {
   assert action.execute();
}
```

With this change made, we can run the tests again to see that the build has finally succeeded.

The example code and test case here may have been a little simplistic, but it does show that it is easy to add unit tests to a Maven project. With this small amount of configuration in place, all that is required is to write test cases and place them in the right location to have Maven run them automatically. We haven't seen it yet, but this has also laid the groundwork for more advanced development scenarios, such as measuring test code coverage.

Getting help

Sometimes, it is necessary to inspect what is going on inside Maven when you need to make a configuration change or are troubleshooting a problem. In these cases, some assistance can be provided by the `help` plugin.

To see the available goals, run the following:

```
$ mvn help:help
```

The selection available covers a variety of needs in telling you about your build or your environment.

For example, one of particular use is to determine which version of a particular plugin is actually being used. This information can be obtained through a command such as this:

```
$ mvn help:describe -Dplugin=compiler
```

The plugin variable given is the short name, or the *prefix*, for the plugin shown in the goal names as it is executed or would use from the command line. If this is not specific enough, you can use the full coordinate of the plugin:

```
$ mvn help:describe -DgroupId=org.apache.maven.plugins \
    -DartifactId=maven-compiler-plugin
```

The resulting output will show the basic information available for the plugin, which in this example would be:

```
[INFO] Plugin: 'org.apache.maven.plugins:maven-compiler-plugin:2.0.2'
------------------------------------------------
Group Id:  org.apache.maven.plugins
Artifact Id: maven-compiler-plugin
Version:     2.0.2
Goal Prefix: compiler
```

It isn't always convenient to visit the Maven web site to access the reference documentation for a plugin to find out the correct way to configure a particular plugin and so another use of the `help:describe` goal is to get that information directly from the plugin:

```
$ mvn help:describe -Dplugin=compiler -Ddetail
```

Some of the other goals of the `help` plugin are described in Appendix A, *Troubleshooting Maven*, later in this book.

Enhancing the development process

The examples so far have shown how to use Maven to automate the build process. However, the information that is already available can also be of use to other types of plugins, which can be of assistance throughout the development process.

While being able to build and install the web application from this chapter into the local repository is useful, deploying that into a running server after every change would be tedious. Many IDEs offer easier ways to manage this step, but you may wish to reuse the setup from Maven instead.

A particularly relevant example for a web application is the Jetty plugin. **Jetty** (http://jetty.mortbay.org/) is a small, fast, and fully compliant Java servlet container that is particularly suited to being embedded in other applications. We will use Jetty's Maven plugin to run the web application in a Jetty container.

First, we need to add the Jetty plugin to the list of plugins in the project so that the goals will be available from the command line. At the time of writing, the Maven coordinate for the plugin is org.mortbay.jetty:maven-jetty-plugin:6.1.14 (though in version 7.x and above it is expected to change the artifact ID to jetty-maven-plugin). Once that is added, starting the server with the web application is simply a matter of running the following command:

```
simple-webapp$ mvn jetty:run
```

The server will start on port 8080, and you can immediately browse the application at http://localhost:8080/simple-webapp/.

The web application is pre-configured from the defaults and values from the project file. This means that you can edit the content under src/main/webapp, and see it reflected in the running web application without a restart.

The Jetty plugin has a large number of configuration options to help you get more out of this environment, which can be found in the Jetty documentation. Because it is using the Maven project model, it can also easily be configured to watch for changes to the source code and dependencies in Maven's local repository, and then recompile and reload the web application on the fly. It is also possible to configure the Jetty server for more complete development options, for example to add JDBC data sources.

Even if you are deploying to a different servlet container, it is still useful to be able to test quickly from the Maven environment using Jetty. However if this is the case, be sure to also test against your target servlet container. We will examine this topic in Chapter 4, *Application Testing with Maven*.

Viewing detailed project information

We have seen many ways to reuse the information stored in the Maven project, but one of the most powerful has yet to be explored. Maven has a documentation rendering framework and large set of plugins that will not only present information about the current project, but will also allow the integration of information from a number of external tools into a one-stop-shop project developer's mini-site.

To get a taste of this now, try the following command:

```
simple-webapp$ mvn site
```

For the basics, no further configuration is needed as the values from the Maven project model are reused. You can now review the content by opening `target/site/index.html` in a browser.

Working effectively with Maven sites, reports, and related practices will be examined in more detail in Chapter 5, *Reporting and Checks*.

 As you may have noticed, this site is rough. Poorly thought out, default Maven project sites can do more harm than good! Be sure to take care in considering what information you are trying to convey and where, then use Maven to make it easier to keep up to date and structure it, rather than relying on it to do all the work.

Multiple module builds

When we defined a Maven project earlier, we saw that it was described as a *unit of work*, typically producing a single output from a single source. However, many software projects are larger than that!

Maven was designed with this situation in mind, and so larger software projects can be composed of multiple Maven projects. This in itself is still referred to as a project, with the other projects that it is composed of referred to as its **modules**.

When multiple projects are built at once in Maven, the builder is referred to as the **reactor**. Whether building a multi-module project or a series of separate projects, the reactor collects the projects to be built and ensures the correct order is used based on any dependencies declared on other projects within the same reactor build.

We won't extend our simple web application to illustrate this at this stage, as we will see much more detail on Maven's support for multi-module projects in Chapter 3, *Building an Application Using Maven*.

What if I need to convert an existing project?

The example we have seen so far has been reasonably complete despite having to provide very little information, because of the pre-defined behavior of the Maven plugins and the conventions used.

That may make it easier to get started with a new project, but what if you wanted to convert to Maven from an existing project? Such a project probably doesn't follow the conventions already, or may have custom or slightly altered behavior to that provided by the default Maven plugins.

There is unfortunately no single way to convert a project from Ant or some other build system to Maven because they frequently use very different approaches.

A typical approach may look something like this:

1. Ensure that the current build behaves like a good "Maven citizen" by publishing builds into a remote repository and starting to consume its dependencies from there.

2. Restructure the existing build into modules and paths that match Maven conventions to simplify the Maven build.

3. Build upon those conventions and the existence of a list of dependencies to produce a concurrent Maven-based build.

4. Gradually migrate any remaining functionality until the Maven-build becomes the only one needed.

Before starting a conversion of any size however, it is best to familiarize yourself with how Maven works on a similar but new project, as this will help identify the best places to adopt Maven's standard practices in a build conversion, and where it will be easiest to retain custom behavior.

Summary

We have now seen a very quick, but comprehensive, introduction to the building blocks that all Maven projects use, and should be confident in putting it to use in a project.

In this chapter, we looked at how to create a new project or module and build some typical Java artifacts. We then looked at how to put it into use with various plugins, and the way to get more out of the Maven project model by generating a site and reports. We then covered some terminology and "theory" of how Maven works, and learned some tips for getting help when it is needed.

In essence, this is all you will ever need to know about Maven to use it well—everything else is about reapplying the same techniques to different applications and learning about the specifics of various plugins.

While some topics, notably profiles, project inheritance, the various management sections of the POM and multi-module builds, were not revised in this chapter, they will be covered in far greater depth in later chapters.

Now that we are confidently using Maven, one of the most important pieces of software anyone will use in a Maven-based infrastructure is **a repository manager**. Hence, in the next chapter Deng will introduce Apache Archiva, and explain how it addresses some fundamental concepts of repository management.

2
Staying in Control with Archiva

Have you ever heard of the term repository manager? If not, then this is the chapter where you will get to know it and get a first-hand experience on the working of a repository manager. If you already know what a repository manager is, you can skip the first few sections of this chapter and go straight to the sections where we install and configure one.

Putting these two words together — **repository** and **manager**, literally means someone who manages a repository. In this case, that *someone* is an application. We will be discussing this application here.

In this chapter, we introduce **Apache Archiva** — one of the many repository managers available. If you are already an experienced user of Archiva or are already familiar with it, Chapter 10, *Archiva in a Team*, covers Archiva more in detail.

For this chapter, you will learn about the importance of a repository manager — why and when you should use one. We will also demonstrate how to set up Archiva and start using it. This includes installation, and basic setup and configuration of an Archiva repository. It also includes the procedure to configure Maven to use Archiva.

Importance of a repository manager

Let us picture a small example. You have just been assigned to a new and big project (let's say its source code is about 5GB). You have finished checking out the project sources, and now it's time to build the project. What are the problems you think you may encounter?

Definitely one of the problems is the slow build time. A big factor of this is the downloading of the dependencies of the project. Remember, if Maven doesn't find a dependency in your local repository, it would get it from the central repository or from other third party repositories that you have specified. Given this, if it is your initial build, just imagine how long it would take you to finish building that project! Also, what if your network connection is having hiccups? Every time an artifact transfer gets corrupted—Eek! You would need to build it from the start again.

Now, let's say in order to solve this download problem, you have asked your system administrator to mirror the Maven central repository and have that mirror hosted locally. That would require your system administrator to synchronize your local mirror regularly, so that its contents are always updated and newly deployed artifacts are added to the mirror. Having a local mirror of the central repository is no easy feat. You have to worry about maintaining it—think along the lines of broken metadata, disk space and so on. Before the year ends, your system administrator might no longer speak to you as you have saddled him with a mirror maintenance headache!

Let's look at another, totally different, scenario—you have a continuous integration server configured to build and deploy your project to a deployment repository each night. We are assuming (again) that the generated project bundle is 5GB. Therefore, each night your CI server deploys a 5GB-sized artifact to your deployment repository. Doing some serious multiplication, which would mean in a week's time, you have already consumed 35GB of disk space in your hard disk! In order to solve that problem, you either write a script that cleans up the repository (don't forget to fix the metadata!) or you delegate someone to regularly clean up the repository (now that would be fun). Either way, you have to exert a lot of effort just to free up some disk space.

This is where a repository manager comes in to picture. Let's take a look at each of the features of a repository manager and see how it addresses the problems that we have identified above.

- A repository manager can act as a **proxy cache**. The ideal setup of a repository manager is to have it running in your local network. You can configure an internal repository to proxy *on-demand* a remote repository thereby making the succeeding download of artifacts faster.

- A repository manager can be used as a local host of your deployment repository. It also usually provides a utility for regularly cleaning up hosted repositories thereby giving you control over the size of your repositories.

- A repository manager provides artifact search of internally hosted repositories. This is very handy when you are looking for a specific class that you want to use and you do not know which JAR it is packaged in.

- A repository manager provides utilities for maintaining repositories. Aside from the regular clean up already mentioned in the second point, a repository manager (usually) also provides other utilities for maintaining a repository such as a utility for fixing up metadata, a utility for generating artifact checksum files and so on.

- A repository manager allows you to monitor the health of your repository via reports. These reports allow you to identify which artifacts are defective and help maintain the quality of your repository.

- A repository manager provides access control to your repositories. It gives you a way of controlling *who* can read and/or write to your repositories.

The above reasons are enough for us to start installing a repository manager. This is where Archiva comes in.

Archiva was one of the first of the open source repository managers available. It is simply a web application where you can host and store, and manage and maintain your enterprise build artifact repositories. Aside from managing artifact repositories, Archiva also provides features such as on-demand remote repository proxying, artifact searching and browsing, reporting and security access control. Archiva is best used with build tools such as Maven, Continuum (a continuous integration server), and ANT. The diagram below shows a high-level view of Archiva and its components, and how it interacts with other build systems.

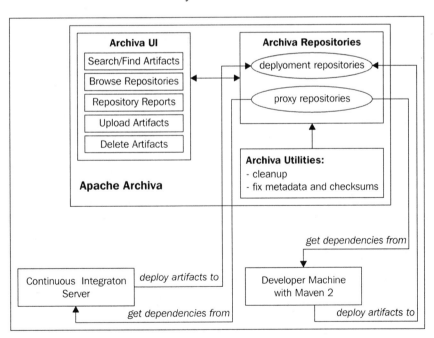

We will get to see some of Archiva's features in the later sections of this chapter and learn in more detail about Archiva in Chapter 10, *Archiva in a Team*.

Installing Archiva

Before we start installing Archiva, let's first take a quick look at how it all started and where it is now.

Archiva became a top-level project at the Apache Software Foundation in March 2008, but it has been around as a sub-project of Apache Maven since 2005. The first-ever release of Archiva was 0.9-alpha-1, followed by the 0.9-alpha-2 release. Joakim Erdfelt re-vamped the whole source code and previewed it to the community. After the re-vamp, development picked up as other developers (including myself) started being active in the project again. Moreover, two years after the project started, 1.0 was officially released to the public. As of the writing of this book, the latest Archiva release is 1.2.1.

We have read the story of Archiva, now let's start installing it! Go to the website `http://archiva.apache.org/download.html` and get the binary or WAR file. We can install Archiva either as a standalone application or as a **webapp (Web Application)** deployed to an application server. If we want to use the standalone application, then we should get the **Archiva Standalone** TAR.GZ or ZIP binary. Otherwise, get the Archiva WAR file.

The Archiva standalone bundle uses an embedded Jetty 6 application server. Wrapper start up scripts for Linux, MacOSX, Solaris, and Windows are included in the binary file. Specific configuration files that we need to take note of are located in the `conf/` directory:

- `jetty.xml`: This file contains Jetty-specific configuration. In the latter part of the configuration file, we will see the Archiva-specific JNDI resources. These are the `validation_mail`, `archiva`, `archivaShutdown`, `users` and `usersShutdown`. The `validation_mail` element defines the mail resource used by Archiva for sending validation mail for newly registered users. `archiva` and `archivaShutdown` on the other hand, are configurations for the Archiva database while the last two resources, `users` and `usersShutdown`, are for the users database created and maintained by Redback. The Archiva standalone comes shipped with an embedded Derby database but if we want to use a different database, we can easily switch it over by simply changing the database connection in this file.

- `jetty-logging.xml`: This is a configuration file for the Jetty logs.

- `wrapper.conf`: This is a configuration file for Archiva's standalone bundle Java service wrapper.

- `archiva.xml`: This is Archiva's default configuration file. If there is no existing `archiva.xml` found in `<USER HOME>/.m2/`, then Archiva will use the default configuration file.

The Archiva log files on the other hand, are located under the `logs/` directory. We will find four types of log files in there—`archiva.log`, `archiva-audit.log`, `archiva-security-audit.log`, and the rolling Jetty log file. `archiva.log` is specific to the Archiva components. The `archiva-audit.log` is for Archiva actions or events and for proxy requests while the `archiva-security-audit.log` is for security-related actions or events. We can configure the log level for these files in the `apps/archiva/WEB-INF/classes/log4j.xml` file of Archiva. All other output outside the boundaries of these three files, such as application server and wrapper logs, goes to the rolling Jetty log file.

If we don't want to use the standalone Archiva and instead would like to deploy the WAR file to a different application server, we can easily follow the steps specified on the Archiva site: `http://archiva.apache.org/docs/1.2.1/adminguide/webapp.html`

Before we start Archiva, we must change the port it will run on, to avoid conflicting with other applications on the default port 8080.

To change the port, edit the configuration below in the `conf/jetty.xml` file and change the default value of the `jetty.port` system property from 8080 to 8081.

```
<Call name="addConnector">
  <Arg>
    <New class="org.mortbay.jetty.nio.SelectChannelConnector">
      <Set name="host"><SystemProperty name="jetty.host" /></Set>
      <Set name="port"><SystemProperty name="jetty.port"
                            default="8081"/></Set>

      ...
    </New>
  </Arg>
</Call>
```

To start the application, go to `bin/` and type in `./archiva console` or `./archiva start` if you are running on Linux, MacOSX or Solaris. Use `archiva.bat` if you are running on Windows.

Starting Archiva using the `start` command means that the application was started as a service. To stop the application, `./archiva stop` must be executed from `<ARCHIVA_INSTALLATION>/bin/`. Starting Archiva using the `console` command would have the output displayed in the console where it was executed. Pressing *Ctrl-C* stops the application.

Archiva can now be accessed at `http://localhost:8081/archiva/`. The **Create Admin User** page is the first page we will see when we access the URL.

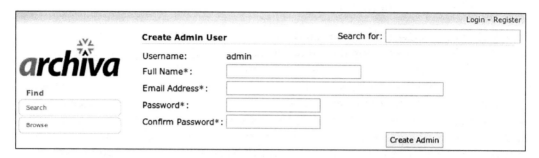

The **admin** user is the ultimate god of Archiva—the **system administrator**. Let's fill out the **Create Admin User** form as follows:

- **Full Name: Administrator**
- **Email Address: admin@example.com**
- **Password: admin1**
- **Confirm Password: admin1**

After we create the **admin** user and log in to Archiva, we will see the webapp view as shown in the following figure:

The navigation menu on the left-hand side of the webapp is divided into three sections: **Find**, **Manage,** and **Administration**. The **Find** section contains the **Search** and **Browse** features of Archiva, the **Manage** section is for **Reports** and **User Management**, and the **Administration** section is for basic configuration of **Repositories**, proxies and consumers.

Before moving on to the next section, let's take a quick look at the **Repositories** page under **Administration**. In there, we see that Archiva comes configured with two managed and two remote repositories.

> A **managed repository** is a repository residing in the local file system where Archiva is installed. It can be set up as a proxy repository or as a deployment repository. A **remote repository** on the other hand, is a repository that is not located on the local file system and is usually configured in Archiva as the repository to be proxied. Only the artifacts in managed repositories can be searched and browsed in Archiva.

For now, our concern is the two managed repositories — **internal** and **snapshots**.

These managed repositories are still empty so performing an artifact search or browsing the repository won't give us anything. As managed repositories reside in the local file system, we can add existing repositories in Archiva. For example, if we already have an internal local mirror of Maven's central repository that our system administrators synchronize regularly, we can add this to Archiva and make it an on-demand proxy cache so that it no longer needs to be synced regularly. Alternatively, we can simply add it to Archiva to provide a UI for searching and browsing artifacts in the repository.

One thing to keep in mind though is that before artifacts can be searched in Archiva, they must first be indexed. When exactly are they indexed?

Artifacts are indexed when a managed repository is **scanned**. Archiva scans a repository in order to gather and process the artifacts in it. Once an artifact is processed, it should show up in the **Browse** page and can be searched. If we look again at the **Repositories** page, there is a **Scanning Cron** field and a **Scan Repository Now** button. These two fields indicate that a repository scan can be explicitly triggered and/or executed on a scheduled basis. There are more to repository scanning than this, as we will learn later in Chapter 10, *Archiva in a Team*.

Separating your repositories

In the previous section, we have learned that a managed repository can be configured as a deployment repository or as a proxy repository. When setting up repositories, there are two points that we need to keep in mind. First, keep deployment and local proxy repositories separate. Second, keep snapshots and released artifacts in separate repositories as well.

Let's tackle the first point. Why do you need to keep your deployment and local proxy repositories detached from each other? The answer is **permissions**. Local proxy repositories are usually used by everyone within the company (or within the local network), and deployment repositories sometimes need to be on a per project basis. You would not want everyone who has access to the local proxy repository to be able to access your project too. It is also easier for the administrator to control and manage who has read and/or write access to the repositories if they are kept separate.

As for deployment repositories, it is recommended that snapshot artifacts are kept separate from released artifacts. There are several reasons for this. First, snapshots are only meant for developers. Clients usually get a hold of new releases of a project by downloading it from a repository, which they have permission to access. If we are also deploying our snapshots to this repository, we are exposing unstable and untested versions of our project to our clients and I am sure you don't want to do that.

The second reason is that it is easier to maintain the repository if it only consists of either of the two—snapshots only or released artifacts only. Snapshots are usually generated often and have timestamped versions when deployed, like from continuous integration builds (we will learn all about CIs in Chapter 8, *Continuum*). Therefore, snapshots usually need to be cleaned up regularly to keep their size at bay. If all your artifacts are jumbled in one single repository, it would be harder to clean it up as you have to make sure that you don't accidentally remove a released artifact.

The third reason for keeping them separate is related to the second reason, but it is concerned with maintaining an artifact's metadata.

> Maven makes use of `maven-metadata.xml` files to keep track of the versions of an artifact in a Maven 2 repository. Their contents change as artifacts are deployed in the repository. There are two types of metadata files — the **artifact-level metadata** and the **version-level metadata**. Artifact-level metadata is located at the artifact-level (for example, `../[groupId]/[artifactId]/maven-metadata.xml`) and lists all the versions of a specific artifact in the repository. The version-level metadata on the other hand, is located at the version-level (for example, `../[groupId]/[artifactId]/[version]/maven-metadata.xml`) and contains the unique versions of a snapshot version of an artifact. It is only present for snapshot versions.

Maven greatly depends on these `maven-metadata.xml` files during build time. It uses them to determine if a specific artifact exists in the repository and to determine which version of the artifact to download when a dependency has a snapshot version.

We will use the `simple-webapp` project that we have created in Chapter 1, *Maven in a Nutshell*, as an example. Let's say we have a single repository where we keep all our snapshots and released artifacts. We will assume that we are still developing our `simple-webapp` project and it is still in version 1.0-SNAPSHOT. We have configured our CI server to build and deploy our project every night; so after a week, we have a number of timestamped versions of our artifact in the repository. Now let's say that it is time to release 1.0, we tag and release our project, deploy 1.0 to our repository and move on to the next development version which is 1.1-SNAPSHOT. After our CI server builds and deploys the 1.1-SNAPSHOT to our repository, this is what the metadata file of our `simple-webapp` artifact in the repository would look like:

```xml
<?xml version="1.0" encoding="UTF-8"?>
<metadata>
  <groupId>com.effectivemaven.chapter01</groupId>
  <artifactId>simple-webapp</artifactId>
  <versioning>
```

```
    <latest>1.1-SNAPSHOT</latest>
    <release>1.0</release>
    <versions>
      <version>1.0-SNAPSHOT</version>
      <version>1.0</version>
      <version>1.1-SNAPSHOT</version>
    </versions>
    <lastUpdated>20080914013919</lastUpdated>
  </versioning>
</metadata>
```

Isn't it strange that we still have 1.0-SNAPSHOT available for download even if the final 1.0 version has already been released? Now if we decide to remove the 1.0-SNAPSHOT timestamped artifacts from our repository, we would have to always keep in mind to update the artifact's metadata file. We must remove the 1.0-SNAPSHOT in the available `<versions>` in order to force everyone using that snapshot version to use the released 1.0. Or else, they would still be left using the 1.0-SNAPSHOT and once it was removed, if the metadata file hasn't been updated, then it would cause a build problem for them because Maven couldn't download the snapshot artifact. A word of caution though, the removal of the artifact from the deployment repository doesn't necessarily mean that the artifact will be removed from a user's local repository. Therefore, if 1.0-SNAPSHOT still exists in the user's local repository, the user would still be able to use it.

The last reason to keep snapshot and release repositories separate comes up when we are looking for a certain artifact. If we are looking for a snapshot, then we just have to go to the snapshots repository — or to the releases repository if we are looking for a released artifact.

Archiva also implements the concept of **virtual repositories**, which is handy when you have multiple proxy caches. We will talk about this in detail in Chapter 10, *Archiva in a Team*.

Hooking up Maven with Archiva

We discussed deployment and local proxy repositories above. Let's get our hands dirty and do some proxying.

Setting up a proxy

Although Archiva can work with different types of clients, we will be mainly using Maven 2 in our examples.

We have learned in the previous sections that there are already managed and remote repositories configured by default in Archiva. We didn't know it earlier but the repository **snapshots** is intended to be a deployment repository where we deploy our artifacts (we will learn how to do this in the later part of this chapter) while repository **internal** is intended to be a proxy repository. How do we know this? If we go to the **Proxy Connectors** page, we will see the **internal** repository and underneath it are two proxy connector entries for **maven2-repository.dev.java.net** and **central** (note that these two are the remote repositories already configured in **Repositories**, which we saw earlier). We can also deploy artifacts in **internal** but it is not recommended as we wish to keep them separate from the proxied artifacts.

The configuration in **Proxy Connectors** signifies that **internal** repository proxies **maven2-repository.dev.java.net** and **central**. For consistency, we will refer to a remote repository being proxied as a **remote proxy** and to a local or managed proxy repository as a **proxy cache**.

By clicking on the **Edit** icon in the configured proxy connector, we will see the different values that we can set for the connector.

We should specify a **Network Proxy** if we are using a proxy in our local area network. Otherwise, we just set it to **(direct connection)**.

A network proxy can be set in **Network Proxies**. The proxies that you defined in that page will be listed in the drop-down **Network Proxy** field in **Proxy Connectors**.

One of the most important things we need to understand with regard to proxy connectors are the policies. There are six types of policies which we can define for a proxy connector.

Return error when specifies that if a remote proxy causes an error, either return the requested artifact if it exists in the proxy cache and return an error if it doesn't exist (**artifact not already present**), or return the error regardless of whether the artifact already exists or not in the proxy cache (**always**). **On remote error** specifies that if there is a remote error, either **stop** and immediately return the error, **queue error** and return all encountered errors after checking other remote repositories, or **ignore** any errors.

The **Releases** and **Snapshots** policies, on the other hand, deal with the frequency of download for these types of artifacts from the remote proxy when they are requested. The **always** policy gets the artifact from the remote proxy each time it is requested, **hourly** and **daily** gets it from the remote proxy if not yet retrieved during the hour or day when it was requested. **once** policy means that if the requested artifact has already been retrieved from the remote proxy at least once, then it would no longer be retrieved again, and finally, **never** retrieve it from the remote proxy. The **Checksum** policy deals with (you have guessed right!) incorrect checksums.

> Checksums are fixed-sized calculated values of a file using a specific algorithm. They are used to determine the integrity of a file. When a file is downloaded, its checksum is calculated then compared to the value contained in the file's checksum file. If they don't match, then there was a problem during the transmission. Maven artifacts always have SHA1 and MD5 checksum files.

We can set the connector to **fix** the checksums, **ignore** the checksum failures, or **fail** the request. Last but not the least, the **Cache failure** policy simply specifies whether to cache encountered failures (**yes**) or not (**no**).

The **White List** and **Black List** patterns are for specifying what types of artifacts should and should not be handled by the connector based on the path of the request respectively.

Let's try configuring one. For this exercise, we will be configuring our managed repository **internal** to proxy the JBoss Maven2 repository.

The first thing that we need to do is add the JBoss Maven 2 repository as a remote repository in Archiva. Go to the **Repositories** page and add a new **Remote Repository**. Fill out the **Add Remote Repository** page as follows and add the repository.

Next, we will go to the **Proxy Connectors** page and click **Add** to create a new connector. We will assume that we will be connecting to the Internet directly so for the **Network Proxy**, choose **direct connection**. Our proxy cache is **internal** and our remote proxy is **jboss.repo**, so that is what we will set for the **Managed Repository** and **Remote Repository** fields respectively. For the policies, let's say we want to stop the build when an error is encountered during proxying and to propagate that error to the requesting client (for example, Maven) so we set **Return error when** to **always** and **On remote error** to **stop**. As the JBoss repository only contains releases and releases should no longer be changed once it is released, we only need to get **Releases** one time. As for the **Snapshots** policies, we will set it to **never** as we are only dealing with released artifacts. For **Checksum** errors, we will set it to **fix** so that Archiva would fix it for us. We don't want to **Cache failures** so we will set that policy to **no**.

We will assume that we only need the `javax` artifacts from the JBoss repository. To narrow this down during download, we shall add the specific path pattern **javax/**** to the **White List**. Finally, we are done! Click on the **Add Proxy Connector** button and we should have a new connector with a configuration similar to the one in the following screenshot:

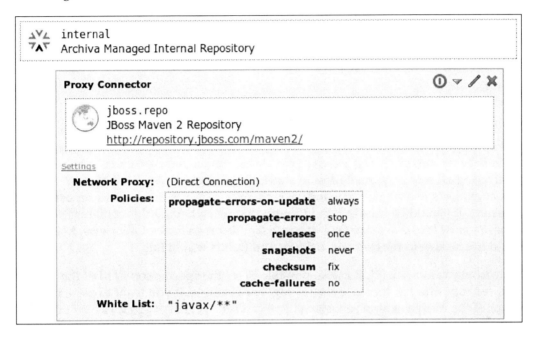

Now let's move on to the next set of configurations that we need to do to hook up Maven with Archiva.

Configuring your settings.xml

Now we need to tell Maven that we want to use a nearby proxy cache for downloading artifacts. In our case, that proxy cache is the **internal** repository. We relay this information to Maven via the `settings.xml` file.

> The `settings.xml` is a Maven configuration file. It is similar to the `pom.xml` except that it contains configuration information that should not be bundled with the project. Maven has a default `settings.xml` file located at `<M2_HOME>/conf/`. It can also be created at `<USER.HOME>/.m2/` for user-specific configuration. Details on what can be configured in the `settings.xml` file can be found at `http://maven.apache.org/settings.html`.

In our case, we will be configuring the proxy cache at the `settings.xml` found in `<M2_HOME>/conf/`. Look for the `<mirrors>` section and add the following inside that section:

```
<...>
<mirror>
  <id>internal</id>
  <name>Proxy Cache - Internal Repository</name>
  <url>http://localhost:8081/archiva/repository/internal</url>
  <mirrorOf>*</mirrorOf>
</mirror>
<...>
```

The `<url>` we specify is the **WebDAV URL** of the **internal** repository displayed in the **Repositories** page. The `<mirrorOf>` tag tells Maven which remote repository or server is being mirrored. The asterisk (*) value signifies that repository `internal` is mirroring **all** remote repositories. In short, we are locking down all Maven artifact requests to a single repository, which, in our case, is the Archiva repository `internal`. It should be kept in mind though that when having this configuration, *the mirror must be able to proxy the requests to the other repositories.* Otherwise, Maven would not be able to retrieve any artifacts and builds would fail.

Aside from the asterisk (*), it is also possible to set the specific server id of the mirrored repository in the `<mirrorOf>` tag. For example, if you want to use a local mirror of the Maven central repository, you can set `<mirrorOf>central<mirrorOf>`.

Another possible value for the `<mirrorOf>` tag is `external:*`. The `external:*` is used to specify that the repository is a mirror of all repositories except those repositories that are running on `localhost` or are file-based. Please take note that this feature is only available in Maven versions 2.0.9 and onwards.

 For more details on how to configure mirrors in Maven, see `http://maven.apache.org/guides/mini/guide-mirror-settings.html`.

Building your project

Most users are afraid of emptying their local repositories because that would mean downloading everything again when you execute Maven. So for now, we will just point our `<M2_HOME>/conf/settings.xml` to a different local repository. In `<USER_HOME>/.m2/`, create a new directory `book-repository` then add the following just inside the `<settings>` section in our `settings.xml`:

```
<localRepository><USER_HOME>/.m2/book-repository</localRepository>
```

By the end of this exercise, we should no longer be afraid of emptying our local repository.

We will be using the `simple-webapp` project we created in Chapter 1, *Maven Best Practices*, so let's open it in the command-line and package it:

`simple-webapp$ mvn clean package`

As your local repository is empty, Maven will download everything again so the beginning output should be similar to the following:

```
[INFO] Scanning for projects...
[INFO] ------------------------------------------------------------------
[INFO] Building simple-webapp Maven Webapp
[INFO]    task-segment: [clean, package]
[INFO] ------------------------------------------------------------------
Downloading: http://localhost:8081/archiva/repository/internal/org/
apache/maven/plugins/maven-clean-plugin/2.2/maven-clean-plugin-2.2.pom
3K downloaded
Downloading: http://localhost:8081/archiva/repository/internal/org/
apache/maven/plugins/maven-plugins/10/maven-plugins-10.pom
7K downloaded
Downloading: http://localhost:8081/archiva/repository/internal/org/
apache/maven/maven-parent/7/maven-parent-7.pom
20K downloaded
Downloading: http://localhost:8081/archiva/repository/internal/org/
apache/apache/4/apache-4.pom
4K downloaded
Downloading: http://localhost:8081/archiva/repository/internal/org/
apache/maven/plugins/maven-clean-plugin/2.2/maven-clean-plugin-2.2.jar
11K downloaded
....
```

Notice that Maven is downloading from our proxy cache **internal** instead of getting everything from the **central** repository. This is the effect of the `<mirror>` setting, which we set earlier and this means that Archiva is already doing the proxying. We can go to the file system path where our **internal** repository is located or we can access the repository in our browser via its WebDAV URL (`http://localhost:8081/archiva/repository/internal`) to verify that the artifacts were downloaded.

When we have finished packaging our project, notice how long it took to build it. In my case, it took almost 12 minutes (**11 minutes 53 seconds** to be exact) to build, as shown in the following output:

```
...
[INFO] [war:war]
[INFO] Packaging webapp
[INFO] Assembling webapp[simple-webapp] in [/home/deng/simple-webapp/
target/simple-webapp]
[INFO] Processing war project
[INFO] Webapp assembled in[151 msecs]
[INFO] Building war: /home/deng/simple-webapp/target/simple-webapp.war
[INFO] -----------------------------------------------------------------
[INFO] BUILD SUCCESSFUL
[INFO] -----------------------------------------------------------------
[INFO] Total time: 11 minutes 53 seconds
[INFO] Finished at: Tue Sep 09 06:14:14 PHT 2008
[INFO] Final Memory: 12M/43M
[INFO] -----------------------------------------------------------------
```

Let's re-build the project again with a clean local repository. We will delete the contents of our `<USER_HOME>/.m2/book-repository` local repository and then package our project.

So, how long did our build go now? For me it took just **13 seconds**!

```
...
[INFO] [war:war]
[INFO] Packaging webapp
[INFO] Assembling webapp[simple-webapp] in [/home/deng/simple-webapp/
target/simple-webapp]
[INFO] Processing war project
[INFO] Webapp assembled in[90 msecs]
[INFO] Building war: /home/deng/simple-webapp/target/simple-webapp.war
[INFO] -----------------------------------------------------------------
[INFO] BUILD SUCCESSFUL
[INFO] -----------------------------------------------------------------
[INFO] Total time: 13 seconds
[INFO] Finished at: Tue Sep 09 06:33:00 PHT 2008
[INFO] Final Memory: 12M/82M
[INFO] -----------------------------------------------------------------
```

Now, that is the power of Archiva.

We have highlighted this as the first reason why we should install a repository manager and we have just experienced it first-hand. In the beginning section of this chapter, we mentioned that the ideal setup of a repository manager is to have it running within a local area network. This would address such cases wherein we have to build our project with a clean repository like when we have to re-format our machine (so we're starting from scratch again) or when a new team member comes in and builds the project for the first time.

Searching for artifacts in Archiva

Let's recall what we did in *Adding Dependencies* in Chapter 1, *Maven in a Nutshell*. You have used `Logger` and `LogFactory` in the `ExampleAction` class and got a compilation failure when you built the project. In order for Maven to build it successfully, you have to add the artifact that has that class as a dependency in your project's POM. However, what if you don't know which artifact that is?

A simple solution to this problem is to search for it in Archiva. As we already did some proxying above, the `slf4j-api.jar` should already be in our proxy cache **internal** so we can try to search for it.

 Newly proxied and deployed artifacts are immediately indexed after they arrive in the repository, which is the why we can already search and find the artifact for `Logger` or `LogFactory`.

In **Quick Search**, simply type **Logger**, hit **Search**, and Archiva will give us the artifact that contains the `Logger` class.

Aside from the Java class or package name search, we can also perform a basic text search. Let's type in **org** in the search box. Archiva will search for all the artifacts that contain the word **org**—whether it is an artifact that has a dependency with the word org in its `groupId` or `artifactId`, or the artifact itself has the word org in its identifiers, as shown in the following screenshot:

Notice in the **Quick Search** that there is a **Search within results** checkbox. If you want Archiva to search for a term within the bounds of the current result set, just tick this checkbox.

Aside from quick search, Archiva also provides an **Advanced Search** option. From the **Quick Search** page, click the **Advanced Search** link and a hidden frame will roll out like the one in the following screenshot:

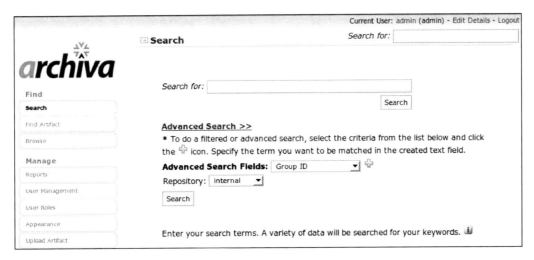

The fields that can be specified when performing an advanced search are listed in the **Advanced Search Fields** drop-down box. These are **Group ID**, **Artifact ID**, **Version**, **Class/Package Name**, and **Row Count**. To use any of these fields, for the search, select it from the drop-down menu and then click on the plus sign (**+**). A text box for the selected field will appear. That is where we will specify the value we want to search for. We can also opt to search for an artifact in a specific repository or search all repositories by selecting the appropriate value in the **Repository** field.

Let's try selecting the **Group ID**, **Artifact ID** and **Version** to see how the fields are created. Make sure that you click the **+** icon after each selection. For example, if we want to search for all artifacts in repository internal whose groupId starts with org.apache then we would specify this value in the **Group ID** field and select repository **internal** from the **Repository** list, then click **Search**. We should see search results similar to the following:

Archiva has another feature called **Find Artifact**. The main use of **Find Artifact** is for instances when we have a JAR file we want to use in our project but we don't know what its identifiers are so we can not add it in our POM.

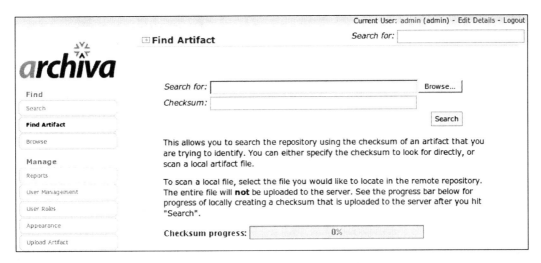

Find Artifact looks for that artifact by calculating the checksum of the specified artifact and searches the index for the checksum that matches it. That is why we can also specify the **Checksum** of our artifact (that is, if we know it) as an alternative to providing the artifact itself.

In the code included with this chapter, you will find the file `mystery-artifact.jar`. Go to the **Find Artifact** page, accept the applet signed by Brett, browse to our `mystery-artifact.jar` then click **Search**. And our mystery artifact is ... JUnit!

Deploying from Maven

We have learned how to use an Archiva repository as a proxy cache, now we will learn how to use it as a deployment repository and how to deploy from Maven. For this exercise, we will be using the `simple-webapp` project again from Chapter 1, *Maven Best Practices*, and the default **snapshots** repository for our deployment repository.

Recalling what we have learned about separating our repositories, we know that snapshots and releases need to go into different repositories. We already have a deployment repository for snapshots configured in our Archiva instance but we don't have a deployment repository for releases yet. We will create one for that. Go to the **Repositories** page again and add a **Managed Repository** with the following configuration:

After creating our deployment repository for releases, we need to create a new user account that we will use to deploy our project.

Creating a new user

In **User Management**, create a new user called `archiva` with `pass123` as its password. Grant the user a **Repository Manager** role for the repositories **releases** and **snapshots** by editing the user account and checking the appropriate boxes in the **Resource Roles** matrix.

As we can see, the **User Roles** page is divided into two groups—**Redback Xwork Integration Core** and **Archiva**. The former is specific to Redback while the latter are Archiva-specific roles. We will learn more about them in Chapter 12, *Maven, Archiva and Continuum in the Enterprise*.

Assigning the user a **Repository Manager** role means that we are granting the user **read** and **write** access to a repository (like what we did above). If we assigned the user with a **Repository Observer** role, it implies that we are just giving the user **read** access to the repository.

Finally, we must return to the user's page and uncheck the **Force User to Change Password** checkbox, then click **Update**. Otherwise, the user will not be able to deploy until their password is changed.

Configuring and deploying from Maven

Now we shall add the credentials for both the **snapshots** and **releases** repositories in our <M2_HOME>/conf/settings.xml file. For security reasons, the <server> configuration must be configured in the <USER.HOME>/.m2/settings.xml especially when the machine is a shared resource. You do not want other people who have access to the machine to be able to see your credentials. In our case, we are assuming that we are the only user of the machine so we are configuring it at the settings.xml in <M2_HOME>/conf/.

Starting with Maven 2.1.0, password encryption is possible. We will use this feature to mask our Archiva repository credentials in our settings.xml.

The first thing that we need to do is to generate an encrypted password by executing the following command:

```
$ mvn --encrypt-master-password [MY_MASTER_PASSWORD]
```

Copy and paste the result in your ~/.m2/security-settings.xml as follows:

```
<settingsSecurity>
  <master>{H76YGRZ4efoHWnMHJsD7ScbggOD3wS/Mt7NPHUYrhN370tdXqNkP6/
OnXFX5rn+O}</master>
</settingsSecurity>
```

Encrypt our Archiva repository password:

```
$ mvn --encrypt-password pass123
```

Copy and paste the result to the <M2_HOME>/conf/settings.xml file as follows:

```
...
<server>
  <id>snapshots</id>
  <username>archiva</username>
  <password>{UJnQYWnvmE8H2mcbITXKz2TGTtwVVcIuKT5upmjXrIw=}</password>
</server>
<server>
  <id>releases</id>
  <username>archiva</username>
  <password>{UJnQYWnvmE8H2mcbITXKz2TGTtwVVcIuKT5upmjXrIw=}</password>
</server>
...
```

More details on password security in Maven are covered in
`http://maven.apache.org/guides/mini/guide-encryption.html`.

> When configuring credentials in `settings.xml`, we must make sure
> that the `<id>` of our `<repository>` or `<mirror>` matches the `<id>`
> of our `<server>` in order for Maven to know which credentials to use
> to access the proxy cache. These IDs may not necessarily be the same as
> the ID of the repository in Archiva, we have just used the same ones for
> consistency purposes.

Aside from setting the credentials in our `settings.xml`, we also need to tell our
project where it will be deployed. To do that, we need to add the following in our
project's `pom.xml`:

```xml
<project>
...
  <distributionManagement>
    <repository>
      <id>releases</id>
      <name>Archiva Managed Releases Repository</name>
      <url>http://localhost:8081/archiva/repository/releases</url>
      <layout>default</layout>
    </repository>
    <snapshotRepository>
      <id>snapshots</id>
      <name>Archiva Managed Snapshots Repository</name>
      <url>http://localhost:8081/archiva/repository/snapshots</url>
      <uniqueVersion>true</uniqueVersion>
      <layout>default</layout>
    </snapshotRepository>
  </distributionManagement>
...
</project>
```

Again, we need to keep in mind that the repository `<id>` we have set in
`<distributionManagement>` must match the server `<id>` we have specified
in our `settings.xml`.

The `<distributionManagement>` tag is required in order to deploy our project, or
else we will get the following error:

```
...
[INFO] ------------------------------------------------------------------------
[ERROR] BUILD ERROR
[INFO] ------------------------------------------------------------------------
```

```
[INFO] Failed to configure plugin parameters for: org.apache.maven.
plugins:maven-deploy-plugin:2.3
```

check that the following section of the pom.xml is present and correct:

```
<distributionManagement>
  <!-- use the following if you're not using a snapshot version. -->
  <repository>
    <id>repo</id>
    <name>Repository Name</name>
    <url>scp://host/path/to/repo</url>
  </repository>
  <!-- use the following if you ARE using a snapshot version. -->
  <snapshotRepository>
    <id>repo</id>
    <name>Repository Name</name>
    <url>scp://host/path/to/repo</url>
  </snapshotRepository>
</distributionManagement>
```

```
Cause: Class 'org.apache.maven.artifact.repository.ArtifactRepository'
cannot be instantiated
[INFO] ------------------------------------------------------------
[INFO] For more information, run Maven with the -e switch
[INFO] ------------------------------------------------------------
[INFO] Total time: 1 minute
[INFO] Finished at: Tue Sep 09 07:45:44 PHT 2008
[INFO] Final Memory: 12M/82M
[INFO] ------------------------------------------------------------
```

If the project's version is a release version, Maven will deploy the project in the <repository> defined in the <distributionManagement> section. However, if the project's version is a snapshot, then Maven will deploy it in the defined <snapshotRepository>. If you want to deploy your snapshots and releases to a single repository, just omit the <snapshotRepository> and Maven will deploy it by default to the <repository> you have defined. This is not recommended though as this contradicts the Maven best practices as we have discussed in the previous sections.

After setting the deployment repository in our pom.xml, we can now deploy our project to our Archiva repository. To do this, just execute:

```
simple-webapp$ mvn deploy
```

And Maven will run the `deploy` goal of the `maven-deploy-plugin` on our project. We will see a similar output to the one below once the deployment is finished:

```
...
[INFO] [deploy:deploy]
altDeploymentRepository = null
[INFO] Retrieving previous build number from snapshots
[INFO] repository metadata for: 'snapshot com.example.chapter01:simple-
webapp:1.0-SNAPSHOT' could not be found on repository: snapshots, so will
be created
Uploading: http://localhost:8081/archiva/repository/snapshots/com/
example/chapter01/simple-webapp/1.0-SNAPSHOT/simple-webapp-1.0-
20080910.231236-1.war
23K uploaded
[INFO] Retrieving previous metadata from snapshots
[INFO] Uploading repository metadata for: 'artifact com.example.
chapter01:simple-webapp'
[INFO] Uploading project information for simple-webapp 1.0-
20080910.231236-1
[INFO] Retrieving previous metadata from snapshots
[INFO] Uploading repository metadata for: 'snapshot com.example.
chapter01:simple-webapp:1.0-SNAPSHOT'
[INFO] ------------------------------------------------------------------
[INFO] BUILD SUCCESSFUL
[INFO] ------------------------------------------------------------------
[INFO] Total time: 12 minutes 30 seconds
[INFO] Finished at: Thu Sep 11 07:12:36 PHT 2008
[INFO] Final Memory: 13M/43M
[INFO] ------------------------------------------------------------------
```

Notice the version of our project. Instead of `1.0-SNAPSHOT`, it became `1.0-20080910.231236-1`. The middle value in between the two hyphens (-) is the build time stamp while the number `1` after the last hyphen (-) is the build number. This is the effect of the `<uniqueVersion>` parameter, which was set to true, earlier for the snapshots repository in the `<distributionManagement>`. So the next time we deploy the same snapshot version of our project, it would get the current build's time stamp and increment the build number (for example, `1.0-20080912.201032-2`) making the versions unique and no overwriting takes place. Otherwise, if it is set to false, then the artifact will be deployed with its version as is (for example, `1.0-SNAPSHOT`) and will be overwritten each time we deploy that snapshot version.

Deploying via web form

As an alternative to command-line deployment, Archiva also provides a web form for uploading Maven 2 artifacts. You can find this page in the **Manage** section's **Upload Artifact**. Only users with **Repository Manager** roles can upload artifacts in the repository, as with deploying from Maven.

As we can see from the following screenshot, the **Upload Artifact** page requires us to specify the `groupId`, `artifactId`, `version`, `packaging`, and the artifact file itself.

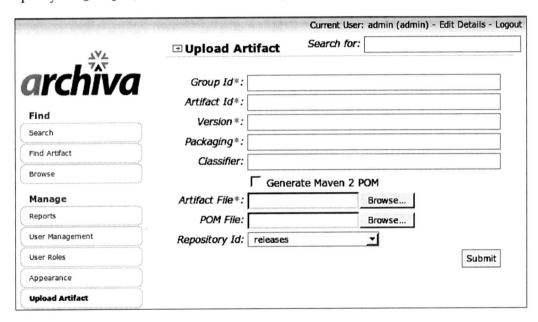

Archiva's **Upload Artifact** behaves like the `deploy-file` goal of the `maven-deploy-plugin`, which is why these five fields are required.

> The `deploy-file` goal is different from the `deploy` goal in that the former is used in cases where we have the artifact file (JAR, WAR, ZIP, and so on.) and not the sources and we want to deploy it to the repository, whereas the latter is used when we have the Maven 2 project sources and we want to build and deploy it to our repository. For more details about the deploy-file goal, checkout `http://maven.apache.org/plugins/maven-deploy-plugin/file-deployment.html`.

The **Artifact File** is where we specify the artifact we would like to deploy while the **POM File** is where we specify that artifact's POM. If we don't have the POM file on hand, we can opt to have Archiva generate the POM for us during deployment by ticking the **Generate Maven 2 POM** field. This feature is equivalent to the `generatePom` parameter of the `deploy-file` goal. We can choose from the list of repositories in the drop-down box where to deploy our artifact.

Summary

In this chapter, we have learned the usual problems encountered with large repositories and how repository managers address these pain points.

We have learned about Archiva and have seen up close some parts of it in action—how to configure and set up a proxy cache, how to make use of Archiva's search and find features, and how to deploy artifacts in an Archiva repository. All of these were demonstrated with a highlight on how Maven and Archiva can work together.

We have been building simple applications using Maven in the exercises of the first two chapters of this book. In the next chapter, we will learn how to efficiently configure and build a complete application using Maven.

3

Building an Application Using Maven

Ok, so you can build Maven projects, but as we saw in Chapter 1, *Maven in a Nutshell*, a Maven project is just a single unit of work and most development efforts produce a number of artifacts to assemble an entire application.

We have already seen a part of how this is done using dependencies. You may have already encountered Maven's inheritance mechanism for assembling multiple projects into a single build elsewhere.

In this chapter, we will take a closer look at these concepts, and introduce a convention for applications that covers all aspects of constructing a multi-module Maven project. We will also introduce a sample project that will be used throughout the other chapters of the book. Finally, we will look at various common scenarios for assembling a project.

Introducing the sample project

Throughout this book, we will look at the development of a sample project called Centrepoint, a basic but useful application that sets up a dashboard of project information.

 Centrepoint is the former name of Sydney Tower in Sydney, Australia. It is an easily recognizable landmark in the skyline. It can also help you get your bearings, as it is located near the center of the central business district and is visible from several different areas of the city.

In this chapter, we will set up the basic structure of the web application, add some documentation, and produce an assembly that can be used to distribute the application easily.

In the sample code associated with this chapter, you will see the result, along with the code to import a Maven project into the application, and display a basic view and links.

In later chapters, we will expand on the tests and quality reports of the project, and use the web services from Archiva and Continuum to view the latest deployments and build results for the project.

To begin with, we will have the following modules in the project:

- `model`: the application's data model for storing projects
- `store-api`: the programming interface for persistent application data
- `store-file`: a simple store implementation on the file system
- `webapp`: a web application for viewing the latest project information
- `maven-importer`: importing a Maven project file into the application

Artifact naming convention

You may have seen two styles of artifact naming conventions — simple names as above, and something like `centrepoint-model` that includes the last part of the group ID at the start of the artifact ID. The longer name should be considered as the convention, particularly if third parties use the artifact, as it makes the filename more recognizable. However, in an application such as this, the shorter names can be more convenient. The important convention that must be always retained is that the source control directory matches the artifact ID.

Setting up a multi-module build

It is rare for a project to contain just a single **module**. Even in a relatively simple application, having a monolithic source tree and build has quickly gone out of fashion, particularly for Java applications.

There are several reasons why having multiple modules is a good idea for a project whether it is using Maven or not:

- **Reusability**: Where appropriate, discrete libraries can be reused in different sections of the application or in other Maven projects as they are shared through the Maven repository.

- **Readability**: In many cases, it can be easier to navigate and understand an application that is broken up into self-contained modules.

- **Development efficiency**: By separating the build into logical subsystems, development can be focused in a certain area. Moreover, the development time can be improved by reducing compilation time and only running tests for modified code. This is particularly useful if different members of a team typically work on different modules.

- **Separate release cycles**: Stable code can be released independently and can be re-used by other projects too.

- **Enforced design constraints**: By making certain code unavailable to other modules, some expected design constraints could be enforced at build time. For example, an API can be separated from the implementation(s) to avoid consumers accidentally depending on implementation details.

Luckily, Maven makes modularization easy. A single POM remains the building block, so adding more modules involves a simple, incremental change. Using Maven's repository and dependency mechanism, the modules can then be linked together, with just a few particular techniques needed to learn for assembling the final application.

By doing so, you can construct your build using the same principles that are beneficial in other areas of software design, using inheritance and composition to simplify and decouple individual segments of the application.

Of course, as with anything, this requires balance. Endlessly adding modules, without justification, will increase complexity rather than decreasing it. Therefore, you must monitor and refactor your build as well, and to whatever extent possible plan for the application design as it affects the source code structure. Chapter 7, *Maven Best Practices*, contains a number of tips for selecting the right level of detail when modularizing your application.

Creating the parent POM

The first step for setting up the application structure is to create the parent POM. This process is the same whether you are starting a new project or expanding on a single module project by adding a common parent for a second module.

 At the time of writing, there is no archetype for creating a parent POM. However, given their simplicity, it is straightforward to create the POM by hand.

The only change that is required to a normal project is that the `packaging` element is set to `pom`. All other information is specified as you normally would, and the information that will be common to various modules should be given in the parent so that they don't need to be repeated, as Maven will ensure that they are inherited.

In our example application, we start by creating a working directory called `centrepoint`, and within it create the `pom.xml` file as follows:

```
<project xmlns="http://maven.apache.org/POM/4.0.0"
  xmlns:xsi="http://www.w3.org/2001/XMLSchema-instance"
  xsi:schemaLocation="http://maven.apache.org/POM/4.0.0
    http://maven.apache.org/maven-v4_0_0.xsd">
  <modelVersion>4.0.0</modelVersion>
  <name>Centrepoint</name>
  <groupId>com.effectivemaven.centrepoint</groupId>
  <artifactId>centrepoint</artifactId>
  <packaging>pom</packaging>
  <version>1.0-SNAPSHOT</version>
  <description>
    Centrepoint is a basic but useful application that sets up a
    dashboard of project information from Maven, Archiva and
    Continuum.
  </description>
</project>
```

We are now ready to create the modules of the application!

Parent POM naming convention

It is a good idea to use the name of the application as it is for the parent POM, rather than suffixing the artifact ID with `-parent`, which is typically more suitable for organization parent POMs. Examples of these types of POMs are illustrated later in this chapter.

Creating the modules

The best way to structure modular applications with Maven is for the application's parent to sit at the top of the directory tree; with the modules sitting in a subdirectory under that (this may occur to multiple levels). Initially our directory structure will look like the following:

```
centrepoint
|-- maven-importer
|-- model
|-- store-api
|-- store-file
`-- webapp
```

With the parent POM in place, we can quickly add the modules we expect to have, as listed earlier, by using the `archetype:generate` command. In each case, the defaults will be suitable, with the exception of the `webapp` module where the `webapp` archetype must be selected from the list rather than the default `quickstart` archetype.

```
centrepoint$ mvn archetype:generate -DartifactId=model \
             -DgroupId=com.effectivemaven.centrepoint
[...]
centrepoint$ mvn archetype:generate -DartifactId=maven-importer \
             -DgroupId=com.effectivemaven.centrepoint
[...]
centrepoint$ mvn archetype:generate -DartifactId=store-api \
             -DgroupId=com.effectivemaven.centrepoint
[...]
centrepoint$ mvn archetype:generate -DartifactId=store-file \
             -DgroupId=com.effectivemaven.centrepoint
[...]
centrepoint$ mvn archetype:generate -DartifactId=webapp \
             -DgroupId=com.effectivemaven.centrepoint
[...]
```

Having run these commands, skeleton modules are in place for the entire application. Though it doesn't yet do much, it can be built in its entirety from the root POM using Maven. The reason for this can be seen if `pom.xml` is inspected, as the archetype plugin added the following elements automatically:

```
    ...
    <modules>
      <module>model</module>
      <module>maven-importer</module>
      <module>store-api</module>
      <module>store-file</module>
      <module>webapp</module>
    </modules>
  </project>
```

These module elements define which modules will also be built whenever the top-level project is built, allowing an aggregated result to be produced in one command.

The trick above is one of the benefits of using the Archetype plugin to generate new modules, as it saves having to remember to type the new modules by hand. However, this is not all that it does. If you inspect the POM of one of the new modules, such as `model/pom.xml`, you will notice an additional `parent` element that is not normally generated:

```
. . .
<modelVersion>4.0.0</modelVersion>
<parent>
  <artifactId>centrepoint</artifactId>
  <groupId>com.effectivemaven.centrepoint</groupId>
  <version>1.0-SNAPSHOT</version>
</parent>
. . .
```

This is a link back to the parent project; it enables Maven's project inheritance mechanism. If you haven't encountered the concept in Maven before, the referenced POM has its fields inherited into the current project where appropriate. The project is intended to be retrieved from the repository, allowing a project to be built regardless of where the parent project is located. However, by default, `../pom.xml` is also used to make development in the standard structure easier. More information on using project inheritance to your advantage can be found in Chapter 7, *Maven Best Practices*.

In this case, we have a bidirectional link between the parent and the child project through the `parent` element and the `module` element. While it is possible to build a set of projects that have different parents (or none at all), it is much less intuitive to those building the project.

While the archetypes we have used here have simplified putting some of the boilerplate in place, they have also generated some information that is no longer necessary. Thanks to project inheritance, values that are inherited can be removed, and some template values should be adjusted:

- The `groupId` and `version` elements are identical to the parent and can be removed in the children
- The `url` element is incorrect and better removed as it will be inherited once set
- The `name` element defaults to the `artifactId`, but is better changed to a more descriptive name such as `Centrepoint Data Store API` and so on.
- The JUnit dependency should be removed and added to the parent project as it is used in all submodules

The resulting POMs for each of the modules now look much friendlier:

```xml
<?xml version="1.0"?>
<project>
  <modelVersion>4.0.0</modelVersion>
  <parent>
    <artifactId>centrepoint</artifactId>
    <groupId>com.effectivemaven.centrepoint</groupId>
    <version>1.0-SNAPSHOT</version>
  </parent>
  <artifactId>store-api</artifactId>
  <name>Centrepoint Data Store API</name>
</project>
```

If the removed JUnit dependency was also added to the parent project, then building from the top level should still succeed.

> **XML namespace declaration**
>
> Though it is not required, if you anticipate editing the pom.xml file in an XML editor, having the namespace declaration that we added to the parent POM is helpful for auto completion.

Dependency management

Even though we have created all the necessary modules for the application, as soon as the code is added, they will need to refer to each other. To achieve this, as with any external library, dependency elements are added to the modules.

In our example, we will add the following dependencies:

- store-api will depend on model
- store-file will depend on store-api and model
- maven-importer will depend on store-api and model
- webapp will depend on store-file and maven-importer

Thanks to Maven's transitive dependencies, the web application actually depends on all of the modules, as you would expect. However, you may be asking why then store-file depends on model, as it is available transitively through store-api. While this is true and the model dependency could be omitted, it is a good practice to explicitly declare all dependencies that you will use directly. This is discussed in Chapter 7, *Maven Best Practices*.

The majority of dependencies can be added in the traditional way. For example, within the `store-api` module, we add the following:

```
<dependencies>
  <dependency>
    <groupId>${project.groupId}</groupId>
    <artifactId>model</artifactId>
    <version>${project.version}</version>
  </dependency>
</dependencies>
```

Note the optional use of expressions to avoid having to retype the values that are the same throughout the application.

Even before code that utilizes the dependencies is in place, you can notice a difference when the application is built. Where previously the build occurred in the order defined in the modules section:

```
[INFO]  Reactor build order:
[INFO]    Centrepoint
[INFO]    Centrepoint Data Model
[INFO]    Centrepoint Maven Project Importer
[INFO]    Centrepoint Data Store API
[INFO]    Centrepoint Data Store (Flat file)
[INFO]    Centrepoint Web Application
```

It now has been adjusted to honor the dependency relationships introduced:

```
[INFO]  Reactor build order:
[INFO]    Centrepoint
[INFO]    Centrepoint Data Model
[INFO]    Centrepoint Data Store API
[INFO]    Centrepoint Maven Project Importer
[INFO]    Centrepoint Data Store (Flat file)
[INFO]    Centrepoint Web Application
```

Regardless of how the modules are ordered in the parent POM, the overall interdependencies of the modules will be considered first, with the module ordering specified in the POM used otherwise.

One further optimization is commonly made in multiple module projects. Rather than declaring the version in every module again, we can add a `dependencyManagement` block to the parent that specifies a template for the use of any dependencies:

```
<dependencyManagement>
  <dependencies>
    <dependency>
      <groupId>${project.groupId}</groupId>
      <artifactId>model</artifactId>
      <version>${project.version}</version>
    </dependency>
    ...
    <dependency>
      <groupId>${project.groupId}</groupId>
      <artifactId>store-file</artifactId>
      <version>${project.version}</version>
    </dependency>
  </dependencies>
</dependencyManagement>
```

This does not mean that every project uses these dependencies (in contrast to the JUnit dependency); otherwise, the model project would depend on itself!

With these in place, the dependency elements in the modules can be reduced to the following format:

```
<dependency>
  <groupId>${project.groupId}</groupId>
  <artifactId>model</artifactId>
</dependency>
```

More information on using the dependency management feature effectively can also be found in Chapter 7, *Maven Best Practices*.

It has previously been discussed that the above behavior might be made the default for dependencies with the same group ID in future versions of Maven. This will make the dependencyManagement element unnecessary for this purpose and used only for the versions of external dependencies. Look out for this change in new releases as a way to simplify your POMs further.

Fleshing out the example application

At this point, we have most of the Maven infrastructure in place, so all that is needed is to write the code!

As we used the default archetype, the first step is usually to rename App.java and AppTest.java to the name of the first class in the package and start adding functionality to replace the placeholders.

We won't examine the development of the application in further detail here. For more information on how it was written, you can see the developer documentation in the source tree (which we will be encountering shortly in this chapter). You can refer to the completed example in the sample code for this chapter. The code in the start directory is the application to this point in the chapter, while the code in the final directory reflects the rest of the changes in the chapter.

We can observe that in this particular application, we have chosen to use TestNG instead of JUnit 3.8, so the dependency in the parent POM earlier has been replaced, and the test classes rewritten accordingly. This will be further discussed and enhanced in the next chapter.

 Thanks to our preemptive use of inheritance earlier, we only had to replace JUnit with TestNG in one place!

Having the first prototype of the application written (including tests) is great, but there are still more improvements that we can make to the Maven project structure for use in a team, distribution of the final application, and further growth of the project. We will continue to explore that throughout the rest of the chapter.

Creating an organization POM

We have already seen the benefits of applying common settings across an application using inheritance, so why not take that one step further?

A commonly utilized concept in this situation is referred to as an **Organization POM**. This means creating a parent POM that is shared among multiple applications within an organization and contains Maven project settings that are relevant to all projects in that organizational unit. The organization may be a team, a division, or an entire company, and multiple levels of inheritance can be used to represent different hierarchies where it makes sense to do so.

While Maven does not have any specialized handling for the use case — the behavior is identical to any other parent POM — the conceptual difference leads to a slightly different structure.

Firstly, the release cycle will be different. The organization unit is likely to be changed less frequently than the application is released, so it tends to be on a separate release cycle. As traditional version numbers don't often have the same meaning for this use case, the commonly practiced convention is to use an integer that increments upwards from 1 as the version.

Let's introduce an organization unit for this book, com.effectivemaven.

Let's create the new parent POM in `../effectivemaven-parent/pom.xml` to look like this:

```
<project xmlns="http://maven.apache.org/POM/4.0.0"
  xmlns:xsi="http://www.w3.org/2001/XMLSchema-instance"
  xsi:schemaLocation="http://maven.apache.org/POM/4.0.0
    http://maven.apache.org/maven-v4_0_0.xsd">
  <modelVersion>4.0.0</modelVersion>
  <name>Apache Maven 2: Effective Implementations Book</name>
  <groupId>com.effectivemaven</groupId>
  <artifactId>effectivemaven-parent</artifactId>
  <packaging>pom</packaging>
  <version>1-SNAPSHOT</version>
  <organization>
    <name>Apache Maven 2: Effective Implementations Book</name>
    <url>http://www.effectivemaven.com</url>
  </organization>
</project>
```

As you can see, we retain the `SNAPSHOT` suffix on the version while it is in development like any other project. Once the parent has been finalized for a first version, it can be released as version `1`, then changed to `2-SNAPSHOT`, and so on.

To refer to the organization POM from a project, the normal Maven parent element is added to the root POM of the Centrepoint build:

```
...
<modelVersion>4.0.0</modelVersion>
<parent>
  <groupId>com.effectivemaven</groupId>
  <artifactId>effectivemaven-parent</artifactId>
  <version>1-SNAPSHOT</version>
</parent>
...
```

Another consequence of having a separate release cycle is that the POM should be stored in a separate source control trunk. This means that the parent must be built and installed in the repository before it can be used, as it will not be in the default location of `../pom.xml`. If you have a consistent structure for checking out these two trunks, however, it is possible to give Maven a hint where to find the latest version without having to install it into the local repository.

```
<parent>
  <groupId>com.effectivemaven</groupId>
  <artifactId>effectivemaven-parent</artifactId>
  <version>1-SNAPSHOT</version>
  <relativePath>../effectivemaven-parent/pom.xml</relativePath>
</parent>
```

The use of `relativePath` can be quite useful in this situation, though it must be remembered that it is only a *hint*, if it is not there then Maven will still refer to the local repository, and eventually in a release scenario the file will not be present and so the parent will be retrieved from the repository. For this reason, it should be used cautiously—it is important that the correct parent is in the repository for consistent behavior.

> The `relativePath` field can also be used in a multi-module build that does not follow the recommended conventions, with the same note of caution as above.

It is worth noting that there is presently no way to automatically select the right version of the organization POM to use. Therefore, when a release of the organization POM is made, all projects will need to be updated by hand. It is not always necessary to do this immediately, depending on the type of change made. However, it is important that parent releases occur reasonably soon after a set of changes so that they don't block the release of one of the projects needing to consume the changes. Like other dependencies, it is not possible to release with a snapshot parent that is not part of the current release, and it is important to lock it to a release version for reproducibility reasons. The Versions Maven Plugin can help keep the version of the organization POM up to date in your projects—for more information see `http://mojo.codehaus.org/versions-maven-plugin/examples/update-parent.html`.

As with any form of inheritance, you have the freedom to include any information that you want to in the organization POM, removing them from the project's POM if necessary to avoid duplication. The most commonly found elements are:

- Infrastructure, and in particular the distribution management section
- The developers on a team
- Standardized plugin versions and configuration

For our project, we will add all three of these elements to the organization POM. Firstly, there is the `distributionManagement` element pointing to Archiva, which we configured in Chapter 2, *Staying in Control with Archiva*:

```
<distributionManagement>
  <repository>
    <id>releases</id>
    <url>http://localhost:8081/archiva/repository/releases</url>
  </repository>
  <snapshotRepository>
    <id>snapshots</id>
```

```
      <url>
        http://localhost:8081/archiva/repository/snapshots
      </url>
    </snapshotRepository>
  </distributionManagement>
```

Next, the developers on this project:

```
<developers>
  <developer>
    <id>brett</id>
    <name>Brett Porter</name>
    <timezone>+10</timezone>
  </developer>
  <developer>
    <id>oching</id>
    <name>Deng Ching</name>
    <timezone>+8</timezone>
  </developer>
</developers>
```

Finally, the now familiar plugin configuration for the compiler plugin to indicate all of our projects will be using Java 5 by default:

```
<build>
  <pluginManagement>
    <plugins>
      <plugin>
        <groupId>org.apache.maven.plugins</groupId>
        <artifactId>maven-compiler-plugin</artifactId>
        <version>2.0.2</version>
        <configuration>
            <source>1.5</source>
            <target>1.5</target>
        </configuration>
      </plugin>
    </plugins>
  </pluginManagement>
</build>
```

In this section, it is quite common just to list plugins and versions to set some basic standards for other projects to use. Another good set of configuration to share is that of the team's standard quality checks, which we will encounter in Chapter 5, *Reporting and Checks*.

We can now confirm that the build still works before continuing:

```
centrepoint$ mvn install
```

Configuring basic reports

Returning now to the application code, one of the best steps to take near the start of a project is to put the framework for documentation and reporting in place. By having this in place early, the chance that it will be maintained throughout the life of the project is increased.

As the structure we established earlier contains all Java code modules, it would be useful to generate some information about it. For that purpose, we can add the Javadoc and JXR (source code cross-reference) reporting plugins to create a reference site.

Establishing this is quite simple when using the standard configuration, and for good measure, we throw in the aggregate flag so that one copy is generated for the whole project instead of a separate set for each module.

```
<reporting>
  <plugins>
    <plugin>
      <groupId>org.apache.maven.plugins</groupId>
      <artifactId>maven-javadoc-plugin</artifactId>
      <version>2.5</version>
      <configuration>
        <aggregate>true</aggregate>
      </configuration>
    </plugin>
    <plugin>
      <groupId>org.apache.maven.plugins</groupId>
      <artifactId>maven-jxr-plugin</artifactId>
      <version>2.1</version>
      <configuration>
        <aggregate>true</aggregate>
      </configuration>
    </plugin>
  </plugins>
</reporting>
```

This plugin configuration is added to the topmost module where the aggregated content will be produced (in this case, centrepoint/pom.xml). Note that we don't put it into the organization POM, as some projects may not be Java projects, or may not be code projects at all. This differs from the Compiler plugin example above, which used pluginManagement to ensure the Java configuration would only be used on Java projects that already use the Compiler plugin.

One of the disadvantages of using the `reporting` element is that it is hard to share configuration across projects, with the lack of a `pluginManagement` equivalent. If you are using the reports in addition to the corresponding checks, it is worth considering using the site build lifecycle instead and manually configuring your site navigation. For more information, see Chapter 5, *Reporting and Checks*.

The reference site can be generated for the project from the `centrepoint` directory using the standard site lifecycle that we saw in Chapter 1, *Maven in a Nutshell*:

```
centrepoint$ mvn site
```

The resulting references will be in `target/site/apidocs` and `target/site/xref`, and linked in from the main site at `target/site/index.html`.

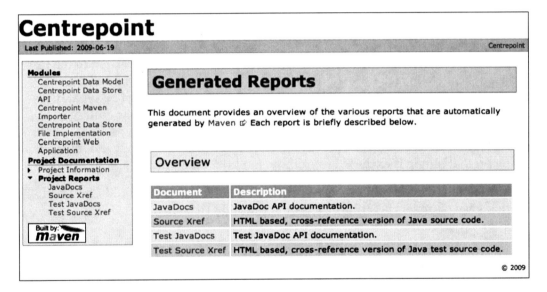

Depending on where you store your development documentation and how much you already have in your Javadoc, you may like to add more content to the main site that provides useful information for developers of the project itself. Note that this is not for end-users of the application! Unless you are writing a framework where the development documentation is part of what the end users need to read, and then end user documentation can be handled separately at a later stage.

The sample application of this chapter provides some development specific documentation on the front page of its site, with the source content in **Almost Plain Text (APT)** formatted files under `src/site/apt` of the project, which provides a working example to think about for your own projects.

For more information on the APT format, refer to
http://maven.apache.org/doxia/references/apt-format.html.

Preparing for non-code modules

I mentioned in the previous section that unless you are writing a framework, the documentation for the code would likely not be the same as the documentation for the rest of the application. If you intend to build that documentation with Maven as well, then it will need to be built separately, outside of the tree of modules that contains the code.

Likewise, there may be other modules that can be built separately. They include the distribution of the application, which depends on all of the others but does not necessarily need to be built every time, and does not have any specific functionality or reporting of its own.

While these modules are apparently separate, they are still closely related to the rest of the application. In fact, they should be part of the overall release and bear the same version number as the modules themselves, so they should not be separated entirely. In addition, we will need a place to configure plugins for the entire application, as well as those specific to the code modules (such as reporting). While most plugins can be configured to exclude certain modules selectively, it will be simpler if that plugin is excluded from those modules altogether.

To address this, we are going to use a convention for such Maven builds, and add another level of project inheritance to our application structure.

Documentation versions

Not all projects distribute their documentation with the application, or even lock it down to a released version. At the time of writing, Maven itself only has one copy of its documentation (which is always for the latest version). Whether this approach suits you will depend on how your documentation is maintained and used, and whether it is to be distributed with the application. For frameworks and applications where a particular version is expected to be used for some time after newer revisions are available, maintaining a copy of the documentation relevant to that particular version either online or as a separate download is highly recommended.

Creating a modules tree

The first step is to create a new POM that will aggregate the existing modules. It is faster to copy the existing one from `centrepoint/pom.xml` into `centrepoint/modules/pom.xml` and adjust the fields, as most of the current parent POM is related to the code modules.

Changing the new POM is simple. Change the artifact ID and project name, and replace the parent reference with the new parent project:

```xml
<modelVersion>4.0.0</modelVersion>
<parent>
  <groupId>com.effectivemaven.centrepoint</groupId>
  <artifactId>centrepoint</artifactId>
  <version>1.0-SNAPSHOT</version>
</parent>
<artifactId>modules</artifactId>
<name>Centrepoint Java Modules</name>
<packaging>pom</packaging>
```

Note that as the parent now has the same group ID and version, we can remove them from the current POM leaving just the new artifact ID. The description and license can also be removed, as they will be inherited.

The next task is to move all of the module subdirectories into the new directory, in this case called `modules`. If you are using version control, you should use the built-in command to move these directories, such as:

centrepoint$ svn mv webapp modules

If you have not yet checked the structure into source control, you can move the directories freely.

Eventually we have a complete directory structure that looks like the following:

```
|-- centrepoint
|     `-- modules
|           |-- maven-importer
|           |-- model
|           |-- src
|           |-- store-api
|           |-- store-file
|           `-- webapp
`-- effectivemaven-parent
```

Moving the directories will ensure that the aggregation side of the relationship works correctly, but each project still points to the original parent. *This is actually a valid Maven configuration so it will not cause an error, even though it may not produce the results you expect.*

 Maven doesn't enforce modules and parents to match up, so when you are moving modules around within a multi-module project, be sure to check that the parents have been adjusted accordingly.

To prevent future confusion, we should change the parent of all of the modules to the new module parent, for example:

```
<parent>
  <groupId>com.effectivemaven.centrepoint</groupId>
  <artifactId>modules</artifactId>
  <version>1.0-SNAPSHOT</version>
</parent>
<artifactId>model</artifactId>
```

Finally, the top-level parent POM needs to be adjusted to the new layout, by adding the new module, and removing the elements that are no longer necessary. The result should look similar to the following:

```
<?xml version="1.0" encoding="UTF-8"?>
<project xmlns="http://maven.apache.org/POM/4.0.0"
  xmlns:xsi="http://www.w3.org/2001/XMLSchema-instance"
  xsi:schemaLocation="http://maven.apache.org/POM/4.0.0
    http://maven.apache.org/maven-v4_0_0.xsd">
  <modelVersion>4.0.0</modelVersion>
  <parent>
    <groupId>com.effectivemaven</groupId>
    <artifactId>effectivemaven-parent</artifactId>
    <version>1-SNAPSHOT</version>
    <relativePath>
      ../effectivemaven-parent/pom.xml
    </relativePath>
  </parent>
  <name>Centrepoint</name>
  <groupId>com.effectivemaven.centrepoint</groupId>
  <artifactId>centrepoint</artifactId>
  <packaging>pom</packaging>
  <version>1.0-SNAPSHOT</version>
  <licenses>
```

```
<license>
   <name>The Apache Software License, Version 2.0</name>
   <url>http://www.apache.org/licenses/LICENSE-2.0.txt</url>
   <distribution>repo</distribution>
</license>
</licenses>
<description>
   Centrepoint is a basic but useful application that sets up a
   dashboard of project information from Maven, Archiva and
   Continuum.
</description>
<modules>
   <module>modules</module>
</modules>
</project>
```

As you can see, this is very similar to the POM that we used in the beginning, but now refers to the `modules` tree containing all of the Java modules that we set up previously.

> With all the directory movements, this may have seemed like the long way around to achieve this result. While this would be the ideal technique to introduce the separation to an existing project, if you were starting with a clean slate it would certainly be easier to create this structure from the beginning.

Note that the reference site that we generated earlier should now be generated only from the `modules` subdirectory, not from the top-level project. As we will see in the next section, we are now able to produce a different type of documentation for the application.

Adding a documentation module

Whether you are building a small application for internal use, or a product that will be shipped to thousands, you will need some form of documentation to accompany it. The amount of documentation needed can range from just a few pages to comprehensive manuals (though the number of pages written usually amounts to much less!)

There are also varieties of tools that can be used to produce the documentation — from simple text files to PDFs that have been carefully and professionally produced.

Maven provides a number of options for dealing with documents in one or more of these forms, either by using plugins or Maven's site capabilities to generate the entire documentation set, packaging up the pre-generated PDFs as is, or some combination of both. It is important to remember that Maven sites don't have to be tied to project reports, nor do they need to be styled with the boring, boxy, default theme that can be found on open source projects all across the web. Regardless of which you choose, if you intend to distribute the documentation with the application and freeze it at release time with a particular version, you should add a module that contains the documentation source and output.

Here we are not talking about a project web site, or documentation that is constantly updated and not released. Such documentation should be stored in a separate version control trunk and, if Maven is even used to manage them, built by a separate Maven project.

For our example application, we will be using Maven to generate a web site by transforming input files into HTML. However, we will also illustrate how to incorporate other resources directly for those that wish to produce the documentation separately. The resulting documentation will be both deployed to a web server and distributed with the application.

The documentation project should be created in the top-level parent directory of the application, so that it resides *alongside* the `modules` directory. Luckily, to get started again we have an archetype. It is shown below:

```
centrepoint$ mvn archetype:generate -DartifactId=documentation \
                -DgroupId=com.effectivemaven.centrepoint \
                -DarchetypeArtifactId=maven-archetype-site-simple
```

This serves as a suitable starting point and generating the site from the documentation directory will already work. Three files were created from the archetype:

- `pom.xml`: the documentation POM
- `src/site/site.xml`: the site descriptor with layout, navigation and additional metadata
- `src/site/apt/index.apt`: a simple front page in plain text format

The content of the site files will not be examined in detail here, however you can refer to the code for this chapter that contains some complete documentation and a site descriptor.

As usual, some customization of the generated POM is needed:

- The redundant group ID and version can again be removed as they match the parent

- The archetype doesn't create a name, so one needs to be added

- As the site will be deployed, the `url` element that specifies which URL will later be used to view it should be added to the POM

- Disable the default reports to keep the site to a minimum by adding the `excludeDefaults` flag to the `reporting` section

- The `distributionManagement` element contains an example value that needs to be replaced

The following is the content of the expected POM:

```xml
<?xml version="1.0" encoding="UTF-8"?>
<project xmlns="http://maven.apache.org/POM/4.0.0"
  xmlns:xsi="http://www.w3.org/2001/XMLSchema-instance"
  xsi:schemaLocation="http://maven.apache.org/POM/4.0.0
    http://maven.apache.org/maven-v4_0_0.xsd">
  <modelVersion>4.0.0</modelVersion>
  <parent>
    <artifactId>centrepoint</artifactId>
    <groupId>com.effectivemaven.centrepoint</groupId>
    <version>1.0-SNAPSHOT</version>
  </parent>
  <artifactId>documentation</artifactId>
  <name>Centrepoint Documentation</name>
  <url>
    http://www.effectivemaven.com/centrepoint/docs/${project.version}/
  </url>
  <packaging>pom</packaging>
  <distributionManagement>
    <site>
      <id>website</id>
      <url>
        file:///${basedir}/www/centrepoint/docs/${project.version}
      </url>
    </site>
  </distributionManagement>
  <reporting>
    <excludeDefaults>true</excludeDefaults>
  </reporting>
</project>
```

The deployment location in this example is contrived, storing it again in the project directory when the `site-deploy` command is run, and would usually be replaced with the remote server to deploy it to that corresponds with the `url` field of the POM. However, it does point out that you can include the project version in the path of the deployed documentation so that over time versions can be retained separately for posterity.

Building the site automatically

The example so far has required that `mvn site` be run from the directory of the documentation. However, this will not be automated or useful when it comes to bundling the documentation.

To overcome this issue, the site goal can be bound to the lifecycle like any other goal. This has obvious advantages for automation, but the disadvantage of missing the rest of the site lifecycle preventing the use of more of the framework.

```
<build>
  <plugins>
    <plugin>
      <groupId>org.apache.maven.plugins</groupId>
      <artifactId>maven-site-plugin</artifactId>
      <executions>
        <execution>
          <id>site</id>
          <phase>generate-resources</phase>
          <goals>
            <goal>site</goal>
          </goals>
        </execution>
      </executions>
    </plugin>
  </plugins>
</build>
```

Here, the goal is bound to the `generate-resources` phase in anticipation that it will be bundled for distribution with the application in the `package` phase. In addition to the above, you may like to add the `deploy` goal to the `deploy` phase as well. This can either be done in the default lifecycle to deploy every snapshot of the site, or can be added to a release profile to perform only the deployment on release. For more information on releases with Maven, see Chapter 9, *Continuum in Depth*.

Assembling the site for distribution

We have not quite come to the point of producing the distribution in this chapter, but it is worth being prepared for that.

When producing artifacts in a multi-module build, one of the best practices to follow is to avoid referencing files outside of the current module directly and using the local repository to share all build artifacts. This will ensure that even if a subset of the project is checked out and built, it will succeed and make the build more resistant to problems, if there are layout changes later. For this reason, we create an assembly of the site contents rather than referring to the generated output directly from other parts of the build.

```
<plugin>
  <groupId>org.apache.maven.plugins</groupId>
  <artifactId>maven-assembly-plugin</artifactId>
  <version>2.1</version>
  <configuration>
    <descriptor>src/site/assembly/docs.xml</descriptor>
  </configuration>
  <executions>
    <execution>
      <phase>package</phase>
      <goals>
        <goal>single</goal>
      </goals>
    </execution>
  </executions>
</plugin>
```

Here, we use the Assembly plugin to produce a ZIP file of the content. By using the `single` goal, it can be bound to the lifecycle, and the resulting ZIP file is added to the list of artifacts to be installed and deployed if those lifecycle phases are run. This means that the ZIP file can later be used as a dependency by other modules.

The format of that ZIP file is described by the assembly descriptor, `src/site/assembly/docs.xml`, which was specified by the assembly plugin configuration.

```
<assembly>
  <id>docs</id>
  <formats>
    <format>zip</format>
  </formats>
  <includeBaseDirectory>false</includeBaseDirectory>
  <fileSets>
    <fileSet>
      <directory>target/site</directory>
      <outputDirectory>/</outputDirectory>
    </fileSet>
  </fileSets>
</assembly>
```

The Assembly plugin will be reviewed in more detail in the next section. However, in this simple example it is clear that the generated site content from `target/site` is being included in the ZIP file. This will allow us to extract the ZIP file directly into a subdirectory of the final application distribution.

If we build the documentation module, we will see that the site is now built and installed into the local repository automatically:

```
documentation$ mvn install
```

Adding site resources

Earlier in the section, it was mentioned that general resources could be included in the documentation. How this is handled depends on whether or not the Site plugin is being used.

The site plugin accommodates resources in the `src/site/resources` directory. Regardless of the type of file, these will be copied into the `target/site` directory as part of the site generation. As you can tell, this makes the process very simple, as the existing assembly descriptor will pick up those resources.

However, what if (unlike the example in this chapter) we were just including resources for the documentation and not generating a site? In this instance, while we would have skipped the Site plugin above, we would still have the Assembly plugin, but with a slight change to the file set that it contained.

Let's imagine that we had all of our documentation pre-generated in the `src/docs` directory. In that case, the assembly descriptor would change as follows:

```
...
<fileset>
  <directory>src/docs</directory>
  <outputDirectory>/</outputDirectory>
</fileset>
...
```

This setup makes for a much simpler build process, however with the added overhead of having to generate the documentation separately and copy it into the build directory (and remember to do so at the right time!)

When only few resources are being used, it might make as much sense to simply include the resources directly into the final application assembly instead of having a separate documentation module. This has some advantages in simplicity and to some extent performance, but on the downside, it makes adding generated documentation more difficult if it is needed later, and does not allow the documents to be reused in multiple different modules as a dependency, so this decision should be weighed carefully.

Adding a skin

So far, in this chapter, we have generated two Maven sites — one for the development documentation, and one for the end user documentation. These were useful, but they were certainly not particularly attractive! Thankfully, the Site plugin includes a mechanism to create a **skin** to produce a reusable set of style information, which can then be used to apply an improved, consistent style to both sets of documentation.

Creating a skin module is just a standard JAR with some specific resources, so the default archetype can be used as before, from the top-level centrepoint directory.

```
centrepoint$ mvn archetype:generate -DartifactId=skin \
              -DgroupId=com.effectivemaven.centrepoint
```

Of course, the regular post-generation cleanup is needed, and in this case, the Java sources and tests should be removed, as the JAR will only need a set of resources.

The resources which can be added are:

- `src/main/resources/css/maven-theme.css` — the CSS for the site
- `src/main/resources/META-INF/maven/site.vm` — the Velocity template for generating XHTML from the input content

In each case, a default will be used if one of these resources is not supplied. Other resources stored under `src/main/resources` (such as an `images` directory) will be copied into the eventual site root.

While demonstrating a new CSS and XHTML layout goes beyond the scope of this book (and my creative abilities!), an improved skin is provided in the example code for this chapter.

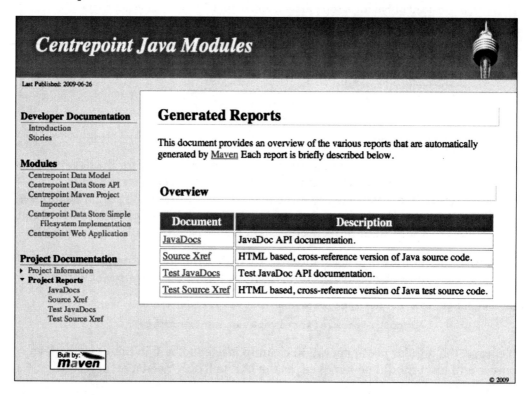

To use the skin from the projects that produce sites, the following needs to be added to the descriptor of each site:

```
<project>
  <skin>
    <groupId>com.effectivemaven.centrepoint</groupId>
    <artifactId>skin</artifactId>
    <version>${project.version}</version>
  </skin>
  ...
```

The skin reference is a normal artifact from the repository, so the JAR that was produced by the new module, once built, will be used from these two projects.

However, there is one problem with this setup. Maven doesn't read into the site descriptor to realize that the project has a dependency on the skin, so the build will not occur in the correct order.

One solution would be to add the skin to the dependency list for the documentation project. However, this is not an option for the modules generation, which happens to occur first. Likewise, it could be added as a plugin dependency for the site plugin. However, this will only work with Maven 2.1.0 and above.

The simplest workaround available is to move the skin to the top of the list of the modules in the POM file.

Regardless, with the new skin available, both sites now look much more attractive and better integrated, and the skin build itself is conveniently included into the build process for the application.

 In many organizations, the skin will be reused across many projects. In this case, rather than being contained in the application build process, it would make sense to build and release the skin separately.

Distributing the application

We now come to the last step in the process of assembling an application—producing the final distribution. This is the process that takes everything that we build and gets it into the hands of our users—whether it is customers using a software product, or system administrators that deploy the application into a production environment.

In our example, we have a web application that we have already built. In some environments, that may well be enough all by itself. The web application can be deployed to a Maven repository and the version is always available for others to retrieve it and deploy it to an application server. The other artifacts of the application are also deployed, such as the Java libraries, and the documentation ZIP file from the previous sections, all for separate consumption.

However, in many cases it also makes sense to bundle several of these into a single artifact for easier consumption. This might be in a compressed archive (ZIP, TAR.GZ, or TAR.BZ2), or an installer generated by one of many different products. Another alternative for Java applications in some cases is a self-executable JAR—an example of producing one of these using the Shade plugin is available in Chapter 6, *Useful Maven Plugins*.

The plugin that will regularly be used for this task is the Assembly plugin. This Maven plugin was designed to take a flexible set of input files, including build artifacts and dependencies, and produce a structured archive in almost any format that can then be compressed and shipped. Whether the distribution is a simple archive of a web application, license, and a *read me* file, or a complex layout of a complete application file system, or a distribution of the source code itself, the Assembly plugin will have it covered.

In our standard application layout that we have been describing, the distribution resides at the top level of the project, alongside the documentation and the modules, as it is not a code module itself.

 You might expect the distribution to be built from the top most project, rather than from a subproject. While this is possible in some cases, and often recommended for source distributions, the flexibility of this option is limited in the current releases of Maven. It can be difficult to select what to include, and ensure proper sequencing of the build so that it occurs last. It is also more difficult to rebuild the assembly without rebuilding the entire project. For this reason, a separate module is currently the recommended approach for producing a distribution.

First, let's create the new module for the distribution. There are no standard archetypes for assemblies at the time of writing, so we create a new project by hand in `distribution/pom.xml`:

```xml
<?xml version="1.0" encoding="UTF-8"?>
<project xmlns="http://maven.apache.org/POM/4.0.0"
  xmlns:xsi="http://www.w3.org/2001/XMLSchema-instance"
  xsi:schemaLocation="http://maven.apache.org/POM/4.0.0
    http://maven.apache.org/maven-v4_0_0.xsd">
  <modelVersion>4.0.0</modelVersion>
  <parent>
    <groupId>com.effectivemaven.centrepoint</groupId>
    <artifactId>centrepoint</artifactId>
    <version>1.0-SNAPSHOT</version>
  </parent>
  <name>Centrepoint Distribution</name>
  <artifactId>distribution</artifactId>
  <packaging>pom</packaging>
</project>
```

Notice that the packaging type is again pom, indicating there is no specific output for the project. This is because the Assembly plugin does not have a packaging type and lifecycle of its own, but is instead intended to be attached to existing builds.

Before continuing, let's not forget to add the new module to the parent POM:

```
<modules>
  ...
  <module>documentation</module>
  <module>distribution</module>
</modules>
```

This new project is now part of the build, so we can move on to adding the functionality to assemble the distribution.

> With all the modules now in place, you will notice that most of the *day-to-day* modules that will be built during development reside under the `modules` directory. This can be used to save time building the project in development when the distribution and documentation are not needed.

Generating the runtime environment with the App Assembler plugin

In our example application, we will distribute the web application along with a pre-configured Jetty servlet container, so that the application can be immediately run after unpacking the archive rather than having to set up your own servlet container. This technique is identical to how Archiva is distributed, and we saw how easy that was to get running in Chapter 2, *Staying in Control with Archiva*.

Like in Archiva, in addition to the Jetty container we will set up **Java Service Wrapper (JSW)** scripts to start Jetty with, and include the documentation for easy reference.

For this task, we will use the App Assembler plugin from the Codehaus Mojo project. This plugin is used to augment the Assembly plugin by generating the necessary framework for the application to be *run* in various scenarios once unpacked from an archive. It includes basic shell and batch scripts for running applications, as well as generation for configuration of the Java Service Wrapper.

> The App Assembler plugin uses an older version of the Java Service Wrapper (v3.2.3), as it was the last to be licensed under the more permissive BSD -style license. Newer versions and documentation can be obtained from the following web site: `http://wrapper.tanukisoftware.org`.

The Assembly plugin will be used to create an archive from this generated content. It is notable that the Assembly plugin does not do very much processing of the build results itself—its role is simply to archive a set of files that have already been produced.

While the App Assembler plugin will simplify the configuration of this environment, we don't have space to cover the entire configuration in this chapter, so will focus on the main points of interest. For the complete example, refer to the sample code for this chapter.

First, we will add the dependencies for the Jetty server to the project so that the App Assembler plugin will pick them up and incorporate them into the server structure:

```
<dependencies>
  <dependency>
    <groupId>org.mortbay.jetty</groupId>
    <artifactId>jetty</artifactId>
    <version>${jetty.version}</version>
  </dependency>
  <dependency>
    <groupId>org.mortbay.jetty</groupId>
    <artifactId>start</artifactId>
    <version>${jetty.version}</version>
  </dependency>
</dependencies>
<properties>
  <jetty.version>6.1.14</jetty.version>
</properties>
```

 Note the use of a property for the Jetty version to avoid duplication and ease the upgrade process in future.

Next, we have the App Assembler plugin itself, which we will break down into sections. First, the configuration contains a set of *daemons*, which are the application scripts to generate for a particular situation. We have just one called centrepoint to start the server using the Java Service Wrapper:

```
<daemons>
  <daemon>
    <id>centrepoint</id>
    <mainClass>org.mortbay.start.Main</mainClass>
    <commandLineArguments>
      ...
```

```
    </commandLineArguments>
    <platforms>
      <platform>jsw</platform>
    </platforms>
    <generatorConfigurations>
      <generatorConfiguration>
        <generator>jsw</generator>
        <configuration>
          ...
        </configuration>
        <includes>
          <include>linux-x86-32</include>
          ...
        </includes>
      </generatorConfiguration>
    </generatorConfigurations>
  </daemon>
</daemons>
```

The daemon contains three sections, as you can see above:

- The command line information for the Java runtime, which includes the main class and the command line arguments (in this example, the Jetty configuration files would be passed in).

- The platforms to generate for the daemon (you can generate Unix or Windows start scripts, or JSW which is capable of generating scripts for many platforms).

- It also contains the configuration for each platform. For JSW, we provide wrapper properties to add to `wrapper.conf` in the `configuration` element and which JSW platforms to support in the `includes` element.

This next section of the configuration lets you construct a repository of artifacts from the dependencies of the project in a certain directory (which is later generated by the `create-repository` goal). In this case it will be generated without repository paths and all the libraries will be placed directly in the `lib` directory.

```
<repoPath>lib</repoPath>
<repositoryLayout>flat</repositoryLayout>
```

Finally, the location to generate the application runtime to is specified in the `assembleDirectory`:

```
<assembleDirectory>
  ${project.build.directory}/generated-resources/appassembler/
                           jsw/centrepoint
</assembleDirectory>
```

To run the App Assembler as part of the build, the following goals are given:

```
<executions>
  <execution>
    <goals>
      <goal>generate-daemons</goal>
      <goal>create-repository</goal>
    </goals>
  </execution>
</executions>
```

There are some final steps needed to get a working server. If we were to generate and run this now, we would find it fails to start up for two reasons:

- The logs directory is missing
- The conf directory that has the Jetty configurations specified as command line arguments is missing

However, the App Assembler plugin does not have any directives for creating these. We could do it later in the assembly plugin, but that would mean we can't test the server directly from the target directory that we have generated it to.

Instead, we can add an instance of the Ant Run plugin to set these two areas up for us in the target directory so that the assembled application is complete and ready for assembly. The execution added to the Ant Run plugin would look like the following:

```
<execution>
  <id>config</id>
  <phase>process-resources</phase>
  <configuration>
    <tasks>
      <copy todir="${project.build.directory}/generated-
                    resources/appassembler/jsw/centrepoint/conf">
        <fileset dir="src/main/conf" />
      </copy>
      <mkdir dir="${project.build.directory}/generated-
                    resources/appassembler/jsw/centrepoint/logs" />
    </tasks>
  </configuration>
  <goals>
    <goal>run</goal>
  </goals>
</execution>
```

In this case, we need the `src/main/conf` directory to exist first. For our example, we have taken `jetty.xml` and `jetty-logging.xml` from the Jetty distribution and included them in that directory.

By this point, we should have a POM that looks identical to the final sample application with the Assembly plugin omitted (which we will cover in the next section). To verify that everything is working as expected, we can generate and run the server from the source directory.

```
distribution$ mvn package
```

Then, from the `target/generated-resources/appassembler/jsw/centrepoint/bin` directory, run:

```
bin$ centrepoint console
```

 On Unix, you may need to change the file mode of the files in the `bin` directory by running `chmod +x bin/*`. In the next section, we will ensure the Assembly plugin makes this unnecessary.

If everything has been configured successfully, the Jetty server will start, but the logs will show that it failed to load any web applications. In the next step, we will bundle the web application itself and produce an archive for redistribution.

Generating the assembly archive

Everything is now finalized and in place, ready to be bundled into an archive for distribution. As mentioned previously, we will use the Assembly plugin for this task.

As the assembly is being generated in a separate module, we are able to bind it to the lifecycle so that the generated archives can be attached to the installation and deployment of the main artifacts into the repository. To do this, we use the `single` goal, and bind it to the `package` phase, just as we did with the documentation earlier.

```
<plugin>
  <groupId>org.apache.maven.plugins</groupId>
  <artifactId>maven-assembly-plugin</artifactId>
  <version>2.1</version>
  <executions>
    <execution>
      <phase>package</phase>
      <goals>
        <goal>single</goal>
      </goals>
    </execution>
```

```
  </executions>
  <configuration>
    <descriptor>src/main/assembly/bin.xml</descriptor>
  </configuration>
</plugin>
```

The configuration for the Assembly plugin is very straightforward with most of the interesting work being done inside the assembly descriptor, which was listed in the configuration section of the plugin.

The format of the assembly descriptor is particularly flexible to different situations. We have already seen a simple example in the documentation section earlier, and we will utilize a few more capabilities here. However, if you are looking for a specific method of assembling a project, refer to the online documentation for the plugin for a full list of configuration options at http://maven.apache.org/plugins/maven-assembly-plugin/.

We will start by configuring the descriptor for the already generated files from the App Assembler. For this purpose, we need to construct a series of filesets (the full set of required filesets can be seen in the sample code for this chapter).

```
<assembly>
  <id>bin</id>
  <formats>
    <format>tar.gz</format>
  </formats>
  <filesets>
    <fileSet>
      <directory>target/generated-
                 resources/appassembler/jsw/centrepoint/lib</directory>
      <outputDirectory>lib</outputDirectory>
      <excludes>
        <exclude>maven-metadata-appassembler.xml</exclude>
      </excludes>
      <fileMode>0755</fileMode>
    </fileSet>
    ...
  </filesets>
</assembly>
```

In this code, we add all of the files from the generated directories. While it would have been ideal to simply add the `target/appassembler/jsw/centrepoint` directory once, as you can see certain `includes` and `excludes` elements are needed in some directories, and more importantly, the file modes and line endings need to be set correctly. The Windows batch files must have Windows line endings to work correctly, and the Unix shell scripts Unix line endings. As we saw in the previous section, all the files in the `bin` directory need to be set to executable.

You can now generate the assembly:

```
distribution$ mvn package
```

When the build completes, the TAR.GZ file will be created in the target directory and can be used to run the Jetty server we had from the previous section.

However, the name of the file is `distribution-1.0-SNAPSHOT-bin.tar.gz` — not a very friendly name for the file! Although in the repository it will use that name regardless, we can use a more appropriate one locally without affecting the artifact ID by using the `finalName` configuration element in the `build` section of the POM:

```
<build>
    <finalName>centrepoint-${project.version}</finalName>

    . . .
```

Upon generating the assembly again, you will see the new name is used.

Now, we need to add our web application into the assembly. We achieve this by adding it as a dependency of the project — no other application dependencies are needed, as they will be brought in transitively from the web application as needed. This is the standard pattern for producing a distribution of a project using a standalone module. As we have here, the module depends on all of the artifacts that you want to include, and then the assembly descriptor is able to refer to the dependencies from the repository, rather than needing to determine relative file paths within the build across projects.

First, the dependency must be added to the distribution POM itself:

```
<dependency>
    <groupId>${project.groupId}</groupId>
    <artifactId>webapp</artifactId>
    <version>${project.version}</version>
    <type>war</type>
</dependency>
```

Next, we need to exclude that dependency from the list added to lib in the assembly descriptor, as it will be added to the webapps directory instead.

```
<outputDirectory>lib</outputDirectory>
<excludes>
  <exclude>*.war</exclude>
  <exclude>maven-metadata-appassembler.xml</exclude>
</excludes>
```

Finally, we must add the dependency to the assembly itself. We do this using the dependencySet descriptor element:

```
<dependencySets>
  <dependencySet>
    <unpack>true</unpack>
    <outputDirectory>webapps/centrepoint</outputDirectory>
    <includes>
      <include>${project.groupId}:webapp</include>
    </includes>
  </dependencySet>
</dependencySets>
```

This new element expresses a simple behavior, that is, retrieve all the dependencies of the project, and those that are included should be unpacked into the output directory. In this case, this means retrieving the web application from the repository (the dependency referred to by group ID ${project.groupId} and artifact ID webapp) and unpacking it into the webapp/centrepoint directory of the final assembly.

As Jetty was configured to run applications in the webapps directory by default, we now are able to rebuild and unpack the resulting distribution, then run the server as before and access the application at http://localhost:8080/centrepoint/.

CENTREPOINT

CENTREPOINT

□ Add a New Project

Centrepoint is a basic but useful application that sets up a dashboard of project information from Maven, Archiva and Continuum.

APACHE MAVEN

Maven is a project development management and comprehension tool. Based on the concept of a project object model: builds, dependency management, documentation creation, site publication, and distribution publication are all controlled from the declarative file. Maven can be extended by plugins to utilise a number of other development tools for reporting or the build process.

CONTINUUM :: PROJECT

Continuum is a continuous integration server for building maven1/2 projects, ant projects and shell projects.

ARCHIVA

Archiva is an application for managing one or more remote repositories, including administration, artifact handling, browsing and searching.

Adding the documentation to the distribution archive

When we created the user documentation in an earlier section, we specifically packaged it up as a ZIP itself with the intention of including it in the distribution once it had been created.

Achieving this now involves steps that are identical to those for the web application above. Firstly, the dependency in the POM:

```
<dependency>
  <groupId>${project.groupId}</groupId>
  <artifactId>documentation</artifactId>
  <version>${project.version}</version>
  <classifier>docs</classifier>
  <type>zip</type>
</dependency>
```

Then the exclusion in assembly descriptor:

```
<outputDirectory>lib</outputDirectory>
<excludes>
  <exclude>*.war</exclude>
  <exclude>*.zip</exclude>
  <exclude>maven-metadata-appassembler.xml</exclude>
</excludes>
```

Finally, the dependency set:

```
<dependencySet>
  <unpack>true</unpack>
  <outputDirectory>docs</outputDirectory>
  <includes>
    <include>${project.groupId}:documentation</include>
  </includes>
</dependencySet>
```

Rebuilding the application will now show the documentation unpacked in the docs subdirectory of the archive, for easy reference wherever it is deployed.

The final directory structure that we obtained was:

```
|-- centrepoint
|   |-- distribution
|   |-- documentation
|   |-- modules
|   |   |-- maven-importer
|   |   |-- model
|   |   |-- store-api
|   |   |-- store-file
|   |   `-- webapp
|   `-- skin
`-- effectivemaven-parent
```

That's it! We can now go to the top level of the project and run the build:

```
centrepoint$ mvn clean install
```

This will produce the entire application, including the web application, a Jetty application server runtime, and all the documentation—ready to unpack and use.

Summary

In this chapter, we have spent quite some time manipulating POM files to arrange the overall project in a particular way. While there are quite a number of changes, they are not very complex, and examining the projects now shows a clean separation that is hopefully easy to understand. It is now very straightforward to add new modules into the overall application structure with a minimal number of changes.

In subsequent chapters, we will look at adding more build functionality into these basic project files to address specific needs related to quality through testing and automated checks, and automating this process through a continuous integration server such as Continuum.

4
Application Testing with Maven

Ok, I admit it—I find testing one of the more rewarding parts of application development. There is something to be said for seeing, for certain, that the application works the way you intended it to, and being able to make sure it stays that way. The whole cycle of firing up the application and viewing your changes by hand is fun the first time, and horribly slow and tedious the next ten times, as you fix the issues that you have found.

Even so, writing these tests is not very enjoyable and there is always great temptation in skipping them *just this once*. One way to keep you honest is knowing that those tests will bring repeated value as they run later. I like to think that if someone manages to break my code with a subsequent change, it is *my* fault for not testing it properly, not theirs. However, for this value to come, the tests need to be automated!

The concept of testing is built right into the Maven lifecycle for this reason, and in this chapter we will expand on our example application to include a variety of types of tests of varying complexity, and look at some other scenarios and how best to incorporate testing into a Maven build. This sets the platform for testing to be a part of our standard development process, and for it to be completely automated as we take a closer look at automated builds in Chapter 8, *Continuum – Ensuring the health of your source code*.

Aside from running various types of tests and reviewing the results, we will look at how to keep ourselves even more honest by integrating code coverage.

While this is not a book about testing, the subject is an important part of application development and so worth covering in some detail. However, we will focus on how to automate tests that have already been written.

Types of testing in Maven

There are many different types of tests that can be automated in a build, which can be categorized in several ways (and often overlap). While testing is built in to Maven, it limits itself to two stages of testing within the build lifecycle: **unit testing**, and **integration testing**. In addition, by building an entirely separate test project a third type of testing can be achieved. In this chapter, we will refer to that as **functional testing**.

These definitions might not match your own or the types of tests you are writing to run at that stage. Particularly for integration tests, there are a varied number of definitions for what it encompasses, and there are various other types of tests such as system tests and acceptance tests, which can fit into other categories. However, the names are not important to Maven as it does very little to constrain the types of tests that can be run in each stage. Instead, it is defined by the three stages of the build in which they can be run, and we use the names to reflect the types of tests *most commonly* run within that stage.

Let's take a closer look at the different stages.

Unit testing (or code testing)

Unit testing is run after compilation but before packaging, therefore it is run on nearly every build. This indicates more accurately that the purpose of tests in this stage is those to be run on every build. They should pass before the build can complete and the artifact can be used.

Note that the phase in Maven are simply called `test`, not `unit-test`. This reflects that the phase is not specific to unit testing, but rather is the main test run for the code of the current project.

Due to their frequency, these tests should be extremely quick. They should be expected to run every time, and if they are slow, there is a greater inclination to skip the tests.

For the same reason, the tests should be expected to never be broken on checked-in code and be resilient to failure. This includes not relying on external resources (for example, a web server or database). Even if the resource can reasonably be expected to be present on every system, the greater chance of variance can be a cause of intermittent failure. Such resources are best tested in a different stage of testing.

Integration testing (or module testing)

Integration tests in Maven are run after the packaging, but before installation into the local or a remote repository. These tests verify that the code is working when put together with other modules that are already built.

Tests that are included in this phase by default can be used to fail the build if the module should not be picked up by other projects as a dependency due to some failure.

You will also need to use this particular phase if the packaged artifact itself must be used to execute the tests. For example, if you have a test that relies on reading the JAR manifest file, it should be in this phase instead of the main test phase before the manifest has been created.

In reality, the occurrence of such use cases is rare, so the phase either serves as a way to separate types of tests logically, or to run optional tests instead. As most developers will still be running the integration-test phase on each build, those that run by default should still be reasonably fast, and expected to pass every time. This pushes many of the use cases for these tests into the functional test category.

Functional and other types of testing

While the Maven lifecycle only accommodates two types of testing within its lifecycle, they don't cover the use cases for which many other types of testing are performed. Other, broader, types of testing fall into this last category.

These types of tests are usually run in one of two ways:

- As a separate project dedicated to running tests, containing only test code and relying on pre-built application artifacts to test
- As an optional part of an existing project through combining profiles and the existing test phases

In general, these tests may be run multiple times to test various different environmental combinations, and are not enabled by default.

Now that we have seen how the various test lifecycles are used in Maven, let's look at specific examples for each case and how they can apply to the example application we started building in Chapter 3, *Building an Application Using Maven*. We will follow along by starting with the code from the final directory of the sample code from Chapter 3.

Working with tests

We have been fortunate to encounter Maven's handling of unit tests on several occasions already in this book. This should come as no surprise, because Maven so closely links this type of test to the build lifecycle of all of the default packaging types.

To revise briefly, in Chapter 1, *Maven in a Nutshell*, we had an overview of the Surefire plugin, how Maven picks up tests automatically, and how to treat unit test failures. We also saw how to write a basic unit test with TestNG and configure that to be used instead of JUnit. If you are interested in learning the basics of how to write your own unit tests and have them configured in the build, take a look back at this section.

In Chapter 3, *Building an Application Using Maven*, though we didn't look at unit tests explicitly, we saw them co-exist with the code of the application that is being constructed, as they were written at the same time as the code. We won't go through them in detail here, however we will see them in action shortly as we take a closer look at how well they work.

One area that we haven't yet examined is how to work with these tests outside of the default mode of running every test on every build.

Surefire plugin configuration

By now, you have encountered the name **Surefire** a few times. Don't worry — this isn't a new testing framework that you need to learn. In fact, the plugin configuration is the only time you are likely to encounter it. Surefire is actually a test runner designed to run tests from any supplied framework in a unified way and feed the results back to Maven consistently. It handles the entire infrastructure for setting up class loaders, forking the JVM, and tracking the total number of tests, passes, and failures. At present, it is compatible with JUnit 3, JUnit 4, TestNG, or tests written as plain Java classes without the use of these frameworks.

To alter the way the tests are run, we provide configuration information to the Surefire plugin. There are two methods for doing this, as with any Maven plugin:

- Configuration of options in the POM that are to apply to the tests every time they are run

- Configuration supplied on the command line for once off alterations during the development cycle

The following are the main configuration options that you will encounter. For a more comprehensive list, refer to the Maven Surefire Plugin documentation online at `http://maven.apache.org/plugins/maven-surefire-plugin/`.

 It is worth noting that most of these configuration options will also be relevant (and in some cases, more so) to the later types of testing we will encounter, not just the main build tests.

Controlling the execution of tests

As the Surefire plugin is designed to run Java tests from one of the supported frameworks, it needs to set up a clean Java environment to run the tests within. By default, this involves starting a new Java virtual machine instance at the start of the test run, and running all the tests from within that new instance.

This is a reasonably well balanced default. While it takes a little extra time to start a new Java virtual machine, it is not going to greatly impact the time it takes to run the tests, and it tends to match the settings used in IDEs, which makes the behavior consistent between the two execution environments.

This behavior is configured by the `forkMode` configuration property. There are three different modes for controlling the execution of tests:

- `once`: The default mode, starting a new virtual machine to run all of the tests
- `never`: Runs all of the tests within the current virtual machine without starting a new instance
- `always`: The opposite mode, that starts a new virtual machine for each test suite

Configuring the **fork mode** is most often done within the POM so that it applies consistently to every execution of the tests. For example, to set the tests to run within the existing virtual machine that is running Maven, the following would be used:

```
<plugin>
  <groupId>org.apache.maven.plugins</groupId>
  <artifactId>maven-surefire-plugin</artifactId>
  <configuration>
    <forkMode>never</forkMode>
  </configuration>
</plugin>
```

There are various reasons that you may wish to change the execution behavior of the tests. While the default mode is usually sufficient, you may find that using the never option provides a small performance boost—which can be very handy if you are frequently running the tests. However, there are definite disadvantages to using no forking, relating to the constraints of the existing virtual machine. There will be less memory to use for the tests, and any increases will need to be applied to the entire Maven execution, not just the tests themselves. Conversely, if the tests have a memory leak or exceed the amount of memory available, the entire build will fail with an error. This may happen not just during the tests, but perhaps, even after the tests have finished running, thus making it harder to track down. In addition to these, while Maven attempts to isolate the environment as much as possible, it is possible that there will be additional classes available and different system properties that may affect the behavior of your tests. Finally, using the never option constrains your tests to the installation and version of the Java virtual machine being used by Maven—it is not possible to take advantage of a different Java installation through the Surefire configuration or a tool chain.

The always option has fewer drawbacks. It will behave identically to the default once mode of operation however with a greater level of isolation between the test suites. As a new virtual machine is started for each suite, any state, system properties, or memory used will be gone by the time the next suite starts. While these reasons make it a helpful option, the extra time that it requires to run the tests can often be too costly for the option to be of value. Consider also that it is a good practice to avoid consuming too many resources or altering the system state from unit tests, so this option is better preserved for cases that have larger test runs where the time to start the virtual machine is not the bottleneck.

Inclusion and exclusion of tests

By default, Maven looks in source files from the test source directory (src/test/java) starting or ending in Test or ending in TestCase for tests to run (that is **/Test*.java, **/*Test.java, **/*TestCase.java). This default is suitable for most scenarios, however in some cases it might be necessary to alter the files included.

This configuration is also added to the Surefire plugin in the POM. For example, to include source files ending in TestSuite instead, the following configuration would be supplied to the Surefire plugin:

```
<configuration>
  <includes>
    <include>**/*TestSuite.java</include>
  </includes>
</configuration>
```

Any number of `include` lines can be added. When the tests are next run, only those ending in `TestSuite` will be executed. A common use case for this is some form of composite test suite that already executes the other test classes using the internal mechanisms of JUnit or TestNG, so Surefire does not need to configure them automatically.

The `include` directives are not additive with the defaults — if you also want to keep the default patterns, those three lines would need to be added to the `include` configuration in the same way.

The same applies for excluding tests. By default, the set of sources found by the supplied `include` patterns is used in its entirety, so to remove specific test classes from being run the corresponding `exclude` pattern needs to be supplied. For example, the following might be used to remove a test that has been broken for some time and needs to be repaired later:

```
<configuration>
  <excludes>
    <exclude>**/MyBrokenTest.java</exclude>
  </excludes>
</configuration>
```

Such temporary exclusion is one use case for exclusions, though it is hopefully a rare one! More commonly, this is used for splitting a test tree across multiple executions of the plugin, often through a profile, for example for a set of slow running tests. We will encounter this variation later in the chapter when configuring Selenium tests.

Differences in TestNG

While Surefire will use the above configuration for TestNG, it is not always necessary. TestNG provides its own, richer mechanism for creating groups of tests, and using XML files to describe test suites. If these suite files are used then the `includes` and `excludes` configuration will be ignored.

Running specific tests from the command line

The previous configuration options were designed for setting up the way the tests are run every time the build is run. However, during development, you might also want to be more selective about the tests that you run rather than running through the whole suite each time.

Surefire provides the `test` configuration option for this purpose. While it doesn't make sense to use it within the POM (where `includes` and `excludes` are more suitable), it can be used to override the configuration from the command line.

For example, to run just the test suite `ViewProjectPageTest` in the `webapp` module of our example application:

```
webapp$ mvn test -Dtest=ViewProjectPageTest
```

This shorthand is the most typical syntax, and in the event that there is more than one class that matches the name, it will run all classes with the given name in the source tree. However, it is also possible to supply the entire package name of the test (or the corresponding path) if it is necessary to be more specific.

In recent versions of Surefire, multiple tests can be run by using a combination of either wildcards or commas to separate the tests to select. For example:

```
webapp$ mvn test -Dtest=*PageTest
```

For those that don't live in the command line during development, typical development patterns will often involve running the tests from the IDE to ensure that they all pass before verifying with Maven through the whole set, reducing the need to use these options. However, even if this is your pattern for development, they are worth remembering for situations where the Maven build may not agree with the original results.

A final note—while it is possible to use the `test` command-line argument no matter what type of Maven build you are running, there are two situations where this should be avoided. When running in a multi-module build, the argument will be applied to all of the modules, causing a number of tests to be skipped because they don't match the expected pattern. Additionally, when running phases beyond `test`, such as `package` or `install`, passing the `test` option allows you to build a complete package while effectively skipping a number of tests—the reason to avoid this will be examined next.

Skipping tests temporarily

A very popular configuration option is the `maven.test.skip` argument. Perhaps a more popular configuration than it should actually be! This option is very simple. A boolean value, when set to `true`, causes all tests to be neither compiled nor executed.

```
webapp$ mvn package -Dmaven.test.skip=true
```

The purpose of this option is primarily to speed up a build, or to avoid tests that are known to be broken.

While both cases are *in rare circumstances* valid, those circumstances should also be avoidable, ensuring that the option does not need to be used frequently. The compulsory tests should be as fast as possible to prevent the temptation to skip them, and chronically broken or unreliable tests should either be fixed or disabled in order to avoid losing confidence in the whole test suite. Otherwise, skipping the tests becomes addictive, it can start being used regularly and eventually test failures will go unnoticed.

For more information on testing best practices, in particular related to skipping tests, see Chapter 7, *Maven Best Practices*.

Producing a report for the test results

In earlier examples of running Surefire through the build, we have seen the results of the tests generated into the `target/surefire-reports` directory in both text and XML format. These are useful for quickly viewing one test suite, particularly to see the reason for a test failure. However, it is also possible to generate a HTML report — in the appearance of the application's generated Maven site — that allows you a unified visual representation.

Let's try this with our example application — in this case from the `modules/webapp` directory. To run the tests and generate the report, simply run the goal from the command line:

```
webapp$ mvn surefire-report:report
```

The resulting output can be found in `target/site/surefire-report.html`, which will look something like the following:

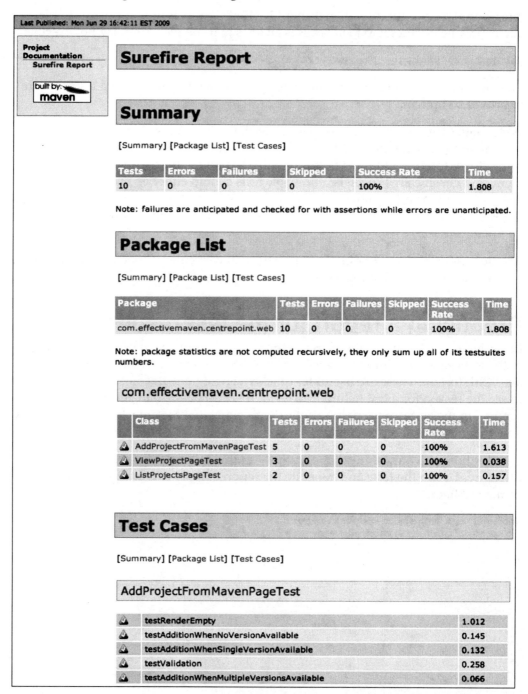

If you have already run the tests and would just like the report generated, for example to see which tests were particularly slow or to quickly access the failures in one page, there is a separate goal to run:

```
webapp$ mvn surefire-report:report-only
```

These goals are very simple and can be used any time you need a one-off HTML report of the results, no matter which test framework is being used.

 If you are using TestNG, it also produces its own HTML report format if it hasn't been suppressed by configuration. If you prefer this report, it can be navigated to from the front page at `target/surefire-reports/index.html`. There is no need to run the `surefire-report` goals in this case.

Another alternative is to have the report run as part of the Maven site by adding it to the reporting element. This ensures that there is always an updated view in the site of the status of the tests, and uses the configured site skin instead of the Maven default. Note again that the default goal will run the tests first, so if you already run them before generating the site, you may want to reconfigure the plugin to use the `report-only` goal.

You may be asking—*Why would I want this? I don't generate my site until the project has been successfully built and all the tests pass.* Now that is a great question! It is true that the report has limited utility as an automated part of the site, at least for the standard test set. Other than to have a view of the performance of your tests (which may also be displayed by your continuous integration server), you would expect it to simply be many green bars.

This is certainly true, so it is less common for the report to be included, especially as many continuous integration servers will offer you a suitably rendered report in the same central location. The possible exception is again more complicated test sets that may be more prone to failure, such as environmental based functional tests, where the main build may not fail but failures will still need to be reported.

Reviewing test coverage

One of the most popular types of tools used related to testing are those that measure the coverage. What this means is that while the tests are run, the tool analyzes which parts of the actual code are run, to give a reasonable idea of how well tested the code is.

Many tools will measure this for you. Some well-known options that have Maven plugins are:

- **Clover** (http://www.atlassian.com/software/clover/)
- **Cobertura** (http://cobertura.sf.net/)
- **EMMA** (http://emma.sf.net/)

Of these, Clover is the most feature-rich and is commercially available from Atlassian. Cobertura and EMMA are both open source projects, each with Maven plugins available from the Codehaus Mojo project (http://mojo.codehaus.org/). Both are excellent choices if you are looking for a free alternative, and at the Maven level, they have roughly comparable functionality.

For this chapter, we have chosen to use EMMA because it is open source (with the more liberal license of the two), and because there are IDE plugins available for both Eclipse (http://www.eclemma.org/) and IntelliJ IDEA (built-in to recent versions).

Before we can start using it in our example application, we need to make sure the project knows how to locate the plugin. To do so, we add the plugin to the build section of the modules/pom.xml file (recall from Chapter 3, *Building an Application Using Maven*, that it is not needed in the top level project, as there are no Java modules or tests outside of the modules tree).

```
<build>
  <plugins>
    <plugin>
      <groupId>org.codehaus.mojo</groupId>
      <artifactId>emma-maven-plugin</artifactId>
      <version>1.0-alpha-2</version>
    </plugin>
  </plugins>
</build>
```

 Don't be put off by the 1.0-alpha-2 version of the plugin—it uses EMMA 2.0 which has been stable for a number of years, and instead reflects the early development stage of the Maven interface to EMMA.

Now, let's start by looking at the store-file module. From that directory, run the following command:

store-file$ mvn emma:emma

Similar to the Surefire report earlier, this command will both run the tests and generate the coverage report. Let's take a closer look at the output. Firstly, after compilation we see the following:

```
[INFO] [emma:instrument {execution: default-instrument}]
[INFO] Instrumenting classes with EMMA
processing instrumentation path ...
instrumentation path processed in 114 ms
[2 class(es) instrumented, 1 resource(s) copied]
metadata merged into [/Users/brett/code/04/centrepoint/modules/store-
file/target/coverage.em] {in 81 ms}
```

Here, the compiled classes have been **instrumented** to include information EMMA needs to keep track of the coverage as the code is later run.

Following this the tests are run, concluding with an indication that EMMA successfully collected data:

```
EMMA: runtime coverage data merged into [/Users/brett/code/04/
centrepoint/modules/store-file/coverage.ec] {in 6 ms}
```

At last we see that the report is generated:

```
[INFO] [emma:emma]
processing input files ...
2 file(s) read and merged in 2 ms
writing [xml] report to [/Users/brett/code/04/centrepoint/modules/store-
file/target/site/emma/coverage.xml] ...
writing [html] report to [/Users/brett/code/04/centrepoint/modules/store-
file/target/site/emma/index.html] ...
```

Fork modes and EMMA

EMMA, and many code coverage tools, are currently relying on a "JVM shutdown hook" to know when to write out the code coverage results at the end of a run of tests. This can be affected by the different **fork mode** settings that we looked at earlier in the chapter. In the case of using the default, coverage data is written once at the end of the tests, which works perfectly as you would expect. The always option also works correctly, writing coverage data out after every suite (which EMMA merges as it progresses to get a complete set). However, the never option causes problems. The coverage data typically won't be written out until Maven itself exits — which will likely lead to an empty, incomplete, or missing coverage report.

The report generated in `target/site/emma/index.html` looks like the following:

EMMA Coverage Report (generated Mon Jun 29 18:03:10 EST 2009)			
[all classes]			

OVERALL COVERAGE SUMMARY

name	class, %	method, %	block, %	line, %
all classes	100% (2/2)	100% (8/8)	92% (488/531)	90% (70.6/78)

OVERALL STATS SUMMARY

```
total packages:         1
total executable files: 1
total classes:          2
total methods:          8
total executable lines: 78
```

COVERAGE BREAKDOWN BY PACKAGE

name	class, %	method, %	block, %	line, %
com.effectivemaven.centrepoint.store.properties	100% (2/2)	100% (8/8)	92% (488/531)	90% (70.6/78)

As you can see, we have some good coverage, but it is not perfect! In the figure, you should be looking most closely for EMMAs **block** level coverage—this is its basic unit of measurement of which pieces of code are being exercised. The **line** coverage offers some information on which lines of code have been covered for visualization purposes, however due to different choices in formatting it can mean very different things about how much code is actually covered. The **class** and **method** coverage metrics indicate how many classes and methods are touched during test execution respectively. This can help to identify whole methods or classes that are not tested at all.

The **package** and **all classes** groupings aggregate information about the type of coverage to those respective levels for a birds eye view. You will notice the report starts at this level, and you can drill down into individual packages, and then individual classes.

A single class view will look like the following example for `PropertiesProjectStore`:

```
 89
 90    private Properties loadProjectProperties()
 91    {
 92        Properties properties = new Properties();
 93        FileInputStream fis = null;
 94        try
 95        {
 96            fis = new FileInputStream( new File( dataLocation, "projects.properties" ) );
 97
 98            properties.load( fis );
 99        }
100        catch ( FileNotFoundException e )
101        {
102            // no error, just doesn't exist yet
103        }
104        catch ( IOException e )
105        {
106            // ignore the error, it'll be recreated if possible
107        }
108        finally
109        {
110            if ( fis != null )
111            {
112                try
113                {
114                    fis.close();
115                }
116                catch ( IOException e )
117                {
118                    // ignore
119                }
120            }
121        }
122
123        return properties;
124    }
125
```

Here you can see a visual representation of the coverage of the class: the lines that are completely executed (Lines: 92, 93, 96, 98, 100, and 123), those that are not executed at all (Lines: 104 and 116), and those that are partially executed (Lines: 110, 114, and 119). Partially executed lines can mean any number of things depending on the code involved — there may be a branch (here it is an `if` condition that is never `true`), or there may be other reasons that byte-code is generated but never executed, possibly highlighting inefficiencies in the code if it was unintentional. For more information, refer to the FAQ on the EMMA web site: `http://emma.sourceforge.net/faq.html#q.fractional.examples`.

Measuring coverage

This technique isn't flawless — One hundred percent coverage doesn't mean one hundred percent tested. Among other things, it won't help you if there are certain boundary conditions on calculations that need special handling, if you have omitted handling a case altogether, or if the test case itself is wrong! As such, it should be treated as just a part of your toolbox (and in some cases, one that will help you with more than just test coverage), but it is not a silver bullet!

Running the coverage on an ad-hoc basis can be quite helpful, but as with many reports, it is most convenient to automate it as part of the Maven site generation. The standard configuration works here — add the plugin to the `reporting` section of the `modules/pom.xml` file and you are done! This has the advantage of ensuring the report is included in the navigation of the module sites without manual configuration.

```
<reporting>
  <plugins>
    <plugin>
      <groupId>org.codehaus.mojo</groupId>
      <artifactId>emma-maven-plugin</artifactId>
      <version>1.0-alpha-2</version>
    </plugin>
```

With the configuration added, generate the Maven site as usual:

```
modules$ mvn site
```

Once it completes, you will notice that each module with tests now contains an EMMA report for reviewing the coverage of that particular module.

Like the Surefire report, by default the EMMA plugin runs the tests every time. This makes sense, as it was unlikely the project had previously compiled the tests to be run with coverage information. However, it can cause large slowdowns to the site generation if the tests need to be run multiple times.

However, what about the main test run? We still have the `package` phase running the tests once, and the `site` phase running it a second time. This becomes even more convoluted in Chapter 5, *Reporting and Checks*, when we want to have coverage over the main test run to determine whether to pass or fail the build!

The best answer to all of these points is that it is often better to run the `site` phase in a separate iteration of Maven to the main `package` phase. There is a good reason for this. The main build is meant to be fast, and even in the build server, you want to see the results of the build as a pass or fail as quickly as possible, and then come back for a second iteration to generate the site with additional information for developers beyond that basic metric. At that time, it is probably acceptable to re-run the tests to generate the information. This extra time spent by the build server will greatly reduce the complexity of your project if you were to attempt to meld all the generations into one attempt with appropriate layering for the initial fast build.

While the Surefire report discussed earlier can often be omitted for the main test suite due to the likelihood of all the tests passing, the same is not usually the case for the coverage report. Unlike tests, there is no binary answer. Coverage will often be considered good enough at a certain percentage level below 100%, though that will vary depending on the type of module. Even then, the coverage should be occasionally reviewed to see if important code is not being tested adequately.

Conversely, just generating the report is not enough. Standing on its own, it is likely to soon be ignored, especially once coverage drops below a certain percentage and it starts suffering from the **broken window syndrome** (`http://en.wikipedia.org/wiki/Fixing_Broken_Windows`).

In the next chapter, we will take a closer look at reporting, and also how to set up enforcement rules that will show a warning or fail the build when there may be reasons that the level of coverage is not good enough, which will prompt the reader of the report to investigate.

Empty or missing report?

You may unexpectedly find that the report in `target/site/emma` is missing, out of date, or empty on some occasions, particularly if you have just started a module. In this case, take a close look at the output from the build after the `[emma:emma]` goal. It will likely tell you that there was no coverage at all (perhaps because there were no tests run), so no report was generated.

Coverage and multimodule projects

When the site was generated earlier, you may have noticed that there was no aggregated view of the coverage. Each module in the project gets a single report, and you must navigate into those particular directories to see the coverage for that code.

While this type of configuration is possible, at the time of writing it is not something that is supplied *out of the box* with the Maven plugins for EMMA and Cobertura. However, if you are using Clover, their website describes how to produce an aggregated report.

We won't cover the manual steps needed to produce the same effect with EMMA, as it requires manually triggering some of the tools outside of the plugin. If you are in need of aggregate data at this time, you might consider simply running the tests together in the IDE plugin to produce a single result.

Integration, functional, and other testing

You may remember from the opening sections of the chapter that there is some limited utility to the `integration-test` phase as part of the default lifecycle. If wired up by default, the tests need to run fast for reasons of practicality, limiting the normal types of tests that can be executed at this stage.

The `integration-test` phase in Maven was partially an afterthought, which has perhaps led to some of these limitations of its use. Unlike the main test phases, it does not have its own source tree and must be manually managed. We can just hope that this will change in a future version of Maven.

One example of the phase's use to consider is a test that verifies that the artifact was built correctly in the previous `package` phase. This need not be a conventional set of tests. For example, something as simple as the following Enforcer rule can be used to verify that the documentation was included in the packaged ZIP file:

```
<plugin>
  <groupId>org.apache.maven.plugins</groupId>
  <artifactId>maven-enforcer-plugin</artifactId>
  <executions>
    <execution>
      <phase>integration-test</phase>
      <goals>
        <goal>enforce</goal>
      </goals>
    </execution>
  </executions>
  <configuration>
    <rules>
      <evaluateBeanshell>
        <condition>
          <![CDATA[zipFile = new java.util.zip.ZipFile(
    "${project.build.directory}/${project.build.finalName}-bin.zip"
  );
```

```
    entry = zipFile.getEntry(
                "${project.build.finalName}/docs/index.html"
    );
    zipFile.close();
    entry != null
        ]]></condition>
      </evaluateBeanshell>
    </rules>
  </configuration>
</plugin>
```

This uses the BeanShell scripting language (http://www.beanshell.org) to run dynamically interpreted Java code in a compact and easy-to-use way.

We can try this example for ourselves by adding it to the distribution/pom.xml file of the example application, and running:

```
distribution$ mvn integration-test
```

These types of tests can be very useful in a distribution module, but what about integration tests for the Java modules? For the answer to this question, we are going to work through the scenario of adding functional tests using Selenium to the web application module. While these may be different to the types of integration tests you might need to incorporate, the principles for configuring them are likely to be the same.

Running integration tests using naming patterns

The simplest technique to incorporate integration tests into an existing project is to add them to the default test tree of src/test/java, under a particular naming convention. The execution of the tests is then controlled by inclusions and exclusions (or additionally in TestNG, groups can be used).

This has the distinct advantage of a single POM and co-located sources with the integration tests. However, it means that the tests are mixed in with the other tests (which may be an advantage or disadvantage based on your situation).

This also means that all the tests will be compiled regardless of what is run. Despite the extra configuration, setting up the separate tree is clearer cut, but the decision on which option to take will depend on your individual circumstances.

Let's try this for ourselves by starting to add Selenium tests to the web application POM, `modules/webapp/pom.xml`.

There are a couple of different ways to author and execute Selenium tests. Within the Maven plugin, it uses **Selenium RC** (which stands for **Remote Control**) to start a Selenium server that will run the test commands through the configured browser(s) available on the system. We can then use the Selenium RC Java client library bindings to write tests in Java to communicate with the server.

First, let's add the first Selenium test case to `src/test/java/com/effectivemaven/centrepoint/selenium/HomePageTest.java`:

```java
package com.effectivemaven.centrepoint.selenium;

import org.testng.annotations.AfterSuite;
import org.testng.annotations.BeforeSuite;
import org.testng.annotations.Test;
import com.thoughtworks.selenium.DefaultSelenium;
import com.thoughtworks.selenium.Selenium;

@Test(groups="selenium")
public class HomePageTest {
  private Selenium selenium;

  @BeforeSuite
  public void startSelenium() {
    selenium = new DefaultSelenium("localhost",
      4444, "*firefox", "http://localhost:8080");
    selenium.start();
  }
  public void homePage() {
    selenium.open( "/" );
    selenium.getTitle().equals( "Centrepoint :: Project List" );
  }
  @AfterSuite
  public void stopSelenium() {
    selenium.stop();
  }
}
```

Note the highlighted lines above that start the Selenium server. The first and second indicates the host and port where Selenium is running respectively. We will configure that shortly to be on the same machine as the build. The third is the browser that it should run the tests in, which will need to be installed on the machine running the build. We have set that to `*firefox` here. If you do not have Firefox installed, try a different value such as `*iexplore`.

For this code to compile, we will need to add the corresponding dependencies to the POM:

```
<dependency>
  <groupId>org.seleniumhq.selenium.client-drivers</groupId>
  <artifactId>selenium-java-client-driver</artifactId>
  <version>1.0.1</version>
  <scope>test</scope>
</dependency>
```

Because the test is in the main test tree, it will be picked up by Maven to run in the default phase. However, at that point the web application will not be built, let alone running, so we need to ensure that the test is excluded from the main set. The preferred configuration for this is as follows:

```
<plugin>
  <groupId>org.apache.maven.plugins</groupId>
  <artifactId>maven-surefire-plugin</artifactId>
  <configuration>
    <skip>true</skip>
  </configuration>
  <executions>
    <execution>
      <id>unit-tests</id>
      <phase>test</phase>
      <goals>
        <goal>test</goal>
      </goals>
      <configuration>
        <skip>false</skip>
        <excludes>
          <exclude>**/selenium/**</exclude>
        </excludes>
      </configuration>
    </execution>
  </executions>
</plugin>
```

This may not have been what you expected. Why not just add the `exclude` element to the top-level configuration like usual? The problem there is that the configuration is inherited to all children. This will include the integration tests we are about to configure, resulting in both an inclusion and an exclusion of `**/selenium/**`, which will cancel each other out.

The approach we have taken instead is to eliminate the pre-configured test run by setting the default configuration of skip to true. We have then re-declared the normal unit testing run using the exclusion we intended, but only to apply to the unit tests. The skip value is configured back to false to override the default and ensure the tests run.

Overriding default goals in Maven 2.2.0

Luckily the above situation can be avoided if you are using Maven 2.2.0 or above. Instead of adding skips and a new test goal, the configuration can be added to the default-test execution and it will be utilized by the built-in lifecycle (and no other executions). However, if taking advantage of this, make sure that the build is not used on earlier versions of Maven where the configuration will not be used!

Next, we need to make sure those tests are run in the integration testing phase. Before we start on that, however, we need to add a **profile** for activating the tests. As these tests will take some time to execute, and will be in the main web application POM, we don't want them to run on every build, but rather in controlled environments at an appropriate interval. This is a practice often known as **build pipelining**, which is covered in more detail in Chapter 7, *Maven Best Practices*.

For our purposes, the profile is very simple, added to the end of the project file:

```
<profile>
  <id>selenium</id>
  <build>
  </build>
</profile>
```

We have no need for an activation section as the command line -P option can be used. If you are interested in more information about profile activation, refer to the Maven documentation at http://maven.apache.org/guides/introduction/introduction-to-profiles.html.

Now we are ready to add the additional execution of Surefire within the profile to run the Selenium tests:

```
<profile>
  <id>selenium</id>
  <build>
    <plugins>
      <plugin>
        <groupId>org.apache.maven.plugins</groupId>
        <artifactId>maven-surefire-plugin</artifactId>
```

```
        <executions>
          <execution>
            <id>integration-tests</id>
            <phase>integration-test</phase>
            <goals>
              <goal>test</goal>
            </goals>
            <configuration>
              <skip>false</skip>
              <includes>
                <include>**/selenium/**</include>
              </includes>
            </configuration>
          </execution>
        </executions>
      </plugin>
    </plugins>
```

As you can see, this configuration looks very similar to the one created above, but this time it is run in the `integration-test` phase, and the Selenium tests are included instead of excluded. Because of the way the `includes` configuration works, all of the non-Selenium tests are excluded from the integration test run.

This is now enough for us to run the test:

```
webapp$ mvn -Pselenium integration-test
```

However, there is a problem—the test fails. As we are using the default configuration, the error report resides in the normal Surefire location of `target/surefire-reports/TestSuite.txt`. Reviewing the file shows that it was unable to locate the Selenium server – perhaps an unsurprising fact as we didn't start it!

There are two tasks that we need to perform for Selenium. They are:

1. Starting the Selenium RC server.
2. Starting the container that runs the web application.

We are spending some time looking at tests very specific to web applications in this section. If your application is not destined for the web, you might like to skip ahead to the section on configuring a separate test module. In addition, though we are focusing on Selenium here, other types of web application testing frameworks exist. While they might not require a server to operate, the other steps outlined in this section should apply in the same way.

Operating the Selenium server

The availability of a Maven plugin for the Selenium RC server makes this process very simple. As our tests are being run in the integration-test phase, we set up the server in the pre-integration-test phase, and then turn it off again in the post-integration-test phase.

The configuration we add to the POM (inside the selenium profile) is as follows:

```
<plugin>
  <groupId>org.codehaus.mojo</groupId>
  <artifactId>selenium-maven-plugin</artifactId>
  <version>1.0</version>
  <executions>
    <execution>
      <id>start</id>
      <phase>pre-integration-test</phase>
      <goals>
        <goal>start-server</goal>
      </goals>
      <configuration>
        <background>true</background>
        <logOutput>true</logOutput>
      </configuration>
    </execution>
    <execution>
      <id>stop</id>
      <phase>post-integration-test</phase>
      <goals>
        <goal>stop-server</goal>
      </goals>
    </execution>
  </executions>
</plugin>
```

As you can see, only basic configuration is needed over the execution of the goals. The background flag needs to be set to true so that execution continues to the integration tests and the server will be stopped by the subsequent stop goal. The default of running in the foreground is designed for those that might want to use Maven as a launcher by using the selenium:start-server goal.

The logOutput configuration will create a log file of the Selenium server that may be useful in troubleshooting issues.

Running headless

Most times, the Selenium tests will be run on a remote continuous integration server. The configuration we have supplied here requires that the browsers being tested (in this case, Firefox), be installed on the same machine as the tests are run. However, it is also common for such systems to be headless. That is, with no windowing system to run the browser in. Servers can be configured to make this possible, and the Selenium plugin provides an xvfb goal to start a virtual frame buffer on Unix systems. If this is something you need in your environment, refer to the documentation for the Selenium xvfb goal for more information at http://mojo.codehaus.org/selenium-maven-plugin/ examples/headless-with-xvfb.html.

Now, if you run the tests again you will notice that they still fail, but that different errors result. The Selenium server can be contacted, but the tests themselves fail, as the browser will not be able to contact the running application. For that, we need to get the web application running in a suitable container.

Deploying the application to a container

If you are testing for a Java web development environment, how you deploy your application is one of the choices that is most specific to your development environment. You may target one type of application server, or you may need to test against multiple different servers (if you are distributing a web application for general use). You may be able to run the server locally where the build is run, or you may need to deploy the web application to a remotely running test server instead. You may even have multiple applications to test, perhaps all together.

A popular framework for this purpose comes from the Cargo project (http://cargo.codehaus.org/). Descended from the Jakarta Cactus project at Apache (http://jakarta.apache.org/cactus/), it has the facility for starting and stopping a variety of Java application servers, and deploying your application into them, which can be very useful for these testing purposes. If you are deploying to a server that doesn't have a more specific Maven plugin of its own, you might consider trying Cargo out.

For our example, we will be using the Jetty plugin directly to achieve this task. We have encountered Jetty and its Maven plugin earlier in the book. Of course, Jetty is a very capable server to use in production—but even if you are deploying to a different type of server you might consider using Jetty as a fast and simple way to run your tests before running a later set of tests on your other environment.

Usually, the Jetty plugin is set up to run in the foreground so that it can be used to preview the application in real time using the `jetty:run` command. However, like the Selenium server, it is possible to set it up to start in the background in the `pre-integration-test` phase (and again stopped in the `post-integration-test` phase).

Add the following to the `selenium` profile of the POM:

```
<plugin>
  <groupId>org.mortbay.jetty</groupId>
  <artifactId>maven-jetty-plugin</artifactId>
  <version>6.1.14</version>
  <configuration>
    <contextPath>/</contextPath>
    <daemon>true</daemon>
    <stopKey>STOP</stopKey>
    <stopPort>8888</stopPort>
  </configuration>
  <executions>
    <execution>
      <id>start-jetty</id>
      <phase>pre-integration-test</phase>
      <goals>
        <goal>run</goal>
      </goals>
    </execution>
    <execution>
      <id>stop-jetty</id>
      <phase>post-integration-test</phase>
      <goals>
        <goal>stop</goal>
      </goals>
    </execution>
  </executions>
</plugin>
```

Here you can see the goals you would expect. As Jetty doesn't have a `start` goal, we use the existing `run` goal, but set the `daemon` flag to true so that it runs in the background. The `stopKey` and `stopPort` are supplied to make it possible to stop the server when required.

The `contextPath` is supplied so that it will be deployed at `http://localhost:8080/` instead of `http://localhost:8080/webapp/` (based on the artifact ID).

Because both have been bound to the `pre-integration-test` phase, it's not determined which order the Selenium and Jetty servers will be started in (and likewise, stopped). However, for this exercise it is not important – the servers do not depend on each other, as long as they both have started by the time the integration tests run.

With all this in place, we should now be in the position to run the tests again and see success:

```
webapp$ mvn -Pselenium integration-test
```

As the tests run, you will notice that Firefox (or the other browser you configured earlier) is started.

Having problems?

As Selenium tests interact heavily with the configuration of your machine, you may run into problems. Check the test results and log files from the Selenium server to see if they indicate what the problem is. If you continue to have problems getting it to work, try reaching the authors on the book's forum.

We have now successfully configured the integration tests for the web application, to be run optionally after the web application is built.

Simplifying test grouping with TestNG

One of the advantages of using TestNG for these types of tests is the availability of **groups**. Each test can optionally be added to one or more groups, which can be used to selectively run certain categories of tests.

These groups can be used to categorize tests in any way that you might like to selectively run them, whether it is categorizing them by a particular feature line across multiple tests, or a type of test such as the `selenium` group we assigned in the previous example.

In our example, we can now use this to our advantage in the POM. The first Surefire configuration would be replaced by the following:

```
<plugin>
  <groupId>org.apache.maven.plugins</groupId>
  <artifactId>maven-surefire-plugin</artifactId>
  <configuration>
    <excludedGroups>selenium</excludedGroups>
  </configuration>
</plugin>
```

Then later integration testing configuration can then be replaced with:

```
<plugin>
  <groupId>org.apache.maven.plugins</groupId>
  <artifactId>maven-surefire-plugin</artifactId>
  <executions>
    <execution>
      <id>integration-tests</id>
      <phase>integration-test</phase>
      <goals>
        <goal>test</goal>
      </goals>
      <configuration>
        <groups>selenium</groups>
        <!-- Override inherited exclusion of selenium -->
        <excludedGroups>none</excludedGroups>
      </configuration>
    </execution>
  </executions>
</plugin>
```

We can see that this configuration is more intuitive and allows multiple classifications of tests if needed. This setup can be useful even if the tests reside in a separate module.

Should the Surefire plugin configuration not offer enough flexibility in the groups to run, you can also use the `suiteXmlFiles` option to run handcrafted test sets using `testng.xml`. For more information, see the TestNG documentation at `http://testng.org/doc/documentation-main.html#testng-xml`.

Using a separate integration test module

Having the tests in the same module may be very convenient, but you will notice that even with the TestNG simplifications, the POM has already grown to be quite large. Moreover, if we were to look at reusing it or adding more variations it would probably be un-maintainable. For this reason, including the tests in the same project tends to be more suited to small projects or examples for frameworks where it is more important to keep the project together.

Consider the case of the Maven integration tests. Plugins tend to be a single module, so the integration tests are configured within the plugin build, so that there is only ever one project to deal with. However, Maven itself consists of multiple modules and the tests might be run against multiple versions, so the integration tests reside in a separate module (or rather, a separate set of modules). The same principles apply to your application when you decide how to design the build.

By setting up the separate module, we are able to cut back on the custom configuration, getting a module that looks more like a standard Maven project. It also allows us to separate the source tree completely, and consequently the dependencies, allowing a more accurate build for the individual tests, as well as more flexibility in how the tests can be constructed.

Let's examine what is needed to take the previous example and construct a separate test module.

First, we construct a new module in the same way that we learned from Chapter 3, *Building an Application Using Maven*. Even though this does not need to be packaged itself, we create a project with a packaging of jar in modules/selenium-tests/ pom.xml, so that we are able to take advantage of the default test lifecycle.

```xml
<?xml version="1.0" encoding="UTF-8"?>
<project xmlns="http://maven.apache.org/POM/4.0.0"
  xmlns:xsi="http://www.w3.org/2001/XMLSchema-instance"
  xsi:schemaLocation="http://maven.apache.org/POM/4.0.0
    http://maven.apache.org/maven-v4_0_0.xsd">
  <modelVersion>4.0.0</modelVersion>
  <parent>
    <groupId>com.effectivemaven.centrepoint</groupId>
    <artifactId>modules</artifactId>
    <version>1.0-SNAPSHOT</version>
  </parent>
  <artifactId>selenium-tests</artifactId>
  <name>Centrepoint Selenium Test Suite</name>
</project>
```

Next, we add this module to the parent POM like the others. However, we still want to retain the optional nature of these tests in a regular build, and rather than encasing the whole project in a profile, it is easier to just do that with the module in the parent. Therefore, in the modules/pom.xml file, we create the same profile that exists in the web application, this time with just the module listed:

```xml
<profiles>
  <profile>
    <id>selenium</id>
    <modules>
      <module>selenium-tests</module>
    </modules>
  </profile>
</profiles>
```

Now we can start to move the rest of the infrastructure from the `webapp` project into the `selenium-tests` project. For the source code, in the new module the normal `src/test/java` directory can be used again, so we move `webapp/src/test/java/com/effectivemaven/centrepoint/selenium` to `selenium-tests/src/test/java/com/effectivemaven/centrepoint/selenium`.

The changes in the POM result in a simplification. We can take the following steps to continue the migration:

1. Move the Selenium dependency from `webapp/pom.xml` to `selenium-tests/pom.xml`.

2. Move the contents of the `selenium` profile from `webapp/pom.xml` to `selenium-tests/pom.xml`. The surrounding profile is not needed in the new POM—they can be entered directly into the build section.

3. Remove the Surefire configuration sections from both POMs, which will not be needed due to the separation of the source trees.

As we will now be using the standard test lifecycle, starting the Jetty and Selenium servers in `pre-integration-test` phase is not suitable; we need to change them to run in the `process-test-classes` phase:

```
<execution>
  <phase>process-test-classes</phase>
```

Likewise, the stop goals can be moved to the `test` phase (where they will run after the tests have completed):

```
<execution>
    <phase>test</phase>
```

We also are no longer in the web application itself, so it is necessary to retrieve that as a dependency and place it in the `target` directory to be used by the `jetty:run` goal. We can do this using a dependency, and the Dependency plugin.

Therefore, first we add a dependency on the web application artifact in `selenium-tests/pom.xml`. This will also ensure that the build order of the multi-module project is correct.

```
<dependency>
  <groupId>com.effectivemaven.centrepoint</groupId>
  <artifactId>webapp</artifactId>
  <version>${project.version}</version>
  <type>war</type>
  <scope>test</scope>
</dependency>
```

Next, we can add the Dependency plugin to unpack it into the
`target/dependency` directory:

```
<plugin>
  <groupId>org.apache.maven.plugins</groupId>
  <artifactId>maven-dependency-plugin</artifactId>
  <version>2.1</version>
  <executions>
    <execution>
      <goals>
        <goal>unpack-dependencies</goal>
      </goals>
      <configuration>
        <includeArtifactIds>webapp</includeArtifactIds>
      </configuration>
    </execution>
  </executions>
</plugin>
```

The only configuration that we needed to add to this goal was the
`includeArtifactIds` option that made sure that only the web application
was unpacked, not the Selenium dependencies that we added earlier.

Finally, we can configure Jetty to use these new locations to launch the web
application by adding these settings to the configuration section:

```
<configuration>
  <classesDirectory>
    target/dependency/WEB-INF/classes
  </classesDirectory>
  <webAppSourceDirectory>
    target/dependency
  </webAppSourceDirectory>
```

Let's try this from the top—building the whole tree from the `modules` directory.

```
modules$ mvn -Pselenium clean install
```

If everything goes to plan, you should see a successful result, including the execution
of the Selenium tests.

As you can see, even with the addition of a new module and some additions to
reference the WAR as a dependency, overall the structure is now more standardized.
This means that, for example, running the Surefire report works the same way that it
used to (though this is not quite the case for EMMA, which we will examine shortly).

Altering integration tests with profiles

If we would like to introduce additional profiles, for example to provide an alternative to Jetty for the application server, or to alter the configuration of the browsers to use, we can now do this within the new POM. It would not have been possible to nest the profiles in the previous POM.

Let's look at a practical example for running the tests against different browsers based on the profile selected.

First, we need to make the browser configurable for the unit tests. In the earlier example, the browser value was hard-coded to *firefox. We can change that to use a system property to make it configurable from the POM.

```
selenium = new DefaultSelenium("localhost", 4444,
  System.getProperty( "selenium.browser", "*firefox" ),
  "http://localhost:8080");
```

It is now possible to alter the browser from the POM, for example:

```
<plugin>
  <groupId>org.apache.maven.plugins</groupId>
  <artifactId>maven-surefire-plugin</artifactId>
  <configuration>
    <systemProperties>
      <property>
        <name>selenium.browser</name>
        <value>safari</value>
      </property>
    </systemProperties>
  </configuration>
</plugin>
```

This is likely to be enough if all you need to do is run one browser at a time, and you can re-run the module tests with a different setting. However, what if you needed to run the test cycle with multiple browsers?

To do this, we will set up multiple executions of the Surefire plugin within the test phase. Therefore, we need to return to some of the configuration we used earlier.

```
<plugin>
  <groupId>org.apache.maven.plugins</groupId>
  <artifactId>maven-surefire-plugin</artifactId>
  <configuration>
    <skip>true</skip>
  </configuration>
</plugin>
```

As in the earlier examples, it is necessary to skip the test plugin by default so that only the configured instances are added.

Next, we add a profile for each of the browsers for which we want to be able to run the tests. For example, the following would be the sample for Safari:

```
<profile>
  <id>safari</id>
  <build>
    <plugins>
      <plugin>
        <groupId>org.apache.maven.plugins</groupId>
        <artifactId>maven-surefire-plugin</artifactId>
        <executions>
          <execution>
            <id>safari</id>
            <goals>
              <goal>test</goal>
            </goals>
            <configuration>
              <skip>false</skip>
              <systemProperties>
                <property>
                  <name>selenium.browser</name>
                  <value>*safari</value>
                </property>
              </systemProperties>
            </configuration>
          </execution>
        </executions>
      </plugin>
    </plugins>
  </build>
</profile>
```

Such a profile can be repeated for all the browsers the project might want to support testing against.

For the best user experience we should also select one (or more) of the browsers as the default. For this, we use the `activeByDefault` configuration for the selected profile, which will cause the given profile to be activated if none are provided on the command line.

```
<profile>
  <id>firefox</id>
  <activation>
    <activeByDefault>true</activeByDefault>
  </activation>
```

This now allows us to run the tests for Firefox by default using the existing command:

```
selenium-tests$ mvn test
```

We can also run the tests just for Safari:

```
selenium-tests$ mvn test -Psafari
```

We can also run multiple copies of the tests:

```
selenium-tests$ mvn test -Pfirefox,safari
```

Of course, there are ways to achieve this programmatically, and such combinations may not be suitable for your other objectives (such as measuring coverage, and test results will be overwritten given the configuration above), not to mention the lengthy POM fragments needed compared to running using the default configuration and a system property. These considerations need to be weighed against the needs of your own projects.

In the example application, we will instead keep the earlier configuration for a single browser for simplicity.

Using TestNG parameters

In the previous section, we saw how to pass configuration parameters into the tests using system properties. While this is quite effective, there is a slightly cleaner method built into TestNG that our example application can use instead, called **parameters**.

Consider the following change to the initialization method:

```
@BeforeSuite
@org.testng.annotations.Parameters( { "selenium.browser" } )
public void startSelenium( String browser ) {
   selenium = new DefaultSelenium( "localhost", 4444,
      browser, "http://localhost:8080" );
```

In this example, we can request that TestNG pass in a parameter to a test method rather than looking up a system property. Surefire uses the same configuration as before to populate these parameters, although `testng.xml` can also be used to configure them if that is in place.

Measuring coverage for integration tests

We have seen earlier the advantages of using a code coverage tool to assess which code is well tested at the unit testing level. However, this was difficult to achieve *out of the box* for multiple module projects, and this likewise affects integration tests — particularly if they are in a separate module.

Unfortunately, in its current alpha state of development, the Emma plugin is not capable of assisting with the task automatically, however with some careful configuration it is possible to establish. These principles should equally apply to other coverage tools (some of which may have better support in the first place).

1. Establish a profile for enabling the use of coverage code in selected environments.

2. Instrument the code, and ensure the coverage tool is configured to use a single database for all modules.

3. Ensure that the instrumented code is included in the artifacts (however, be cautious not to install them in the local or remote repositories).

4. Run the application with the instrumented code and run any necessary tests against it (ensure it is run in a separate JVM so that coverage data is written when it is stopped).

5. Generate a report from the coverage data.

In these cases, if the Maven plugin is not giving you enough flexibility to gather the necessary data or generate the report from a given data set, you may need to fall back to the Ant tasks for the coverage tool. For more information on using Ant from your Maven projects, refer to Chapter 6, *Useful Maven Plugins*.

Summary

We've now seen a variety of different configurations for automated testing within Maven. We've also applied these to the example application that we encountered in the previous chapter and seen them in action.

There is a much wider range of ways to address testing needs by using the variety of available testing libraries and toolkits, particularly as the type of test becomes more specific or encompasses a larger part of the application. However, the techniques above should be applicable to other tools equally when run in the same scenario.

We have also had a close look at integrating EMMA into the application—and though our examples were specific to EMMA the concepts tend to match other coverage tools with a Maven plugin such as Cobertura and Clover. In the next chapter, we will look at EMMA in more depth as we start enforcing the coverage rules to the point of failing the build.

Tests are the predominant method of ongoing measurement of quality in application code. However, there are a number of other tools available in the Java ecosystem that can be used to identify current or potential problems or otherwise analyze your code. In the next chapter, we will look at integrating some of these into your Maven build.

5
Reporting and Checks

So far, in this book we have learned about how Maven projects are established. With the exception of the integration of specific tools that might be required for the build, everything that is needed should be in place—the application can be built, tested, packaged, and shared.

We might well stop at this point and be happy with what we have achieved. However, we are not done yet!

There are a number of tools available, particularly for Java projects, which are useful for keeping track of other metrics and information about the project. We have encountered some of these already when the Javadoc and cross reference were set up in Chapter 3, *Building an Application Using Maven*, and the Surefire and EMMA reports in Chapter 4, *Application Testing with Maven*.

While these tools may be used to help you set your own personal standards, they become especially important in the team environment where shared standards can help team members work together effectively, and the availability of a common source of information about the project can keep them aligned.

Maven is particularly well suited to the integration of these tools by allowing them to reuse the standard project model that is at its heart, as well as other techniques such as team project inheritance for shared settings. While admittedly, the reporting mechanism in Maven hasn't entirely lived up to its promise in this regard (perhaps by being associated too closely to the rendering of the Maven site itself), when used conscientiously and deliberately it can bring great value to your team's project development infrastructure.

In this chapter, we'll be continuing with the example application that we have been working with to illustrate how these concepts can be applied to a typical project layout. We will look at the principles behind how reports are configured, some of the reports that are available for use in Java projects, and how to correctly configure them. We will also look at how to enforce certain constraints related to the reports, and how to use this to our advantage in ensuring code quality.

Review: Example application

Even though we have only lightly touched on Maven's site and report capabilities to this point, we have already achieved quite some functionality:

- Setting up a basic site for developers with shared information about the project's code and development
- Including some simple reports in Javadoc and the source cross reference to the developer's site, aggregated across all of the Java modules
- Creating a separate site for user-oriented documentation for the project
- Applying a skin to both of the sites
- Configuring the Surefire and EMMA HTML reports to be run from the command line or integrated into the developer's site if desired

As we now move to enhance the project, we will be focusing on the `modules` subdirectory, enhancing both the developer-oriented site through reports, and the build itself through the addition of enforcement based on these reporting tools.

Constructing the developer's site

In Chapter 3, *Building an Application Using Maven*, we saw that you could generate a small site with information for developers by running the following from the `modules` directory:

```
modules$ mvn site
```

When this command is run, the site can be viewed from `target/site/index.html`. From what we have done already, there is a short description of the project as well as aggregated Javadoc and a source cross reference.

You will also see a menu for individual modules in the left-hand navigation. The purpose of this is to link to the same sites for each of the individual modules in the project, as Maven generates a site on a per-project basis. However, if you attempt to click on the link, you will find that the page is not found, even though the previous command would have generated sites for those modules.

The reason this occurs is that the relative link on the eventual site will be the artifact ID of the module. However, in the generated content it will be under the module's `target` directory. For example, for the model module, it will be in `model/target/site` instead of `target/site/model`.

As you can see this can make it quite tedious to test a multi-module site, and to make matters worse, the Site plugin (as of version 2.0) contains a number of bugs and feature gaps related to multiple module sites, such as:

- The `site:stage` goal, intended to ensure sites are aggregated into one directory, incorrectly constructs links for the modules

- The `site:run` goal does not support multi-module projects

- Site menu inheritance and the parent module menu have a number of outstanding issues reported against them

- The Site plugin's dependence on using the `url` from the POM and the `distributionManagement` URL for constructive relative links causes regular problems and confusion, particularly if not deployed to the eventual location

Given all of these problems, you might wonder why we would recommend using the Site plugin at all! It is true that you must think seriously about whether it is the right technology for your project. At present if you are using it to write developer documentation then you should expect to either house the majority in the root project (which might not be feasible for very large multi-module projects with independent functions), or maintain your own navigation between the modules.

One of the main advantages of the plugin in the reporting aspect is the automatic generation and linking of configured reports for each module, which we will look at in the following section. Some of these reports aggregate to the top level (such as Javadoc and JXR). However, some will generate one report per module and need additional navigation. We will be looking at the addition of some types of reports in the following sections.

Later in this chapter, we will look at setting up enforcement checks on the thresholds of some of the reporting plugins. That means that consulting the generated site is only needed infrequently when the check fails (and in that case, there may also be alternatives). In this instance, the structure of the site becomes less important.

Finally, we will also look at Sonar, which provides a different representation of the data from the reports, and becomes an alternative to using the site plugin for the reporting aspect.

But coming back to our site for now—what if we needed to preview the multi-module site in a single directory? As site deployment generally works in the end, it is best for us to use that now, but instead of using the final destination, we can choose a known location on the filesystem.

To be able to deploy a site, you must first add a distributionManagement element to the POM, so we add the following to modules/pom.xml:

```xml
<distributionManagement>
  <site>
    <id>website</id>
    <url>${siteDeploymentUrl}</url>
  </site>
</distributionManagement>
```

We have already encountered the distributionManagement element when we were adding a repository to deploy the artifacts of the project. Our new addition in this case is the site element, which looks much like a repository but instead provides a URL for deploying the sites. Like a repository, this can be a URL using protocols such as scp://, file://, http://, and so on. However as you can see we have provided a property reference instead. This will allow us to choose a default deployment URL, but to override it from the command line so that we can do our test deployment.

First, let's add the default property value in the POM:

```xml
<properties>
  <siteDeploymentUrl>
    file:///${basedir}/www/centrepoint/dev/${project.version}
  </siteDeploymentUrl>
</properties>
```

This value is similar to the one used for the documentation in Chapter 3, *Building an Application Using Maven*, but as you can see we create a new location for the development documentation. Typically, a WebDAV, SSH or FTP location would be given here instead that points to a shared web server to view the documents from. For now, we can generate the site locally with the following command, overriding the property:

modules$ mvn site-deploy -DsiteDeploymentUrl=file:target/staged

We have used a shortened file URL here, which will resolve to a relative path within the modules directory and acts most consistently. You might consider a more complete URL with an absolute path (for example, file://localhost/www/staged-projects/centrepoint/) in some cases, however be aware that file URLs behave differently based on the operating system and version of the JDK being used.

You might like to set this value of the property in a profile to reduce the amount of typing you need to use when generating the site, by activating the profile instead of typing the full command. In addition, if you use this frequently you might consider setting it as the default and instead having your build server set the actual deployment location instead.

Of course, if all this seems like too much hassle, you can just browse to the subdirectory of the module and into `target/site` from there—it just won't be an integrated navigation in the web site! This may be more practical for some reports as you may wish to just regenerate them for a single module while you are fixing a problem anyway.

Maven reports

Let's now take a closer look at Maven's reporting infrastructure. We have encountered several reports built on top of it already—the EMMA coverage report, the Javadoc and source cross reference, and even the **Project Information** submenu on the generated site. You will notice that not all of these are the same, or even strictly reports about the project in the true sense of the word. What they do have in common is that they integrate automatically into the Maven generated site and are configured in a separate part of the project. This is the main service of Maven's reporting infrastructure today—to stitch them together into the site without having to run each individually and to remain separate from the main build process.

This might lead you to believe that the reporting mechanism and the site generation mechanism (or rendering) are the same thing. While it is true that they are closely related, it is important to realize there is a difference and that they can be used independently for different tasks.

For example, it is possible to render a site without any reports at all for the purposes of generating documentation—we saw this in Chapter 3, *Building an Application Using Maven*, when we created the documentation module for our sample application. Likewise, plugins such as EMMA and Javadoc render a report without using the Maven site generation mechanism at all, and some plugins such as PMD are able to generate a data set in XML instead of a rendered report for different forms of consumption.

As Maven's support in this area evolves, it is likely that the latter forms of output will be used solely to produce analytical and historical information without the need to render it to a site, using the same configuration that exists today in the `reporting` section. Therefore let's look at this in more detail.

Adding reports to the project

When you first generate a site for a project, you will notice that there is a **Project Information** menu, but no **Project Reports** menu. This is because the former, supplied by the `maven-project-info-reports-plugin`, is configured to run by default (unless disabled), but no other reports have been added.

The standard information reports are useful for sharing information with others — particularly the newcomers to the project who have encountered other Maven projects and will already know where to look for the information that they need to get started. However, the focus of this chapter is on the reports that generate some analytical information about the project on which they are operating.

As we have seen, adding reporting plugins to the project is very much similar to adding build plugins to the `build` section of the project — they are just added to the `reporting` section instead. For example, take this configuration for the Javadoc plugin that we added in Chapter 3, *Building an Application Using Maven*:

```
<reporting>
  <plugins>
    <plugin>
      <groupId>org.apache.maven.plugins</groupId>
      <artifactId>maven-javadoc-plugin</artifactId>
      <version>2.5</version>
      <configuration>
        <aggregate>true</aggregate>
      </configuration>
    </plugin>
  </plugins>
</reporting>
```

This adds the report to the top-level project, and as a result, it will be inherited by all of the child modules and will appear on their respective sites (unless, as with the Javadoc and JXR plugins, they are configured to aggregate their information in the parent).

Where reports start to differ from build plugins is in how they are *bound* to execution. The above, if placed in the `build` section of the project, would only reconfigure already configured executions of goals from the plugin, not run anything new, as there is no `executions` section. In contrast, the above report definition tells the Site plugin to run every report contained within it, using the configuration given.

Note that this is not currently a lifecycle as it is for the build — the Site plugin simply takes the declaration given and executes the reports specified. The order in which they are run is much less important than in the build lifecycle.

However, what about if you needed to run a particular report more than once, or exclude a particular report? For this, there is the `reportSets` sub-element, which is roughly equivalent to the `executions` element used in the main build section.

Firstly, let's look at how we can use this to limit the standard reports included on the project web site. Let's exclude those that have no information in the example project (such as continuous integration and mailing lists). This is as straightforward as listing the reports within a report set, again in `modules/pom.xml`:

```
<plugin>
  <groupId>org.apache.maven.plugins</groupId>
  <artifactId>maven-project-info-reports-plugin</artifactId>
  <version>2.1</version>
  <reportSets>
    <reportSet>
      <reports>
        <report>index</report>
        <report>license</report>
        <report>dependencies</report>
        <report>dependency-convergence</report>
        <report>dependency-management</report>
        <report>plugin-management</report>
        <report>plugins</report>
        <report>summary</report>
        <report>project-team</report>
        <report>scm</report>
      </reports>
    </reportSet>
  </reportSets>
</plugin>
```

As you can see in the previous code, the report names are like goal names in other plugins. This is no coincidence, they are in fact the goal names of each report if it were to be run on its own from the command line (which is also a possibility, as demonstrated by the use of the Surefire report in Chapter 4, *Application Testing with Maven*). If you need to know which reports a plugin contains, take a look at the plugin site for the goals that it lists.

Check the report names!

The Site plugin does not currently validate that the report names are correct and will silently ignore any that are mistyped. Make sure to double check them by validating the resulting site.

It is also possible to add a `configuration` element within the `reportSet`. Like in the `build` section, this will be added to whatever configuration was given at the plugin level but applied only to that set. This allows you to produce a second report set with different configuration, perhaps to be able to repeat a particular report with a different input source. Note that in that case the report must have the option to reconfigure its output file name so that both will be visible on the site and the reports won't overwrite each other!

In practice, `reportSets` are used infrequently, as the default tends to be sufficient. In fact, many reporting plugins only contain one report that needs to be run once.

Configuring plugins for both reporting and the build

We have already used the Javadoc plugin in the reporting section so that it can be added to the site for the benefit of developers working on the project. However, what if we wanted to generate the Javadoc as part of the build process so that it can be included in a release?

The technique remains the same—it is added to the build and is configured to execute at a certain stage. In fact, this is such a common behavior for Java projects that it is configured by default for the release profile (for more information on the release profile, refer to Chapter 9, *Continuum in Depth*).

However, the Javadoc plugin commonly requires some kind of configuration to render as expected, and it would be frustrating to have to configure it twice so that the report and the released version look the same. Luckily, Maven considers this, and so all configurations in the `reporting` section are *applied to the build*.

The reverse does not apply though—configuration in the build section is **not** added to the configuration of the report when it is run. The reason for this will become apparent when we move on to the enforcement checks in the later sections of this chapter.

To be more explicit, the rules for configuration of a given goal or report is as follows:

- Top level reporting configuration is applied to build plugins at the top level, as well as any report sets and executions
- Top level build configuration is not applied to reporting plugins when run in the site lifecycle
- Report set and execution configuration is confined to that execution within the lifecycle or the site
- Command line execution picks up both top level configuration elements, but not executions or report set

At first, this might seem a bit complicated, but in practice, it is quite simple. Just follow these rules when considering where to add your configuration for a reporting plugin:

- Place the configuration only in the build section if the report should never be included in the site, or the piece of configuration is only relevant to the build (For example, if it causes the build to fail under some circumstances)
- In all other instances, place the configuration in the reporting section

Of course, configuration can be split across the two depending on the type to maximize reuse without conflict.

Configuring reports in the site life cycle

All that we have seen so far has assumed that the Site plugin will be responsible for executing the reports. In most cases, this is a reasonable assumption, but there is one limitation in Maven that may make this difficult: the lack of a `pluginManagement` equivalent for the `reporting` section.

Consider the case where you have a corporate standard configuration for the Checkstyle plugin (we will look closer at this plugin in the next sections). If you were to configure it in the `reporting` section of the organization POM then due to inheritance it would be applied to every child project for execution, whether it was needed or not, with no mechanism to disable it. In many cases, this is acceptable as reports won't execute on projects for which they are irrelevant (such as those with a `packaging` of `pom`), but the universal nature of it may be a concern for projects of other types added in the future.

The alternative is to use `pluginManagement`, from within the `build` section. Now, if you are thinking "but you just told me the build configuration isn't used for reports", you are correct! This means we'll need to also configure the reports in the build lifecycle.

Luckily, site generation can also utilize a build lifecycle, so it is possible to configure reports to run before the site is generated, resulting in similar behavior to that if the reporting section had been used.

Let's take a look at how this might be configured for the Checkstyle plugin example given. We won't be retaining this configuration as we progress with the example project, but it can serve as an illustration of the concept for now. First, we add the configuration we want to share to a pluginManagement section in our effectivemaven-parent/pom.xml file:

```
<plugin>
  <groupId>org.apache.maven.plugins</groupId>
  <artifactId>maven-checkstyle-plugin</artifactId>
  <version>2.2</version>
  <configuration>
    <configLocation>config/maven_checks.xml</configLocation>
  </configuration>
</plugin>
```

Now if we move to one of our sub modules, such as store-file, and run the checkstyle command we will see the report generated using the new configuration:

store-file$ mvn checkstyle:checkstyle

Checking the configuration

The checkstyle goal doesn't tell us what checks it is actually using in the default output, so how can you be sure that the configuration was used? In this case, you could run the command with the -X flag and look for the section that shows the arguments including the new value for configLocation being passed to the checkstyle goal just before the [checkstyle:checkstyle] marker.

The report now exists in target/site/checkstyle.html. However, if you were now to run the site, you will notice that the Checkstyle report is **not** generated:

store-file$ mvn clean site

This is to be expected, as we only put Checkstyle in a management section, not in the build or reporting sections. To ensure it does run, we would add the following to the build section of the modules/pom.xml file:

```
<plugin>
  <groupId>org.apache.maven.plugins</groupId>
  <artifactId>maven-checkstyle-plugin</artifactId>
  <executions>
    <execution>
      <phase>pre-site</phase>
```

```
        <goals>
          <goal>checkstyle</goal>
        </goals>
      </execution>
    </executions>
  </plugin>
```

You will notice that unlike in the `reporting` section, just listing the plugin is not sufficient: we must actually execute the goal, and the execution phase we choose is called `pre-site`. However, we did not need to list the configuration already given in the `pluginManagement` section of the organization POM. If we now try generating the site, we will see the report is generated:

`store-file$ mvn site`

However, there is another problem—let's look at the site now:

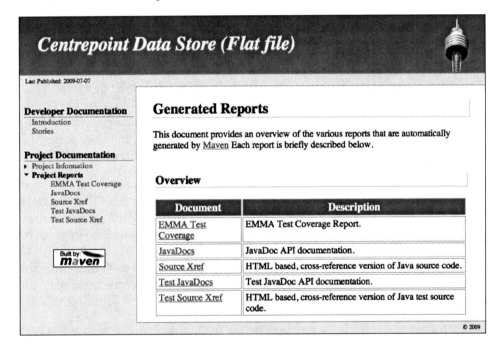

Notice the **Project Reports** menu. You will realize that it has not detected the Checkstyle report like it usually would if it were declared in the `reporting` section. We can correct this by adding it manually to an extra reports menu in `modules/src/site/site.xml`:

```
<menu name="Additional Reports">
  <item name="Checkstyle report" href="/checkstyle.html" />
</menu>
```

There is one final downside: the navigation of the report itself will no longer match the site, so users will need to use the browser back button to go back to the main index after viewing the report.

Overall, this configuration is a little more complicated and less declarative, and also means that you have opted out of potential future enhancements to the reporting mechanism. However, despite this, the practice can be more flexible—and is particularly useful if you don't intend to use the site functionality entirely but just run the reports as part of the build. Until the Maven project allows *mix-ins* to include fragments of configuration more easily, or supports a `pluginManagement` element in the `reporting` section, this is one workaround that you might need to consider.

We now know everything we need to be able to configure reporting plugins effectively for our project, so let's look at using the same tools to force a build failure on certain reporting conditions.

Setting up quality checks

Before we start looking at these examples, it is worth noting that Maven has no special notion of a quality check or a reporting enforcement rule at this time. The examples we will see here are just regular Maven goals that will trigger the build to fail under certain conditions. The behavior for what is judged a pass or fail is up to the plugin itself and the configuration that you supply for it. In many ways, this is similar to the Enforcer plugin that we have encountered in Chapter 1, *Maven in a Nutshell*, however the rules that it uses are not specific to any particular plugin.

Now, why do we need this? Well, I am sure you are all familiar with the war stories from your own projects. How often do the lower priority problems get fixed up if nobody is keeping an active eye on them? Very little—and they tend to grow over time until it gets to the point where some drastic action is needed to get things coordinated again. Even high priority problems—like the build not succeeding at all—can go left unattended if they are not continuously monitored and the appropriate people *nagged* to fix them.

Therefore, a group of reports on a web site may well look impressive to your management team, but if it starts trending in the wrong direction without enforcement, it is going to start looking less impressive very quickly! Therefore, what we need is to start configuring the build to fail when certain conditions are not met, so that they can be fixed before getting any worse. Let's start by looking back to the EMMA coverage report for an example.

Setting a minimum coverage requirement

Back in Chapter 4, *Application Testing with Maven*, we configured the EMMA plugin to run as part of the developer site generation process to report on the code coverage of the unit tests ran within the project. Now, what if we noticed that coverage was slipping over time, and not just in unimportant areas of the code? For this reason, the EMMA plugin has the emma:check goal.

 It is a convention in Maven to name such goals as check so they are easily recognized, but as we have already mentioned, any goal could perform this function.

To try this out, we must first add the EMMA plugin to the build configuration in modules/pom.xml if you have not already:

```
<plugin>
  <groupId>org.codehaus.mojo</groupId>
  <artifactId>emma-maven-plugin</artifactId>
  <version>1.0-alpha-2</version>
</plugin>
```

Before we can use this, we need to set some parameters for what to check. The EMMA plugin supports four different metrics:

- classRate: The percentage of classes that have some coverage
- methodRate: The percentage of methods that have some coverage
- blockRate: The percentage of actual executable code that is covered
- lineRate: The percentage of source code lines that were covered

 As explained on the EMMA site, the **line rate** can be an unreliable measure of coverage as simple formatting changes can affect it, and blocks of code can actually span multiple locations. For this reason, it is better used only as a visual indication.

As you can imagine, this actually gives us a useful ramp for introducing coverage—we can start by just ensuring all the classes are covered to some extent, then increase the number of methods, and then finally the code itself. For our example, let's start with one hundred percent coverage of classes and blocks, then work backwards to a more realistic expectation. To achieve this, we need to add the following configuration to the plugin element that was just added:

```
<configuration>
  <check>
    <blockRate>100</blockRate>
    <classRate>100</classRate>
  </check>
</configuration>
```

With that in place in the parent, let's test it out on the `maven-importer` module:

```
maven-importer$ mvn emma:check
```

It seems we still have some work to do! The build fails with the following messages:

```
[INFO] [emma:check]
[INFO] Checking EMMA coverage results
[WARNING] Insufficient code coverage for blocks: 90% < 100%
```

So, we **could** change the block rate to be 90 and leave it, right? Doing so at the parent POM configuration would be a bad idea, for starters as other modules that have higher coverage will then be given more leeway. At the `maven-importer` module level that might be a reasonable first step, to at least maintain the current amount of coverage, but what if we wanted to be more specific?

First, let's see exactly what the results look like by generating the report:

```
maven-importer$ mvn emma:emma
```

Opening the report in `target/site/emma/index.html`, we see that the package `com.effectivemaven.centrepoint.maven.repository` is the culprit.

To be more specific in the check, we can use patterns to configure different coverage rates within a single module. Even though the package is unique to this module and could be set from the `modules/pom.xml` file as before, we want the configuration to be set in the same context as it will be used. Therefore, with the following added to `maven-importer/pom.xml`, we could reduce the global configuration but increase it on the packages that are well tested to ensure they do not slip by later.

```
<build>
  <plugins>
    <plugin>
      <groupId>org.codehaus.mojo</groupId>
```

```
      <artifactId>emma-maven-plugin</artifactId>
      <configuration>
        <check>
          <classRate>0</classRate>
          <blockRate>0</blockRate>
          <regexes>
            <regex>
              <pattern>com.effectivemaven.centrepoint.maven</pattern>
              <blockRate>100</blockRate>
              <classRate>100</classRate>
            </regex>
            <regex>
              <pattern>
                com.effectivemaven.centrepoint.maven.repository
              </pattern>
              <blockRate>90</blockRate>
              <classRate>67</classRate>
            </regex>
          </regexes>
        </check>
      </configuration>
    </plugin>
  </plugins>
</build>
```

If we run the check again now, you will see that it passes:

```
[INFO]  Checking EMMA coverage results
[INFO]  EMMA coverage results are valid
```

> Note that the top-level values are not overridden by the later regular
> expressions—they apply globally and must be satisfied in addition to
> the specific checks listed underneath! This is why each package is listed
> individually and the main checks are disabled by setting them to 0.

You may have wondered why it wasn't recommended to just go ahead and write
more tests at this point to raise the coverage percentages. While that is likely the
eventual outcome in many applications that have insufficient testing, just doing it
blindly is not recommended. Instead, by putting a stable configuration in place you
are well positioned to at least maintain it, and set objectives for increasing testing in
areas *where it is needed*. As we already saw, testing is a balancing act in this regard
that no metric can fully capture—the value of writing tests up to one hundred
percent may diminish rapidly for code that is not particularly crucial, and conversely
there are some circumstances where one hundred percent still does not actually
cover all the possibilities.

In the example code for this chapter you will notice that we have retained the 100% check requirements in the top level POM and then gone on to override that for individual modules as needed. The reason for this is that when new modules are later added, they are started with a stricter requirement and can lower it as appropriate.

Having this configuration available is helpful for those diligent developers that may check it before committing their work, or as a separately configured goal in your continuous build environment. However, for true enforcement you will need to add this to the default lifecycle at some point. The execution for this (to be added to modules/pom.xml) will look familiar already:

```
<configuration>
  <check>
    <blockRate>100</blockRate>
    <classRate>100</classRate>
  </check>
</configuration>
<executions>
  <execution>
    <goals>
      <goal>check</goal>
    </goals>
  </execution>
</executions>
```

Note that the configuration element remains *outside* of the executions. This ensures that if you run emma:check from the command line, the configuration will still be applied. This would not be the case if it were associated with the lifecycle bound check execution.

We can now try this again under the maven-importer module:

```
maven-importer$ mvn verify
```

The verify phase is used as that is the default phase that the check goal is bound to.

Firstly, you should notice the EMMA goal was run as expected:

```
[INFO] [emma:check {execution: default}]
[INFO] Checking EMMA coverage results
[INFO] EMMA coverage results are valid
```

If you scroll further up though, you may notice something else—the tests were run twice! This is because EMMA needs to instrument your class files, and the tests are re-run using those class files instead of the normal ones (however, these are instrumented in a separate directory, so are not packaged in your application). There are a number of ways to approach this problem.

Firstly, the execution can be added to a profile. This is in fact a good idea regardless to keep the default build as fast as possible, only adding the EMMA instrumentation (and additional test run) when required for the check. Let's adjust `modules/pom.xml` for this scenario by moving the execution that we just added:

```xml
<profile>
  <id>checks</id>
  <build>
    <plugins>
      <plugin>
        <groupId>org.codehaus.mojo</groupId>
        <artifactId>emma-maven-plugin</artifactId>
        <executions>
          <execution>
            <goals>
              <goal>check</goal>
            </goals>
          </execution>
        </executions>
      </plugin>
    </plugins>
  </build>
</profile>
```

You will notice that we have only moved the execution here—the configuration (now without the execution) remains in the main build section. This allows us to continue to run `emma:check` correctly from the command line, but to trigger the check in the default build we would need the profile:

maven-importer$ mvn verify -Pchecks

This is a good practice because it balances out the responsibilities. The developers can largely ignore the profile, ensuring they have a fast default build that will encourage them to continue running the unit tests in the first place, and can use their IDE tools for the extended checks such as code coverage. On the flipside, the continuous build server can vigilantly monitor the coverage, where the profile can always be activated, and generate the reports at the same time so that failures can be visualized.

While the purists may want to run the tests twice regardless to confirm that the behavior is the same with and without coverage information, what if you would prefer to run them only once? Unfortunately, at the time of writing the EMMA plugin does not have a `check-only` style of goal similar to the `surefire-report:report-only` goal, but this is something to look out for in future versions.

Of course, none of this affects the site generation. If it contains the EMMA report it will run the tests again as well and it is expected that the site generation is run at a different time to the main build tests. For more information on staggering this appropriately, see Chapter 9, *Continuum in Depth*.

This raises the question—why continue to generate reports if we now have a build check that fails? To some extent, it becomes less necessary, and it depends on the type of report in question, but the web site also provides a permanent record of a project's health which everyone can see at any time. It provides additional information to help determine the reasons for a failed build, and whether the conditions for the checks are set correctly.

This is important, because if the bar is set too high, there will be too many failed builds. This is unproductive as minor changes are prioritized over more important tasks, to get a build to pass. Conversely, if the bar is set too low, the project will meet only the lowest standard and go no further. This issue is important enough to look at in more depth now.

Best practices for configuring coverage checks

Choosing appropriate settings is the most difficult part of configuring any of the reporting metrics in Maven. Some helpful hints for determining the right code coverage settings are:

- Like all metrics, involve the whole development team in the decision, so that they understand and agree with the choice.

- Don't set them too low, as it will become a minimum benchmark to attain and rarely more.

- Don't set them too high, as it will discourage writing code to handle exceptional cases that are not being tested.

- Set some known guidelines for what type of code can remain untested.

- Remain flexible—consider changes over time rather than hard and fast rules. Choose to reduce coverage requirements on particular classes or packages rather than lowering them globally.

In particular, don't become obsessed with the numbers. There is more to assessing the health of tests than success and coverage. These reports won't tell you if all the features have been implemented — this requires functional or acceptance testing. They also won't tell you whether the results of untested input values produce the correct results.

Reporting and quality tools

There are already a range of both open source and commercial tools that have been integrated with Maven to supply reports and policy enforcement to projects. In this section, we will look at some practical examples of some of the most popular and well established of the tools.

You may already be using these tools, or others that are quite similar, and if you have already configured them and added them to your build, you can quickly step over that section. If not, this section may illustrate some new tools to consider in your own projects.

Dependencies

Before looking at the external tools, let's look at one that comes with Maven itself. Amongst the project information pages there are a set of reports on the dependencies of the project. These are primarily for informational purposes, but there is one that provides some metrics — the **Dependency Convergence Report**.

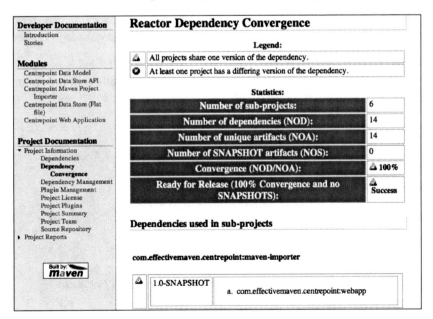

The report only appears in a multi-module build (so you will see it in the `modules` site of our generated sites above, but not any of the sub-modules sites), and was originally designed for confirming that throughout the build only one version of each particular dependency is used. This is particularly helpful if you do not use the `dependencyManagement` element consistently for defining the versions of your dependencies.

The other metric is the number of snapshots there are from outside of the current build. As long as such snapshots exist, it will not be possible to perform a release, so the report gives some indication of the release readiness of the project without needing to perform a dry run using the release plugin.

Unfortunately, there are no corresponding enforcement checks for either of these metrics within the plugin itself so you must rely on manually checking the report. Luckily, the Enforcer plugin does provide an enforcement rule for external snapshots instead, and if dependency management best practice is being followed, dependency convergence should not be of any concern for your projects. For more information on how to achieve these, see Chapter 7, *Maven Best Practices*.

Javadoc

By this point, we are certainly familiar with this tool! It requires little explanation here — put plainly, it serves as a complete wrapper around the Javadoc command line tool and works to integrate the result into the Maven site.

As far as reports go, it possibly contains the most configuration options, exposing most if not all of the options available to the command line version. The defaults will generally give you satisfactory results. However, you may wish to review the options available to see if they can improve your report.

One useful option to configure is links. In the online mode, this will link to an external Javadoc reference at a given URL.

For example, the following configuration, when added to `modules/pom.xml`, will link the JDK 6 and Wicket API documentation directly:

```
<plugin>
  <groupId>org.apache.maven.plugins</groupId>
  <artifactId>maven-javadoc-plugin</artifactId>
  <version>2.5</version>
  <configuration>
    <aggregate>true</aggregate>
    <links>
      <link>http://java.sun.com/javase/6/docs/api/</link>
```

```
        <link>http://wicket.apache.org/docs/1.4/</link>
      </links>
    </configuration>
  </plugin>
```

If you regenerate the site again, you will see that all references to the standard JDK classes such as `java.lang.String` and `java.lang.Object`, are linked to API documentation on the Sun Web site, as are the Wicket references in the classes from the web application.

Checkstyle

Checkstyle is a tool that does exactly what it says—checks the style of the code, to see if it conforms to a coding standard. Based on this behavior it has also added some additional rules for code issues, though other tools for this purpose come in the following sections with **PMD** and **FindBugs**. If you would like to know about the other modules that it has available, refer to `http://checkstyle.sf.net/availablechecks.html`.

How important this function is depends on the team involved in a project. While some might view it as pedantic, having a consistent style is important for readability of the code—it can be hard to follow if spacing changes regularly or you can't find your usual reference points as you scan the code. In addition, if your development environment relies on *diffs* in some way, then maintaining consistent formatting is essential to keeping the differences to a minimum. This means that reviewing commit logs is faster, and submission of patches or merging of changes from another source is significantly easier.

Of course, if you are going to require a particular style then having a corresponding formatter for the IDEs used by all the developers on the project is crucial. Nobody should have to spend time fiddling with the formatting when they should be able to run the built-in rules to do it automatically. There is very little point to choosing a style guideline that cannot be achieved by one or both of these tools.

Let's take a look at how Checkstyle operates on our example project. For testing, try running the following from the command line:

```
modules$ mvn checkstyle:checkstyle
```

You will see that this generates a report for each module individually, in the normal site location under `target/site/checkstyle.html`. The following is the start of the report that is created for the `store-file` module:

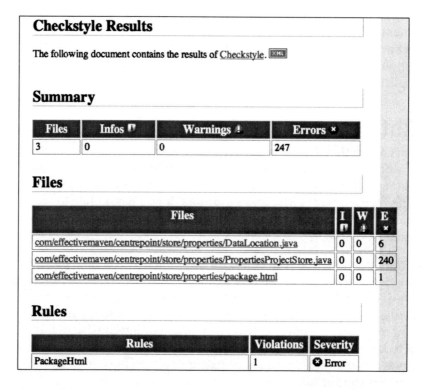

Checkstyle Results

The following document contains the results of Checkstyle. [XML]

Summary

Files	Infos	Warnings	Errors
3	0	0	247

Files

Files	I	W	E
com/effectivemaven/centrepoint/store/properties/DataLocation.java	0	0	6
com/effectivemaven/centrepoint/store/properties/PropertiesProjectStore.java	0	0	240
com/effectivemaven/centrepoint/store/properties/package.html	0	0	1

Rules

Rules	Violations	Severity
PackageHtml	1	⊗ Error

The report has two sections—a **summary** at the top, and then the **individual errors** broken down by file. The line number is also shown, and if the JXR plugin is being used this will link to the line in the source code cross reference.

> Unfortunately, at the time of writing, this technique of linking is not compatible with aggregated cross references, so even if the site is eventually deployed all together, the links from sub modules will not work, as the Checkstyle plugin does not aggregate itself. If this is important to you, you might consider turning off aggregation for the source cross reference.

As you can see, there are many errors! This is because the default style definition is the Sun coding standard, however this code uses a style closer to the current Maven coding standard, which uses quite a bit more whitespace.

Before we move on to fixing this, let's look at how to set an enforcement check. As is conventional, the goal for this is called `check`. Much as we did for EMMA in the previous section, we can then add the following to our `checks` profile:

```
<plugin>
  <groupId>org.apache.maven.plugins</groupId>
  <artifactId>maven-checkstyle-plugin</artifactId>
  <executions>
    <execution>
      <goals>
        <goal>check</goal>
      </goals>
    </execution>
  </executions>
</plugin>
```

This can now be run using the same command as earlier:

modules$ mvn verify -Pchecks

Of course, if you would like to run just the individual test, you can also run Checkstyle directly:

modules$ mvn checkstyle:check

In either case, the build will fail due to the style violations in the first module where they are encountered, showing the number of errors that have occurred.

```
[INFO] [checkstyle:check {execution: default}]
[INFO] --------------------------------------------------------
[ERROR] BUILD FAILURE
[INFO] --------------------------------------------------------
[INFO] You have 311 Checkstyle violations.
```

In the report earlier, you would have seen that there are different severities of violation—informational, warnings, and errors. In the default check, only errors cause the build to fail, however this can be configured via the plugin configuration if a stricter mode is desired.

Now, to resolve the failure, we need to switch the style definition to one that matches the code (rather than reformat all of the code!). As we are using a similar style to the Maven project itself, we can use one of the other built-in definitions from the plugin by adding the following to the `reporting` section of `modules/pom.xml` (also adding the report to the generated site when that is later built):

```
<plugin>
  <groupId>org.apache.maven.plugins</groupId>
  <artifactId>maven-checkstyle-plugin</artifactId>
  <version>2.2</version>
  <configuration>
    <configLocation>config/maven_checks.xml</configLocation>
  </configuration>
</plugin>
```

If you were to run either of the above commands now you would see that the build still fails, but with fewer errors:

```
[INFO] You have 67 Checkstyle violations.
```

Now, we could tweak the code to match these last few rules. This is convenient as we used one of the built-in styles, but what if you needed to configure one that matches your existing code?

The `configLocation` parameter can be set to a file within your build, an URL, or a resource on the classpath. We have taken advantage of the last alternative here by taking the file `config/maven_checks.xml` from the classpath of the plugin itself. This technique is typically the best available, as URLs can cause offline build and reproducibility problems, while standalone files are difficult to locate in a multi-module build.

To achieve this in our example, we need to create a small bundle that contains the necessary resources and add it to the build when the plugin is running. Let's consider how you might create a custom bundle to incorporate into the standard application structure.

As Checkstyle will be executed for all of the Java modules, we can't include it within the `modules` directory, so we create a module at the top level of the project, alongside the `skin`, `documentation`, and `modules` directories. Let's call the artifact simply `build`.

```
centrepoint$ mvn archetype:generate -DartifactId=build \
          -DgroupId=com.effectivemaven.centrepoint
```

While the template files can be removed, the project will remain as a standard JAR project. The resources we will look to add are in `src/main/resources`, as you can see from the sample code associated with this chapter. This includes not only the Checkstyle configuration for our project, but a copy of the project license header.

Writing your own Checkstyle configuration

While this chapter will not go into an example of how to do this, the Checkstyle documentation provides an excellent reference at `http://checkstyle.sf.net/config.html`.

Now that we've created this bundle, let's install it in the local repository to make it ready for use:

```
build$ mvn install
```

Finally, we need to modify the `modules/pom.xml` file to refer to the new build resources. The first step is to adjust the Checkstyle plugin configuration to match the new paths and to add the `headerLocation` configuration for the license header we've included:

```
<configuration>
  <configLocation>checkstyle/checks.xml</configLocation>
  <headerLocation>checkstyle/header.txt</headerLocation>
</configuration>
```

The next step is to add the build resources to the classpath for the plugin. This can be achieved using the `dependencies` element within the plugin—however, it comes with a catch. In many versions of Maven, the element was not allowed inside a reporting plugin. To work around this, we must declare the plugin in the `build` section with the dependency we want to add, like so:

```
<plugin>
  <groupId>org.apache.maven.plugins</groupId>
  <artifactId>maven-checkstyle-plugin</artifactId>
  <version>2.2</version>
  <dependencies>
    <dependency>
      <groupId>${project.groupId}</groupId>
      <artifactId>build</artifactId>
      <version>${project.version}</version>
    </dependency>
  </dependencies>
</plugin>
```

Note that the entire configuration is not needed there and according to the practices we discussed earlier, should actually remain in the reporting section.

 Prior to Maven 2.1.0, plugin dependencies were not taken into account when considering the build order. To ensure that your build works from a clean repository with older versions of Maven, you should consider moving the build resources module to the top of the modules list in the parent POM.

With all of this in place, we can run the site to see the final, cleaned up report:

```
modules$ mvn site
```

You will see that Checkstyle has been included under the **Project Reports** menu for each project where it was generated. Likewise, the check goal will now pass, so we are all set to be confident of maintaining a consistent code style for the project.

PMD

PMD takes a set of either predefined or user-defined rule sets and evaluates the rules across your Java source code. The result can help identify bugs, copy-and-pasted code (through a separate but included tool, **CPD**), and violations of a coding standard.

PMD won't operate on our Java 5 sources without some configuration, so to get started let's add this report to the main set for the project in modules/pom.xml in the reporting section:

```
<plugin>
  <groupId>org.apache.maven.plugins</groupId>
  <artifactId>maven-pmd-plugin</artifactId>
  <version>2.4</version>
  <configuration>
    <targetJdk>1.5</targetJdk>
  </configuration>
</plugin>
```

Now we can take a look at the PMD results with the default rulesets as we did for Checkstyle:

```
modules$ mvn pmd:pmd
```

When the command is run, the report is generated in `target/site/pmd.html` for each module (where appropriate). Again looking at the `store-file` module, we would see the following report:

PMD Results

The following document contains the results of PMD 4.2.2.

Files

com/effectivemaven/centrepoint/store/properties/PropertiesProjectStore.java

Violation	Line
Avoid empty catch blocks	100 - 103
Avoid empty catch blocks	104 - 107
Avoid empty catch blocks	116 - 119
Avoid empty catch blocks	180 - 182
Avoid empty catch blocks	191 - 193

This report looks very similar to the one that we encountered for Checkstyle earlier (and as we noted previously, some of the rules such as the empty catch block discovered above are also present in Checkstyle), however the errors generally relate to the functionality of the code rather than the style.

PMD uses **rule sets** to determine what to check and report on from the source code. When we run this report right now, we are getting the default settings, which include the **basic**, **unused code**, and **imports** rule sets. The basic rule set includes checks on empty blocks, unnecessary statements, and possible bugs such as incorrect loop variables. The unused code rule set will locate unused private fields, methods, variables, and parameters. Finally, the imports rule set will detect duplicate, redundant, or unused import declarations.

However, PMD is one tool where you rarely want the defaults. The above are a good, achievable starting point but you would be missing much of the power to not try some of the others rule sets which are available.

Adding new rule sets is easy, by passing the `rulesets` configuration to the plugin. However, if you configure these, you must configure **all** of them, including the defaults, explicitly. For example, to include the default rules, and the `finalizer` rule set, add the following to the plugin configuration you declared earlier:

```
<plugin>
  <groupId>org.apache.maven.plugins</groupId>
  <artifactId>maven-pmd-plugin</artifactId>
  <version>2.4</version>
  <configuration>
    <targetJdk>1.5</targetJdk>
    <rulesets>
      <ruleset>/rulesets/basic.xml</ruleset>
      <ruleset>/rulesets/imports.xml</ruleset>
      <ruleset>/rulesets/unusedcode.xml</ruleset>
      <ruleset>/rulesets/finalizers.xml</ruleset>
    </rulesets>
  </configuration>
</plugin>
```

We will revisit configuring the rule sets in a moment. However, as we have learned by now, being able to generate the report is not enough—we need to have an enforcement check in place! Let's get that into the build now, then work at gradually enhancing the rule sets we want to use.

The process for this is identical to Checkstyle. You can start by testing the check from the command line:

```
modules$ mvn pmd:check
```

This will run through all of the modules of the build and stop if it encounters a problem in the source code as evaluated by the PMD rules selected. We can now see the error we saw earlier:

```
[INFO]  [pmd:check]
[INFO]  ----------------------------------------------------------
[ERROR]  BUILD FAILURE
[INFO]  ----------------------------------------------------------
[INFO]  You have 5 PMD violations. For more details see:.../modules/store-file/target/pmd.xml
```

You might find the XML file that it refers to a little hard to read. However, we still have the report that we generated before to reveal to us that the problem is the empty catch blocks.

Before we go on to fix it, let's also add this to the `checks` profile so that it is automated:

```
<plugin>
  <groupId>org.apache.maven.plugins</groupId>
  <artifactId>maven-pmd-plugin</artifactId>
  <version>2.4</version>
  <executions>
    <execution>
      <goals>
        <goal>check</goal>
      </goals>
    </execution>
  </executions>
</plugin>
```

By default, the `pmd:check` goal is run in the `verify` phase, which occurs after the `package` phase. If you need to run checks earlier, you could add the following to the execution block to ensure that the check runs just after all sources exist:

```
<phase>process-sources</phase>
```

We can now run the build to confirm the same result as above:

`modules$ mvn verify -Pchecks`

Of course, with three checks in place this is getting a bit slower—so you may wish to just use `pmd:check` for testing, and reserve this profile for the full-blown cycle on the build server.

Getting back to the reported issues, there are three ways that this issue could be fixed:

- Fix the offending code—in most cases this is the most likely solution
- If the code is valid and needs an exemption, a marker can be added to the source code
- If the rule is not one you are interested in, it can be excluded from the rulesets

The first option is hopefully self-explanatory from the rule that has failed. In this case, we could add some code, such as logging, to the empty catch blocks. But what if it is intentional, such as the case of the failed `close()` operations? In this case, we could mark it as special so PMD will ignore it:

```
catch ( IOException e ) // NOPMD
{
}
```

This will skip the rule we set above — but note that it will also skip any other rules on that line of code!

We could go ahead and do the same for the all the catch blocks, but we may decide that we are going to require this regularly, and that it is better to disable that rule while retaining all the others. To do this in PMD, you will need to create a custom rule set, which can refer to existing rule sets or add new ones.

 I don't recommend disabling the EmptyCatchBlock rule in anything other than example code! As the PMD documentation says, "In most circumstances, this swallows an exception which should either be acted on or reported."

As with Checkstyle, you can supply several locations for the new rule set — including a file or a resource on the classpath resource (as we did above with /rulesets/*). To review the pros and cons of each see the previous section on Checkstyle. In this case, we already have a build resources module that is perfect for reusing, not only will it span the whole project, but also we could promote the artifact to represent an entire team so that we can easily reuse a predefined set of rules elsewhere without copying files around.

To create the custom rule set, let's add the following file to build/src/main/resources/pmd/rules.xml:

```
<?xml version="1.0"?>
<ruleset name="custom">
  <description>
    Default rules, no empty catch block errors
  </description>
  <rule ref="/rulesets/basic.xml">
    <exclude name="EmptyCatchBlock" />
  </rule>
  <rule ref="/rulesets/imports.xml" />
  <rule ref="/rulesets/unusedcode.xml" />
  <rule ref="/rulesets/finalizers.xml" />
</ruleset>
```

Here, we have retained the same configuration as previously but have excluded one particular rule from use. Now, to activate this rule set we must make two changes. First, we must add the build resources as a dependency of the PMD plugin. Recall from the previous section that this must be a new element in the build section, rather than the `reporting` or `profile` sections:

```
<plugin>
  <groupId>org.apache.maven.plugins</groupId>
  <artifactId>maven-pmd-plugin</artifactId>
  <version>2.4</version>
  <dependencies>
    <dependency>
      <groupId>${project.groupId}</groupId>
      <artifactId>build</artifactId>
      <version>${project.version}</version>
    </dependency>
  </dependencies>
</plugin>
```

Secondly, we must adjust the configuration in the `reporting` section to refer to the new ruleset:

```
<rulesets>
  <ruleset>/pmd/rules.xml</ruleset>
</rulesets>
```

Now, we are ready to test it all out again! Remember, we must install the build resources to the local repository first as they have been updated. In fact, a simple way may be to run an install from the top level of the project:

```
centrepoint$ mvn install -Pchecks
```

For more examples on customizing the rule sets, see the instructions on the PMD web site at `http://pmd.sf.net/howtomakearuleset.html`. It is also possible to write your own rules if you find that existing ones do not cover recurring problems in your source code.

There we have it—a fully customized and reusable PMD setup, ready to start adding more rules to, and gradually improving the source code quality accordingly. This now raises the question of how to select the right rules to use. For PMD, try the following guidelines from the web site at `http://pmd.sf.net/bestpractices.html`:

- Pick the rules that are right for you. There is no point having hundreds of violations you won't fix.

- Start small, and add more as needed. `basic`, `unusedcode`, and `imports` are useful in most scenarios and easily fixed. From this starting point, select the rules that apply to your own project.

Before moving on to other tools it is worth noting the additional goal that PMD has for copy/paste detection, `cpd`. This tool includes a list of duplicate code fragments discovered across your entire source tree. As we enabled the PMD plugin in the reporting section earlier, it will be included in the site by default. However, to include the check, you would need to add `cpd-check` to the list of goals, alongside check, in `modules/pom.xml`:

```
<goals>
  <goal>check</goal>
  <goal>cpd-check</goal>
</goals>
```

Unlike PMD, CPD does not take a set of rules – it solely performs copy/paste detection. There is one configuration option that it accepts: `minimumTokenCount` (which defaults to 100). This can be fine-tuned to the right size that identifies an identical code block, and should likely be reduced if your code already passes at the default level. Like the EMMA report, you may wish to configure this setting on a module-by-module basis to match the type of code that it contains.

If you find that this rule is distracting, you do not have to use this particular check, and can disable the report by using the `reportSets` element of the PMD report plugin.

FindBugs

FindBugs is a tool for detecting potential bugs in Java software. Where PMD performs analysis on source code, FindBugs performs static analysis on the Java byte code to detect common bug patterns. For example, let's try running FindBugs on the `store-file` module to compare the results. Unlike the previous examples, running the goal from the command line does not generate a standalone report, so we must add the configuration to the site in `modules/pom.xml`:

```
<plugin>
  <groupId>org.codehaus.mojo</groupId>
  <artifactId>findbugs-maven-plugin</artifactId>
  <version>2.0.1</version>
</plugin>
```

We can then go ahead and create the site. Note that FindBugs uses quite a lot of memory, and so you may need to alter the Maven execution options from the default:

```
store-file$ MAVEN_OPTS=-Xmx256m mvn site
```

When you open the report, you will notice that it contains a problem the others were unable to detect, with an ignored return value:

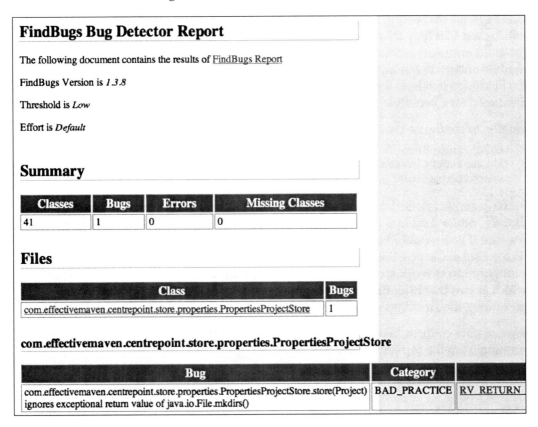

The configuration for the FindBugs plugin follows the same pattern that we have seen earlier, through the addition to the `reporting` section and the `check` goal execution to the `checks` profile, which we can go ahead and add to the example application.

Several configuration options to the plugin are available that match the original FindBugs command-line options. For complete information on these options, you can refer to the plugin web site at `http://mojo.codehaus.org/findbugs-maven-plugin` and the FindBugs command line options reference at `http://findbugs.sourceforge.net/manual/running.html#commandLineOptions`.

These are configured in the same way as the other reporting plugins that we have encountered. For example, to limit the problems listed to those of a medium or higher priority, we can add the following to the configuration in the `reporting` section of `modules/pom.xml`:

```
<configuration>
  <threshold>Normal</threshold>
</configuration>
```

FindBugs can also accept a filtering file to determine which rules to include and exclude, which class files they should operate on, and so on. Such files may also be included in the build resources artifact that we created earlier. An example is given in the `build` module under `src/main/resources/findbugs/excludes.xml`. To utilize this, we add the FindBugs plugin to the main `build` section of `modules/pom.xml` in the same way illustrated for Checkstyle.

Finally, to configure the exclusions filter file, we add the following option:

```
<configuration>
  <excludeFilterFile>findbugs/excludes.xml</excludeFilterFile>
</configuration>
```

In the example application, you will notice that this was added into the `checks` profile directly, rather than into the `reporting` section as you may expect. This is a valid use case if you would like the site to show all of the problems but only fail based on a subset of the possible problems. However, in this case we have had to use this configuration to work around a bug in the FindBugs plugin at the time of writing which means that filter files from plugin dependencies are not supported when generating the FindBugs report for the site (but work correctly for the check goal).

We can now confirm that the project passes our FindBugs checks using the profile, running from the top-level directory `centrepoint`:

```
centrepoint$ mvn install -Pchecks
```

Clirr

An important tool in determining whether a project is ready to be released is Clirr, which is a tool that detects whether the current version of a library has introduced any binary incompatibilities with the previous release. Catching these before a release occurs can eliminate problems that are quite difficult to resolve once the code is *in the wild*.

This is particularly important if you are building a library or framework that will be consumed by developers outside of your own project. Libraries will often be substituted by newer versions to obtain new features or bug fixes, but then expected to continue working as they always have.

Because existing libraries are not recompiled every time a version is changed, there is no verification that a library is binary-compatible. Incompatibility will be discovered only when there is a failure.

However, does binary compatibility apply if you are not developing a library for external consumption? It certainly does! It is likely that you are developing some small reusable modules that will spread across applications and start to have differing versions. This is particularly true in a Maven-based environment, where the dependency mechanism is based on the assumption of binary compatibility between versions.

For the most part, configuring the Clirr plugin follows the same process as for the others we have seen so far. There is a default report, as well as a `check` goal that fails if there are any compatibility errors.

However, instead of taking a set of rules to process, Clirr takes a previous release artifact. This can either be explicitly specified with a version, or with a different artifact if it has moved, but by default it will look for the latest release in the repository that is earlier than the version currently being built.

Other than a minimum severity threshold, Clirr's main configuration is the list of classes to include and exclude in the comparison. By using these extra options it is possible to ignore a class that has had a deliberate and managed API break without removing the check altogether.

We won't run through Clirr on the example application, as we are not yet at the point of having a release ready for it, let alone a past one to which we can compare! However, if you are building your own artifacts that have to maintain an external API, strongly consider adding the `clirr:check` goal to your build immediately after the first release so that binary compatibility can be monitored.

Other tools

Here, we have touched on just some of the most common tools that are available for analysis of your code using Maven. However, there are many more open source and commercial tools that can provide such services, and it is worth researching what best fits your needs and culture. Even if the tool does not have a Maven plugin, it is likely they can be integrated into the build in some way using the `antrun` plugin or the `exec` plugin which we will look at in the next chapter.

With our toolbox now well understood, let's look at some practices for how to choose and use them most effectively.

Reporting best practices

Like any system in Maven, there are particular sweet spots for how to use reports, and some common practices that are not to be recommended at all. In this section, we will browse through some best practices to keep in mind if you choose to use the reporting and check capabilities available.

Choosing reports

We have seen that there are a few reports at your disposal, and as you search for those available online you will find that there are many more. In most cases, they are trivial to add, just requiring the plugin definition to get started with the defaults. So it might be tempting to just go ahead and add everything you can find, right?

Report selection is actually a very important choice. If developers are faced with too much information or irrelevant information, it devalues the entire set and makes it harder to find what is really needed and what the real problems are. Of course, each report also adds to the build time and memory requirements that should be kept to a minimum.

What this boils down to: only include something if it is really going to be used! The report results and the checks performed should be accurate and conclusive – every developer should know what they mean and how to address them.

When it comes to choosing which reports you intend to include in your project, consider the following:

- Reference documentation is a good start. These are reports such as Javadoc and the source cross reference that provide a complete set of particular information about the project. They tend to be linked in from other reports to provide the necessary context, and are available to developers that need a single place to look up something in particular if it isn't immediately available in their development environment.

- Decisions about including other reports must be accompanied by a decision about a quality check. If the report has one, a corresponding check execution to fail the build at a certain threshold will provide a good enforcement point to check the report for problems.

How reports are configured once they are selected also needs consideration. We have seen this as we looked at some examples in the previous sections for specific tools. While the defaults are usually sensible, be sure to understand what they mean and customize the configuration to your environment as necessary.

These points might seem obvious, but they are worth keeping in mind. After all, how many times have you seen a project that lists a Checkstyle report that uses the default style guidelines, which doesn't match their source and routinely reports **thousands** of errors? How useful is that report in actually getting any errors fixed?

This extends to the standard project information reports as well. We saw in an earlier example how to configure these for a particular project so that only a subset is rendered. It makes sense to omit those that will not display useful information for your project, or may be plain misleading.

We should also be reminded at this point of the significance of the documentation structure in the example application. In a very deliberate move, the project code reports (under the `modules` directory) was separated from the user-facing documentation (in the top-level directory) and from any project web site content. Really, the only reports that belong on those documentation-style sites are some of the most basic project information reports such as mailing lists, the location of the source repository, the team, and the license.

Site deployment

Being able to generate the site is an important first step, but it is often a task that takes some time, and is best automated in your build server. However, what happens with it after that?

It is important that there is a centralized location to deploy all of the reports so that developers in the team know where to go to get the latest information, and are operating from the same source. They can also use this information to visualize problems or see what errors triggered a failed build due to a check going below a certain threshold.

If there are multiple branches of development, then it is a good idea to include the version in the site URL so that it can represent that particular branch of development. This also becomes useful at release time as reference documentation such as Javadoc can be deployed to a location that is permanent for that version.

Introducing and selecting failure thresholds

Just like choosing reports, choosing how and when to fail the build if a certain metric is not met is an important decision. If the requirement is too low, developers will tend to stop when they meet that minimum and go no further (30.5% coverage—done!). However, if it is too high it will become too discouraging and result in it being turned off or ignored. "*Yeah, that build has always been failing because we only have 99.95% coverage.*"

Here are some guidelines we might find helpful in introducing quality goals to a project:

- Use those that fit with the **current** culture, and add them gradually. Choose an achievable baseline (probably a measure of the current state of the code), and get used to monitoring it. Increase the target levels as the code evolves.

- Choose checks that have clear benefits through early bug detection and improved quality. Don't fail the build on style issues that the team weren't committed to in the first place!

- Remain consistent across teams and projects—use the organization POM to set rules consistently. Shifting developers should not have to learn new rules or change their culture.

- If starting a new project, decide the quality goals from day one and code it right into the template build—it is always harder to catch up later!

- Just do it! Too often getting started is in the too hard basket—it isn't going to get any easier, so make the commitment and get the checks running today.

Tying it all together

Previously in this chapter, a large amount of information was presented about a project, each in discrete reports. Some of the reports linked to one another, but they didn't relate information from one report to another, and very few of the reports aggregated information across a multiple module build.

Finally, none of the reports presented how the information changes over time. These are all important features required to have an overall view of the health of a project.

There are a number of projects that have started to integrate well with Maven to provide this information. Here we will look briefly at two that take quite a different approach.

Dashboard plugin

Still in the beta level of development, the dashboard plugin has started to achieve a reasonable level of functionality. Though it does not presently aggregate information in a multi-module build, it does aggregate the results of various different metrics into one report for each module and presents the ability to start capturing the information over time.

To try it out on the example application, you must first add the following to the `build` section of `modules/pom.xml` (as we will be running it from the command line initially, not as a report):

```
<plugin>
  <groupId>org.codehaus.mojo</groupId>
  <artifactId>dashboard-maven-plugin</artifactId>
  <version>1.0.0-beta-1</version>
</plugin>
```

Next, we will take it for a spin:

```
modules$ MAVEN_OPTS=-Xmx256m mvn site
modules$ mvn dashboard:dashboard
```

As you can see, at present the plugin requires that you have run the site goals in a separate execution first.

 This separation can be problematic when being used in a continuous integration server.

The resulting output for the store-file module will look similar to the following:

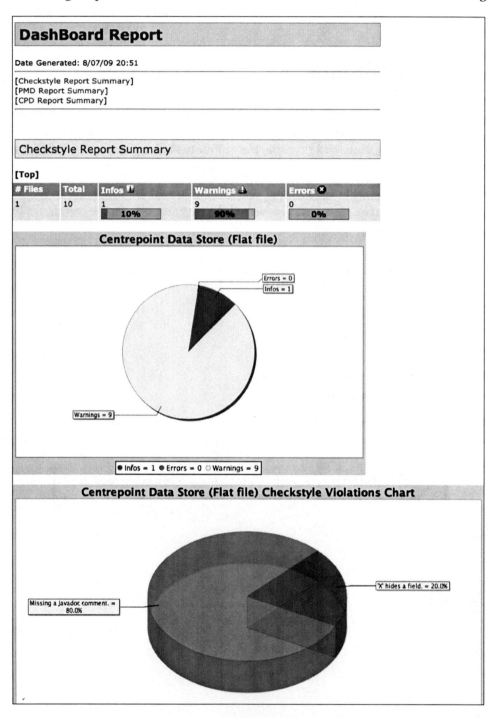

As you can see, the information is represented together, however because we have fixed all the issues that we are testing, the information in the PMD section is not particularly revealing! For this reason, such reports will be more of use where active checks were not deemed practical or are operating on a threshold that is lower than what might be desired and reported upon (such as is the case with Checkstyle above).

Sonar

The **Sonar** project (`http://sonar.codehaus.org/`) takes quite a different approach. It was built from the outset to accommodate historical information. While it uses the same tools and configuration as above, it is in fact a complete replacement for the reporting mechanism of Maven in those respects. If you are using it you may wish to simply link your Maven site to the Sonar installation instead of including PMD, Checkstyle, and so on as reports.

Sonar runs as part of the regular build lifecycle, integrated into your continuous build schedule. It is designed to push the results of all of the tools configured for the build to a common server. As above, this may mean that it is less effective to use active checks and instead follow the trends within Sonar to see how your quality is trending over time.

Discussing how to install Sonar is beyond the scope of this book, as it is another piece of development infrastructure on the order of Archiva or Continuum to maintain, however if this is the type of reporting functionality that you are looking for it may be worth investigating for your environment.

Summary

Maven reports and the tools they are associated with are under-utilized in many projects. While to some extent this may be because of the awkwardness of the Maven site that they tend to be housed in, even the comparatively simple task of establishing a quality check in the automated build is balked at—because of what it will take to bring to keep the code up to that level. For this reason, taking a slow but steady approach will bring the most benefit.

- For reports that are added, add a corresponding enforcement check if applicable.
- Add both the reports and the checks to a continuous build system so that the quality is monitored and does not degrade over time. Make it easy to meet at first, and make it part of the teams' culture to maintain it.

- Add a profile for the checks so that they do not slow the default build and can be enabled optionally or as part of the build system. It is likely easier to use IDE tools for the developers to check the quality metrics rather than the reports.

We have seen in this chapter that the power of Maven's declarative model is that it is very simple to set up new tools and this information can be shared with your team to visualize the quality of the project. We have also learned to set up automated enforcement checks on certain metrics, and about the tools that are available for these tasks.

So far, we have expanded on the example application to add a number of quality metrics that we can monitor. Later in the book we will examine how best to automate the site and report generation, as well as the new enforcement rules.

By this point, we have a relatively complete build environment for our application. Further additions will only need to be to incorporate specific functionality for the needs of the project, and so in the next chapter we move on to examine a cookbook of sorts for common tools and tricks that might be beneficial in some builds.

6
Useful Maven Plugins

Nobody can tell exactly how many Maven plugins exist today—since, like dependencies they can be retrieved from any specified remote repository, there are likely hundreds to choose from, and likely even more that have been custom written for use within the infrastructure of particular organizations.

A common practice for frameworks and tools that require build integration is to publish a Maven plugin to accomplish the task—and it is becoming increasingly common to encounter this as a standard part of the getting started section of a project you might hope to use. However, there are also a number of plugins that would be considered general purpose and handle some extended build cases in a wider variety of projects.

In this chapter, we will take a closer look at some of these plugins from two locations: those hosted as part of the **Apache Maven** project (`http://maven.apache.org/plugins/`), and a number of plugins from the **Codehaus Mojo** project (`http://mojo.codehaus.org/plugins.html`), which is oriented directly towards Maven plugin development. Some of these have been covered already in this book, so this will be an opportunity to examine their use in more depth, while others are new.

Where possible, we will apply the plugins to our example application to see how they can be used in practice, and then cover some of the other use cases and best practices for their use.

While this won't come close to covering all the plugins you are likely to encounter, with these common tools in your arsenal it will cover many of your Maven build needs, reducing the need for you to write your own plugins.

The Remote Resources plugin

Most projects will use the Resources plugin at some point, even if it isn't configured directly—it is standard in the default life cycle for any packaging that produces some type of artifact, bundling the resources found in `src/main/resources`.

However, what if you wanted to share those resources among multiple projects? The best approach to doing that is to store the resources in the repository and retrieve them for use in multiple builds—and that is where the Remote Resources plugin comes in.

First, we should note that this is not the only alternative for handling the scenario. The Dependency plugin's `unpack` goal is also quite capable of unpacking an artifact full of resources directly into the location that will be packaged.

However, the Remote Resources plugin offers several advantages:

1. Re-integration with the resources life cycle so that retrieved resources will automatically be processed in any goals in the `process-resources` phase.
2. The ability to perform additional processing on the resources (including the optional use of Velocity templates to generate the resources) before inclusion.
3. A specific bundle generation goal for creating the resource artifact in the first place.

These advantages can make the plugin very effective at dealing with some common scenarios. For example the inspiration for the creation of the plugin, and one of its more common uses, is to place aggregated license files within the final artifact.

There are other scenarios where the `dependency:unpack` goal remains more suitable—for example, the bundling of plugin configuration as seen in Chapter 5, *Reporting and Checks*. It is best to select the Remote Resources plugin when the files will be incorporated into the resources life cycle and the Dependency plugin when the files will be utilized independently.

Let's look at how to create a license file for our **Centrepoint** application. We will do this in two steps—the creation of the resource bundle that provides the generic resources for any project by the same organization, and the processing of the module resources.

Creating a Remote Resource bundle

Remote Resource bundles are regular JAR files packaged with additional information generated by the remote resource plugin's `bundle` goal. Creating a module follows the same process as with other JAR files.

In the example application, we will create the module outside of the Centrepoint multi-module hierarchy, so that it could (theoretically) be used by other projects from the same organization. This could be anywhere in source control, but we will assume it sits side-by-side with the `effectivemaven-parent` module in the workspace.

```
$ mvn archetype:generate -DartifactId=license-resources \
                    -DgroupId=com.effectivemaven
```

As this is not going to be a code project, the `src/main/java` and `src/test` directories can be removed from the generated content. We then continue to add the parent project to the POM, so the result looks like the following:

```xml
<project xmlns="http://maven.apache.org/POM/4.0.0"
  xmlns:xsi="http://www.w3.org/2001/XMLSchema-instance"
  xsi:schemaLocation="http://maven.apache.org/POM/4.0.0
    http://maven.apache.org/maven-v4_0_0.xsd">
  <modelVersion>4.0.0</modelVersion>
  <parent>
    <groupId>com.effectivemaven</groupId>
    <artifactId>effectivemaven-parent</artifactId>
    <version>1-SNAPSHOT</version>
    <relativePath>../effectivemaven-parent/pom.xml</relativePath>
  </parent>
  <artifactId>license-resources</artifactId>
  <version>1.0-SNAPSHOT</version>
  <name>License Resource Bundle</name>
</project>
```

We will add the Remote Resources plugin shortly, but first let's create the resources that will be bundled. These are added to the `src/main/resources` like regular resources.

Consider the following Velocity template file, `src/main/resources/LICENSE.vm`:

```
## License Generator
#macro(showUrl $url)
  #if($url)
    ($url)
  #end
#end
```

```
This software is distributed under the following license(s):
#foreach ($l  in $project.licenses)
  - $l.name #showUrl ($l.url)

#end

#if (!$projectsSortedByOrganization.isEmpty())
The software relies on a number of dependencies. The individual
licenses are outlined below.
#set ($keys = $projectsSortedByOrganization.keySet())
#foreach ($o in $keys)
From: '$o.name' #showUrl($o.url)
#set ($projects = $projectsSortedByOrganization.get($o))
#foreach ($p in $projects)
  - $p.name #showUrl ($p.url)
    $p.artifact
#foreach ($l  in $p.licenses)
    License: $l.name #showUrl ($l.url)

#end
#end
#end
#end
```

For those not familiar with Velocity, the purpose of this is to first iterate through the project's licenses and list them, then secondly iterate through the project's dependencies (grouped by the organization they are from) and list their license. The $projectsSortedByOrganization variable is a special one added by the Remote Resources plugin to assist in this task.

Before we can move on to use the bundle, we need to add the plugin to the bundle project like so:

```xml
<build>
  <plugins>
    <plugin>
      <groupId>org.apache.maven.plugins</groupId>
      <artifactId>maven-remote-resources-plugin</artifactId>
      <version>1.0</version>
      <executions>
        <execution>
          <goals>
            <goal>bundle</goal>
          </goals>
        </execution>
      </executions>
    </plugin>
  </plugins>
</build>
```

This goal is required to generate a *bundle manifest*, the contents of which tell the plugin which resources to process when it is later called on to do so.

With this all in place, we can now install the bundle into the local repository, ready for use:

```
license-resources$ mvn install
```

If you were to inspect the contents of the generated JAR file, you would see both the LICENSE.vm file in the root, and the bundle manifest in META-INF/maven/remote-resources.xml. You would also find that the Velocity template is unmodified — the contents will be *executed* when the bundle is later processed in the target project, which we will proceed to look at now.

Processing Remote Resources in a project

Using the resource bundle we have created is now quite straightforward. We start by adding the folllowing to the build section of modules/pom.xml file of Centrepoint:

```
<plugin>
  <groupId>org.apache.maven.plugins</groupId>
  <artifactId>maven-remote-resources-plugin</artifactId>
  <version>1.0</version>
  <executions>
    <execution>
      <goals>
        <goal>process</goal>
      </goals>
    </execution>
  </executions>
  <configuration>
    <resourceBundles>
      <resourceBundle>
        com.effectivemaven:license-resources:1.0-SNAPSHOT
      </resourceBundle>
    </resourceBundles>
  </configuration>
</plugin>
```

Here we have added a list of resource bundle artifacts to the configuration for the process goal, in the familiar shorthand artifact notation of groupId:artifactId:version. It has been added to the modules POM so that the license is included in the JAR files, but not included in the other non-code modules such as the documentation (which already generates a copy of the license from the reporting plugins).

Normally, you should use a released version of the license bundle, not a snapshot as we have here (as we have not yet covered the release process!). Since the bundle is configured directly and not through a dependency, the Release plugin will not detect this unresolved snapshot later.

Now, if we build a module such as `store-api`, we will see the license included in the root directory of the JAR file with the following content:

```
This software is distributed under the following license(s):
  - The Apache Software License, Version 2.0
      (http://www.apache.org/licenses/LICENSE-2.0.txt)
```

```
The software relies on a number of dependencies. The individual
licenses are outlined below.
```

```
From: 'Apache Maven 2: Effective Implementations Book'
      (http://www.effectivemaven.com/)
```

```
  - Centrepoint Data Model
    com.effectivemaven.centrepoint:model:jar:1.0-SNAPSHOT
    License: The Apache Software License, Version 2.0
      (http://www.apache.org/licenses/LICENSE-2.0.txt)
```

```
From: 'Google'
      (http://www.google.com/)
```

```
  - Guice
      (http://code.google.com/p/google-guice/)
    com.google.code.guice:guice:pom:1.0
    License: The Apache Software License, Version 2.0
      (http://www.apache.org/licenses/LICENSE-2.0.txt)
```

This is a good start, but we don't really need to include our own artifacts in the list, so we go back to the plugin declaration in `modules/pom.xml` and add another line of configuration:

```
<configuration>
  <excludeGroupIds>${project.groupId}</excludeGroupIds>
  <resourceBundles>
  ...
```

Regenerating the above artifact will alter the license to remove the dependencies from the project's group.

A different case is the final distribution. As this is not part of the `modules` hierarchy, first we need to include the plugin definition identical to the one added previously.

In the sample code for this chapter, you will notice that this has been taken a step further with the version and common configuration pushed into a pluginManagement section of the Centrepoint parent POM, and just the execution of the plugin goal remains in the modules and distribution POM files.

We can now build the assembly as usual:

```
distribution$ mvn clean install
```

Upon inspecting the generated assemblies, you will not see the license file included yet. This is because the Assembly plugin does not pick up Maven resources by default, as it does not participate in the normal life cycle.

To include the license file, we must alter the assembly descriptor distribution/src/main/assembly/bin.xml and add the following file set:

```
<fileSet>
  <directory>target/maven-shared-archive-resources</directory>
  <outputDirectory>/</outputDirectory>
</fileSet>
```

The directory given is the standard location in which the Remote Resources plugin stores the resources it has processed, so if you decide to configure that differently in your own projects you would need to change this to the corresponding location.

Upon building the assembly again we will see that the license has been generated, and that it includes the licenses of dependencies outside of the Centepoint application. As you can see, the distributed application depends on Jetty (also under the Apache License 2.0), which includes some portions of Glassfish (under the CDDL 1.0 License).

While the above technique can be very helpful in constructing some useful information about your project and its dependencies, it cannot be guaranteed to produce complete licensing information for a project. The method relies on accurate information in the POMs of your dependencies, and this can sometimes be inaccurate (particularly when using public repositories such as the Maven Central Repository). If you are redistributing your files, always confirm that you have correctly recorded any necessary licensing information that must accompany them!

The Remote Resources plugin is also capable of covering other scenarios that are particularly suited to license handling or more generally recording information about the project it is being processed for. These include:

1. The `supplementalDataModels` configuration option that allows you to fill in incomplete or incorrect metadata for a project dependency before the resources are processed (to avoid particular problems as described above).

2. The `appendedResourcesDirectory`, which allows you to store the above models in a separate file.

3. The `properties` configuration, which allows the injection of other build properties into the Velocity templates.

However, with this in mind, remember that the Remote Resources plugin is often just as suitable for any type of reusable resource, even if it is a static file.

The Build Number plugin

In Maven Mojos, the goals within a plugin are always designed to be simple tasks. Their aim is to do one thing, and do it well. A good example of this is the Build Number plugin. This simple plugin has one goal (`create`), with one purpose — to obtain a suitable build number and expose it to the build through properties or a file.

> While the plugin focuses on exposing the current Subversion revision, it is capable of generating an incremented build number (stored in a specified properties file), and a representation of the current system date and time. This feature can be very useful in identifying the exact heritage of a particular build. The build number generated by the plugin is different to that used by Maven to identify snapshots or artifact versions. While it is possible that you might mark your version using the information it generates, this plugin is typically used to record information about a particular build — whether it is a snapshot, or a release — within the artifact itself as a permanent record.

Using the plugin is straightforward. By adding the goal to the project, the Subversion revision and a timestamp property will be exposed from the point that it is run onwards.

```
<plugin>
  <groupId>org.codehaus.mojo</groupId>
  <artifactId>buildnumber-maven-plugin</artifactId>
  <version>1.0-beta-1</version>
```

```
<executions>
  <execution>
    <phase>generate-resources</phase>
    <goals>
      <goal>create</goal>
    </goals>
  </execution>
</executions>
</plugin>
```

In this example, we execute the plugin in the `generate-resources` phase so that the properties are available to any resource processing. Note that the values could be used with the Remote Resources plugin that we have just seen.

There are two things to take into consideration with this configuration, however. Firstly, not all source builds will be Subversion checkouts, but the plugin does not verify that. To work around this potential problem, you can put the goal into a profile:

```
<profile>
  <id>buildnumber</id>
  <activation>
    <file>
      <exists>.svn</exists>
    </file>
  </activation>
  <plugin>
    <groupId>org.codehaus.mojo</groupId>
    <artifactId>buildnumber-maven-plugin</artifactId>
    . . .
```

This particular activation check will cause the profile to be used within a Subversion checkout (that is, if `.svn` exists in the current directory), and to skip the plugin if not. In this case, the properties will not be set (or the file will not be created), so the code using these must take that into account.

Secondly, how the values will be accessed needs to be given careful consideration. For example, it is unlikely that you want to create a convoluted build processing step to filter the value into a particular JSP file to appear in a web application. For the sake of keeping the build simple (and speedy), it is best to write the values into a single file that the application can then load from its classpath.

This can be achieved by creating a filtered resource that contains references to the values. The advantage of this method is that it is automatic if you have already configured filtered resources, and automatically ends up in the classpath of the application code that can load the file as a resource.

The plugin also supports a number of formatting options, in the event that you do not wish to use the raw build number and timestamp integers. These options are also used to trigger the manual build number increment feature of the plugin in the event that Subversion is not used.

As our example application is one such case, let's apply this technique ourselves. We will only need to include the build number plugin in one location—if it were to be run on every module, the number would end up being different for each. Some seemingly sensible options may not actually be appropriate here:

- The parent project will cause the build number to be included in every module, and executing it just in the parent may result in it not being executed at all.

- The final distribution might be the best place in some situations, but what if you needed to reference the build number from the application itself?

Considering these factors, the best location is the web application module, as this will be the code which will eventually display the build number. In another application where multiple modules were to require it, it might be best generated in a common dependency instead.

The `modules/webapp/pom.xml` file requires two modifications. First, to enable filtering, we must add *both* the new filtered resources location and the original resources location to the `build` section (as Maven inheritance overrides resources instead of adding to them). This will look like the following:

```
<resources>
  <resource>
    <directory>src/main/resources</directory>
  </resource>
  <resource>
    <directory>src/main/filtered-resources</directory>
    <filtering>true</filtering>
  </resource>
</resources>
```

Depending on what resources you have in `src/main/resources`, you may choose to do away with it and include them in the `filtered-resources` directory instead. However, if some resources may be corrupted by filtering (such as images and other binary files), you will need to retain both.

Next, the addition of the build number plugin is needed with some particular configuration:

```
<plugin>
  <groupId>org.codehaus.mojo</groupId>
  <artifactId>buildnumber-maven-plugin</artifactId>
  <version>1.0-beta-1</version>
  <configuration>
    <format>Build: #{0} ({1,date})</format>
    <items>
      <item>buildNumber\d*</item>
      <item>timestamp</item>
    </items>
  </configuration>
  <executions>
    <execution>
      <phase>generate-resources</phase>
      <goals>
        <goal>create</goal>
      </goals>
    </execution>
  </executions>
</plugin>
```

Note the formatting options being used. The first, `format`, specifies what the configured property (by default called `buildNumber`) will look like, using the Java `MessageFormat` syntax. The `items` configuration provides a list of variables to substitute into the message format for {0}, {1}, and so on. Here, the first configured variable is `buildNumber\d*`, which is used to trigger the automatic number generation. The second is the integer timestamp that represents the current system date and time.

> You may also configure the location of the file to be generated that contains the incremented build number, with the default being `buildNumber.properties` in the current directory. It is important to place this in a location that will not be purged over time—for example, in the `target` directory, as this is regularly cleaned!

The exposed property is referenced from the resource files using the normal filtering syntax, so we can create `src/main/filtered-resources/build.properties` like so:

```
build.message=${buildNumber}
```

When we build the application, we will see the build number generated and incremented each time:

```
[INFO] Storing buildNumber: Build: #1 (27/03/2009) at timestamp:
1238074038389
```

All that is left to do is to access the build number from the application, which you can see in the `BuildNumber` class:

```
ResourceBundle bundle = ResourceBundle.getBundle( "build" );
msg = bundle.getString( "build.message" );
```

As you can see, if you are using Subversion it is likely a simpler option to use the revision number instead of creating a new build number, or perhaps passing the build number in from your build server using its own build numbering scheme. Using an incremented number as we have above can be inconsistent depending on the build order and build successes, with the additional requirement of maintaining the separate tracking file.

The Shade plugin

Maven's dependency-based nature promotes the practice of proper componentization of a build and producing a set of discrete artifacts that can be aggregated into an application. Throughout a dependency tree, dependencies may appear multiple times and can be mediated to the correct version so that a single version can be used. However, circumstances will occur where, rather than the discrete list of dependencies, it is necessary to merge, hide, or alter the parts of a number of dependencies into a single artifact. This is the purpose for which the Shade plugin was developed, and in this section we will look at two use cases in more detail.

Building a standalone artifact

In Chapter 3, *Building an Application Using Maven*, we learned how to build a suitable distribution for our example application. This was a suitable set up for a server where there are multiple configuration files, startup scripts, as well as the application itself. But for some Java applications, all that is needed is to run `static void main()`.

Distributing such applications if they have dependencies on other JAR files has always been problematic. Java has a mechanism to run a JAR on its own through the `Main-Class` manifest attribute, providing us with a simple command such as the following:

```
client$ java -jar centrepoint-client-1.0-SNAPSHOT.jar
```

However, this will generally fail as the dependencies required are not present on the classpath. From here, you might add the `Class-Path` element to the manifest. However, this requires that the JARs be placed in a particular location relative to the other files, and we are back to distributing a complete archive.

To make this easier, the Assembly plugin contains a pre-built descriptor called `jar-with-dependencies`. This simply collapses the JAR and all it's dependencies into one large JAR so that the above type of execution can work. In some cases, this configuration will work correctly, and no more work needs to be done.

One of the issues with the naïve approach of the assembly plugin is that many of the dependencies will house files with identical names, and it is given little choice but to pick just the last file that it encounters rather than dealing with the overlap properly.

This is where the Shade plugin can be useful, by providing hooks to transform these resources into a single resource as appropriate.

This is similar in intent to the Uberjar plugin that you may have used in Maven 1, however the technique is improved. In the assembly plugin and the shade plugin, the resulting artifact collapses the dependency JARs and corrects references instead of having to unpack and construct classloaders, making it a much faster alternative.

For example, consider the following configuration:

```
<plugin>
  <groupId>org.apache.maven.plugins</groupId>
  <artifactId>maven-shade-plugin</artifactId>
  <version>1.2</version>
  <executions>
    <execution>
      <phase>package</phase>
      <goals>
        <goal>shade</goal>
      </goals>
      <configuration>
        <transformers>
          <transformer implementation="org.apache.maven.plugins.shade.
                          resource.ComponentsXmlResourceTransformer" />
        </transformers>
        <artifactSet>
          <excludes>
            <exclude>xerces:xercesImpl</exclude>
```

```
        </excludes>
      </artifactSet>
    </configuration>
  </execution>
</executions>
</plugin>
```

Here we have the `shade` goal bound to the `package` phase to produce the collapsed JAR file as we might expect. In the `transformers` section, a transformer is added that merges all encountered Plexus descriptor files under `META-INF/plexus/components.xml`. Finally, we have the ability to configure the transitive dependencies that are included and excluded from the final artifact using the `artifactSet` configuration.

As of Shade version 1.2, the following transformers are supplied with the plugin:

- `ApacheLicenseResourceTransformer` and `ApacheNoticeResourceTransformer`: Specific to Apache license files such as those we created with the remote resources plugin earlier

- `AppendingTransformer`: To concatenate plain text resources

- `ComponentsXmlResourceTransformer`: For merging Plexus descriptors

- `ManifestResourceTransformer`: For merging Java JAR file manifests

- `ServicesResourceTransformer`: For merging Java services metadata in `META-INF/services`

- `XmlAppendingTransformer`: To concatenate XML resource files with appropriate nesting

These transformers will cover many of your needs when using the Shade plugin. You may eventually need your own custom transformer if there are certain types of resources that must be merged between two artifacts that are not accommodated by the above. In that case, a transformer can be written in a separate artifact and added as a plugin dependency, then referenced directly from the configuration. This is similar to the technique illustrated for sharing other build resources such as the reporting configuration files in Chapter 5, *Reporting and Checks*.

Shading dependencies

Another interesting use case of the Shade plugin is to hide or alter the dependencies of an artifact. This can be helpful in several situations, such as:

- Distributing classes from JARs that are difficult to access as dependencies (as long as such redistribution is allowed). For example, you may need to use a patched version of a common library and not want to cause conflict for projects that might depend on both your library and the original version.

- Avoiding conflicts with other instances of the dependency within a classloader or to work around incompatible versions in a dependency tree.

- Reducing the amount of code shipped by selectively including code from a particular dependency.

These situations are all similar and boil down to including some or all of the classes from a set of dependencies into the current artifact and altering the transitive dependency tree to compensate.

Let's consider this example within the context of the example application. In the example code for this chapter, we have extended the model to use commons-lang, which is used to construct the equals and hashCode methods. Now, if we were to share the API and model with third party developers to create their own store implementations, it would raise the same issues:

- Requiring the dependency of commons-lang (about 260K in size) for just a couple of classes.

- Introducing a dependency with a potentially stricter requirement than the rest of the application may later require (for example, if an incompatible, Java 5 enabled, commons-lang 3.0 is made available), again for very few classes.

In this situation, *shading in* just the portions of commons-lang that are needed may be a viable alternative. It is important to note that we can only do this if the license of the dependency allows such a combination, which in this case is true.

 An important part of this scenario is that the dependency is being shared outside of the current application. Inside an application, where you have full control of the dependency tree, you are less likely to benefit from shading dependencies for this purpose.

To start with, we will add the Shade plugin configuration to the `model/pom.xml` file:

```
<plugin>
  <groupId>org.apache.maven.plugins</groupId>
  <artifactId>maven-shade-plugin</artifactId>
  <version>1.2</version>
  <executions>
    <execution>
      <phase>package</phase>
      <goals>
        <goal>shade</goal>
      </goals>
      <configuration>
        <artifactSet>
          <includes>
            <include>commons-lang:commons-lang</include>
          </includes>
        </artifactSet>
      </configuration>
    </execution>
  </executions>
</plugin>
```

Running the `package` command with this in place will show the following:

```
[INFO] [jar:jar]
[INFO] Building jar: /Users/brett/code/06/centrepoint/modules/model/
target/model-1.0-SNAPSHOT.jar
[INFO] [shade:shade {execution: default}]
[INFO] Including commons-lang:commons-lang:jar:2.3 in the shaded jar.
[INFO] Replacing original artifact with shaded artifact.
[INFO] Replacing /Users/brett/code/06/centrepoint/modules/model/target/
model-1.0-SNAPSHOT.jar with /Users/brett/code/06/centrepoint/modules/
model/target/model-1.0-SNAPSHOT-shaded.jar
```

Multiple things are happening here. First, we can see that the normal JAR is produced as usual, and then the shade goal runs (consistent with the execution we added to the project). The plugin next shows that because of the `artifactSet` that we gave, `commons-lang` will be included in the JAR. If there were other dependencies, they would remain a regular dependency and not be included. Finally, we see that using the Shade plugin's default configuration, the original artifact is replaced with the shaded artifact so that this version will be installed or used in the reactor instead.

However, we still have some work to do. Notice the size and contents of the JAR for the model now — so far, we have added **all** of commons-lang. We would only like to include the builder classes, so for that purpose we add **artifact filters** to the Shade plugin configuration:

```
<filters>
  <filter>
    <artifact>commons-lang:commons-lang</artifact>
    <includes>
      <include>org/apache/commons/lang/builder/**</include>
    </includes>
  </filter>
</filters>
```

If we rebuild the project, we see that the JAR has reduced in size and upon inspection would find that only the files under the given path are included. This also ensures other files that might cause confusion (such as the pom.properties file under META-INF from commons-lang) are not included.

Of course, some caution is required here — these classes may well have required some of the now-excluded classes that are no longer present. In your own projects, ensure that your integration test cases adequately exercise the code being used; so that inadvertent runtime errors don't occur later.

 Beware the catch here that unit tests won't exercise this change! Unit tests run before the shading process occurs, so the tests need to occur in the integration test phase or in a separate testing module.

The next thing that we might notice about the contents of the JAR file is that the classes are still in their original packages under org/apache/commons/lang. This poses a potential problem for other projects that use commons-lang and depend on this API. There will now be two copies of these classes on the classloader that contains both JARs, and depending on the order, either copy of the classes could be used. If the wrong version is silently picked up, confusion will ensue on the part of the developer that appears to be getting the right version of the dependency, but the wrong behavior.

To prevent this, the Shade plugin allows us to encapsulate the use of commons-lang entirely by using the **relocations** feature.

```
<relocations>
  <relocation>
    <pattern>org.apache.commons.lang</pattern>
  </relocation>
</relocations>
```

Now when we build the artifact, we will see that the class names have changed, for example:

```
hidden/org/apache/commons/lang/builder/EqualsBuilder.class
```

This is more than a simple renaming—the Shade plugin has also adjusted the bytecode of these classes and the references in our own Java classes to rename the package to include `hidden` at the start. This will now avoid any conflict with other instances of `commons-lang`!

> Though this conflict is removed, you may still need to consider the converse case, if a class depends on only being instantiated once to operate correctly, or is accessed by a string using `Class.forName` for example, shading may not work.

One slight adjustment should be made here, as the default pattern of prepending `hidden` is not always a good choice. This can be confusing to see in stack traces, and if two different dependencies shade the same classes in the same way then the likelihood of conflict occurs again. Instead, we can choose to include them within the namespace of our own package instead by a slight adjustment to the relocation configuration:

```
<relocation>
  <pattern>org.apache.commons.lang</pattern>
  <shadedPattern>
    com.effectivemaven.centrepoint.model.shaded.lang
  </shadedPattern>
</relocation>
```

A final thing is worth noting about the configuration we have used so far. Initially, the shaded artifact replaces the original artifact and is installed in the local repository. In addition to replacing the original artifact, you may notice that the POM file installed in the local repository is also replaced with a different version that removes the `commons-lang` dependency. This is what we would expect as we have completely incorporated our `commons-lang` needs within the classes of the JAR through the shading process. This is thanks to the `createDependencyReducedPom` configuration option being enabled by default.

In some scenarios, you may not wish to replace the artifact, but instead create an additional artifact, with a different classifier, that contains the shaded alternative. This can be a good middle ground to give users the choice between an all-in-one artifact, or the default artifact that allows Maven to manage the dependencies normally. In this case, the `createDependencyReducedPom` option should be set to `false`, and the `shadedArtifactAttached` option set to `true`. Bear in mind, however, that the dependency representation for the classified artifact in this instance will be incorrect as the main artifact POM is used for classified artifacts as well.

The Shade plugin configuration contains a number of other configuration options for altering inclusions and exclusions at each step of the process that we have seen here and in particular for altering the technique and naming of artifacts that are attached with a classifier. Refer to the Shade plugin documentation for more information: http://maven.apache.org/plugins/maven-shade-plugin/shade-mojo.html

Before we move on, you may have observed a potential side effect of this change; that there will now be *two* instances of each class in the application should another use commons-lang. If multiple dependencies shade in the same classes, there may be multiple copies so even though this is powerful it is worth being judicious about using the technique, particularly if you have good control over how your artifact will be used as a dependency. Maven's dependency mechanism and version management is there for a reason. If it is possible to continue using discreet artifacts as they are, then that may be the best and simplest alternative too!

The Build Helper plugin

Within Maven, there are a number of common tasks which plugins can perform to alter the current project for changes occurring during the build. We have seen the inclusion of new resources in the Remote Resources plugin, and the attachment of a new artifact from the Shade plugin. It is also possible to have a plugin generate new source code and include it for compilation, even though the directory is not included in the POM file.

The role of the Build Helper plugin is to provide a set of goals that can help achieve a collection of small but common tasks for which it would not be worth writing a custom plugin.

Adding source directories

Maven's inability to have multiple source directories in the project model has often been called into question. However, as time has progressed the request has died down as the idea of a standardized source structure took hold.

The Build Helper plugin offers the ability to add another source directory or test source directory to that configured in the POM. This is not necessarily to allow a workaround for the deliberate limitation in the project model, but rather to facilitate other use cases that require it. The most common need to use this technique is to assist with the migration of a project in an existing layout to Maven temporarily.

Even with this capability it is still recommended not to add multiple source directories without a particular reason—apart from breaking with convention, you may find that some tools that operate based on the values in the POM will not recognize the additional directories as containing source code.

The following example illustrates the addition of a source directory:

```
<plugin>
  <groupId>org.codehaus.mojo</groupId>
  <artifactId>build-helper-maven-plugin</artifactId>
  <version>1.1</version>
  <executions>
    <execution>
      <id>add-source</id>
      <phase>generate-sources</phase>
      <goals>
        <goal>add-source</goal>
      </goals>
      <configuration>
        <sources>
          <source>src/main/more-java</source>
        </sources>
      </configuration>
    </execution>
  </executions>
</plugin>
```

The need to use the Build Helper plugin for adding sources is now becoming more rare. Maven plugins that generate source code would be likely to add the extra directory to the project internally without the need for additional configuration. If some other means is used to generate the sources—for example, from a scripting plugin—it is common for the scripting plugin to have a way to add the source directory with fewer configurations than using the Build Helper plugin. However, if the need does arise, the Build Helper plugin will prove itself useful.

Attaching arbitrary artifacts

A similar scenario that can occur is the generation of additional artifacts that need to be *attached* to the build process. This means they use the same POM to define them, but are different types of related build artifacts, with their own classifier. The artifacts are installed and deployed to the repository alongside the original.

Typically, this will be in the form of another JAR file, possibly generated by one of the scripting plugins that did not attach the artifact itself.

However, it could be used for any number of files that need to be stored in the repository alongside the main artifact. Consider the example of deploying the license to the repository—if you were to run the install phase on the given project, you would be able to have the license installed into the local repository alongside the main artifact and its POM.

In reality, this particular configuration may be overkill, especially if the licenses are identical across many projects, or can be derived from the POM. However, depending on your deployment needs this possibility can be helpful in ensuring the repository contains the information about an artifact that you need, at the time it was deployed, in addition to any extra build artifacts that might be generated.

In our example application, we generated the license in two places—in all the Java modules, and the final distribution. Deploying it along with the final distribution makes some sense, so let's add it to the `distribution/pom.xml` file:

```
<plugin>
  <groupId>org.codehaus.mojo</groupId>
  <artifactId>build-helper-maven-plugin</artifactId>
  <version>1.1</version>
  <configuration>
    <artifacts>
      <artifact>
        <file>
          target/maven-shared-archive-resources/LICENSE
        </file>
        <type>txt</type>
        <classifier>license</classifier>
      </artifact>
    </artifacts>
  </configuration>
  <executions>
    <execution>
      <goals>
        <goal>attach-artifact</goal>
      </goals>
    </execution>
  </executions>
</plugin>
```

This goal will execute after the packaging has occurred, but before installation so that it can be attached to the installation (and deployment) process. The file to attach is the license generated earlier by the Remote Resources plugin and is given an extension of `.txt` and classifier of `-license`. When running the `install` phase, we now see the file being processed:

```
[INFO] [build-helper:attach-artifact {execution: default}]

[INFO] [enforcer:enforce {execution: default}]

[INFO] [install:install]

[INFO] Installing /Users/brett/code/06/centrepoint/distribution/target/
pom-transformed.xml to /Users/brett/.m2/repository/com/effectivemaven/
centrepoint/distribution/1.0-SNAPSHOT/distribution-1.0-SNAPSHOT.pom

[INFO] Installing /Users/brett/code/06/centrepoint/distribution/target/
centrepoint-1.0-SNAPSHOT-bin.zip to /Users/brett/.m2/repository/com/
effectivemaven/centrepoint/distribution/1.0-SNAPSHOT/distribution-1.0-
SNAPSHOT-bin.zip

[INFO] Installing /Users/brett/code/06/centrepoint/distribution/target/
centrepoint-1.0-SNAPSHOT-bin.tar.gz to /Users/brett/.m2/repository/com/
effectivemaven/centrepoint/distribution/1.0-SNAPSHOT/distribution-1.0-
SNAPSHOT-bin.tar.gz

[INFO] Installing /Users/brett/code/06/centrepoint/distribution/target/
maven-shared-archive-resources/LICENSE to /Users/brett/.m2/repository/
com/effectivemaven/centrepoint/distribution/1.0-SNAPSHOT/distribution-
1.0-SNAPSHOT-license.txt
```

Other goals

The Build Helper plugin also contains some other goals in the latest release at the time of writing (v1.1) of more specific interest:

- `remove-project-artifact`: To clean the local repository of artifacts from the project being built to preserve space and remove outdated files. This may occur if the build no longer produces those files, or if it is necessary to remove older versions.

- `reserve-network-port`: Many networked applications may want to use a network port that doesn't conflict with other test cases. This goal can help reserve unique ports to use in the tests. This is useful for starting servers in integration tests and then referencing them in the test cases. However, note that it won't be available when running such tests in a non-Maven environment such as the IDE.

The goals available in the Build Helper plugin may increase over time, so if you have some small, common adjustments to make it is a good place to look to first for those utilities.

The AntRun plugin and scripting languages

Maven was designed to be extended through plugins. Because of the fact that this is so strongly encouraged, there are now many plugins available for a variety of tasks, and the need to write your own customizations, particularly for common tasks, is reduced. However, no two projects are the same, and in some projects, there are likely to be some customizations that will need to be made that are not covered by an existing plugin.

While it is virtuous to write a plugin for such cases so that it can be reused in multiple projects, it is also very reasonable to use some form of scripting for short, one off customizations.

One simple option is to use the AntRun plugin. Ant still contains the largest available set of build tasks to cover the types of customizations that you might need in your build, and through this plugin you can quickly string together some of these tasks within the Maven life cycle to achieve the outcome that you need.

Running simple tasks

We have already used the AntRun plugin in the distribution module of the example application. This snippet was used to copy some configuration files into place and create a `logs` directory, ready for the Assembly plugin to create the archive from:

```
<plugin>
  <groupId>org.apache.maven.plugins</groupId>
  <artifactId>maven-antrun-plugin</artifactId>
  <version>1.1</version>
  <executions>
    <execution>
      <id>config</id>
      <phase>process-resources</phase>
      <configuration>
        <tasks>
          <copy todir="${project.build.directory}/generated-
                      resources/appassembler/jsw/centrepoint/conf">
            <fileset dir="src/main/conf" />
          </copy>
          <mkdir dir="${project.build.directory}/generated-
                      resources/appassembler/jsw/centrepoint/logs" />
        </tasks>
      </configuration>
      <goals>
```

```
            <goal>run</goal>
          </goals>
        </execution>
      </executions>
    </plugin>
```

This shows how quick and useful the AntRun plugin can be for simple tasks. However, it also contains a number of other features that can be of benefit to the build for more significant tasks.

Interacting with the Maven project

As we mentioned in the section, *The Build Helper plugin*, you can tell the plugin to map some directories to new source directories. This functionality is identical to that of the Build Helper plugin, but is more conveniently located when the directories are being generated by Ant tasks.

This can be useful because even though tools are increasingly supplying native Maven plugins in addition to Ant tasks, you might come across a source generation tool that only has an Ant task. In this scenario, you can use the AntRun plugin to run the tool, generate the source code, and use the sourceRoot parameter to have that directory added back into the build life cycle.

In addition to injecting source directories back into the life cycle, the AntRun plugin also injects Maven project information into Ant's context. Probably the most important of these is the availability of the project's and plugin's dependencies as Ant path references:

- maven.compile.classpath: The dependencies in the compile scope (this syntax will look familiar to those that used Maven 1's built in Ant-based files)

- maven.runtime.classpath: The dependencies in the runtime scope (including the above)

- maven.test.classpath: The dependencies in the test scope (including both of the above)

- maven.plugin.classpath: The dependencies of the AntRun plugin itself, including any added via the POM

Though we have not needed it in the example application, to illustrate how these two options would work, consider if you needed to use the XJC Ant task from JAXB to generate some sources.

JAXB is a **Java-to-XML** binding framework that can be used to generate Java source code from XML schema (among many other things), using its XJC tool. Though it serves as a suitable example here, you would not be faced with this issue with JAXB itself, as it now offers a Maven plugin.

In this example, you might add the following configuration to an AntRun execution in a POM file:

```
<plugin>
  <groupId>org.apache.maven.plugins</groupId>
  <artifactId>maven-antrun-plugin</artifactId>
  <version>1.3</version>
  <executions>
    <execution>
      <id>xjc</id>
      <phase>generate-sources</phase>
      <configuration>
        <tasks>
          <taskdef name="xjc"
              classname="com.sun.tools.xjc.XJCTask"
              classpathref="maven.plugin.classpath" />
          <xjc destdir="${project.build.directory}/xjc"
              schema="src/main/jaxb/schema.xsd">
            <classpath refid="maven.compile.classpath" />
          </xjc>
        </tasks>
        <sourceRoot>${project.build.directory}/xjc</sourceRoot>
      </configuration>
      <goals>
        <goal>run</goal>
      </goals>
    </execution>
  </executions>
  <dependencies>
    <dependency>
      <groupId>com.sun.xml.bind</groupId>
      <artifactId>jaxb-xjc</artifactId>
      <version>2.1.9</version>
    </dependency>
  </dependencies>
</plugin>
```

We see here that the XJC Task is defined using the plugin classpath to locate the task and its dependencies (and that task's artifact is added as a plugin dependency to accommodate this). Additional built-in Ant tasks would also be added as plugin dependencies (such as `ant-nodeps`).

AntRun and Ant versions

While in some cases they might be compatible, generally you should use the same version of the Ant optional tasks as the version of Ant itself. The version of Ant used by the plugin is predetermined by what it has been built against. In AntRun v1.3, that is Ant 1.7.1. To use a different version of Ant, consider a different version of the AntRun plugin.

Next, the task is run—being passed the project's dependencies and schema to generate the source code from. The source code is output to `target/xjc`, which is also added as a source directory by the AntRun plugin because of the configuration specified. As the task runs in the `generate-sources` phase, it is available for compilation in the same way as any other source code.

Again, the configuration of AntRun here has been relatively simple, and is completely integrated with the Maven artifact handling and build life cycle such that it would not likely be needed to write a plugin to wrap the tool completely if you were faced with this decision in your environment.

Converting Ant or Maven 1 builds

The AntRun plugin can be most useful when it comes to converting an existing build from Ant or Maven 1 (if it used custom Ant-based plugins or `maven.xml` heavily).

The approach to converting such a build varies depending on the project. For some projects, it is easier to start over on the build and map in modules one by one, interacting via the repository. For others, it might be a matter of gradually turning the existing script into a POM file and using AntRun to execute the existing code for the unconverted parts, keeping the flow wrapped in the new Maven life cycle.

The topic of build conversion is covered in more depth in the Better Builds with Maven section in Chapter 8, available at `http://www.maestrodev.com/better-build-maven`.

Let's look at another example. The following execution might be added to the AntRun plugin, with the same pattern repeated for other such examples in different parts of the life cycle:

```
<execution>
  <id>gen-src</id>
  <phase>generate-sources</phase>
  <configuration>
    <tasks>
      <ant antfile="build-migration.xml" target="gen-src" />
    </tasks>
  </configuration>
  <sourceRoot>${project.build.directory}/gen-src</sourceRoot>
  <goals>
    <goal>run</goal>
  </goals>
</execution>
```

In this source generation example, the previous build file is executed to perform a certain task. As before, the resultant directory is added back into the Maven project so that Maven can continue to control the build.

You will notice that the original script (perhaps broken up) is retained and called rather than pasting the script fragment into the POM. While either is acceptable (as long as the script does not contain multiple targets), it is a good idea to keep the POM as trim as possible. Unless the Ant script is just one or two lines long, it is better to put those commands into an external build file to execute.

This advice applies even if not performing a build conversion. If your Maven build contains script fragments that are longer than a few lines, consider placing them outside of the POM file. However, bear in mind that in doing so it will not be available when reading the POM from the repository later.

In some conversions, a particular task may be reusable in multiple places or projects (particularly if migrating a Maven 1 plugin). In this case, instead of the AntRun plugin, you may consider writing your own plugin for the task. Luckily, to reduce the work involved Maven also offers the ability to run plugins written in Ant.

Maven plugins written in Ant

While the AntRun plugin offers a convenient way to string some simple tasks together, as with any part of the build process in Maven it is worth taking into consideration a simple rule of thumb: if you might use it twice, consider writing a plugin.

Of course, if you do take that step, it is not required to write the plugin in Ant. However, having the option available is useful as:

- It will be easier to use for converting from a previous Ant/Maven 1 build
- Ant tasks may be more familiar to your team than writing Maven plugins in another language
- It can be easier to put together a set of Ant tasks for certain procedures than to write the corresponding code in another language such as Java

The process for creating Ant plugins involves the following steps:

1. Create a Maven project of type `maven-plugin`.
2. Add the `maven-plugin-plugin` to the `build` section, including a plugin dependency on `maven-plugin-tools-ant`.
3. Add an Ant build script for each goal to `src/main/scripts` directory under the name `goalName.build.xml`. This should be a completely executable Ant script containing one target definition.
4. Add a Mojo definition for each goal to `src/main/scripts` directory under the name `goalName.mojo.xml`. This defines the mapping of Maven information to the Ant target.

Plugin authoring (in Ant or other languages) is not something we will go into detail on in this chapter. For more information on writing plugins in Ant, see the documentation: `http://maven.apache.org/guides/plugin/guide-ant-plugin-development.html`.

Other scripting languages

While this section has focused on Ant as one of the most common scripting tools for builds, it is worth noting that other scripting languages can be used both for executable fragments (such as the fragments that AntRun is used for) and whole plugins (such as the Ant plugin tools are used for).

If you have expertise in a particular scripting language, and would like to use that for your own plugins or to add fragments to the build, you might consider one or more of the following projects:

- **GMaven**: This is a mature solution for writing plugins in Groovy, and running Groovy scripts from the POM. For more information, see `http://groovy.codehaus.org/GMaven`.

- JRuby Maven Plugin: This is an early but functional tool for writing plugins in JRuby, or running Ruby scripts from the POM. For more information, see `http://mojo.codehaus.org/jruby-maven-plugin/howto.html`.

- Script Maven Plugin: This uses **BSF (Bean Scripting Framework)** for running scripts in other languages directly from the POM. Supports a larger number of languages, but does not allow the creation of native Maven plugins from the source. For more information, see `http://mojo.codehaus.org/script-maven-plugin`.

 At the time of writing, the Script Maven Plugin has not had an official release and needs to be built from source.

The Exec plugin

In some build situations, the best (or only!) way to get something done might be to run an external application, or a piece of Java code. It was for this purpose that the Exec plugin was created.

The plugin contains two goals: `exec:exec` and `exec:java`. They are similar in purpose, however the `java` goal sets up an easier way to pass Java configuration and execution parameters to a forked JVM instance, whereas the `exec` goal simply runs any executable available on the system.

To use the `exec` goal, you pass the path of the executable program in the `executable` configuration option, and optionally can add the `environmentVariables` or `arguments` configuration to run the command as desired.

 Portability

Keep in mind the question of portability when using the `exec` goal. Some executables may not be available on all platforms that the build will run on. You may need to clearly state the requirement in the build's documentation, gracefully degrade the functionality, or use a profile to run a different executable on a different platform.

In contrast, the `java` goal automatically locates the JVM executable to run, and instead you provide the `mainClass` configuration option. The `arguments` configuration can again be given, but can also include a `classpath` option that helps construct Java `-classpath` arguments from the Maven build (though it is also possible to pass this to the `exec` goal if you happen to be running a particular `java` executable with it). You may also configure `systemProperties` for the plugin to pass to the forked JVM instance.

By default, the `java` goal will construct its base classpath from the current project's dependencies, though it is also possible to have it pass the plugin's dependencies as well or instead of the project dependencies. For more information on configuring either of the plugin goals, refer to the plugin website at: `http://mojo.codehaus.org/exec-maven-plugin`.

Both of these goals provide a useful way to run external processes, depending on what type of application it is. However, the context that it will be used in is also important. For execution there are often two scenarios—integrating the external process into the build life cycle (much like the examples we have seen with AntRun previously), or pre-configuring the plugin to be able to be run from the command line for a given project.

Adding the Exec plugin to the Build life cycle

In the first scenario, there may be an external tool or Java application that needs to be run at a certain point in the build for which the plugin should be configured. This occurs in the same way as for any other plugin, using a particular execution.

In *The AntRun plugin and scripting languages*, we looked at running the XJC tool from Ant. Another alternative could be to run the tool from the command line (assuming it had been pre-installed in the path):

```
<plugin>
  <groupId>org.codehaus.mojo</groupId>
  <artifactId>exec-maven-plugin</artifactId>
  <version>1.1.1</version>
  <executions>
    <execution>
      <id>xjc</id>
      <phase>generate-sources</phase>
      <goals>
        <goal>exec</goal>
      </goals>
      <configuration>
        <executable>xjc</executable>
```

```
    <arguments>
      <argument>-d</argument>
      <argument>${project.build.directory}/xjc</argument>
      <argument>src/main/jaxb/schema.xsd</argument>
    </arguments>
    <sourceRoot>${project.build.directory}/xjc</sourceRoot>
  </configuration>
    </execution>
  </executions>
</plugin>
```

For this particular scenario of source generation, the Exec plugin also contains a `sourceRoot` and `testSourceRoot` parameter for adding any generated sources into the build for later—exactly like the AntRun plugin.

Notice in the example that the configuration is inside the execution element, and therefore will not be able to be run from the command line. This is usually the best course of action when binding to the life cycle so that multiple instances are possible.

Running the Exec plugin standalone

There are also a number of uses for running the Exec plugin directly from the command line. This might be used with a particular project, or run independently.

A common reason to use this approach is if a particular Maven project produces an executable JAR—we looked at such an example with the Shade plugin earlier. By pre-configuring the Exec plugin with the necessary information, the JAR can be easily run by Maven itself. The following POM snippet from the Archiva XMLRPC Client illustrates this:

```
<plugin>
  <groupId>org.codehaus.mojo</groupId>
  <artifactId>exec-maven-plugin</artifactId>
  <version>1.1.1</version>
  <configuration>
    <mainClass>
      org.apache.archiva.web.xmlrpc.client.SampleClient
    </mainClass>
    <arguments>
      <argument>http://127.0.0.1:8081/xmlrpc</argument>
      <argument>admin</argument>
      <argument>${password}</argument>
    </arguments>
  </configuration>
</plugin>
```

Here, the project dependencies are included and the given arguments passed to the main function of the class specified. Notice that in contrast to the previous example, the configuration is not in an execution, both because it is not bound to the life cycle, but also so that it can be run from the command line.

Executing this is now a matter of running the following command:

```
$ mvn exec:java -Dpassword=ADMIN_PASSWORD
```

Clearly, this is much easier to remember than the full set of arguments!

In similar scenarios, the Exec plugin can become very useful in being able to give a simple demonstration or quick use of an application while in development. In some ways, it can be compared to jetty:run for web applications as bringing the same functionality to executable standalone applications.

Summary

As we learned early in the first chapter, once you have the right framework in place with Maven, it is a matter of finding and selecting the right combination of plugins to assemble your build from there on. Here, we have seen a selection of such plugins to help achieve some common builds goals.

The list doesn't stop here though. If you are looking to integrate a particular tool or framework into your build, see if a plugin is already available for it. A number of plugins such as the Dependency plugin, Enforcer plugin, Assembly and App Assembler plugins, discussed elsewhere in the book, have more goals and configurations that are worth investigating as well. If you have some other needs that might apply to multiple builds, search for a plugin to serve that case, or beyond that write one yourself in a scripting language, as a set of Ant tasks, or your own Maven plugin. Online Maven repository search engines can be helpful in finding other plugins to use.

In the first half of this book, we have covered all the pieces of the build puzzle needed to build an application with Maven—from the basics to dependency management, multi-module applications, distribution, reporting, and now a variety of plugins to augment build functionality.

With this in place, in the next chapter we are going to review what we have learned about Maven so far and lay out some best practices to keep in mind as you write or review your own builds.

7
Maven Best Practices

Poor Maven has a reputation for being too complicated, overly restrictive, and more trouble than it is worth. Just try entering a word expressing frustration along with Maven into Google, and see what results you get!

Of course, Maven is not perfect and it does suffer from a number of these failings (perhaps more often than it should). However, it does not have to be that way — in many cases it is because unnecessary flexibility is sacrificed for consistency and conciseness, and trying to fight against that can make Maven harder to use than it needs to be.

If you are frustrated with Maven *right now*, the troubleshooting appendix may be of more use to you. In this chapter, we will look at the preventative medicine for you and your teammates in the future. As you already know how to use Maven, we will investigate a number of strategies for using Maven *well*.

Of course, this whole book is about Maven best practices, and some of the most important decisions you will make about your environment came in the preceding chapters, so we are already well on the way to using Maven effectively. It is always helpful to learn about Maven from "first principles", so that you are prepared when you work with it to recognize the techniques that look right, and those that have a funny smell about them. However, here we will shift our context slightly to the general principles that you can use at any stage of establishing a project, or to review an existing project.

There are a number of day-to-day tips that we will cover that can improve the way in which we use Maven. This includes some tips for avoiding the pitfalls that you may have already seen, and other practices that you may not have encountered that can take your Maven usage to the next level.

Preparing the development environment

You may remember from the earlier chapters that Maven is best used as part of a bigger picture. It has a capability to be the focal point for continuous integration, repository and dependency management, source control management, testing, project reporting and metrics, and even issue tracking and other tooling.

Surprisingly few projects take full advantage of this. While changes are inevitable, it is likely that most of your project infrastructure is in place before a project even begins, and the more that you can have established and documented, the more successful it will be as a part of the project's development.

When preparing Maven for use within your development environment, you need to look at all levels of configuration available:

- If you share a Maven installation, the **installation settings** are where you specify what you share with others in your environment, such as the location of team repositories and network proxy servers.
- The **user settings** are for those settings that are not shared at all, such as server usernames and passwords, and any local paths. They can also be used for sharing settings across multiple installations of Maven on a single machine.
- The **project settings** are those, declared in the POM, that are shared with everyone building the project anywhere (that is, enough to make it work *out of the box*).

We will first look at how each of these relate to the development environment.

 As of Maven 2.0.9, additional settings (**toolchains**), are also supported. However, at the time of writing plugin support is not sufficient for regular use. These are worth considering for use in the future, as a way to centralize paths to JDK installations and so on. However, in the mean time this is best addressed through carefully defined properties in both projects and settings.xml.

Maven installation and user settings

We have already encountered the Maven settings.xml file earlier in the book. In many situations, the few simple settings that we have already added will be sufficient for your environment.

This is an important fact to take note of—if you find that you require a lengthy settings file then you might be establishing a bad practice that will be time consuming for new members of the team to set up, and for existing members to keep track of.

Use the Maven settings files for those settings that apply to any project built in a particular development environment. Above all, keep your Maven settings files simple!

Now, what about those settings that you do include? It is rarely mentioned that there are two locations for the Maven settings file, in the installation and the user's home directory, and it is worth examining how best to use each.

Many prefer to use just the `~/.m2/settings.xml` file. This is, of course, perfectly fine, as it has the benefit of always being in the same location, and even when you upgrade Maven (or change between versions you have installed) the file does not need to be changed.

However, there are good reasons to consider using the installation settings file (in `conf/settings.xml` where Maven was installed) as well, and these relate to the situation where multiple users might be sharing a single Maven installation. The most likely settings to share in this case will be the `proxies` and `mirrors` — in other words, how to access remote files consistently.

 To reduce the effort in keeping a large group of developers up-to-date, share installation settings among users where appropriate.

However, **don't share the local repository** used by multiple developers! A lack of synchronization and separate workspaces will cause problems as multiple users write conflicting changes to the same directory.

How you go about sharing the settings will be highly dependent on which environment you find yourself using. In some cases, it will only be necessary to share the `settings.xml` file, in some it may make sense to ensure everyone is using the same version of Maven itself by sharing the entire installation. Some alternatives are:

- Shipping or updating the settings file using desktop management tools.
- Checking the Maven installation into SCM so that a simple `update` command will update the settings and Maven version.
- Using a shared location, such as a network path or system-wide installation when multiple users are on the same server.
- Shipping a re-bundled distribution where the default settings file is replaced. This option will also allow for adding custom components by default, though bear in mind that any such changes limit the reproducibility of building a project on different Maven versions.

Encrypting server passwords

For those using Maven 2.1.0 and above, a healthy practice to observe is to encrypt the passwords in the server section of `settings.xml`. For more details on how to achieve this, refer to Chapter 2, *Staying in Control with Archiva*, where this was explained.

Project settings

An important step that you can take is to ensure as much of the infrastructure as possible is registered in the POM. Even if your build may not use all of the information immediately, it ensures the information is available later when a new tool is introduced or a new use case is formed.

Consider the following elements to describe the project's infrastructure:

- **Distribution management** (`distributionManagement`): We encountered this element earlier; it is a prerequisite to deploying your artifacts into a repository and to deploying the project web site. Note that when deploying a site, the project's `url` element should correspond to the eventual location given in this section.

- **Source control** (`scm`): Even if only for documentation purposes, it is valuable to include information about the location of source control in your project descriptor. However, it is used by Maven and other tools for more practical reasons as well, as we will examine in the next chapter, which covers continuous integration.

- **Issue management** (`issueManagement`): This straightforward element is used to point users and developers to the issue, bug or task tracker for the project.

- **Build management** (`ciManagement`): Much like the issue tracker, this element points users and developers in the direction of the continuous integration or build server for the project. We will look at this in greater depth in the next chapter.

- **Mailing lists** (`mailingLists`): While mailing lists are a staple communication mechanism in open source projects, they are also quite common in some form in many corporate environments. If a project has such a list, it is helpful to add it to the POM. This is another good candidate for inheritance. In some cases, a team distribution list placed in an organization POM will be sufficient.

- **Participants** (`contributors` and `developers`): Don't be shy! Information such as the `id` and `email` are used to link a developer to their commits in a number of places, and it can be of benefit to be able to search for what projects a particular developer has been involved in. Inheritance should be used as much as possible to avoid repetition, and you should be as specific as you feel is necessary. Developer `roles` can be used to keep track of an individual's current role in the project, or to mark that they have moved on and keep a record for historical purposes.

Provide as much useful information as possible in every Maven POM

While here we are looking at the importance of describing development infrastructure, it is just as important to supply descriptive project information such as the `name`, `description`, `license`, and so on. For example, consider what happens when your project is deployed to Archiva—all of the information that you have referred to in your project is captured and associated with a given release for the future. In a large organization, the `description` element that you have given can be used by others to search for a project they may not have been aware they could use.

Project inheritance can be utilized to avoid repeating these elements in every project. For example, the `distributionManagement` element may only need to be specified once for your entire organization. Some elements that work with directories provide additional assistance during inheritance if the conventions are being followed: `scm`, `url` and the corresponding `site` section of `distributionManagement`. When these are inherited, the artifact ID of the module is automatically appended to the path of each. This assumes that the artifact ID of the module matches the directory name used in source control. Should the automatic values not be correct, you would need to redefine the elements with the correct values in the modules.

One set of elements we did not consider here are repositories (at least those used for downloading dependencies and plugins). As they span both the POM and the settings files they deserve some special attention.

Configuring repositories

Because the repositories can be specified in several places, it can often be confusing, so let's look at the best practices for using repositories in your project.

A repository can be assigned three ways for retrieving dependencies or plugins. They are:

- A `repository` element in the POM (including the default definition for the central repository)
- A `repository` element in a profile in `settings.xml`
- A `mirror` element in `settings.xml` (replacing an existing repository above)

The `mirror` settings that have been demonstrated so far should be considered as the primary means of managing your repositories in your environment when used in conjunction with a repository manager. They have the ability to give you full control over your dependencies, preventing other projects from introducing repositories you were not expecting and reducing build times by avoiding consultation of multiple repositories.

 Use mirrors to lock down external access to your repository manager, which can in turn manage any further external use as needed.

In particular, be sure to use the following in at least one of your mirrors to ensure the environment is properly locked down to a repository manager for which you have full control of:

```
<mirror>
  <id>archiva.public</id>
  <url>http://localhost:8081/archiva/repository/public</url>
  <mirrorOf>external:*</mirrorOf>
</mirror>
```

This will instruct Maven to use this repository manager for all repositories except those on the filesystem (which are special cases used by some projects).

If needed, you can specify additional repository mirrors, for example:

```
<mirror>
  <id>archiva.public</id>
  <url>http://localhost:8081/archiva/repository/public</url>
  <mirrorOf>external:*, !my.snapshot.repo</mirrorOf>
</mirror>
<mirror>
  <id>archiva.snapshots</id>
  <url>http://localhost:8081/archiva/repository/snapshots</url>
  <mirrorOf>my.snapshot.repo</mirrorOf>
</mirror>
```

In this example, the repositories declared in projects using the identifier my.snapshot.repo will be directed to Archiva's snapshot repository, while all other repositories will be directed to the public repository group. The exclusion on snapshots (!my.snapshot.repo) is not needed if the public definition is given last, however it is a good practice to be explicit rather than relying on ordering to avoid problems with an accidental cut and paste later. The external:* and ! notations are only available in Maven 2.0.9 and above.

This example does rely on a repository—my.snapshot.repo—being declared in a project at some point, though. While declaring repositories in a project is increasingly becoming a less necessary procedure, there are still some reasons to do so.

For a project intended to be consumed by the general public, it is best to ensure that their first experience building the project is a positive one – after all this is one of the advertised strengths of Maven. Failing with missing dependencies won't help that cause! For this reason, it can be a good idea to declare any repositories that the project needs to find its dependencies. However, this use should be minimized as much as possible.

Addition of repositories means that the user needs to trust new sources, and it decreases efficiency as the additional repositories are searched. It is particularly problematic if your project will be consumed as a dependency by another project, as this then transitively includes a new repository, almost unsuspectingly. In addition, any repository in the POM must be perpetually available to all users that will be attempting to build the project.

If your project is to be consumed by third parties as a dependency and you need to access specific repositories, weigh up the pros and cons of introducing a repository for them, or requiring them to add it to their own build.

In an organization where the repositories are added consistently, it can make sense to add them to an organization POM to share amongst all projects. This is particularly useful for snapshot repositories as Maven does not declare a default snapshot repository. However, note that the location of the organization POM must be able to be found from existing repository definitions or the Maven settings. If this is not possible, you may need to declare the repository in each user's settings file.

Consider the following `settings.xml` example, which picks up from the snapshots example earlier:

```xml
<profile>
  <id>global.repositories</id>
  <repositories>
    <repository>
      <id>my.snapshot.repo</id>
      <url>
        http://localhost:8081/archiva/repository/snapshots
      </url>
      <releases>
        <enabled>false</enabled>
      </releases>
    </repository>
  </repositories>
</profile>
```

In this example, we add a snapshot repository to every project in the environment, directing requests for snapshots (note that releases are disabled) to the repository manager. It is important that we have named the repository `my.snapshot.repo` as that was excluded from the mirror setting earlier. Likewise, the profile needs to be enabled, so the following should be added to your settings file as well:

```xml
<activeProfiles>
  <activeProfile>global.repositories</activeProfile>
</activeProfiles>
```

Even though these repositories are configured to define where the default locations are, it is still best to use the mirror settings to lock down the environment to a repository manager housing these.

Another reason to declare repositories in the POM is to change the characteristics of the repository that are not available through the mirror settings — to enable or disable the use of snapshots or releases, and to change update policies. These could be set in either the settings file as above or the POM depending on whether they are specific to the environment or the build of the project.

For example, due to issues in Central, the default repository sets checksum failures to warn only. This can avoid problems with bad metadata, but also means that situations where incorrect content is received will go undetected and corrupt the local repository.

To change this configuration, we can use a similar profile to that given above and set the following override for Central in our settings:

```
<profile>
  <id>global.repositories</id>
  <repositories>
    <repository>
      <id>central</id>
      <url>http://repo1.maven.org/maven2/</url>
      <releases>
        <checksumPolicy>fail</checksumPolicy>
      </releases>
    </repository>
  </repositories>
</profile>
```

This will override the default definition (not add a new repository) which has the same ID of central, and all mirrors will still be used.

 As we saw in Chapter 2, *Staying in Control with Archiva*, Archiva can also control how checksums are managed, including correcting problems from remote repositories to ensure you have a trusted source that makes enabling the above even more beneficial.

Having looked at various environmental properties of the POM and ways to make it as complete as possible, we now turn our attention to the structural construction of the project, and the build section in particular.

Keeping it simple

One of the great temptations in putting together a build environment, or to make changes to it, is to do it as fast as possible. After all, once that is out of the way, the *real* work can begin! As much as this makes sense, builds constructed without enough thought can end up much like code approached in a similar way—bloated, inconsistent, hard to understand, and hard to maintain.

Maven takes some measures to avoid this by enforcing build modularity through plugins and encouraging reuse. However, there are still plenty of opportunities for these problems to occur and measures need to be taken to avoid them.

The best recommendation that can be taken here is to think of the build file like any other piece of code. Good development practices tend to apply in both areas. Plan, design the build structure, and examine user stories to keep the scope for what you are trying to achieve when you want to add a new feature.

Of course, don't over-do it! Over-architected code can be even harder to do anything with than spaghetti code, and the same applies to build files. The build is no place to try and get creative — it should be boring, reliable, and above all, simple. Avoiding complexity wherever possible will lead to better long-term maintainability and comprehension. Nobody wants to deal with 42 modules where four will do!

This advice applies to any build system, but luckily, Maven specifically provides the tools to help, and we'll now look at some techniques to take advantage of its strengths, while avoiding the temptation to get out of control.

Using conventions

If the goal is to keep the POM simple, then the first step is surely to reduce the amount of information present. In the previous sections, we looked at *adding* more information into the POM in the interest of *adding* value, now it is time to *remove* information that isn't adding value.

This is one of the reasons Maven emphasizes conventions. Many choices are arbitrary and one option or another may just be a matter of preference or policy. In such a case, it is better to adopt a common convention for a number of reasons:

- Developers familiar with the convention do not need to learn new options
- Unimportant information can be omitted so that important information is more obvious
- A bonus for the indecisive — there is no need to make a decision

There are many areas in Maven that use conventions that we can take advantage of, with the most common examples being:

- The build life cycle itself is a fixed convention for all Maven builds
- The POM contains a number of fields that are preset for the project type
- The rules of inheritance for the POM construct paths and inherit fields in a certain way
- The configuration of plugins usually have sensible default values
- In many of the above cases they work together to dictate a standard directory structure for a project

Consider the following example of identical projects that use a slightly different directory layout. Firstly, the project that follows the conventions:

```
<project>
  <groupId>com.effectivemaven</groupId>
  <artifactId>test-project</artifactId>
  <version>1.0-SNAPSHOT</version>
  <packaging>war</packaging>
</project>
```

And now, the one that makes slight alterations:

```
<project>
  <groupId>com.effectivemaven</groupId>
  <artifactId>test-project</artifactId>
  <version>1.0-SNAPSHOT</version>
  <packaging>war</packaging>
  <build>
    <sourceDirectory>src/java</sourceDirectory>
    <testSourceDirectory>src/test</testSourceDirectory>
    <resources>
      <resource>
        <directory>src/java</directory>
        <excludes>
          <exclude>**/*.java</exclude>
        </excludes>
      </resource>
    </resources>
    <plugins>
      <plugin>
        <groupId>org.apache.maven.plugins</groupId>
        <artifactId>maven-war-plugin</artifactId>
        <configuration>
          <warSourceDirectory>src/web</warSourceDirectory>
        </configuration>
      </plugin>
    </plugins>
  </build>
</project>
```

As you can see, this is a lot more information that needs to be specified, understood, and maintained — without adding much value other than changing some perhaps arbitrary paths. While directory structures are not always to blame for these occurrences, they are often the ones that require the most contortion of a build to fit a certain layout, and often the most unnecessary.

But I have to!

For many reasons you may need to have a different directory structure. This may be due to a policy, some other tooling, or an in-grained convention or preference within a team. This is entirely possible, and can still be effectively managed through judicious use of inheritance. However, take this opportunity to consider whether adopting a common convention might just make your life a little easier.

Using inheritance

Removing information that is part of a convention is a great start, but every build needs to be customized. Inheritance is one of the easiest ways to adopt the principle of **Don't Repeat Yourself**, though it can be applied in many other areas such as the *management* sections and by creating plugins.

Consider the previous example, where a particular directory structure did need to be adopted across a set of projects. With some slight modifications, the parts of the web application that would be reused could be moved to a parent POM for the team:

```
<project>
  <groupId>com.effectivemaven</groupId>
  <artifactId>test-parent</artifactId>
  <version>1-SNAPSHOT</version>
  <build>
    <sourceDirectory>src/java</sourceDirectory>
    <testSourceDirectory>src/test</testSourceDirectory>
    <resources>
      <resource>
        <directory>src/java</directory>
        <excludes>
          <exclude>**/*.java</exclude>
        </excludes>
      </resource>
    </resources>
    <pluginManagement>
      <plugins>
        <plugin>
          <groupId>org.apache.maven.plugins</groupId>
          <artifactId>maven-war-plugin</artifactId>
          <configuration>
            <warSourceDirectory>src/web</warSourceDirectory>
          </configuration>
        </plugin>
      </plugins>
    </pluginManagement>
  </build>
</project>
```

The two changes are highlighted. This project is now declared as the parent project. The WAR plugin configuration has been moved into a pluginManagement section so that the configuration will be ignored for different types of projects that do not already use the WAR plugin.

The pluginManagement section operates like the dependencyManagement section in Maven—the configuration and executions are applied to any instance of that plugin encountered (including if it is introduced implicitly by the packaging life cycle), but if the plugin is never encountered then that pluginManagement section is ignored.

The individual web application now looks much more like the original example:

```
<project>
  <parent>
    <groupId>com.effectivemaven</groupId>
    <artifactId>test-parent</artifactId>
    <version>1-SNAPSHOT</version>
  </parent>
  <artifactId>test-project</artifactId>
  <version>1.0-SNAPSHOT</version>
  <packaging>war</packaging>
</project>
```

The only addition is that of the parent reference, while all the changes are now centralized to that project, avoiding repetition and allowing us to version certain configurations and change between them based on the version of the parent. As an added bonus, because the group is the same, we can use the inheritance convention to avoid re-specifying it.

In this instance, we have used one level of **organization POM** to factor out conventions common to a team. It has the separate, sequential versioning, and is typically located outside of the project as we saw in Chapter 3, *Building an Application Using Maven*.

The other situation for inheritance is in a multi-module build. The same changes can be applied in that situation, though the emphasis will shift towards project specific settings such as dependencies. In addition to this, there are a number of methods for using modules to keep projects simple.

Decomposing the build into modules

Managing modularity is an important concern to address as it covers multiple aspects of software development—the structure of the code itself, the packaging and distribution for consumption by others, and the structure of the build. For this reason, Maven builds the concept in to align these concepts and take advantage of the common principles.

In Chapter 3, *Building an Application Using Maven*, we examined a reusable module structure for Maven builds, and some of the advantages of modularizing a project, including:

* Re-use
* Readability
* Development efficiency
* Release cycles
* Enforced design constraints

Deciding on how to modularize is not a clear-cut choice, but rather a balance based on experience. We don't want to under-modularize—one JAR that contains 15,000 classes and is 22MB might be OK for the prerequisite Java runtime class library but if all you wanted from it was `java.util` then you would be hesitant to use it. On the other side, over-modularizing can cause problems as well:

* Needing to hunt around for the right module
* Starting to drag in a large number of dependencies
* Increasing the likelihood of version conflict problems
* Circular dependencies
* General maintainability problems such as longer build times, large numbers of artifact deployments, and increased repository maintenance needs

The following are some tips that can help when making decisions about when to create a new module.

Aligning the source structure

In the examples that we have seen so far, it has been assumed that there is some alignment between the source structure, the module structure, and the inheritance structure. That is, a single releasable project is in one source tree, where the modules are in subdirectories that match the artifact ID (and their parent project is then in the parent directory).

This is certainly encouraged by Maven with several advantages:

- Source control is a single checkout, and matches the structure of the eventual source distribution
- The build always occurs from the top level project, following convention
- The Maven release mechanism and Continuum set up are trivial to use
- SCM elements and URLs can be automatically derived for modules

The limiting factor of using this structure in the past has been the inability of Eclipse to handle nested projects (which occurs if you wish to add the parent and the modules as separate projects). Recently, Eclipse integrations have learned to cope with this well and should not be a concern, so the hierarchical module structure is to be highly recommended.

Selecting group and artifact identifiers

As the number of modules being created grows, the challenge of choosing a unique identifier can also increase. There is room to be flexible on this as long as it is consistently applied in your organization, but the following tips may be useful.

The first consideration is the group ID. The main question here is when to nest another level. Ideally, this would occur with each level of organization POM. So in our example application this was `com.effectivemaven` and `com.effectivemaven.centrepoint`. However, note that additional nesting was not added for `modules`, or corresponding Java packages such as `store`. In most cases, a single releasable project can use the same group ID no matter what nesting is present. New levels should only be needed if there is a true subproject, or a need to segregate similar artifact IDs.

Choosing artifact IDs was covered in Chapter 3, *Building an Application Using Maven,* and it was noted that short forms such as those in the example application could be of benefit if they are unlikely to be used outside of the current application. However, even though the group and artifact ID combined may be unique, often the artifacts are used with just the artifact ID in the filename. For example, the JARs which are included in a web application's `WEB-INF/lib` directory. If interacting with other frameworks, there is a good chance that the simple name of `model` used in the example might clash. If this is a possibility, or if the libraries are expected to be used by others, a common practice is to prepend the last part of the group ID to the artifact ID. Therefore, the module in the example would have an artifact ID of `centrepoint-model`. For consistency, all other modules in the build should do the same.

While this is often enough, it is a judgment call based on expected usage, and you may wish to use other variants. For example, it is common for **OSGi** applications to use a filename equivalent to `com.effectivemaven.centrepoint.model-1.0`. To meet this particular convention, you might use a group ID of `com.effectivemaven.centrepoint` and an artifact ID of `com.effectivemaven.centrepoint.model`. In many cases, this is unnecessary duplication, but the opportunity is there if it makes sense, as long as it is applied consistently.

Building modules together

Break the build into sections that you would tend to build together. If you build a certain set of modules together frequently, making them their own subtree can make building them easier.

The structure of an application outlined in Chapter 3, *Building an Application Using Maven*, achieves this by keeping all of the Java modules together, while others such as the distribution and documentation can be built separately, though if needed all can be built together. If there were a large number of Java modules, they could be further broken down (if it was found to be useful). For example, by grouping all of the back-end modules, the web modules, and so on.

Each module should be independently useful

A single module should be useful when used on its own (along with its dependencies). If you always need to include another module alongside it that is not a direct dependency, it may have been broken down too far.

Watching the dependencies

If your module has a number of optional dependencies, then it may be too large and can be broken down along the lines of the dependencies. This can ensure that projects that use only one portion of the code need not drag in unnecessary dependencies and you can avoid the complexity of declaring optional dependencies.

Separating API from implementation

It is not always useful to be able to provide an alternate implementation of an API, but in those instances it is a good idea to separate the API from the implementation in the packaging and make it clear from the artifact names. Users can then depend on the API without polluting their dependency tree with the dependencies of the default implementation. In some cases, the API may even go onto a separate release cycle so that implementers can code against something stable across product versions.

For example, consider the store API from the example application in earlier chapters. While initially implemented against a flat file, it might later store the information in a database using Hibernate through a different implementation. Now, if there were a reporting library that needed to query the project store without being concerned about the implementation it could depend on the API module and avoid making the decision to include the Hibernate modules. The application that then uses the reporting API could choose just to include the Hibernate module, or both, depending on what it needed, without having to get additional transitive dependencies.

Trimming dependencies

We have just seen some recommended ways of breaking down a project into modules, and saw how that positively affected the handling of dependencies within the project. Such techniques can make the project a better player in the Maven ecosystem.

However, what can be done when dealing with third party dependencies that are outside of your control?

It is important to keep a close eye on your dependencies as you make changes over time to ensure you are only using what you need. If you are producing a library to be used by others, your dependencies will be passed on transitively, so you want to limit them as much as possible. If you are packaging an application that will bundle its dependencies, you will want to keep the size down.

Maven provides tools to help manage these situations, in the **Dependency plugin**. From the command line, the first goal you will likely need is `dependency:tree`. To try that for yourself, run the command on the `maven-importer` module in the example application from earlier chapters:

```
maven-importer$ mvn dependency:tree
```

This reveals all of the dependencies used, both those used directly and those acquired transitively. We can notice at least one, JUnit, that looks out of place:

```
[INFO] [dependency:tree {execution: default-cli}]
[INFO] com.effectivemaven.centrepoint:maven-importer:jar:1.0-SNAPSHOT
...
[INFO] +- org.codehaus.plexus:plexus-container-default:jar:1.0-alpha-10:
compile
[INFO] |  +- junit:junit:jar:3.8.1:compile
[INFO] |  \- classworlds:classworlds:jar:1.1:compile
```

Some research would show that Plexus requires this artifact for a specialized test case that it includes, which is not used by our application. Effectively, JUnit is an optional dependency, though it has not been marked as such by Plexus in its POM.

Others will use the `maven-importer` library, and we don't want to pass on the JUnit dependency. We already have such an example where it is unnecessarily included in Centrepoint's web application under the `WEB-INF/lib` directory.

To ensure JUnit is not included, add the following to the dependency where it came from:

```
<dependency>
  <groupId>org.codehaus.plexus</groupId>
  <artifactId>plexus-container-default</artifactId>
  <version>1.0-alpha-10</version>
  <exclusions>
    <exclusion>
      <groupId>junit</groupId>
      <artifactId>junit</artifactId>
    </exclusion>
  </exclusions>
</dependency>
```

As you can see by running the command again, JUnit is no longer included. In fact, the same can be seen by running `mvn clean install` from the top-level `modules` directory and examining the `WEB-INF/lib` directory of the web application that is built.

While Maven currently does not support *global exclusions*, if you would like to ensure a dependency never occurs the Enforcer plugin can be used to set up some global rules. For an example of such a case, refer to Chapter 1, *Maven in a Nutshell*.

There are two ways that the Plexus developers could have avoided propagating this issue had this been foreseen. The first would be to mark JUnit as optional in the Plexus POM, such as this:

```
<dependency>
  <groupId>junit</groupId>
  <artifactId>junit</artifactId>
  <version>3.8.1</version>
  <optional>true</optional>
</dependency>
```

This indicates that consumers of the library may or may not need to use the specified dependency. Obviously, this is not very specific! This makes the dependency become a hint, where it will not be used by default, but will be considered for scope and version calculations. If you decide to use the library, it would need to be included in the target POM again.

A better alternative is to split modules along functional lines where dependencies are optional. In this case, the Plexus library could become `plexus-container-default` (classes not depending on JUnit) and `plexus-testcase` (classes depending on JUnit). Afterwards, `plexus-container-default` would depend on `plexus-testcase` with a scope of test, so that the JUnit dependency is not passed on. While this is ideal, the decision to split a library would need to be taken carefully as it is not always a straightforward separation of classes (perhaps they have circular dependencies that need to be further separated), and you would need to consider backwards compatibility across versions.

Another piece of information that can be of benefit to reducing the size of the transitive dependency tree is the **scope** of the dependency. In the previous example, the JUnit dependency could be specified like the following if it is only used for test cases:

```
<dependency>
    <groupId>junit</groupId>
    <artifactId>junit</artifactId>
    <version>3.8.1</version>
    <scope>test</scope>
</dependency>
```

Without the scope, this dependency would be passed on to any other projects that used the library. However, the test scope indicates that it should not be exported at all.

This seems obvious when declaring JUnit for testing. However, how about other libraries that contain implementations having no direct dependency in the code? In this case, the dependency can be declared as `runtime` scope to ensure they are not accidentally used during compilation in either the current project or those that depend on it, but are still passed on and bundled for use at runtime.

An additional tool to help with trimming dependencies is the `dependency:analyze` goal. This goal will examine your code and estimate which direct dependencies could be removed. It will also identify those that are being used directly and should be added to the POM to be more explicit. Let's try this command on the `maven-importer` module:

maven-importer$ mvn dependency:analyze

This results in the following output:

```
[dependency:analyze {execution: default-cli}]
Used undeclared dependencies found:
  org.apache.maven:maven-model:jar:2.1.0:compile
  org.apache.maven:maven-artifact:jar:2.1.0:compile
Unused declared dependencies found:
  org.apache.maven.wagon:wagon-http:jar:1.0-beta-5:runtime
  org.apache.maven.wagon:wagon-file:jar:1.0-beta-5:test
```

Here you see the two dependencies that contain classes that have been directly used by the code (`maven-model` and `maven-artifact`). It is a good practice to declare these explicitly, in case the transitive tree changes in future versions and removes these required libraries. Therefore, we should add the following to `maven-importer/pom.xml`:

```
<dependency>
  <groupId>org.apache.maven</groupId>
  <artifactId>maven-model</artifactId>
  <version>2.1.0</version>
</dependency>
<dependency>
  <groupId>org.apache.maven</groupId>
  <artifactId>maven-artifact</artifactId>
  <version>2.1.0</version>
</dependency>
```

We also see two unused dependencies listed. This is expected as one is used by dynamic loading only at runtime and the other in test cases respectively. Should a `compile` scope dependency appear here, you would want to assess if it should be removed, or changed to `runtime` or `test` scope.

Unfortunately, the goal cannot make an assessment about what transitive dependencies will be used. This requires knowledge of the dependencies that you are using. However, as a first step to pruning unused dependencies the `analyze` goal can be quite helpful.

Dependency version management

There is one final area to attend to with regard to dependencies in the project, and that is the version of dependencies being used. While Maven is able to take two dependency versions and decide which is best to use and discard the other, it makes the build simpler — and faster — to reduce the variance for any versions across a multi-module build.

This can be achieved using the `dependencyManagement` section of the POM in the parent to assign a version for a particular dependency wherever it is encountered throughout the build—whether it is declared directly or is found through the tree of dependencies. This is most useful in incidences where Maven selects a different version to the one desired, but can also be of benefit in making the build more explicit.

We have already seen examples of this use in the example application, with the `modules/pom.xml` file specifying unified versions for the application modules and Guice, and overriding the version of `plexus-utils` transitively.

Managing dependencies has the added benefit of centralizing the specification of versions. This ensures that a change need only be made once, and it is obvious where that change should be made. However, much like modularity, caution and balance is also needed in taking advantage of this ability—for dependencies that are only ever used once it can be very verbose to list them in the parent POM and it adds a level of indirection to finding the version for a given dependency when reviewing the POM.

While the `dependencyManagement` section lets you consistently set a version for a single artifact at a time, there are some groups of dependencies that will have the same version that you might want to set just once. For example, in the `maven-importer` module, we now have three dependencies on Maven 2.1.0 libraries. The best way to unify these at present is to use a property.

We can make this modification to `maven-importer/pom.xml` to illustrate. First, we must add the property:

```
<properties>
  <mavenVersion>2.1.0</mavenVersion>
</properties>
```

With this property in place, it can now be referenced from all of the dependencies:

```
<dependency>
  <groupId>org.apache.maven</groupId>
  <artifactId>maven-model</artifactId>
  <version>${mavenVersion}</version>
</dependency>
```

This simple change can allow easy upgrading of a Maven version rather than searching through multiple entries, as well as allowing experimentation with different versions from the command line using `-DmavenVersion=2.2.0`, for example.

Profiles and pipelining

The addition of profiles to a build, when used properly, can be an effective way to segment a build into multiple functions to be run at different times. Though profiles can add some complexity, they can help to ensure that the default build remains as simple as possible.

This is sometimes referred to as **build pipelining**, where the most basic needs of the build are addressed by default, and more advanced features are added optionally. Often these additional levels are more time consuming to run and may be limited to running mostly in an integration build environment. We have already seen an example of this in Chapters 4 and 5 (*Application Testing with Maven* and *Reporting and Checks* respectively), and in Chapter 9, *Continuum in Depth*, we will use Continuum to put that into practice.

How to segment your build most effectively will depend on your team and their development practices. It is important to have a build that is fast so that it can be run frequently, though it is valuable to be able to run as many tests as possible in the default build so that problems can be caught early. By the time they get to the continuous integration server they may already be checked into source control and in some ways it may be "too late" to avoid a broken build.

The best approach to creating profiles should include the following:

- Run as much as comfortable by default—keep the default build fast enough that there is no inclination to skip tests.

- Make it easy to run additional checks and tests so that they can be done before commit on the developer's machine (where reasonable).

- Ensure all additional checks and tests are run as soon as possible to give feedback that ensures failures are fixed. Use additional layering if needed to get earlier feedback on a particular set of tests.

 Though profiles are very useful for this purpose, always take note of the potential pitfalls of using them improperly as discussed later in this chapter with regard to portability!

While profiles do participate in the project inheritance mechanism, it should be noted that profiles cannot inherit from other profiles. This can mean that combined profiles are hard to construct without some amount of duplication.

This can be eased by using properties for any values that must be duplicated between profiles.

However, ideally you would avoid duplicated sections by separating profiles into distinct uses and require the user to enable each individually. For example, consider a set of Selenium tests that can run on combinations of multiple browsers and multiple application servers. Instead of configuring how Internet Explorer and Tomcat are run in one profile using `-Ptomcat-over-iexplore`, the application server setup and Selenium setup can be split into profiles for each, ran with `mvn -Piexplore,tomcat`.

Scripting and writing plugins

While the large (and growing!) suite of plugins available for Maven cover many build use cases, it is still common to need to add some functionality that cannot be found elsewhere. This will usually lead to the urge to add a small piece of scripting to the project. Such urges could soon lead to a much more complicated build, and so it is worth weighing the pros and cons of scripting with regard to keeping the build simple.

As we saw in Chapter 6, *Useful Maven Plugins*, there are a number of plugins available that will allow you to introduce a small amount of scripting using Groovy, Ruby, and other dynamic languages. The most commonly used is probably the *Ant Run* plugin, which can be very beneficial in using existing tasks to achieve those small one-off needs.

Exercise some caution though. Maven is declarative by design. If you find yourself saying *the life cycle is too restrictive!*, it is possible you are trying to unnaturally cram in tasks in a particular order rather than using the defined order.

These plugins should only be used for small fragments of script. Large chunks will complicate the build and make the POM hard to read and large to deploy. If there is a reason for a large script, consider executing it from an external file.

However, if a non-trivial task could be parameterized and used in more than one project, consider writing a plugin instead. As an added bonus, the build will likely be more portable because of it. Writing a plugin is not as hard as it may appear at first. From a Maven perspective, they are constructed in the same way as any other module, and though they lack the quick *run and test* scenario of most scripting solutions, they can be written using existing tools and automated testing where appropriate.

To illustrate how they can fit into a build, in the example code for this chapter we have created a `server-setup-maven-plugin` module to replace the AntRun functionality in the `distribution/pom.xml` file. Normally, this would be more work than is necessary for these simple commands, but if this were a repeated task used in other applications where changes needed to be made consistently, the value of adding it to a plugin would start to show.

Whether a plugin is built as part of the application (that is, in the `centrepoint` directory), or released separately (as is the case here), is determined by the scope of where the plugin is expected to be used. The same principles are used as for the license resources we have already encountered, and other organization level modules.

Creating and using archetypes

Sometimes all that is needed to keep on top of a project is to start on the right foot. For this reason, it is a good idea to create archetypes specifically tailored to your environment so that new projects fit right in. For example, you can ensure that all new projects start with something as simple as inheriting from the organization POM parent.

We have encountered archetypes already, using them to create small projects quickly from the shared set of template projects. This can be taken a step further by creating projects specifically set up for an environment where new modules and projects are created often.

This gives the advantage of simplifying the landscape of projects and increasing consistency, which will help in the long term with keeping projects simple.

For more information on creating archetypes, see Chapter 11, *Archetypes*.

Build portability

Have you ever felt the frustration of getting your hands on a project for the first time and finding the build fails?

Maven strongly encourages making builds portable. This is a very important trait—a single build needs to run in a large number of locations with a minimum number of customizations. It will be shared by other developers, run in automated environments, and possibly be built again at some time in the future when your own environment has changed. Portability is not just about the ability to work cross-platform, but building successfully anywhere. The last words you want to hear from your team mates is *works in my backyard* when you are struggling against a failing build.

Setting expectations

The first step is to set the right expectations. While this is not a technical problem with the build, it can be possible to change the build so that it behaves differently to how an average Maven user expects.

As we have seen, Maven is heavily convention based, so a POM fragment such as this can lead to confusion in the hands of a different developer:

```
<execution>
  <phase>generate-sources</phase>
  <goals>
    <goal>install-file</goal>
  </goals>
</execution>
```

If the developer is only running the tests, but finding things added to the local repository, confusion is bound to occur at some point. Such practices are best avoided.

But sometimes, it can be more subtle. What is wrong with this picture?

```
$ mvn -Dmaven.test.skip=true test
```

Perhaps this is just because the tests are slow. There is no harm in that... until they fail for someone else. At that point, you discover they have been failing for you as well, or would have if you had been running them. Perhaps everyone has been ignoring continuous build results because it has *always been that way*. The story probably sounds familiar.

If you need to skip the tests, reconsider why—are they unstable? Could they be faster? Perhaps this is a case for build pipelining.

Hard coding

A common cause for portability problems is hard coding values into a project. Hard coding refers to anything that relies on a particular environment—whether it is a particular developer's machine, or the central build environment itself.

While this might seem obvious, these can often be subtle, like relying on a single database. Such scenarios work while one person is building, but as soon as two people build at the same time, random tests fail.

- Don't hard code paths
- Don't hard code databases

- Don't hard code property values
- Don't hard code URLs
- Don't do it in the tests either!

The last point is often overlooked. As test cases are run throughout a build, hard coding inside the test code has the same effect as doing so in the build file.

If it is necessary through some system requirement to have a hard coded path, the best way to handle it is to use a property that can be overridden. The property should also have a sensible default value so that most builds require minimal set up.

For example, you might add the following property with a sensible default to your POM:

```
<properties>
  <weblogic.home>/usr/local/weblogic</weblogic.home>
</properties>
```

If a particular developer installs it in a different location, they can change it from their `settings.xml` file:

```
<profiles>
  <profile>
    <id>global.settings</id>
    <properties>
      <weblogic.home>C:\Program Files\WLS</weblogic.home>
    </properties>
  </profile>
</profiles>
<activeProfiles>
  <activeProfile>global.settings</activeProfile>
</activeProfiles>
```

Databases, services, and other resources are generally more difficult to deal with. Sometimes, they can be incorporated into the build itself by using the Dependency plugin to download a resource, or an in-memory, pre-loaded database for testing against. However, if you specifically need to test against an external resource because of its nature or because you are specifically testing integration with that implementation, you will be best to use some form of provisioning to be able to get a unique resource for the given builder to avoid conflicts and minimize up-front configuration.

Portable profiles

Profiles are very useful for breaking up the build into different objectives, such as the case for build pipelining examined earlier. They also have a number of activation triggers that are based on the environment being used to build. These triggers can be used to make a build **more** portable, by ensuring a build supports multiple platforms where it might not otherwise. However, they can also be used to make a build **less** portable by making the build significantly different between environments.

When it comes to introducing a profile, follow some simple guidelines:

- Don't use profiles to cause the build to behave differently based on the environment, use them to make sure the build works the same across different environments

- Document the existence of each profile so that users know which to enable and when

- Ensure the build works as expected without any profiles enabled, setting default activation where necessary

- Use profiles for **additional**, **optional**, build functionality

- Keep the number of profiles to a minimum

Portable artifacts

One of the most frequently asked questions by Maven users is how to manage artifacts for different target environments, and how to manage resource filtering for different target environments.

This is obviously an important feature. Projects need to be run in development, staging, and production environments with different configuration. Java EE applications often need to be deployed on multiple application server types that require modifications or configuration. Some libraries for redistribution need to be altered depending on the JDK it will be used on.

However, this would seem to be at odds with Maven's setup, as there is only one repository where it can deploy. This is another case where Maven encourages a particular development practice to promote consistency.

In remote repositories, where artifacts are finally deployed, artifacts are required to be *unique*. It should not be possible to redeploy a version that has already been placed there with a different one due to the confusion it would cause.

This leaves some options (or possibly combinations of options) for your artifact configuration needs:

- Utilize classifiers to produce tailored artifacts for each target environment within a given artifact version.

- Incorporate a default configuration, but post-process the artifact before use to replace it with the actual configuration.

- Incorporate all known configurations, and require the user select which environment to target (for example, using a system property).

- Don't make any environment-specific settings into an artifact.

Let's look at when each is appropriate:

An example quoted for classifiers earlier was targeting various JDKs. As much as Java is a backwards compatible language, there are cases where this is necessary. For example, if you have developed the code using Java 5 syntax such as generics, but would like to run it on 1.4 JRE's by using **retro-translation**. Classifiers are designed for variant output based on the same set of source files, so they make sense to use in this instance. Consumers can then choose either the `jdk14` version or the leaner `jdk15` version depending on their own minimum requirement.

You might also consider classifiers when you produce `mywebapp-1.0-dev.war`, `mywebapp-1.0-stage.war`, and `mywebpp-1.0-prod.war` to include alternate configuration files containing the database connection information for each environment.

This might make sense at first, but it could easily get out of control as you need to produce a different version of each for Tomcat, JBoss, and Websphere. Next, you might need different versions for each server in a deployment—ten different production copies. As you can see, the multiples would become unmanageable because of the combinations that would need to be built, as well as chewing up disk space with mostly redundant information in each build. In addition, changes cannot be made without re-releasing.

A better way to handle this situation is to make the artifact in the repository unique. However, the configuration still needs to reside somewhere, so that leads to the other alternatives and their individual pros and cons.

Post-processing the artifact for the target environment before deployment requires the most complicated deployment steps for the application. However, it can provide a single representation of the deployed system at a given time, which can be of benefit if configuration options change with the application releases.

Baking in the available configurations gives the same result with a reduced deployment complexity, but it makes it harder to change once it has been released, particularly for new target environments. The inclusion of the actual settings for non-production environments also introduces additional risk—you certainly don't want to point your production systems at a testing database!

Finally, you can externalize the configuration. This alternative means not including any *hard coded* configuration at all, instead ensuring that the application is written to be able to locate it from an external source.

For maximum portability, this alternative is worth investigating if it is possible. This requires a conscious design choice for the application in question, and libraries that it might depend on. It is particularly beneficial if you are authoring a library for others to use, as it is unlikely that configuration would be baked in to the artifact you distribute without a way to manage the configuration externally.

Most common needs have technology available to facilitate this practice already. In Java EE, JNDI can be used to push the resource and environment configuration into the server set up so that the web application can remain unmodified using data sources, mail sessions, and context properties. Frameworks such as Spring allow configuration of beans outside of a packaged application by using the Java class path. For other applications, there are frameworks to use designed specifically for the purpose such as **Commons Configuration** (`http://commons.apache.org/configuration/`) or the Java Preferences API.

Let's consider this with a common example from a Spring application. The following may be a common set of configuration included into a web application that is released into the repository:

```
<bean id="dataSource"
      class="org.springframework.jdbc.datasource.
DriverManagerDataSource">
  <property name="driverClassName"
          value="org.hsqldb.jdbcDriver" />
  <property name="url" value="jdbc:hsqldb:database" />
  <property name="username" value="sa" />
  <property name="password" value="" />
</bean>
```

As you can see, the application is hardcoded to a built-in database. Perhaps suitable for a default development deployment, but hardly likely to be the production database settings.

Instead, replace the configuration with the following:

```
<bean id="dataSource"
      class="org.springframework.jndi.JndiObjectFactoryBean">
   <property name="jndiName"
             value="java:comp/env/jdbc/database" />
</bean>
```

This allows you to configure the database however you need to in the application server or other runtime environment, change the configuration at runtime, target different databases from different servers, and so on.

Of course, this then raises the question—how can Maven help with managing the configuration, getting the artifacts onto the server, or post-processing artifacts as described earlier?

The simple answer is that it does not. While there may be Maven plugins for tools that do, Maven's life cycle ends with deployment into the repository. It can be used to ensure the artifact gets there, and to push up any amount of configuration alongside it, but when it comes to using the artifacts, it is time for other tools to come in.

With artifacts only being built once into the repository, there is an obvious impact on the need for resource filtering, which is usually used to populate the values of those configuration files.

Resource filtering

As we saw above, one of the main use cases for resource filtering—to populate environment-specific configuration values in the generated artifact—is best avoided by keeping the artifact and its configuration separate.

For that reason, I tend to avoid resource filtering as much as possible. It risks introducing inconsistencies between builds of the same artifact, or baking in harmful defaults to release artifacts such as build server test settings.

They do have a purpose though, when used wisely.

Firstly, they can be used to filter Maven project values into the artifact. This is valuable to provide a simple way to provide the value to existing configuration without the need to process the additional pom.xml and pom.properties files that are already included. We saw an example of this in Chapter 6, *Useful Maven Plugins*, with the Build Number plugin that can be seen in the example application. This also covered the best practice of setting up an additional filtered-resources directory to minimize the amount of filtering needed.

Filters can still be used for more generalized properties too, however. Of particular value is **centralization** of properties, where they have the same value in multiple places in the artifact but can be centralized to avoid repetition, increase visibility and make them easier to change. For example, properties like the following could be filtered into a web application's templates:

```
google.analytics.code=UA-1234567-1
```

This leads into the final case of one-off alterations. If there is a configuration property that is generally the same in all environments, but might be changed for one-off occasions, using a filter can help centralize the configuration location. For example:

```
debug.mode=false
```

Even in development, this might be turned off by default, and in rare occasions enabled by a build property or system profile to be filtered into the artifact as `true`.

Shared resources

In the previous sections, we have discussed application configuration and the best ways to manage it, including externalizing the configuration. The same can be applied to pieces of the build process itself, and in the process assist with some instances of hard coding.

A number of Maven plugins require a configuration file with which they can operate. To use this, the build author seems faced with a few choices:

- Include the file in the build, duplicating it in every project even if it is the same.

- Require it be installed on each developer's machine and reference it from a certain path name (perhaps configured by a property to be a little less hard coded). This might be the case software licenses, but in general is impractical.

- Refer to it from an external URL, avoiding the duplication but risking long-term reproducibility if it moves location.

- Include some sort of materialization of the resource from a reliable location.

The last option sounds ideal, but also the most complicated—but thankfully Maven already has all of the tools to achieve this. By placing configuration in the remote repository, you can take advantage of the same versioning and management techniques as all of the other project dependencies. The configuration can be stored either as it is if it is a single file, or as a ZIP archive of one or more files.

As we have seen in Chapter 5, *Reporting and Checks*, some reporting plugins such as Checkstyle and PMD already support directly consuming files from the repository in this manner. We have also seen similar behavior from the Remote Resources plugin in Chapter 6, *Useful Maven Plugins*. However, it is worth noting that the more general purpose dependency:unpack goal can also be used for other, similar situations.

> **Sharing resources with the Dependency plugin**
>
> This technique can even be extended for use beyond build resources. In fact, if you have any set of files that need to be included in another artifact and need to avoid duplication, you can share them via the repository in this way too.

Let's update the example application by moving css/flavour.css into a separate resource ZIP so that it can later be used by other modules.

In the example code, you will see the web-resources module created. This will seem familiar from the other examples in Chapter 3, *Building an Application Using Maven*, and its purpose is to create a ZIP file, uploaded to the repository, containing the shared resources (in this case, css/flavour.css).

We have then removed that CSS from the web application, added the web resources as a dependency, and then added the following plugin to webapp/pom.xml:

```
<plugin>
  <groupId>org.apache.maven.plugins</groupId>
  <artifactId>maven-dependency-plugin</artifactId>
  <version>2.0</version>
  <executions>
    <execution>
      <id>configuration</id>
      <phase>validate</phase>
      <configuration>
        <outputDirectory>
          ${project.build.directory}/webapp
        </outputDirectory>
        <includeArtifactIds>web-resources</includeArtifactIds>
      </configuration>
      <goals>
        <goal>unpack-dependencies</goal>
      </goals>
    </execution>
  </executions>
</plugin>
```

Because of this, the ZIP will be unpacked in the `target/webapp` directory for packaging by the WAR plugin. We use the `includeArtifactIds` configuration to limit the unpacking to just the `web-resources` dependency.

Note that it was important that a ZIP dependency be used here and not a JAR. The latter would have also been copied into `WEB-INF/lib` as a dependency.

Alternatively, we could not use the `unpack-dependencies` goal and instead use the generic `unpack` goal that takes a list of artifacts to resolve and unpack. However, this would lose the ordering we gain from having a project dependency in the reactor, and is only suitable if the resources are external to the current project.

Build reproducibility

Have you ever checked out a project from its last release and found the build no longer worked? Or, maybe a project that you had just built yesterday seems to have magically stopped building today.

If build portability is the ability to run a build anywhere with a minimum amount of configuration, reproducibility is the ability to run the build the same way every time, particularly at some point in the future.

This is particularly relevant for releasing, which we will examine in more detail in later chapters. Once that build is locked down, you want to make sure it is already equipped to be reproduced *exactly* at a point in the future.

The portability that we have just examined is a prerequisite to reproducibility, particularly if the source code is being distributed to third parties to build instead of consuming the official binary releases. To ensure reproducibility, the build must be isolated from change, so dependence on external resources and configuration is likely to be a problem unless they are guaranteed to be maintained over time.

Within Maven, there are several sources of variance that can hinder reproducibility:

- The use of remote repositories, particularly metadata and POM files
- Use of dependency ranges for versions
- Open ended plugin versions
- Use of snapshots
- Varying versions of Maven itself
- Other environmental factors

These are all manageable when given proper consideration.

Remote repositories can be locked down as we examined at the beginning of the chapter, using the repository manager we have set up to ensure that metadata that has been used is never altered.

Versions require a closer look as Maven allows some to be defaulted to irreproducible values. In present incarnations of Maven, dependency ranges are best avoided unless you have an alternate method for tracking the version used. Plugin versions should be specified wherever possible, including those built in to Maven's life cycles such as the Compiler plugin. While ideally the plugins will remain backwards compatible, this introduces significant risk of altering the behavior between builds.

 Recent versions of Maven lock down the built in versions of plugins by default, unless they are overridden in the POM. However, they will change between releases. If you choose not to specify all plugin versions used, you might consider specifying a required Maven version to build with to ensure these remain consistent.

Snapshots are somewhat easier to manage through the update policies, repository management, and their removal in advance of a release (which is a requirement of the Maven release tools by default).

For the Maven version and the surrounding environment, you cannot control most of the parameters from the build directly. However, you can verify that those that are important to you are set correctly and fail the build if not.

Earlier in the book we have encountered the Enforcer plugin. This plugin is particularly useful in ensuring a build is prepared for reproducibility.

Let's start with ensuring the plugins in the build are all released versions, and that no automatic values have been used, by adding the following to the `centrepoint/pom.xml` file:

```
<plugin>
  <groupId>org.apache.maven.plugins</groupId>
  <artifactId>maven-enforcer-plugin</artifactId>
  <version>1.0-beta-1</version>
  <executions>
    <execution>
      <goals>
        <goal>enforce</goal>
      </goals>
      <configuration>
        <rules>
          <requirePluginVersions>
```

```
              <banLatest>true</banLatest>
              <banRelease>true</banRelease>
            </requirePluginVersions>
          </rules>
        </configuration>
      </execution>
    </executions>
  </plugin>
```

As you can see, the familiar plugin configuration has been added, with the new rule that requires plugin versions are set, and that the automatic values for the latest snapshot or release may not be used.

Now we can try validating the project:

```
centrepoint$ mvn validate
```

We will notice that initially there are some failures:

```
[WARNING] Rule 0: org.apache.maven.plugins.enforcer.RequirePluginVersions
failed with message:
Some plugins are missing valid versions:(LATEST RELEASE SNAPSHOT are not
allowed )
org.apache.maven.plugins:maven-install-plugin.  The version currently in
use is 2.3
org.apache.maven.plugins:maven-site-plugin.     The version currently in
use is 2.0.1
org.apache.maven.plugins:maven-deploy-plugin.   The version currently in
use is 2.4
org.apache.maven.plugins:maven-clean-plugin.    The version currently in
use is 2.3
```

These are built-in plugins that we have used but not supplied the version for (even though they are built in to Maven). In some cases, the Enforcer plugin was able to tell us what version was already being used. To resolve the issue, we can add the versions to the pluginManagement section of the POM, for example:

```
<pluginManagement>
  <plugins>
    <plugin>
      <groupId>org.apache.maven.plugins</groupId>
      <artifactId>maven-site-plugin</artifactId>
      <version>2.0</version>
    </plugin>
```

Running the command again will progress to further modules where more missing plugin versions will be found. Repeating the above, we will eventually get a build success.

Now, how about validating the environment? This is simply a matter of adding a new rule or two such as the following:

```
<rules>
  . .
  <requireMavenVersion>
    <version>[2.2.0,)</version>
  </requireMavenVersion>
  <requireOS>
    <family>!windows</family>
  </requireOS>
</rules>
```

In this example, Maven versions 2.2.0 and above will successfully build the project, but others will not (perhaps to avoid a more confusing failure on an earlier version of Maven due to a build incompatibility). Likewise, it will fail to build on a Windows platform (perhaps because the tests require X11 libraries).

This ability to fail fast makes the build easier to understand and self-documenting for current users, and those seeking to reproduce a build on a distant environment in the future.

Summary

There you have it—the secrets to reducing a number of pain points when using Maven! They may well appear obvious. However, when used from the beginning of a project they can save a lot of time.

If you have already been using Maven for some time, review the topics here against your environment. How many have you already been using? How many did you know you should be using but had not had the time to put in place? Perhaps now is the time to start!

By this point we have established a complete application structure, learned how to implement various testing techniques, and the best practices as we proceed to build a project. Now it is time to automate it!

We already have one critical piece of infrastructure in place with a repository manager. In the next chapter, we will look at setting up continuous integration and automated builds for the project using Continuum.

8
Continuum: Ensuring the Health of your Source Code

In this chapter, we will learn about the importance of a continuous integration, or CI, server in a project (especially gigantic ones!).

We will be using Continuum to show you first-hand the formidable role of a CI server in the development life cycle. We will learn the essentials of how to set up Continuum, plus the basics of how to configure it so you will know when your project's build breaks.

The first part of the chapter deals with setting up a source repository, installing any required applications or tools, and setting up Continuum. The remaining sections cover the systematic process of adding and building projects in Continuum.

Knowing when your build breaks

First, let us define a **continuous integration**, or **CI server**. A CI server is an application that is used to monitor your project's build and ensure the health of your source repository.

In a software development setup, a project includes a number of developers. If it is a big project, expect the team to be larger as well. Apart from this, a team can be physically distributed in different locations. An open source project is a good example of this. Developers in open source communities are often located in different parts of the world. All these developers commit or check their code into a central source repository. Sometimes though, people only tend to build the component which they have made changes to (especially when building the entire project takes a while!). Moreover, when that component builds successfully, they commit their changes without checking whether there are dependent components that had been affected by these changes. Now, what if it turned out that one dependent component's build failed because of those changes? No one would know until someone from the team updated his or her local copy and ran a full build. How can everyone else proceed if they were then unable to build the project?

If the developer who discovered the broken build were a Good Samaritan, he would try to fix the build on his own (which would probably take a while). Tracking down and identifying which changes caused the build to break is a tedious job. Either that or the developer would notify his team mates about the broken build so that whoever caused the build to fail would know and would be able to fix the build. However, what if the person who caused the build to break has just left for a vacation? His teammates could either track him down and bug him while he is on vacation, or they could fix it themselves. Either of which would eat up a lot of development time!

If only they had their project source in a CI server:

- They would know that they broke some component in the project when the build failed — whether it was a compilation failure or a test failure, because a CI server ensures that the entire source code builds and all the tests pass.

- They would know that the build is broken because the CI server would notify them when it encountered the build failure.

- They would know who caused the build to break, and they can contact that person and help them to fix it.

- They would know which changes caused the build to break as this information is available in the CI server.

- They would know when there is a problem in their build and deployment infrastructure. For example, when their source repository is down or their deployment repository is not accessible. We did not see these issues in the scenario above but they do happen.

It is obvious from our definition and list above what the importance of a CI server is. However, we will see in the following sections that it's useful for more than just that.

Setting up Continuum

Continuum is an open source continuous integration server that has support for different types of projects such as Maven 2, Maven 1, Ant, and shell projects. Some of its features include build automation, release management, source control management, and build statistics.

Archiva and Continuum used to be sub-projects of Maven. Continuum officially became a top-level project at the ASF in February 2008, just a couple of months before Archiva.

In this section, we will deal with basic source repository setup, the installation of other applications or programs needed by Continuum, and the setup and configuration of Continuum.

Setting up a source repository

We start off by setting up our source repository where we will be adding the example application that we have been utilizing in the previous chapters. The source repository server that we will be using is Subversion or SVN for short. More details about Subversion can be found at http://subversion.tigris.org/.

First, let's download and install Subversion as specified from their site http://subversion.tigris.org/getting.html#binary-packages. We can then set up our local SVN repository by executing the following command:

```
$ svnadmin create /path/to/data/svn
```

Make sure that you replace /path/to from the above command with the actual directory path where you will put your SVN data. This applies to all the commands with the same convention in this chapter.

Before we add our example application centrepoint and its parent POM effectivemaven-parent in the SVN repository, let's first create the appropriate directories in the source repository by executing the following commands:

```
$ svn mkdir file://localhost/path/to/data/svn/effectivemaven-parent/
$ svn mkdir file://localhost/path/to/data/svn/effectivemaven-parent/trunk
$ svn mkdir file://localhost/path/to/data/svn/effectivemaven-parent/
                        branches
$ svn mkdir file://localhost/path/to/data/svn/effectivemaven-parent/tags
$ svn mkdir file://localhost/path/to/data/svn/centrepoint/
$ svn mkdir file://localhost/path/to/data/svn/centrepoint/trunk
$ svn mkdir file://localhost/path/to/data/svn/centrepoint/branches
$ svn mkdir file://localhost/path/to/data/svn/centrepoint/tags
```

The `trunk/` directory is where the latest or current development happens. To use software lingo, this is the **bleeding edge**. The `branches/` directory contains development code of certain versions of the project for maintenance purposes. It may also contain temporary copies of the source code in `trunk/` specifically for developing major features or fixing critical bugs that may possibly break the code (they eventually get merged back to `trunk/` once the changes made are stable). The `tags/` directory on the other hand, contains all the released or **tagged** versions. A tagged version should no longer be modified as that version has already been frozen.

> It is a convention to structure your SVN repository as such because it makes it easier to identify or to know where to look for specific sources. Maven and Continuum both use this structure in determining the default tag URL when releasing a project.

Now, let's import our example projects `centrepoint` and its parent project, `effectivemaven-parent`, to our SVN repository. In the sample code for this chapter, `cd` to the `effectivemaven-parent` first then execute the following command:

```
$ svn import . file://localhost/path/to/data/svn/effectivemaven-parent/trunk
```

Do the same with `centrepoint`. `cd` to the `centrepoint` directory and execute:

```
$ svn import . file://localhost/path/to/data/svn/centrepoint/trunk
```

> Before importing new projects in a source repository, make sure that there are no unnecessary files (like the Maven generated `target/` directory or IDE descriptor files) present. Execute `mvn clean` to cleanup `target/` directories or `mvn eclipse:clean` and `mvn idea:clean` to remove Eclipse and IntelliJ IDEA descriptor files before adding the project in source control.

Installing prerequisites

We know that Continuum supports four different types of projects: Maven 1, Maven 2, Ant, and Shell projects. In order for Continuum to build them, of course we need to have the necessary tools installed. Not all of them are required to be installed though, it really depends on the projects you will be adding to and building in Continuum. It does not make sense to have Ant installed if all of your projects are in Maven 2.

To install Maven 2, we can refer back to Brett's Installing Maven guide from Chapter 1, *Maven in a Nutshell*. We can also follow these steps to install Maven 1, but instead of using `M2_HOME` as our environment variable, we use `MAVEN_HOME` to point to our Maven 1 binaries. Maven 1 can be downloaded at `http://maven.apache.org/maven-1.x/start/download.html`.

To install Ant, we can follow the steps specified at the following web page `http://ant.apache.org/manual/index.html`.

Apart from the build tools above, we will also need a mail server. If you do not have a mail server installed in your machine, you can use **Apache James** (`http://james.apache.org`). Following steps 1 to 4 in `http://wiki.apache.org/james/JamesQuickstart` should be enough to get you started.

Installing and configuring Continuum

Now that we have everything ready, we can proceed with the installation and setup of Continuum.

Continuum can be downloaded from `http://continuum.apache.org/download.html` either as a standalone bundle or as a WAR file (just like Archiva). In our case, we will be using the standalone bundle.

To use the WAR file and deploy it to an application server, just follow the steps specified in `http://continuum.apache.org/docs/1.3.3/installation/installation.html`.

As of the writing of this book, the latest version of Continuum is 1.3.3. Just download the bundle and unpack it.

In Chapter 2, *Staying in Control with Archiva*, we saw the different directories included in the Archiva bundle. Both binaries have the same directories included in their respective bundles. We will simply do a quick run through on some of them with Continuum's.

I have identified below the directories and configuration files that we need to take note of in Continuum:

- `conf/continuum.xml`: This contains Continuum-specific configuration such as the location of the build and release output directories, working copy directory, and the base URL for accessing the webapp. The base URL is used for emails and such, which provides a URL back to the application.
- `conf/jetty.xml`: This is a Jetty-specific configuration. This is where the Continuum and Redback databases and mail resources are configured.

- `data/`: This is the default location of the Continuum and Redback databases as seen in the `jetty.xml` file. This is also the default base location of the working directory, build output directory, and release output directory for projects being built in Continuum.

- `logs/`: This is the default location of the Jetty and Continuum log files. The location of the log files can be set in the `jetty-logging.xml` for Jetty and `apps/continuum/WEB-INF/classes/log4j.xml` for Continuum-specific logs. Once we start up Continuum, we will be seeing different types of log files created in this directory. These are composed of the Continuum rolling log file, audit logs, Jetty logs and wrapper log.

We can see in the `bin/` directory that there are multiple Java wrappers for starting up Continuum. The following OS platforms are supported: `linux-x86-32`, `linux-x86-64`, `windows`, `macosx-universal-32`, `solaris-sparc-32`, `solaris-sparc-64` and `solaris-x86-32`.

Before we start Continuum, we must change the port it will run on. Otherwise, we will encounter an `Address already in use` error during startup.

To change the port, edit the configuration below in the `conf/jetty.xml` file. Change the default value of the `jetty.port` system property from `8080` to `8082`.

```
<!-- START SNIPPET: jetty_port -->
<Call name="addConnector">
  <Arg>
    <New class="org.mortbay.jetty.nio.SelectChannelConnector">
      <Set name="host"><SystemProperty name="jetty.host" /></Set>
      <Set name="port"><SystemProperty name="jetty.port"
                                        default="8082"/></Set>
      <Set name="maxIdleTime">30000</Set>
      <Set name="Acceptors">2</Set>
      <Set name="statsOn">false</Set>
      <Set name="confidentialPort">8443</Set>
      <Set name="lowResourcesConnections">5000</Set>
      <Set name="lowResourcesMaxIdleTime">5000</Set>
    </New>
  </Arg>
</Call>
```

Now let's fire up Continuum. In the `bin/` directory, execute `./continuum console` if you want to see the logs in the console or `./continuum start` to run it in the background. If you are running on Windows, you need to execute `continuum.bat console` to execute it in console mode or `continuum.bat install` then `continuum.bat start` to run Continuum as a service.

I am sure you have noticed during startup that the Continuum standalone uses an embedded Jetty server similar to the one Archiva uses.

Did you know that the Archiva and Continuum standalone bundles were created using Maven plugins? These are the `appassembler-maven-plugin` that was used to generate the **Java Service Wrappers** including the wrapper configuration, and the `maven-assembly-plugin`, which was used to package the binaries bundle. You can refer back to Chapter 3, *Building an Application Using Maven*, for more details about these plugins.

Once Continuum has started up successfully, we can access it in the web browser via the URL `http://localhost:8082/continuum`.

 You can easily change Continuum's URL either by setting it in the webapp through the **General Configuration** page or by manually setting it in the `<baseUrl>` of `continuum.xml`. One thing to keep in mind when changing the host or the context from the default in Jetty (or in the application server), is to make sure that you change the `<baseUrl>` in the configuration file as well.

Accessing the above URL gives us the **Create Admin** page (Yes, this is just like Archiva.)

For consistency purposes, we will use the same credentials we used in Archiva for the default `System Administrator` user. Fill in the required fields as follows:

- **Full Name: Administrator**
- **Email Address: admin@example.com** (this is our official phony admin email address)
- **Password: admin1**

After creating the **admin** user, we will be directed to the **General Configuration** page, which looks like the following:

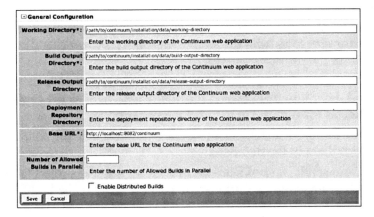

The **Working Directory** is where Continuum keeps the local checkouts of the projects it is building, while the **Build Output Directory** and **Release Output Directory** are where Continuum stores the respective output of the project builds and the releases done in Continuum. We have already tackled what the **Base URL** is for, so we will be skipping that. As for the last two fields—**Number of Builds in Parallel** and **Enable Distributed Builds**, we will learn what these two are for when we get to Chapter 9, *Continuum in Depth*. The contents specified in the fields above will be saved in the `continuum.xml` file once we hit the **Save** button.

 As a general practice, the **Working Directory, Build Output Directory** and **Release Output Directory** should be kept separate from the Continuum installation. This is to avoid accidentally deleting these directories when upgrading Continuum.

Using Continuum

In Chapter 1, *Maven in a Nutshell*, you learned about Maven's build life cycle. Now, we will see how Continuum builds a project, and how it uses and works with Maven.

At a glance

Outlined below is a brief step-by-step explanation of how Continuum builds a project:

- Project build is triggered (either by the user explicitly triggering the build or through the schedule).
- Continuum adds the build to the build queue and determines the build definition and the build environment to be used for the build. You will understand what it is I am talking about once we get to the middle parts of this chapter.
- Continuum checks out a fresh copy or updates the project's working copy (or *working directory*) from the source repository. A working directory is just a checkout of the project's sources.
- Once the checkout or update is finished, Continuum builds the project using the build definition from Step 2. It actually just invokes the configured build tools such as Maven or Ant to build the project.
- When the build is finished, Continuum would collects the results of the build and stores them in the database.
- Continuum sends out notifications or messages to the project team regarding the result of the build execution—the build is broken, the build is fine, and so on.

> If you later install Continuum on a server where you do not have access to the file system, you can browse the working directory through the **Working Copy** tab of the project in the Continuum web application.

Now enough with these concepts and let's start exercising our fingers with some CI action.

The first thing we need to do is to check out our example application and its parent POM locally. As we did not host our SVN repository to be accessible via HTTP, we will be adding our project from the filesystem. Execute:

```
$ svn co file://localhost/path/to/data/svn/effectivemaven-parent/trunk
effectivemaven-parent
```

```
$ svn co file://localhost/path/to/data/svn/centrepoint/trunk centrepoint
```

Now we will be adding our example application to Continuum from the filesystem. In order to be able to do this, we must first enable the `file://` protocol in `apps/continuum/WEB-INF/classes/META-INF/plexus/application.xml`. Otherwise, we will encounter a **The specified resource isn't a file or the protocol used isn't allowed** error message, if we attempt to add it without enabling it first.

> By default, the `file://` protocol for adding projects is disabled in Continuum due to security reasons. Only `http`, `https` and `ftp` are allowed.

Let's stop Continuum first. As we are running on console, we will stop it via *Ctrl+C*. Use `./continuum stop` if Continuum is running in the background or as a service.

Now edit `apps/continuum/WEB-INF/classes/META-INF/plexus/application.xml` and uncomment the `file://` scheme in the following section:

```
<plexus>
...
  <component>
    <role>org.apache.maven.continuum.utils.ContinuumUrlValidator
                                                      </role>
    <role-hint>continuumUrl</role-hint>
    <implementation>
      org.apache.maven.continuum.utils.ContinuumUrlValidator
    </implementation>
    <configuration>
      <allowedSchemes>
        <allowedScheme>http</allowedScheme>
        <allowedScheme>https</allowedScheme>
```

```
        <allowedScheme>ftp</allowedScheme>
        <!-- <allowedScheme>file</allowedScheme> -->
      </allowedSchemes>
    </configuration>
  </component>
  . . .
</plexus>
```

Start up Continuum again and so that we can add our projects. We need to add `effectivemaven-parent` to Continuum first since it is our practice project's (`centrepoint`) parent and we will not be able to add `centrepoint` without it. Otherwise we will get a **Missing artifact trying to build the POM. Check that its parent POM is available or add it first in Continuum** error.

 It is possible to add the `centrepoint` project to Continuum without having to add `effectivemaven-parent` first *if and only if* the `effectivemaven-parent` POM is already installed in the local Maven repository where Continuum is running. In our case, we will need the parent when we get to the releasing part in Chapter 9, *Continuum in Depth*, so we will be adding ours to Continuum.

Now, let's add `effectivemaven-parent` through the **Add Maven 2.0+ Project** page.

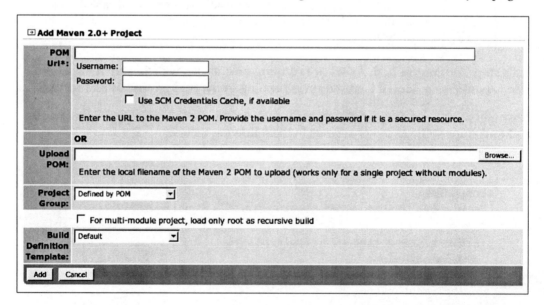

We provide the filesystem path to our check out of our example project's POM in the **POM Url** field, which is `file:///path/to/local/checkout/of/effectivemaven-parent/pom.xml`. We can leave the **Username** and **Password** fields empty, as we did not set up security in our SVN repository. We will leave the rest of the fields as they are.

We can tell Continuum whether to use the default group configured in the project's POM or add it to a specific project group via the **Project Group** field. If we choose the default Defined by POM, a new **Project Group** will be created based on the `<name>` element set in the project's POM. The project (and its submodules) will be added under that group. Now if we choose a specific **Project Group**, then that's where our new project will be added.

Now, click **Add** and we will get a **Missing "scm" element in the POM, project Apache Maven 2: Effective Implementations Book** error. This is Continuum telling us that we don't have the required information configured in our POM. Therefore, here is what we will do:

In our local checkout of the project, we add the `<scm>` tag in the topmost POM.

```
...
<scm>
  <connection>scm:svn:file://localhost/path/to/data/svn/
effectivemaven-parent/trunk</connection>
  <developerConnection>scm:svn:file://localhost/path/to/data/svn/
effectivemaven-parent/trunk</developerConnection>
  <url>file://localhost/path/to/data/svn/effectivemaven-parent/trunk
                                              </url>
</scm>
...
```

> Continuum requires the `<scm>` configuration because it uses that for checking out and updating the project from the source repository. For multi-module projects, Continuum determines the SCM URLs of the sub-modules based from the SCM URL of the parent or topmost POM. For more details about the SCM URL format used by Maven and Continuum, check out `http://maven.apache.org/scm/scm-url-format.html`.

Then we commit our changes to the source repository.

```
effectivemaven-parent$ svn commit
```

Do the same for our `centrepoint` project and set the appropriate SCM URLs in its POM.

```
...
<scm>
    <connection>scm:svn:file://localhost/path/to/data/svn/centrepoint/
trunk</connection>
    <developerConnection>scm:svn:file://localhost/path/to/data/svn/
centrepoint/trunk</developerConnection>
    <url>file://localhost/path/to/data/svn/centrepoint/trunk</url>
</scm>
...
```

(Don't forget to commit the changes you made.)

Add the `effectivemaven-parent` project in Continuum again and... success! We now see it being added and after a while, we are directed to the **Project Group Summary** page.

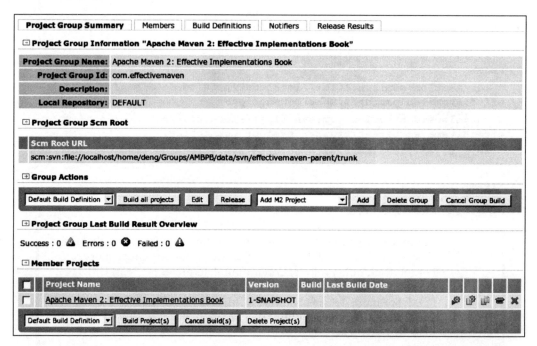

As we can see from the screenshot above, most of the information in the **Project Group** were captured from the POM. The **Project Group Id** of the created project group was from the `<groupId>` specified in the POM. If, for example, you add another project which has the same `groupId` (and you specified the **Project Group** field when you added the project as **Defined by POM**), the project will be added to this **Project Group**.

Continuum groups its projects making it easier and far more flexible to build a set of projects with just one click. This is designed to handle cases such as **multi-modules**. We can build the entire project tree by building the group as opposed to triggering the build for each one. Think about the Maven reactor which was discussed in Chapter 1, *Maven in a Nutshell*. When a build is triggered at the group level, all the projects underneath it will be built sequentially with respect to their inter-dependencies.

Now, let's add our `centrepoint` application. Go back to the **Add Maven 2.0+ Project** page, and add this **POM Url** `file:///path/to/local/checkout/of/centrepoint/pom.xml`. After it is added, we should see the project's **Project Group Summary** as follows:

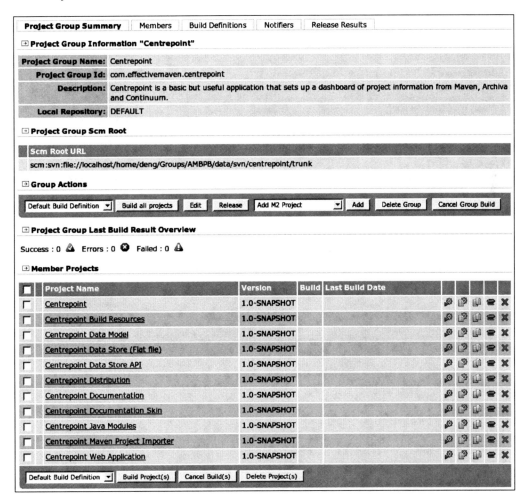

As `centrepoint` has a different `groupId` from its parent `effectivemaven-parent`, it was added as a separate **Project Group**.

Project groups are especially handy when we have *a huge project with a lot of components that may be released independently*. As releases are done by **Project Group** in Continuum, we can add each component as a separate group so we can easily release that component without the need to release the entire project.

The build queues

In Continuum, when a project build is triggered — either forced or from the schedule, the project is added to a build queue. This build queue can be viewed via the **Queues** page. The **Queues** page is divided into six sections, as we can see below:

⊞ **Current Build**

Build Queue	Project Name	Build Definition	
DEFAULT_BUILD_QUEUE	Centrepoint	Default Maven 2 Build Definition	⚙

⊞ **Build Queue**

☐ Build Queue	Project Name	Build Definition	
☐ DEFAULT_BUILD_QUEUE	Centrepoint Build Resources	Default Maven 2 Build Definition	⚙
☐ DEFAULT_BUILD_QUEUE	Centrepoint Java Modules	Default Maven 2 Build Definition	⚙
☐ DEFAULT_BUILD_QUEUE	Centrepoint Data Model	Default Maven 2 Build Definition	⚙
☐ DEFAULT_BUILD_QUEUE	Centrepoint Data Store API	Default Maven 2 Build Definition	⚙
☐ DEFAULT_BUILD_QUEUE	Centrepoint Data Store (Flat file)	Default Maven 2 Build Definition	⚙
☐ DEFAULT_BUILD_QUEUE	Centrepoint Maven Project Importer	Default Maven 2 Build Definition	⚙
☐ DEFAULT_BUILD_QUEUE	Centrepoint Web Application	Default Maven 2 Build Definition	⚙
☐ DEFAULT_BUILD_QUEUE	Centrepoint Documentation	Default Maven 2 Build Definition	⚙
☐ DEFAULT_BUILD_QUEUE	Centrepoint Distribution	Default Maven 2 Build Definition	⚙
☐ DEFAULT_BUILD_QUEUE	Centrepoint Documentation Skin	Default Maven 2 Build Definition	⚙

[Cancel Entries]

⊞ **Current Checkout**

No current checkout

⊞ **Checkout Queue**

Checkout Queue is empty

⊞ **Current Prepare Build**

No current prepare build

⊞ **Prepare Build Queue**

Prepare Build Queue is empty

The **Current Build** section contains the project currently being built. The **Build Queue**, on the other hand, contains the projects waiting in line to be built next. The **Build Queue** column in each section shows in which **Build Queue** the project is going to be built. This is in relation to **parallel builds**, which we will cover, in the next chapter.

The **Current Checkout** section contains the project currently being checked out from the source repository. This would have a value, if and only if a new project was just added to Continuum or a project which was set to be built fresh (checkout a fresh copy of the project) each time was triggered to be built. The **Checkout Queue** contains the projects waiting in line to be checked out from the source repository.

The **Current Prepare Build** section contains the project being prepared to be built. When a project is in the prepare build stage, its build state and working directory (if it already exists) is updated, making it ready for building. Once it is out of the prepare build phase, the project will be added either to the **Checkout Queue** or the **Build Queue**, depending on whether the project has already been checked out or not. The **Prepare Build Queue** on the other hand, just lists the projects waiting to be prepared for building.

After a project has finished building, it will be removed from the **Queues** page. Administrators can access queues to stop the current build or remove builds from the queue.

The build definition

As we have seen in the Continuum build life cycle overview earlier, Continuum uses build definitions for building the projects.

We can think of build definitions as instructions for Continuum on how to build the project. There are two levels of build definition: project group level and project level.

Project group build definition

Let's go back to the **Project Group Summary** page of our `centrepoint` application and click on the **Build Definitions** tab. Continuum configures a default build definition for each project group created. The content of the build definition depends on the type of the project. For Maven 2 projects, goals such as `clean install` and `clean deploy` need to be defined while Ant and shell projects do not require this. Instead, they configure their respective command-line goals.

As we can see from the **Project Group Build Definition** of our **Centrepoint** project group below, the goals to be executed for the build can be configured as well as the schedule of its execution.

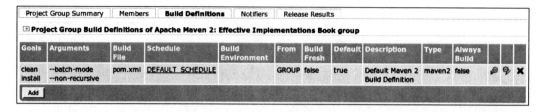

The default **Project Group Build Definition** has **clean install** as its goals. Having **install** as a goal means that the project's artifacts will only be available locally (in the local Maven repository) to where our Continuum instance is running. Consumers of the project (for example, the project's Quality Assurance team) will not necessarily have permission to access the machine itself and it is out of the question to obtain the latest build from the local repository. Instead, the right way to do is to set up a deployment repository for snapshot artifacts, configure Continuum to build the project, and deploy the built artifacts to the snapshot repository, so that there is a new build each day that can be consumed by the QA team for testing.

In previous chapters, we configured our project to deploy to the Archiva snapshots repository that we created in Chapter 2, *Staying in Control with Archiva*:

```
...
<distributionManagement>
  <repository>
    <id>releases</id>
    <name>Archiva Managed Releases Repository</name>
    <url>http://localhost:8081/archiva/repository/releases</url>
    <layout>default</layout>
  </repository>
  <snapshotRepository>
    <id>snapshots</id>
    <name>Archiva Managed Snapshots Repository</name>
    <url>http://localhost:8081/archiva/repository/snapshots</url>
    <uniqueVersion>true</uniqueVersion>
    <layout>default</layout>
  </snapshotRepository>
</distributionManagement>
...
```

We don't need to configure anything else in our `settings.xml` and
`security-settings.xml` as we are using the same `<id>` for our repositories
as what we have configured already in Chapter 2, *Staying in Control with Archiva*,
when we deployed to Archiva.

Now let's create a new build definition for our **Centrepoint** project group. Click the
Add button on the group build definitions page, then fill in the **Build Definition**
as follows:

⊞ **Add/Edit Build Definition**	
POM filename*:	pom.xml
Goals:	clean deploy
Arguments:	--batch-mode --non-recursive
	☐ Build Fresh (Run always a clean checkout instead of an SCM update)
	☐ Always Build
	☐ Is it default?
Schedule:	DEFAULT_SCHEDULE ▾
Build Environment:	▾
Type:	maven2 ▾
Description:	Build and deploy project to snapshots repository
Save Cancel	

The **POM filename** is the actual filename of our project's `pom.xml` that will be used
for the build. The **Goals** are the goals we want to execute when using this build
definition. As we want our artifacts to be available to the snapshots repository,
we will set **clean deploy** as our goals. The **Arguments** specify the additional
arguments that will be used when building the project. In our case, these are
Maven 2 arguments, as our project is a Maven 2 project. If you had wanted to do a
fresh checkout instead of just updating from the source repository during the build,
you would tick the **Build Fresh** checkbox.

One behavior of Continuum to take note of is that if there were no changes to the
SCM in the last build; Continuum would no longer build the project. This sometimes
causes people to panic and think their CI is broken, but it is actually not. When you
think about it, it makes sense that this is the default behavior. There were no changes
in the code, so why build it? To countermand this behavior, you would tick the
Always Build checkbox in the build definition. This would tell Continuum to always
build the project whether there were any changes in the SCM or not.

The **Is it default?** field signifies that the build definition is the default one that will
be used when the project build is explicitly triggered (forced build) from the **Project
Group Summary** and **Project Summary** pages. This field can only be edited if there
are multiple build definitions defined for the project.

We will discuss schedules next, but for now we will just use the DEFAULT_SCHEDULE. The same goes for **Build Environment.** We will cover this at the end of this chapter. For now, we will leave as it is.

As for the last two fields, they simply specify the type of project the build definition is for and the description of the build definition respectively.

Click **Save** and our build definition is created.

Now for each project group, we can define multiple build definitions and attach it to a **schedule**. A schedule is just a plain old schedule of when a build will be triggered or executed. The diagram below, which Wendy Smoak created for Continuum effectively shows how the project group, build definitions, schedules, build queues, and notifiers (which we will discuss later on) work together.

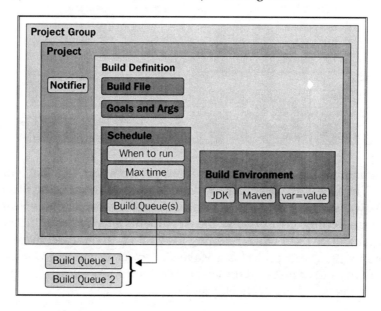

Going back to the schedules, a default schedule running every hour is already pre-defined in Continuum and that is where the default build definition is attached. We will create a schedule for our project's nightly builds where we will attach the build definition that we created so that there is a fresh snapshot each day which the QA team can test for all the changes or fixes in the code from the previous day. From the Schedules tab on the left you can add a new schedule. Fill in the form as follows:

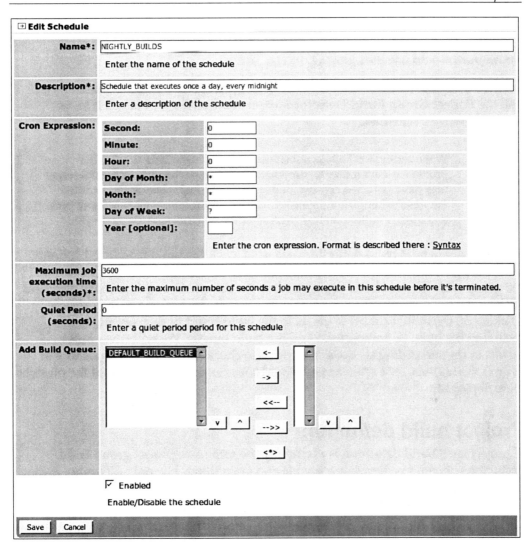

The important field to take note of in the **Schedule** is the **Cron Expression**.

 A **Cron Expression** is a representation of a time or times at certain intervals. This is used typically to fire or trigger a schedule to do or execute something.

From the **Cron Expression** we have specified above, we are configuring our schedule to build each night at 12 midnight.

The other field to take note of is the **Build Queue**. This simply defines where the project(s) attached to this schedule will be queued. If no build queue were set, Continuum would use the DEFAULT_BUILD_QUEUE.

Save the schedule that we created. Go back to Centrepoint's **Build Definitions** tab, edit the **Project Group Build Definition** we created earlier and attach it to our NIGHTLY_BUILDS schedule.

> When setting a schedule, sometimes an hour is too long to wait. If a problem occurs it may be drowned out by other changes, or the developer may have switched context. Builds should be kept short and scheduled frequently. Long-running tasks, such as performance and functional tests, and nightly builds can be run on separate schedules.

To demonstrate how build definitions are used, click the build icon (third column from the right) of our snapshot deployment build definition. After the projects in the group have finished building, go back to the **Project Group Summary** page and click on the build number link (fifth column from the left) of one of the projects. Clicking on the build number leads us to the build result of that specific build including the build definition used and the build output. We will cover build results in the succeeding sections. You can also check the snapshots repository at http://localhost:8081/archiva/repository/snapshots to see that the projects were deployed.

Project build definition

A project level build definition is essentially the same as a project group build definition—it could be tied to a schedule and everything. The only difference is that it's on a *per project level*. Therefore, when only that project was triggered to be built, Continuum would use the default project level build definition.

The notifiers

We mentioned earlier in the chapter that one of the benefits of using a CI server is that when the build breaks, the project members would immediately know of it. This is where notifiers come in. Notifiers are a configuration in the CI, which send out **notifications** to the project members regarding the status of the build.

Different types of notifiers

In Continuum, there are **five** types of notifiers that can be configured. These are the:

- **Mail notifier**: The mail notifier sends out an email to a specific address regarding the status of the build. For the mail notifier to work, it's good to keep in mind to set up a mail server first. Remember, we did this whilst installing prerequisites at the beginning of the chapter.

- **IRC notifier**: This notifier sends out a message to a specific IRC channel alerting the channel of the project's build condition.

- **Jabber notifier**: This notifier sends out a message to a specific Jabber account.

- **MSN notifier**: This notifier sends out a message to a specific MSN account.

- **Wagon notifier**: This notifier deploys the build results to a specific URL (for example, to the project's site) using Wagon.

These notifiers can be configured to notify the project team on certain conditions of the build. They can be set up to **Send on Success**, **Send on Failure**, **Send on Error**, and/or **Send on Warning** as seen in the following screenshot:

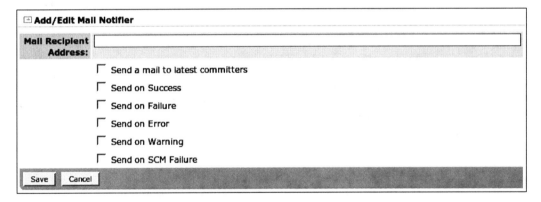

They are self-descriptive, but we will give each one a quick run through:

- **Send on Success**: Send out a notification if the build was successful.

- **Send on Failure**: "Code red! Code red! Code RED!!!". Need we say more? Okay, just to elaborate... a notification will be sent out when the build fails. By fail, we mean that a problem was encountered **during** build execution. This can be a compile failure, a test failure, or simply a dependency not being found.

- **Send on Error**: A notification will be sent out when there was an error **outside** of the build execution. A good example of this is when the source repository goes offline and Continuum cannot update its working copy.

- **Send on Warning**: A notification will be sent out if the build was not a successful build, a failed build, or an erroneous build.

A notification is sent only when a project's state is modified. For example, if the previous state of all the projects in the group is **SUCCESS** and on the next build, all the projects in the entire group were built successfully again, no notification will be sent. However, if the second build of one of the projects failed (state is **FAILURE**), a notification will be sent specific to that project.

The **Send a mail to latest committers** field for the **Mail Notifier** tells Continuum to send a notification mail to those developers who committed changes to the source repository as part of the last build. The **Mail Recipient Address** does not have any effect on the **Send a mail to latest committers** as the email addresses where the notification mail will be sent are retrieved from the list of project developers.

Like build definitions, notifiers can also be configured at the project group level and/or at the project level. Notifiers are cumulative, which means notifiers configured at the group level always takes effect whether or not there are notifiers configured at the project level. This is similar to the concept of inheritance in Maven.

Now, let's create a group mail notifier for our `centrepoint` application. In our exercise, we will use our own valid email address for the mail notifier. We want to know everything that is happening to our project build so we tick all the checkboxes except for **Send a mail to latest committers** (we don't have usernames in our SVN repository so we don't have any use for this). Let's build our project by pressing the **Build All Projects** button on the **Project Group Summary** page. We should get a successful build and the build states of all the projects in the group should show the **SUCCESS** icon. However, no notification mail was sent. This is because there were not any changes in the build state nor were there any changes in SVN.

Now, let's edit the test case of one of the modules of our **Centrepoint** application. Go to your local checkout of the project and open `PropertiesProjectStoreTest.java` located at `modules/store-file/src/test/java/com/effectivemaven/centrepoint/store/properties/` either in your IDE or in a text editor. Add the following failing test to the class:

```
@Test
public void failingTest()
{
    assert false;
}
```

Commit the changes that we made and then let's build the **Centrepoint** project group in Continuum. Now, we will see that we got an email notification (similar to the one in the following screenshot) that contains a summarized build result status for **Centrepoint Data Store (Flat File)** project, which had the failing test case.

 Before continuing, make sure to remove the broken test and commit again so that the build succeeds!

```
Build statistics:
State: Failed
Previous State: Ok
Started at: Thu 30 Jul 2009 15:08:01 +0800
Finished at: Thu 30 Jul 2009 15:08:17 +0800
Total time: 16s
Build Trigger: Forced
Build Number: 8
Exit code: 1
Building machine hostname: marya
Operating system : Linux(unknown)
Java Home version :
    java version "1.5.0_11"
    Java(TM) 2 Runtime Environment, Standard Edition (build 1.5.0_11-b03)
    Java HotSpot(TM) Server VM (build 1.5.0_11-b03, mixed mode)

Builder version :
    Maven version: 2.0.9
    Java version: 1.5.0_11
    OS name: "linux" version: "2.6.20-17-generic" arch: "i386" Family: "unix"

***************************************************************
SCM Changes:
***************************************************************
Changed: oching @ Thu 30 Jul 2009 15:05:07 +0800
Comment: fail test
Files changed:
/centrepoint/trunk/modules/store-file/src/test/java/com/effectivemaven/centrepoint/store/properties/PropertiesProjectStoreTest.java ( 203 )

***************************************************************
Dependencies Changes:
***************************************************************
com.effectivemaven.centrepoint:model:1.0-SNAPSHOT

com.effectivemaven.centrepoint:store-api:1.0-SNAPSHOT

com.effectivemaven.centrepoint:modules:1.0-SNAPSHOT


***************************************************************
Build Definition:
***************************************************************
POM filename: pom.xml
Goals: clean install
Arguments: --batch-mode --non-recursive
Build Fresh: false
Always Build: false
Default Build Definition: true
Schedule: DEFAULT_SCHEDULE
Description: Default Maven 2 Build Definition

***************************************************************
Test Summary:
***************************************************************
Tests: 4
Failures: 1
Errors: 0
Success Rate: 75
Total time: 1.928

***************************************************************
Test Failures:
***************************************************************

TestSuite
  testStoreMinimalProject :
java.lang.AssertionError
java.lang.AssertionError
    at com.effectivemaven.centrepoint.store.properties.PropertiesProjectStoreTest.testStoreMinimalProject(PropertiesProjectStoreTest.java:64)
```

To learn more about how to configure the different types of notifiers in Continuum, visit http://continuum.apache.org/docs/1.3.3/user_guides/notification/index.html.

Configuring notifiers in Maven

The Maven 2 project model allows configuration for the CI server officially used by the project. This can be achieved through the `<ciManagement>` section, wherein the type of CI server, the URL where it is running and the build notifiers to use can be configured.

As we can see in the sample configuration below, it has similar parameters to what we can configure in Continuum.

```
...
<ciManagement>
  <system>continuum</system>
  <url>http://localhost:8082/continuum</url>
  <notifiers>
    <notifier>
      <type>mail</type>
      <sendOnError>true</sendOnError>
      <sendOnFailure>true</sendOnFailure>
      <sendOnSuccess>true</sendOnSuccess>
      <sendOnWarning>false</sendOnWarning>
      <configuration>
        <address>continuum@example.com</address>
      </configuration>
    </notifier>
  </notifiers>
</ciManagement>
...
```

The value in the `<configuration>` section varies depending on the type of notifier extended and used.

If a notifier is configured in the POM of a project when it was added to Continuum, that notifier would be automatically configured in Continuum and will be used to send out build notifications. Take note though that notifiers declared in the POM cannot be edited or deleted through Continuum. It must be removed by hand in the POM and checked in to the source repository.

In the case of some open source projects (like Maven for example), a notifications mailing list specific for build notifications is set up and a mail notifier is configured in the project's parent POM to send build notifications to that mailing list. So whoever would like to be notified of the builds can just subscribe to that list and there is no need to add specific email addresses in the build server's notifier configuration.

The Build results

We already had a peek at the build results in our discussion on build definitions. Now let's go back to the **Centrepoint Data Store (Flat File)** project. Click the **Builds** tab. You should see a list of all the build results from building the project in the previous section. Click the **Result** link (first column from the right) of the build whose **State** shows FAILURE. We can see that it contains information about the build (how it was triggered, the duration of the build, and such), the changes in SCM and project dependencies, the build definition used, generated reports, and the build output (which can also be downloaded).

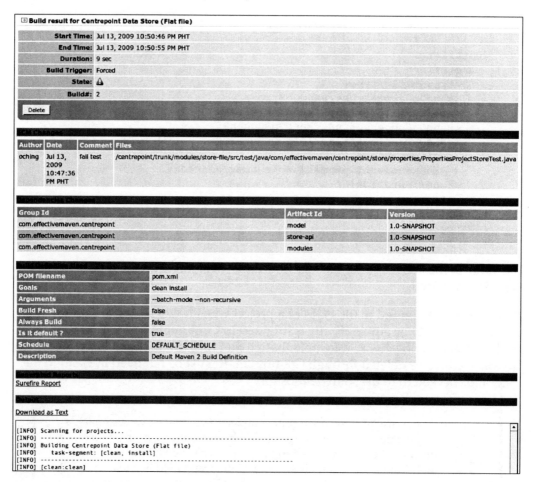

One other important piece of information to take note of is the generated reports. As we can see, one of these reports is the **Surefire Reports**.

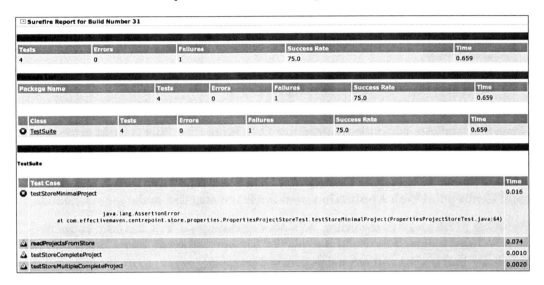

As we can see from the screen shot above, **Surefire Reports** is divided into three sections. The first is the **Summary**, which contains the summary of the executed tests. It is similar to what we see at the end of the test phase when we build a project from the command line. The second section is the **Package List**. This contains the packages and test classes that were executed during the build. It also includes the number of test cases that passed, failed, or were in error. The last section is **Test Cases**, which is a list of all the test methods that were executed, including the cause (or causes) of the error or failure.

Surefire Reports is handy when there are test failures during the build. It is easy to identify which test case(s) failed, as the reports are broken down to this level.

Dependency changes

Continuum builds the project when there are changes in its dependencies. These dependencies must be projects that are also in the Continuum instance and is usually evident in inter-dependent modules. Project dependencies are tracked from the Maven POM, and this can be seen from the project information page.

Let's go back again to our **Centrepoint Data Store (Flat File)** project. Looking at the pom.xml of the **Centrepoint Web Application** project, we can see that it has a dependency on **Centrepoint Data Store (Flat File)**.

```
. . .
<dependency>
  <groupId>${project.groupId}</groupId>
  <artifactId>store-file</artifactId>
</dependency>
```

Given this scenario, when the **Centrepoint Data Store (Flat File)** is build is triggered from the schedule, Continuum will see that the **Centrepoint Web Application** project has a dependency on it. If Continuum detects any SCM changes when it updated the working copy of **Centrepoint Data Store (Flat File)**, then it will also build **Centrepoint Web Application** even if it is not attached to the same schedule.

One thing to take note of regarding dependency changes is that this only happens for scheduled builds. If the build is explicitly triggered (forced), then Continuum will only build that project and not the dependent projects.

Installations and build environments

In company settings, different projects have different build environments. Some projects require a specific version of Java to be used while other projects need additional environment variables to be set in order for them to be built. Because of this, it is better to have different environments where we can build and test our projects to ensure that they are platform independent and can be built on these environments.

To address this need, Continuum has **installations** and **build environments**.

Installations

Installations or builders are tools or environment variable settings, which can be configured if some projects require a different or specific tool apart from the default tools installed in the server. An **installation** may be a tool, such as Java or Maven, or it can even be an environment variable setting such as MAVEN_OPTS.

Let's say we want to increase the memory allocation for Maven when building our example application. This can be achieved by setting the MAVEN_OPTS environment variable before building the project. Now, we only want that to be used when building our example application and not when building other projects in Continuum. What we can do in this case is create a build environment in Continuum where the MAVEN_OPTS environment variable is set.

In the navigation menu, click on **Installations** and add a new one. Create an **Environment Variable** type installation. Fill in the form as follows:

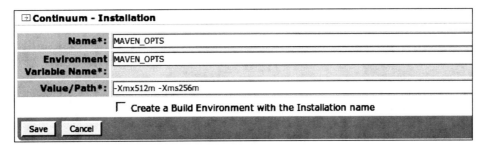

The **Name** field is just a name for the installation used by Continuum as reference. The **Environment Variable Name** is the actual environment variable we want to set and the **Value/Path** is the value we want to use for the environment variable. As for the checkbox, ticking that box means a **Build Environment** (which we will discuss in the next section) with a similar installation name will automatically be created.

Now click **Save** to create the Continuum installation.

Build environments

We can define multiple installations in a build environment. The purpose of this is so that we can simulate and configure all the different variables that compose or affect the environment. For example, we want to make sure that our project builds using certain Maven versions.

Now lets create a build environment for our project where we will use the MAVEN_OPTS installation we created in the previous section.

Click **Build Environments** from the navigation menu and add a new one. Fill in the **Build Environment** form as follows:

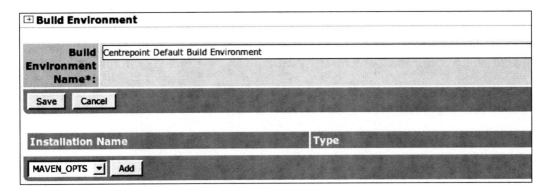

To configure our MAVEN_OPTS installation to the build environment, just select **MAVEN_OPTS** and click the **Add** button. Then click the **Save** button to create the build environment.

We can use this to build our example application. Let's go back to the **Project Group Summary** page of **Centrepoint** and go to the **Build Definitions** tab. Edit the default build definition and set **Centrepoint Default Build Environment** as the **Build Environment**.

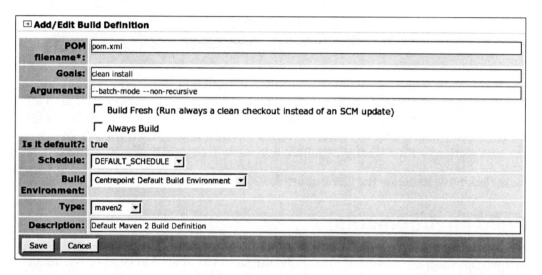

Save the changes and click the build icon (third column from the left) of our default build definition. We can check the build result and see from the **Build Definition Used** that the build environment we have just configured was used.

Summary

In this chapter, we have learned the proper way of setting up and using Continuum to our best advantage.

We have learned what build definitions are, how to schedule a build in Continuum, how to set up notification, and how to configure and use build environments.

We will learn more about Continuum's advanced features in the following chapter.

9
Continuum in Depth

In this chapter, we will learn more about the nitty-gritty details of Continuum. We will delve into the Maven release process and see step-by-step how Continuum adopts the same process. However, it has been made simpler and easier. We will also learn different strategies that we can use for building our projects in Continuum.

The two main approaches for how to build multiple projects at the same time will also be covered in this chapter. Last, but certainly not the least, we will cover maintenance. We will learn how to manage local repositories, working and build output directories used by Continuum.

Releasing projects

As we saw earlier, Maven clearly distinguishes released projects from snapshots of projects in the middle of development. A project release is simply a distribution of the project or application containing specific changes to the project, fixed at that point in time with an attached version. It does not necessarily need to be the final production version, but something that you want to lock down for using later. While developing software, it is crucial to segment the development of the project into multiple iterations. Each iteration has its own development, release, and test phase. It should aim to accomplish a specific set of features of the project. Making releases easy and reliable is important for keeping this moving smoothly.

Release early, release often

When dealing with releases, it is always good to keep in mind the mantra *release early, release often*. Why should you release early? You don't want to be dealing with release difficulties for the first time at the end of a project with a deadline. Why should you release often? If you keep the iteration too long, a lot of features tend to be jammed into the release, making it more prone to bugs and resulting in a more painful release process. Releases should also be reproducible so that if you need to go back to something you've released in the past, you can ensure you can build it (perhaps after fixing some critical bug) the same way that it was built before. In Chapter 7, *Maven Best Practices*, some tips were given for making your Maven builds reproducible.

Producing a release tends to be tricky and involves proper planning and a lot of discipline. Releases are traditionally manual processes that require a number of error-prone steps and changes that need to be checked. Maven aims to automate as much of the tedium as possible, making releases easier and more reliable. Let's start by looking at Maven's release capabilities directly.

Maven release process

Maven uses the Release plugin when releasing a project. While we will only discuss the two most important goals of this plugin, there are other goals to help with related tasks such as creating new development branches. To get a list of all of its available goals and how to use them, visit `http://maven.apache.org/plugins/maven-release-plugin/`.

A typical Maven release involves two stages (in the form of goals) and these are — **prepare** and **perform**.

 Only projects with SNAPSHOT versions can be released. If the `<version>` in the POM does not contain the SNAPSHOT keyword, Maven will not go through the release process.

As the name signifies, the **prepare** stage is when the project is prepared for the release. The following phases are executed in order at this stage:

- `check-poms`: POM(s) are checked to see if they are in the right state for a release. For example, an error will be thrown if the current version of the project during the release process is not a SNAPSHOT version. Without the SNAPSHOT keyword in the version, Maven will expect that the project has already been released.

- `scm-check-modifications`: The local checkout of the project is checked if there are modifications that are not committed in the SCM repository, which would make the release inconsistent with the current build.

- `check-dependency-snapshots`: The working copy is checked for dependencies with SNAPSHOT versions. The release will not continue if there are any SNAPSHOT dependencies as they are not stable and may still change over time. So, releases should not depend on them.

- `create-backup-poms`: Backups of the current POM(s) will be created, as they will be updated to the release version and committed to the source repository when the release version is tagged. These backup POM(s) are used for rolling back the release if it fails.

- `map-release-versions`: The user will be prompted for the release version in this phase if the release was triggered to be interactive. The projects will then be mapped to the specified release version.

- `input-variables`: Determine other input variables that are not yet configured. For example, the tag or label of the release.

- `map-development-versions`: The user will be prompted for the next development version in this phase if the release was triggered to be interactive. The projects will then be mapped to the specified development version.

- `rewrite-poms-for-release`: The POM(s) will be updated with the release version. The SCM URLs in the `<scm>` section are also updated to the new URL of the tag to be created.

- `generate-release-poms`: The POM(s) that will be used for the release will be generated.

- `run-preparation-goals`: The project will be built using the preparation goals specified. This verifies that the build is still correct with the new values in the POM(s). The default goals are `clean verify`.

- `scm-commit-release`: Commit the project with the modified POM(s) to the source repository.

- `scm-tag`: The release tag is created and committed to the source repository. For example, `svn copy` is performed from the trunk if the SCM is Subversion.

- `rewrite-poms-for-development`: The POM(s) are updated to the next development version specified at the start of the preparation stage.

- `remove-release-poms`: The generated POM(s) used for the release (if there were any) are cleaned up.

- `scm-commit-development`: The local changes for the development versions are committed to the source repository.

- `end-release`: The release is finalized. This is the equivalent of the `release:clean` goal of the release plugin.

Now, we will try releasing `effectivemaven-parent` project to see how each of these phases are executed during release preparation.

 If a project's parent is a SNAPSHOT version, the parent should be released first. Otherwise, you will not be able to release the project until the parent has been released and the project is referencing the released parent version.

Let's go to the local checkout of our parent project from Chapter 8, *Continuum – Ensuring the Health of your Source Code*, and execute the following command:

```
effectivemaven-parent$ mvn release:prepare
```

As Maven executes the prepare stage, you will be prompted for the release version, the release tag, and the new development version. As we will be using the default values, just hit *Enter* for each prompt. You can of course specify the specific values for each if you do not want to use the default values. After the prepare stage is finished, you should see an output similar to the following:

```
[INFO] ------------------------------------------------------------
[INFO] Building Apache Maven 2: Effective Implementations Book
[INFO]     task-segment: [release:prepare] (aggregator-style)
[INFO] ------------------------------------------------------------
[INFO] [release:prepare]
[INFO] Verifying that there are no local modifications...
[INFO] Executing: svn --non-interactive status
[INFO] Working directory: ...
[INFO] Checking dependencies and plugins for snapshots ...
What is the release version for "Apache Maven 2: Effective
Implementations Book"? (com.effectivemaven:effectivemaven-parent) 1: :
What is SCM release tag or label for "Apache Maven 2: Effective
Implementations Book"? (com.effectivemaven:effectivemaven-parent)
effectivemaven-parent-1: :
What is the new development version for "Apache Maven 2: Effective
Implementations Book"? (com.effectivemaven:effectivemaven-parent) 2-
SNAPSHOT: :
[INFO] Transforming 'Apache Maven 2: Effective Implementations Book'...
```

```
[INFO] Not generating release POMs
[INFO] Executing goals 'clean verify'...
[INFO] Executing: mvn clean verify --no-plugin-updates
[INFO] Scanning for projects...
        [INFO] ------------------------------------------------------
        [INFO] Building Apache Maven 2: Effective Implementations Book
        [INFO]    task-segment: [clean, verify]
        [INFO] ------------------------------------------------------
        [INFO] [clean:clean]
        [INFO] [site:attach-descriptor]
        [INFO] ------------------------------------------------------
        [INFO] BUILD SUCCESSFUL
        [INFO] ------------------------------------------------------
        [INFO] Total time: 7 seconds
        [INFO] Finished at: Sat Aug 01 18:39:17 PHT 2009
        [INFO] Final Memory: 7M/82M
        [INFO] ------------------------------------------------------
        [INFO] Checking in modified POMs...
[INFO] Executing: svn --non-interactive commit --file /tmp/maven-scm-
845985696.commit --targets /tmp/maven-scm-30757-targets
[INFO] Working directory: ...
[INFO] Tagging release with the label effectivemaven-parent...
[INFO] Executing: svn --non-interactive copy --file /tmp/maven-scm-
1973080933.commit . ...
[INFO] Working directory: ...
[INFO] Transforming 'Apache Maven 2: Effective Implementations Book'...
[INFO] Not removing release POMs
[INFO] Checking in modified POMs...
[INFO] Executing: svn --non-interactive commit --file /tmp/maven-scm-
1477535264.commit --targets /tmp/maven-scm-30758-targets
[INFO] Working directory: ...
[INFO] Release preparation complete.
[INFO] ------------------------------------------------------------
[INFO] BUILD SUCCESSFUL
[INFO] ------------------------------------------------------------
```

We should be able to match some of the phases we have discussed to the output logs above and determine at which part of the build they were executed. For example, the **Verifying that there are no local modifications...** log signifies the `scm-check-modifications` phase, the prompt for the release version signifies the `map-release-versions` phase, and so on.

While dealing with multi-module projects, you will be asked for the release version and the next development version for each module.

If all of them have the same values for these parameters, you can add the `-DautoVersionSubmodules=true` parameter when executing `mvn release:prepare` so that you will be asked for these parameters only once.

You may also notice by browsing the `effectivemaven-parent` project directory that there were two files generated: `pom.xml.releaseBackup` and `release.properties`. The first one is the backup of the original POM that was created during the `create-backup-poms` phase. This will be cleaned up later on once the release has been finalized. As for the `release.properties` file, this contains the configuration parameters used by the Release plugin all throughout the release process.

Next up, the **perform** stage is when the tagged version is built and deployed to the deployment repository. Contrary to the prepare stage which involves a lot of phases to be executed, the perform stage only has three phases:

- `verify-completed-prepare-phase`: Checks whether the release preparation stage has already been executed. It is a pre-requisite of the perform stage.

- `checkout-project-from-scm`: The tagged version is checked out from the source repository which will be built in the next phase.

- `run-perform-goals`: The specified release perform goal(s) are executed on the checked out tag. The default goal is `deploy`.

You may also want to take a look at the Maven Stage Plugin, which is very useful if you are staging your releases first before pushing them to the public or official releases repositories. More details about this plugin is available at `http://maven.apache.org/plugins/maven-stage-plugin/`.

To see how these phases are executed, we will finalize the release of our `effectivemaven-parent` project. From the command line, execute the following:

```
effectivemaven-parent$ mvn release:perform
```

We should see a build output similar to that below after the `release:perform` goal
has finished executing.

```
[INFO] ------------------------------------------------------------
[INFO] Building Apache Maven 2: Effective Implementations Book
[INFO]    task-segment: [release:perform] (aggregator-style)
[INFO] ------------------------------------------------------------
[INFO] [release:perform]
[INFO] Checking out the project to perform the release ...
[INFO] Executing: svn --non-interactive checkout file://localhost/path/
to/data/svn/effectivemaven-parent/tags/effectivemaven-parent checkout
[INFO] Working directory: /path/to/local/checkout/of/effectivemaven-
parent/target
[INFO] Executing goals 'deploy'...
[INFO] Executing: mvn deploy --no-plugin-updates -DperformRelease=true -f
pom.xml
[INFO] Scanning for projects...
        [INFO] ----------------------------------------------------
        [INFO] Building Apache Maven 2: Effective Implementations Book
        [INFO]    task-segment: [deploy]
        [INFO] ----------------------------------------------------
        [INFO] [site:attach-descriptor]
        [INFO] Preparing source:jar
        [WARNING] Removing: jar from forked lifecycle, to prevent
                 recursive invocation.
        [INFO] No goals needed for project - skipping
        [INFO] [source:jar {execution: attach-sources}]
        [INFO] [javadoc:jar {execution: attach-javadocs}]
        [INFO] Not executing Javadoc as the project is not a Java
                 classpath-capable package
        [INFO] [install:install]
        [INFO] Installing /path/to/local/checkout/of/effectivemaven-
                 parent/target/checkout/pom.xml to /path/to/.m2/repository/
                 com/effectivemaven/effectivemaven-parent/1/effectivemaven-
                 parent-1.pom
        [INFO] [deploy:deploy]
        altDeploymentRepository = null
        Uploading: http://localhost:8081/archiva/repository/releases/com/
        effectivemaven/effectivemaven-parent/1/effectivemaven-parent-
        1.pom
        1K uploaded
```

```
[INFO] Retrieving previous metadata from releases
[INFO] repository metadata for: 'artifact com.effectivemaven:
       effectivemaven-parent' could not be found on repository:
       releases, so will be created
[INFO] Uploading repository metadata for: 'artifact com.
       effectivemaven:effectivemaven-parent'
[INFO] -----------------------------------------------------------
[INFO] BUILD SUCCESSFUL
[INFO] -----------------------------------------------------------
[INFO] Total time: 6 seconds
[INFO] Finished at: Sun Aug 02 13:27:02 PHT 2009
[INFO] Final Memory: 14M/80M
[INFO] -----------------------------------------------------------
[INFO] Cleaning up after release...
```
```
[INFO] -----------------------------------------------------------
[INFO] BUILD SUCCESSFUL
[INFO] -----------------------------------------------------------
```

Glancing at the output, you will see the different phases being executed — such as when the tagged version was checked out from the source repository or when the perform goal deploy was executed. Notice also the **Cleaning up after release...** log at the end. This is executed by the plugin to remove all the generated files that we saw earlier. If you browse the project directory again, the pom.xml.releaseBackup and release.properties files have been removed.

You may also notice the execution of the [source:jar] and [javadoc:jar] goals above. While they didn't have anything to do in this POM-only project, they provide some default behavior that is helpful to other types of projects. Let's see how these defaults are defined and can be customized.

Release profile

The Maven 2 super POM has a profile that is activated during the release process. As all POMs inherit from the super POM, this profile is inherited by all Maven 2 projects.

```
<profile>
  <id>release-profile</id>
  <activation>
    <property>
      <name>performRelease</name>
      <value>true</value>
```

```xml
        </property>
      </activation>
      <build>
        <plugins>
          <plugin>
            <inherited>true</inherited>
            <groupId>org.apache.maven.plugins</groupId>
            <artifactId>maven-source-plugin</artifactId>
            <executions>
              <execution>
                <id>attach-sources</id>
                <goals>
                  <goal>jar</goal>
                </goals>
              </execution>
            </executions>
          </plugin>
          <plugin>
            <inherited>true</inherited>
            <groupId>org.apache.maven.plugins</groupId>
            <artifactId>maven-javadoc-plugin</artifactId>
            <executions>
              <execution>
                <id>attach-javadocs</id>
                <goals>
                  <goal>jar</goal>
                </goals>
              </execution>
            </executions>
          </plugin>
          <plugin>
            <inherited>true</inherited>
            <groupId>org.apache.maven.plugins</groupId>
            <artifactId>maven-deploy-plugin</artifactId>
            <configuration>
              <updateReleaseInfo>true</updateReleaseInfo>
            </configuration>
          </plugin>
        </plugins>
      </build>
    </profile>
```

The above snippet from the super POM indicates that if the project is in the release stage, Javadocs and sources will be generated and packaged along with the main build artifact. Another configuration you will notice is the `maven-deploy-plugin`, wherein the `updateReleaseInfo` parameter is set. This indicates that the artifact being deployed is a released artifact and the artifact's metadata should be updated as a release.

The release profile is activated through the property `performRelease`. Behind the scenes in the previous build perform stage, the following goals were executed:

```
mvn deploy --no-plugin-updates -DperformRelease=true -f pom.xml
```

Now, let's say you want to customize your release and you want to add additional steps such as signing the artifacts before they are deployed to the repository, or creating a source distribution of the entire project aside from the packaged per-module sources JAR. You can do this by extending the existing `release-profile` profile.

However, you may decide that you do not need the original Javadoc and source configuration, and would rather create and configure your own release profile. As they won't be needed for the bundle, let's do this for the `license-resources` module before we release it.

We have not yet added the License Resources to our Subversion repository, so we need to do that now. First, we create the space in the same way that was done in Chapter 8, *Continuum - Ensuring the Health of your Source Code* (replacing `/path/to/data/svn` with your Subversion repository location):

```
$ svn mkdir file://localhost/path/to/data/svn/license-resources/
$ svn mkdir file://localhost/path/to/data/svn/license-resources/trunk
$ svn mkdir file://localhost/path/to/data/svn/license-resources/branches
$ svn mkdir file://localhost/path/to/data/svn/license-resources/tags
```

We can then import the code from this chapter into the repository:

```
license-resources$ svn import . file://localhost/path/to/data/svn/
license-resources/trunk
```

Now get a clean checkout of the location above and update the POMs with the `scm` section for this location:

```xml
<scm>
  <connection>
  scm:svn:file://localhost/path/to/data/svn/license-resources/trunk
  </connection>
  <developerConnection>
```

```
    scm:svn:file://localhost/path/to/data/svn/license-resources/trunk
    </developerConnection>
  </scm>
```

We also need to adjust the parent POM to the newly released version for our release to succeed:

```
<parent>
  <groupId>com.effectivemaven</groupId>
  <artifactId>effectivemaven-parent</artifactId>
  <version>1</version>
  <relativePath>../effectivemaven-parent/pom.xml</relativePath>
</parent>
```

Now we can adjust our release profile by declaring the `maven-release-plugin` in the `<build>` section of `license-resources/pom.xml` with the following configuration:

```
<plugin>
  <groupId>org.apache.maven.plugins</groupId>
  <artifactId>maven-release-plugin</artifactId>
  <version>2.0-beta-9</version>
  <configuration>
    <useReleaseProfile>false</useReleaseProfile>
    <arguments>-Plicense-release</arguments>
  </configuration>
</plugin>
```

The `<useReleaseProfile>false</useReleaseProfile>` parameter from the configuration above disables the execution of the inherited `release-profile`. The `-Plicense-release` argument will be included as an additional argument when the release perform goal is executed to activate your custom release profile. We then need to add this profile, with just the minimal configuration needed:

```
<profiles>
  <profile>
    <id>license-release</id>
    <build>
      <plugins>
        <plugin>
          <inherited>true</inherited>
          <groupId>org.apache.maven.plugins</groupId>
          <artifactId>maven-deploy-plugin</artifactId>
          <configuration>
            <updateReleaseInfo>true</updateReleaseInfo>
          </configuration>
        </plugin>
      </plugins>
    </build>
  </profile>
</profiles>
```

After committing these changes, we can proceed with the release, accepting the defaults:

```
license-resources$ mvn release:prepare release:perform
```

This time, you will notice that the source and Javadoc JARs are not produced, as we requested. With the two pre-requisites released, we are now able to look at releasing Centrepoint itself, and for that we will use Continuum.

Releasing projects using Continuum

In Continuum, the release process also involves the two stages we saw in Maven's release process. The only difference is that the release can be done via a GUI and in a centralized location. By a centralized location, we mean that all releases are done in just one place, compared to executing the release process via the command line where anyone can do it locally. In the succeeding sections, we shall see how easy it is to do a release in Continuum.

Preparing a release

Before a project can be prepared for release in Continuum, it must be in a **SUCCESSFUL** build state. This is again one of the best practices implemented by both Maven and Continuum. In Maven, the release process would fail in the middle of the execution of the prepare goal when the build failure is encountered. However, in Continuum, the build failure can be caught during the scheduled builds and the build state of the project would be flagged as in **FAILURE** or in **ERROR**, and Continuum would not allow the release process to start until the build state of the project is in a **SUCCESSFUL** state.

We shall again use the Centrepoint project which we set up in Chapter 8, *Continuum – Ensuring the Health of your Source Code*.

 Remember what we did in Chapter 2, *Staying in Control with Archiva*, when we deployed our project to an Archiva repository? We will see in the later parts of this section how this is related to the release process.

Before we start preparing Centrepoint for a release, let's first update its parent to the released version which we released earlier using the Release plugin. From the local checkout of Centrepoint, edit the topmost POM and change the `<version>` of the `<parent>` as follows:

```
<parent>
  <groupId>com.effectivemaven</groupId>
  <artifactId>effectivemaven-parent</artifactId>
  <version>1</version>
  <relativePath>../effectivemaven-parent/pom.xml</relativePath>
</parent>
```

We need to update its parent to the released version. Otherwise, the release will fail because Continuum will see that it is still dependent on a `SNAPSHOT` version, which is considered unstable.

Likewise, we should change the `license-resources` version:

```
<resourceBundles>
  <resourceBundle>
    com.effectivemaven:license-resources:1.0
  </resourceBundle>
</resourceBundles>
```

Don't forget to commit the changes that you made.

> The Release plugin will not actually detect snapshots in the resource bundles automatically (a limitation we already discovered in Chapter 6, *Useful Maven Plugins*).

Now, let's take a look at the **Project Group Summary** page of our **Centrepoint** project in Continuum. To start the release process, click the **Release** button in the **Group Actions** frame. This takes us to the **Release Goals** page as follows:

Choose Release Goal for Centrepoint

⊙ Prepare project for release
○ Perform project release
| Provide Release Parameters ▾ |

Submit

Notice that the two release stages are listed and the **Prepare project for release** stage is ticked by default. Click the **Submit** button and we should see the **Prepare Project for Release** page.

Prepare Project for Release

⊟ **Release Prepare Parameters**

SCM Username:	
SCM Password:	
SCM Tag*:	centrepoint-1.0
SCM Tag Base:	file://localhost/path/to/data/svn/centrepoint/tags
SCM Comment Prefix:	
Preparation Goals*:	clean integration-test
Arguments:	
Build Environment:	▼

☐ Use edit mode

☑ Add a schema to the POM if it was previously missing on release

⊟ **Centrepoint**

Release Version*	1.0
Next Development Version*	1.1-SNAPSHOT

⊞ **Centrepoint Documentation Skin**

Release Version*	1.0
Next Development Version*	1.1-SNAPSHOT

⊞ **Centrepoint Java Modules**

Release Version*	1.0
Next Development Version*	1.1-SNAPSHOT

⊞ **Centrepoint Data Model**

Release Version*	1.0
Next Development Version*	1.1-SNAPSHOT

⊞ **Centrepoint Maven Project Importer**

Release Version*	1.0
Next Development Version*	1.1-SNAPSHOT

Preparing the release requires a couple of parameters to be set as shown above. Quickly running through the form, take notice of the similarities of the required parameters here to those from the Release plugin.

As we don't have authentication configured for our source repository, we will leave the **SCM Username** and **SCM Password** blank.

 Configuring security in a source repository is not within the scope of this book. However, in practice, source repositories *must always be secured.*

The **SCM Tag** is the name of the release tag that will be created in the source repository. You can set a different value from the default, but in our case, we will use the standard convention. Next, the **SCM Tag Base** is the URL or identifier of the source repository where the tag will be created. Continuum determined the default path based on the project's Subversion URL and using the standard structure of having `trunk/`, `tags/`, and `branches/` at the same directory level in the source repository.

The **Preparation Goals** are the goals that will be executed during the prepare stage. In our case, we will be using **clean install** instead of the default **clean integration-test**. The Centrepoint project has inter-dependent modules. Therefore, once the snapshot version has been changed to the released version, Maven will try to resolve these new versions and will look for them in the local repository when it builds the project. These artifacts need to be installed in the local repository so that the project can be built successfully during release preparation.

The **Arguments** are any arguments that we want to add when the preparation goals are executed. It is also possible to use a specific **Build Environment** during the release, but in our case we won't be using one. While not included here, another option to consider is using the build environment we defined in Chapter 8, *Continuum – Ensuring the Health of your Source Code*. You might also consider adding the `checks` profile to the arguments to ensure they pass at release time. We'll take a closer look at building this regularly later in the chapter.

On the lower half of the **Prepare Project for Release** page, each module of our project has its own section with a **Release Version** and **Next Development Version** fields defined for each. These fields are already filled in with their defaults. The **Release Version** field's value contains the current version of the project minus the `SNAPSHOT`, and the current version was incremented by one for the **Next Development Version** field.

We will leave everything other than the preparation goals as it is and submit the form. After doing this, we should be directed to the **Executing Release Goal** page like the one we see in the following screenshot:

	Status	Release Phase
Executing Release Goal		
⚠		update-working-copy
⚠		generate-reactor-projects
⚠		check-poms
⚠		scm-check-modifications
⚠		check-dependency-snapshots
⚠		create-backup-poms
⚠		map-release-versions
⚠		input-variables
⚠		map-development-versions
⚠		rewrite-poms-for-release
⚠		generate-release-poms
⚙		run-release-prepare-goals
⚙		scm-commit-release
⚙		scm-tag
⚙		rewrite-poms-for-development
⚙		remove-release-poms
⚙		scm-commit-development
⚙		end-release
Refresh		

As I'm sure you've already noticed, the release prepare phases executed are similar to that of the prepare stage when using the Release plugin. The only difference is that Continuum has two additional phases at the start: update-working-copy and generate-reactor-projects.

In the update-working-copy phase, Continuum's local checkout of the project is updated in order to get the latest changes from the source repository. In our case, as we are using Subversion, svn update is performed. In the generate-reactor-projects phase, the modules or projects under the group are identified and the build and release order of these projects are determined.

After all of these phases have been executed, we should see the **View Output** link, the **Rollback Changes** button, and the **Done** button afterwards.

> The **Rollback Changes** button is specifically for rolling back the release in cases when you want to abort the release or if something failed somewhere in the release preparation stage. However, this does not remove a release tag (if one was already created) from the source repository. It only reverts the changes made to trunk. You need to explicitly delete the created tag.

To view the output logs of the preparation stage, just click on the **View Output** link and you should be able to see something similar to the following:

To finish the preparation stage, go back to the previous page and click **Done**. We should be brought back to the **Release Goal** page.

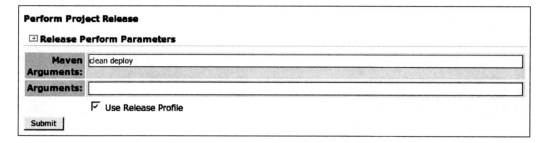

This time the version that we have just prepared for release is available in the list box under **Perform project release**, telling us that the release is now ready to be finalized.

Finalizing a release

To finalize the release, select **Perform project release** with **1.0** selected from the drop-down box and click **Submit**. The next page that should appear is the **Perform Project Release** page where we can provide the **Maven Arguments** (these are actually goals that will be executed during the perform phase). By default, this is set to **clean deploy**. We will be pushing our project to the releases repository so we will use the default goals.

Perform Project Release

⊞ **Release Perform Parameters**

| **Maven Arguments:** | clean deploy |
| **Arguments:** | |

☑ Use Release Profile

Submit

The **Arguments** are the additional arguments that we want to add when the goals are executed. In case you have a customized release profile, you can activate that profile by adding a `-P[PROFILE ID]` in this field.

On the other hand, if you want to activate the inherited release profile from the Maven 2 super POM which we covered earlier in the Maven release process, the **Use Release Profile** checkbox must be ticked. Similar to the Release plugin's behavior, this is enabled by default. Now, let's click the **Submit** button to trigger the release perform process and we should see the following page showing the release perform phases as they are executed.

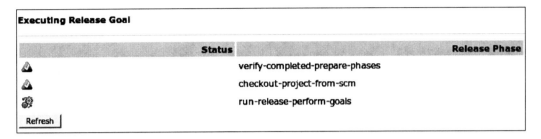

These three phases are the same phases of the perform stage using the Release plugin. Similarly to the release preparation stage, the **View Output** link, the **Rollback Changes** button, and the **Done** button should appear once the last phase has finished executing. Click **Done** and we're finished with the release! You can check our **releases** repository in Archiva for the deployed artifacts.

Continuum and the Release plugin use the same underlying code in the Maven Release component. This is the reason why both have the same release process, their almost similar release preparation, and release perform phases.

Viewing release history

Another advantage of using Continuum for releasing projects is that you will be able to preserve the history of all the project releases done in the server. The summary and output of each release is tracked by Continuum and can be viewed from the web application.

From the **Project Group Summary** page of **Centrepoint**, click the **Release Results** tab and you should be able to see the list and summary of all the project's releases.

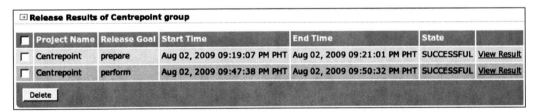

Clicking the **View Result** of one of the release results should show us the output log similar to what we saw when clicking the **View Output** link, after the respective release prepare and release perform phases have been executed during the release.

Other types of releases

There are cases when the modules of a project have different release cycles. To handle these instances, what you can do is to treat your modules as separate projects. You will have to break the multi-module structure where the relationship between the parent and its module is two-way. You need to make the relationship one-way, so the module references the parent. This is similar to how `effectivemaven-parent` and `centrepoint` relate to each other. If you take a quick look at `effectivemaven-parent`'s POM, you would notice that it does not have any `<modules>` configured, but `centrepoint` references it as its `<parent>`. After structuring your projects this way, you should be able to release each one separately.

It is also possible to release only a set of projects within a group. You can do this by clicking the **Release** icon (second column from the left) corresponding to the project you want to release from the **Project Group Summary** page. The condition that its parent and all of its dependencies have been released still applies, so make sure that you are releasing the projects in the correct order.

Troubleshooting releases in Continuum

Not all releases run as smoothly as ours did earlier. We've identified below the usual suspects that may cause you trouble during a release:

- *There is a snapshot dependency found in one of the POMs.* Using plugins with snapshot versions would also block the release. You need to either release the dependency or plugin and upgrade to the released version, or downgrade to the previous released version.

- *The tag base is incorrect.* For example, the `tags/` directory does not exist yet or the structure of the source repository does not conform to the standard layout and the **SCM Tag Base** property was not properly set.

- *The tag already exists.* A bad release was rolled back and the tag was not explicitly removed.

- *Unable to resolve artifacts.* Sometimes the goals to be executed just need to be tweaked. Going back to the release prepare stage in Continuum, we changed the **Release Preparation Goals** from `clean integration-test` to `clean install` so that the dependent modules would be able to see the other modules they depend on and avoid this problem.

- *Unable to deploy to the artifact repository.* The usual causes for this are:
  - ○ The credentials weren't set in the build server's `settings.xml`
  - ○ The repository IDs and the server IDs do not match
  - ○ The user does not have write permission to the deployment repository

- *The build simply failed.* It could be because something went wrong during the execution of your release profile or an additional argument was forgotten in the preparation or perform goals.

- *The pom.xml already exists bug during release perform when using Subversion 1.5.x.* This is a known issue with Subversion and affects the underlying Maven SCM component. You can take a look at `http://jira.codehaus.org/browse/SCM-406` for more understanding of the issue. The easiest workaround is to downgrade Subversion to 1.4.x.

- *Infrastructure problems.* For example, if the source repository suddenly went down or the build server machine's disk is full.

Now that we understand how to use Continuum to release, let's get back to its regularly scheduled builds.

Build pipelining and multiple build definitions

Recall what you have learned about multiple profiles and build pipelining from earlier chapters:

- Where it makes sense, layer advanced optional build features into profiles with increasing scope.
- Run as much as possible in your own environment while keeping the default build fast.

From a best practices perspective, profiles that take a while to build should be put on an integration server. Examples of these profiles are integration tests, Selenium tests, and site generation. In this section, we shall see how to make this work in Continuum.

The Centrepoint project has two profiles configured: `selenium` and `checks`. We will see how we can configure each of them in Continuum.

Make sure that you have the necessary browsers that will be used for the Selenium tests installed in the build server machine. Otherwise, the tests will not run.

First, we will configure the build to run the checks against the source code of the Centrepoint project. We will configure this to execute in a separate schedule from the nightly builds. From the **Schedules** page, add a new schedule and fill it in as follows:

⊞ **Edit Schedule**	
Name*:	TEST_VERIFY_BUILDS
	Enter the name of the schedule
Description*:	Schedule for running checks and tests that executes once a day, at 12nn
	Enter a description of the schedule
Cron Expression:	**Second:** 0
	Minute: 0
	Hour: 12
	Day of Month: *
	Month: *
	Day of Week: ?
	Year [optional]:
	Enter the cron expression. Format is described there : Syntax
Maximum job execution time (seconds)*:	0
	Enter the maximum number of seconds a job may execute in this schedule before it's terminated.
Quiet Period (seconds):	0
	Enter a quiet period period for this schedule
Add Build Queue:	DEFAULT_BUILD_QUEUE
	☑ Enabled
	Enable/Disable the schedule
Save Cancel	

We scheduled it to execute at the middle of the day in between development so that problems in the source code will be caught early on.

Now, return to the **Build Definitions** page of Centrepoint and add a new build definition as follows:

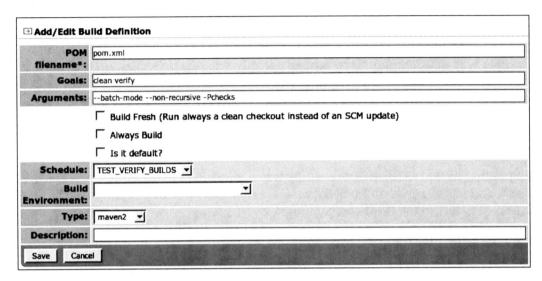

To activate our checks profile, we added the -Pchecks parameter in the **Arguments**. We have also configured the goals to be executed as clean verify as our plugins for verifying the source code are attached to the verify phase.

There is one potential problem with this — if there have not been any recent changes then the build won't occur. To correct this, check the **Always Build** option on the build profile. This will ensure it builds whether there have been SCM changes or not.

If there have been SCM changes, this profile will "steal" the build from the normal process. As this build covers everything the default build would have, this should not be a problem. So, it is a good practice to ensure that this is the case.

Building the Site

The above profile would also be a good time to build the site (before the checks are run), so that any failures can be reviewed visually. If you have a suitable site deployment location already configured, this can be achieved with the goals `clean site-deploy verify`.

The use of multiple schedules and build definitions is one way of build pipelining. Another way in Continuum is by having a totally separate project group for building only a subset of modules as needed. When the modules themselves change, or their dependencies change, the build will be triggered, but the separate group allows us to easily change the scheduling and build definitions for just these special modules. One good example to use here is the `selenium-tests` model from our example application. Let's see how this works.

Notice that the `selenium-tests` module was not included in the release process above and still depends on 1.0-SNAPSHOT. We first need to adjust that value to 1.1-SNAPSHOT in the POM and commit it.

Now, let's add the project to Continuum. As the `selenium-tests` module is not part of the regular build, we will add it in a separate project group. From the **Group Summary** page, create a new project group with the following details.

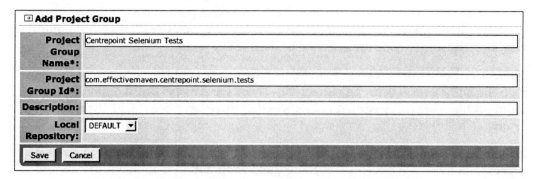

Add the `selenium-tests` module to this project group as we learned in Chapter 8, *Continuum – Ensuring the Health of your Source Code.*

After successfully adding it to the group, go to the **Build Definitions** tab and edit the default build definition. Fill in the form as follows:

⊞ **Add/Edit Build Definition**
POM filename*: pom.xml
Goals: clean test
Arguments: --batch-mode --non-recursive
☐ Build Fresh (Run always a clean checkout instead of an SCM update)
☐ Always Build
☐ Is it default?
Schedule: TEST_VERIFY_BUILDS ▾
Build Environment: ▾
Type: maven2 ▾
Description:
Save   Cancel

We attached the above build definition to the **TEST_VERIFY_BUILDS** schedule as we want it to be executed in the middle of the day as well.

To verify the builds we configured, explicitly execute both of them from their respective build definitions pages. You should be able to see the results for the checks and also Firefox windows being opened and closed as the Selenium tests run.

Since only the `verify` phase is run, you may get an error about missing dependencies on Centrepoint 1.1-SNAPSHOT in some modules. This happens if it hasn't been built using the `install` phase yet—in this case you should run the default build definition before re-running the verification build definition.

Parallel builds

As more projects are added to the build server, the build schedule becomes too crowded, especially if each project takes a while to build. Instead of having hourly builds, you might end up with daily builds (and that is not the best practice).

To remedy this problem, concurrent or parallel builds were implemented in Continuum (beginning at version 1.3). In this section, we will learn how to configure and utilize parallel builds to our advantage.

How it works

Continuum makes use of multiple build queues to build projects concurrently. If you look back at the diagram from Chapter 8, *Continuum – Ensuring the Health of your Source Code*, which shows how project groups, build definitions, schedules, and build queues are related, you will see the two build queues at the bottom. Those two represent parallel builds.

 Projects belonging to the same project group are always queued on the same build queue.

Let's take a look at how it works exactly in the scenario when a scheduled build is triggered.

When a schedule executes, Continuum gathers all the projects attached to that schedule. It then determines the build order of the projects and groups them together based on their interdependencies and project groups. Assuming that we have two build queues available for parallel builds, Continuum will add each group of projects to the build queue which has the least amount of projects queued in it at the time of checking. For example, **Build Queue A** has three projects queued while **Build Queue B** has only two, Continuum will queue the group of projects in **Build Queue B**. If both **Build Queue A** and **Build Queue B** each have three projects queued to them, Continuum will queue the project to whichever of the two comes first in the build queues list attached to the schedule.

Configuring parallel builds

Parallel builds are enabled by default in Continuum. However, this is not obvious because only one build queue is pre-configured. To be able to add a new build queue, we must first set the maximum allowed number of builds to be built in parallel in the **Configuration** page. Change the value of **Number of Allowed Builds in Parallel** field from **1** to **2** then click **Save**.

> There is no limit to the number of allowed builds in parallel but make sure that you consider the capacity of your build server machine. More concurrent builds means more CPU memory and resources used, which may actually make the builds slower.

We will use the builds we have configured in the previous section to demonstrate how parallel builds work.

Let's create a new build queue. Go to the **Continuum - Add/Edit Parallel Build Queue** page by clicking **Build Queue** from the navigation menu and add a new one as follows:

After creating the build queue, go to the **Schedules** page again and edit the **TEST_VERIFY_BUILDS**. Add **BUILD_QUEUE_2** to the schedule as shown below:

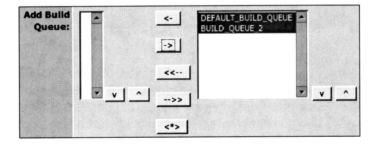

Save the changes. Now, let's try building the **Centrepoint** and **Centrepoint Selenium Tests** project groups by clicking their build icons on the verification build definition from their respective group pages. We can then go to the **Queues** page and see both projects being prepared or in the prepare build queue. After a while you should be able to see the projects in the **Centrepoint** group queued or being built in one of the build queues, while the **Centrepoint Selenium Tests** group is being built in the other build queue similar to what we have below.

⊞ Current Build			
Build Queue	**Project Name**	**Build Definition**	
BUILD_QUEUE_2	Centrepoint Selenium Test Suite	clean test	⚙
DEFAULT_BUILD_QUEUE	Centrepoint	clean verify	⚙

⊞ Build Queue			
■ Build Queue	**Project Name**	**Build Definition**	
☐ DEFAULT_BUILD_QUEUE	Centrepoint Build Resources	clean verify	⚙
☐ DEFAULT_BUILD_QUEUE	Centrepoint Java Modules	clean verify	⚙
☐ DEFAULT_BUILD_QUEUE	Centrepoint Data Model	clean verify	⚙
☐ DEFAULT_BUILD_QUEUE	Centrepoint Data Store API	clean verify	⚙
☐ DEFAULT_BUILD_QUEUE	Centrepoint Data Store (Flat file)	clean verify	⚙
☐ DEFAULT_BUILD_QUEUE	Centrepoint Maven Project Importer	clean verify	⚙
☐ DEFAULT_BUILD_QUEUE	Centrepoint Web Application	clean verify	⚙
☐ DEFAULT_BUILD_QUEUE	Centrepoint Documentation	clean verify	⚙
☐ DEFAULT_BUILD_QUEUE	Centrepoint Distribution	clean verify	⚙
☐ DEFAULT_BUILD_QUEUE	Centrepoint Documentation Skin	clean verify	⚙

Cancel Entries

And that is how to utilize parallel builds!

Even though these projects do depend on each other (with the Selenium tests depending on the web application), they are allowed in parallel as they were placed in separate groups. This can be advantageous as the Selenium tests use different types of resources to the main build and will eventually take much longer. However, be aware that they might be building with an older version of the web application while the main application is still building in the mean time.

One final thing to note about parallel builds is that they don't apply to releasing. Meaning, only one release at a time can be done in Continuum even if there are multiple build queues.

Distributed builds

Project builds can also be distributed among different machines. A few reasons why to distribute your project builds include:

- To build the project in different platforms. Some projects may need to be built on a Windows machine, while others must be built on Linux. You can use distributed builds to accomplish this.

- To lessen the load on the server.

 Parallel builds and distributed builds cannot be used simultaneously. You can either build all projects concurrently in the build server or distribute each build to a build agent.

This feature was implemented at the same time as parallel builds, so it is available starting with Continuum 1.3.

Master and slave

Distributed builds in Continuum are implemented in a master-slave setup. A Continuum instance is the master, while a Continuum build agent is the slave. A **build agent** is a standalone light-weight web application, whose function is simply to build the project(s) dispensed to it by its master. The **master** is the one who distributes the build among the build agents registered to it. They have a one-to-many relationship, where a master can have multiple build agents, but a build agent can only have one master at a time. The master and build agents communicate with each other using the **XML-RPC** protocol.

 The XML-RPC protocol is a specification which allows separate or dispersed applications that may be operating in different environments to communicate with each other through **Remote Procedure Calls (RPC)**. It uses HTTP for transport and XML for encoding. For more details about XML-RPC, visit http://www.xmlrpc.com/.

To give you a high-level view of how distributed builds are designed, look at the descriptive diagram below, which Wendy Smoak prepared for her Continuum talk at ApacheCon EU in March, 2009.

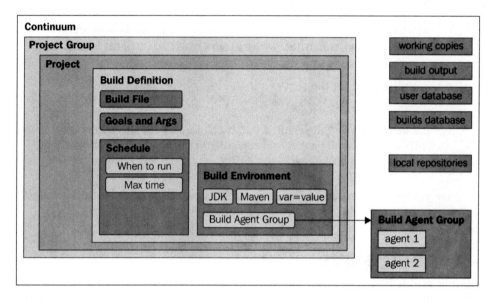

Comparing this with parallel builds, instead of **Build Queues** attached to the **Schedule**, what we have instead are sets of build agents attached to a **Build Environment**. The reason behind this is related to the first reason we identified concerning why we use distributed builds. For example, if you have a master Continuum server running on Linux but you want to test if your project builds on Windows. You can accomplish this simply by:

- Installing a build agent on a Windows box
- Creating a build environment (in the master Continuum instance) specific to a Windows environment, then adding it to a build definition
- Attaching the build agent to the created build environment

Afterwards, you should be able to test if your project builds on Windows by building your project using the build definition, where you attached the build environment.

Configuring distributed builds

Now, let's go through the process of configuring distributed builds in Continuum. The first thing that you need to do is to enable distributed builds. From the **Configuration** page, just tick the **Enable Distributed Builds** checkbox and save the changes. You should be able to see the **Parallel Builds** section replaced by **Distributed Builds** in the navigation menu. Before you can register a build agent to the master Continuum server, you must install a build agent first.

 It is possible to build a project locally to the machine where the master Continuum instance is running by installing a build agent on the same machine where the master is installed. The master Continuum instance will simply treat it as a regular build agent.

In our case, we will install our build agent on our local machine. The steps are no different if you will be installing it to a separate machine.

Download the Continuum Build Agent binaries from `http://continuum.apache.org/download.html`. Unpack it to your build agent machine. By default, the Continuum build agent runs on port 8181. If you want to change it to a different port, just edit `conf/jetty.xml` in the same way as we have done for Continuum previously. This also allows you to install multiple build agents in one machine.

You also need to configure `conf/continuum-build-agent.xml` and add the following fields:

```
<continuum-buildagent-configuration>
  <buildOutputDirectory>
    /path/to/build/agent/data/build-output-directory
  </buildOutputDirectory>
  <workingDirectory>
    /path/to/build/agent/data/working-directory
  </workingDirectory>
  <continuumServerUrl>
    http://localhost:8082/continuum/master-xmlrpc
  </continuumServerUrl>
  <installations>
    <installation>
      <name>Maven 2 Home</name>
      <type>maven2</type>
      <varValue>/path/to/apache-maven-2.2.1</varValue>
    </installation>
  </installations>
</continuum-buildagent-configuration>
```

The first two specify where the build agent would put the build output and where to check out the project it would be building respectively. The `<continuumServerUrl>` is the URL of the master Continuum server. Make sure to replace the base URL with the actual URL you are using. The `/continuum/master-xmlrpc` is necessary to be specified in the URL in order for the master Continuum server to determine that the requests came from a build agent. The `<installations>` contains the list of installations (for example, Maven, JDK, and so on) that are available for use by the build agent.

 Continuum 1.3.3 and earlier contain a bug that was fixed in Continuum 1.3.4. If you are using these versions, you must also copy all the `wagon-XXX.jars` from `apps/continuum/WEB-INF/lib/` in your master Continuum server to the `continuum-build-agent` installation's `apps/continuum-buildagent/WEB-INF/lib/`. This is needed for retrieving parent POMs with snapshot versions. Otherwise, you will not be able to build projects whose parent POM is a snapshot version.

Now, to get the build agent up and running, go to `bin/` and execute:

```
bin$ ./continuum-build-agent console
```

Windows users should execute `continuum-build-agent.bat console` instead.

Once the build agent is started, you can register it in your master Continuum server. In the master Continuum instance, go to the **Build Agent** page and create a new build agent. Fill in the form with the following values:

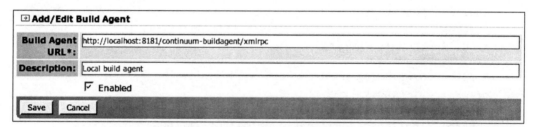

Make sure to replace the base URL of the **Build Agent URL** with the actual value of where your build agent is running.

Now, create a build agent group that will be used with a build environment. For our sample configuration, we will create a **Build Agent Group** for all build agents running on Linux, where we will add the local build agent configured earlier.

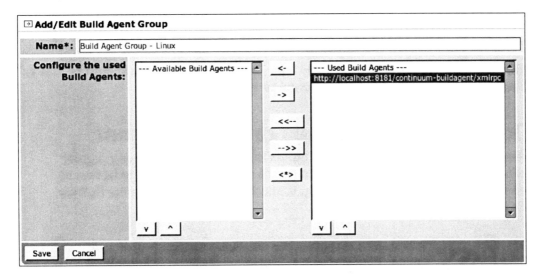

In order to build a project to a specific group of build agents, you need to add the build agent group to a specific build environment.

We will attempt to build our **Centrepoint Selenium Tests** project on the Linux build agent. Create a new build environment named **Linux Build Environment** then add the **Build Agent Group - Linux** to it. Go back to **Centrepoint Selenium Tests Build Definitions** tab and edit the default build definition **clean test**. Set the **Build Environment** to **Linux Build Environment** and save the changes. Now, build the project using this build definition. If you go to the **Queues** page, you should see the **Centrepoint Selenium Tests** project being built in the build agent similar to the following:

⊟ **Current Build**

Project Name	Build Definition Label	Project Group Name	distributedBuild.table.agentUrl	
Centrepoint Selenium Test Suite	Default Maven 2 Build Definition	Centrepoint Selenium Tests	http://localhost:8181/continuum-buildagent/xmlrpc	🔧

⊞ **Build Queue**

Build Queue is empty

⊟ **Current Prepare Build**

No current prepare build

⊞ **Prepare Build Queue**

Prepare Build Queue is empty

The `<scm>` configuration needs to be added to the project's POM in order to avoid encountering this bug in Continuum 1.3.3 during release preparation, using distributed builds: `http://jira.codehaus.org/browse/CONTINUUM-2322`.

After the **Centrepoint Selenium Tests** have finished building, you should be able to view its build results in the master Continuum server.

Doing project releases on a build agent

Releasing a project when distributed builds is enabled is the same as a regular release. The only difference is that you need to specify the **Build Environment** where the specific **Build Agent Group** is attached when providing the **Release Prepare** parameters.

 With distributed builds, you can release multiple project groups simultaneously as long as you are using different build agent groups for each release.

Now, let's try releasing **Centrepoint Selenium Tests**. The first thing that we need to do is to update the version of its parent to the released version. As we already released `Centrepoint 1.0` earlier, we can just flip the `<version>` of the parent POM reference as follows:

```
<parent>
  <artifactId>modules</artifactId>
  <groupId>com.effectivemaven.centrepoint</groupId>
  <version>1.0</version>
</parent>
```

As we updated the parent to the released version, we must add a `<version>` field in the project itself. Otherwise, the parent's released version will be inherited and we will not be able to release the project. We must also update the `<version>` of the `com.effectivemaven.centrepoint:webapp` as it is using the `project.version` property. See the following configuration:

```
<artifactId>selenium-tests</artifactId>
<version>1.0-SNAPSHOT</version>
<name>Centrepoint Selenium Test Suite</name>
<dependencies>
  <dependency>
    <groupId>com.effectivemaven.centrepoint</groupId>
```

```
      <artifactId>webapp</artifactId>
      <version>1.0</version>
      <type>war</type>
      <scope>test</scope>
    </dependency>
  </dependencies>
```

Commit the changes. Go to the **Centrepoint Selenium Tests** project group and start the release process. There's no difference with the regular release process, all you need to do is set the appropriate **Build Environment** in the **Release Prepare** input form. Once the release has started, you can take a look at the **Releases** page (under **Distributed Builds** section in the navigation menu) for the releases currently in progress. It should show which build agent is executing the release and should look similar to this:

⊡ **View Releases**		
Release ID	**Release Goal**	**Build Agent URL**
com.effectivemaven.centrepoint:selenium-tests	prepare	http://localhost:8181/continuum-buildagent/xmlrpc

Before continuing, we should now set the parent and web application versions back to their original values so Continuum will test 1.1-SNAPSHOT.

That's it for Continuum's distributed builds. For further reading on this feature, you can visit the following site:

```
http://continuum.apache.org/docs/1.3.3/administrator_guides/
distributed-builds.html.
```

Maintenance

This section is targeted specifically for administrators and deals with maintaining local repositories and directories used by the running Continuum server.

Configuring multiple local repositories

One of the enhancements recently added to Continuum is the ability to set different local repositories for each project group.

By default, the local repository that Continuum uses is the `<localRepository>` defined in `~/.m2/settings.xml` and if it is not defined, then it uses `~/.m2/repository` under the home directory of the user running Continuum. We can configure other local repositories by adding one from the **Local Repository** page.

⊡ **Add/Edit Local Repository**
Name*:
Location*:
Layout: default ▾
Save   Cancel

As we can see in the screenshot above, the **Name** and **Location** of the local repository is required. Fill in **ALTERNATE_LOCAL** and **<USER_HOME>/.m2/alternate** for these two fields, and select **default** for the layout.

Let's say we want our **Centrepoint** project group to use our alternate repository instead. To do this, we'll just go to the **Project Group Summary**, click the **Edit** button, and set **ALTERNATE_LOCAL** as the **Local Repository** to be used. The next time the build is triggered for our Centrepoint project, Continuum would use the **ALTERNATE_LOCAL** repository to build and install our project.

Why would you want to do this? Consider that you had two different build definitions that were scheduled to run concurrently and you wanted to avoid the builds conflicting with each other in the local repository. By using different local repositories you can ensure they won't conflict. This does come with two drawbacks though. First, both schedules must ensure to completely build all the projects needed (or obtain them from the remote repository), as it won't be able to find them in the local repository as it usually does. Secondly, it will *re-download all of the dependencies* from the remote repository, taking up bandwidth (best solved by using a locally installed repository manager) and disk space. For this reason, you may need to occasionally clean up your local repositories.

Cleaning up local repositories

In the early sections of this chapter, we learned the best practice of *release early, release often*. As more projects are released, more versions are consistently being added and old snapshots of these released artifacts are left in our local repository. We may also have multiple copies of artifacts in multiple local repositories. As time goes by, the size of our local repositories grow. Before we know it, it has consumed a large chunk of our hard disk space.

If our artifacts and dependencies are huge ones, we'll constantly be bothering our system administrators to ask for help in freeing up some disk space. We know how busy these guys are and we wouldn't want to bother them with that now, would we?

Don't worry, because Continuum has a built-in feature of cleaning up its local repositories. All we need to do is configure it and set the schedule for when it should run. Let's take a peek at the **Purge Configurations** page below.

⊟ **Repository Purge Configurations**

Repository	Days Older	Retention Count	Delete All	Delete Released Snapshots	Schedule	Default	Enabled	Description			
DEFAULT	100	2	false	false		true	true		🖉	🖉	✖
ALTERNATE_REPOSITORY	100	2	false	false		true	true		🖉	🖉	✖

Add

⊟ **Directory Purge Configurations**

Directory Type	Days Older	Retention Count	Delete All	Schedule	Default	Enabled	Description			
releases	100	2	false	PURGE_SCHEDULE	false	true	Purge release output directory	🖉	🖉	✖
buildOutput	100	2	false	PURGE_SCHEDULE	false	true	Purge build output directory	🖉	🖉	✖

Add

We can see our two repositories listed with some corresponding figures set. The purge or cleanup can be configured to behave in two ways:

1. Clean up the repository by removing snapshot artifacts older than a specific number of days.
2. Clean up the repository by retaining only a specific number of timestamped artifacts of each snapshot version.

The **Days Older** and **Retention Count** fields signify these two behaviors. In order to activate the purge by **Days Older** behavior, just set the **Days Older** field to a number greater than zero. Otherwise, if you want to activate the purge by **Retention Count** behavior, you must set the **Days Older** field to zero.

The two columns on the right of **Retention Count** are **Delete All** and **Delete Released Snapshots**. The **Delete All** field tells Continuum to wipe out the entire contents of the local repository. On the other hand, the **Delete Released Snapshots** field tells Continuum to remove a snapshot version from the local repository if it sees a released version of the artifact in that local repository.

The remaining fields are self-descriptive so we shall go over each briefly. The **Schedule** field is the schedule of the clean up. This is the same schedule we have learned about in Chapter 8, *Continuum – Ensuring the Health of your Source Code*, and used in build pipelining earlier. We can attach a local repository cleanup to a schedule the same way we attach a build definition.

 It is good practice to have an entirely separate schedule for the purging, so that it would not affect the build. If you use the same schedule for purging and building, it is possible that the maven-metadata.xml is being updated at the same time and Maven would have trouble resolving snapshot artifacts.

The last two fields to take note of for the purging are **Default** and **Enabled**. These two are important if there are multiple purging or cleanup configurations for a local repository. There can only be one default configuration (purging configuration whose **Default** field is set to true) for a local repository and it would be the one used for scheduled purging.

 The purging can also be forced by clicking on the **Purge** icon. It's the one in the middle of the three icons on the rightmost part of the table.

Cleaning up directories

In the earlier sections of this chapter, we learned how to release projects in Continuum. During the release process, Continuum creates a release directory specifically for that release where it keeps the results of the release. This directory, including its contents, is left for viewing and history purposes. The same also goes for the results of each build (called the build results, which we have learned in the previous chapter). They are also kept in a build output directory.

As time goes by, more and more historical data is created each time a build or a release is made. This in turn means more files to fill up our server.

Continuum has got this covered too, so there is no need to worry about it. Going back to the **Purge Configuration** screenshot in the previous section, notice the **Directory Purge Configuration** table. That is the configuration for purging the releases and build output directories. The same configuration and process applies for these as with the repository purging.

Summary

In this chapter, we have discovered the more advanced features of Continuum. We walked through the Maven release process and saw how the same process is also applied in Continuum except that it was quicker to do. We have also learned how to utilize distribute builds and how to build projects concurrently in Continuum. And last but not the least, we learned about its built-in maintenance features and how to make use of them properly.

In the next chapter, we will recall what we have learned about Archiva in Chapter 2, *Staying in Control with Archiva*. We will tackle its more complex features and at the same time, learn how we can utilize them in a project team.

10
Archiva in a Team

A continuation of Chapter 2, *Staying in Control with Archiva*, this chapter showcases the different techniques and ways for getting the best out of using an Archiva repository. We will learn a little bit about access control in Archiva, how to configure and use a virtual repository, and a whole lot about maintenance.

Roles and permissions

In preparation for the latter sections of this chapter, let's familiarize ourselves with the user roles and permissions available in Archiva. The list of available roles can be seen by clicking a user account in **User Management** and then clicking on the **Edit Roles** link.

 Some of the roles in Archiva are resource-based with each repository treated as a resource. This means that access is controlled at the repository level.

There are eight types of roles available in Archiva. They are:

1. **System Administrator**: Provides access to Manage and Administration sections, user administration privileges, and read and write permissions to all repositories.

2. **User Administrator**: Provides access to **User Management** and **User Roles** pages.

3. **Global Repository Manager**: Provides read and write permissions to all repositories.

4. **Global Repository Observer**: Provides read permission to all repositories.

5. **Repository Manager** (resource level): Provides read and write permissions to a given repository.

6. **Repository Observer** (resource level): Provides read permission to a given repository.

7. **Registered User:** The default role assigned to a user who has registered in Archiva.

8. **Guest**: Provides the same permissions that are enabled for the built-in guest user account, which we will discuss later on.

A user assigned with a **Global Repository Manager** or resource level **Repository Manager** role automatically gains the **Global Repository Observer** or resource level **Repository Observer** role respectively.

> Users assigned with a **Repository Manager** role should be able to access the **Find** section as well as **Upload Artifact** and **Delete Artifact** menu in the web application. On the other hand, users with a **Repository Observer** role should only be able to access the **Find** section. Repository-level security applies to each corresponding operation. This means that a user will only be able to search, browse, and upload to or delete artifacts from those repositories that they have permission to access.

When managing roles and permissions, another thing to take note of is the **guest** account. To enable access without authentication for a specific resource or operation, just assign the guest user the appropriate role. By default, the guest user is already assigned the **Repository Observer** role for **internal** and **snapshots** repositories. This allows anyone to be able to browse and search for artifacts from these repositories. If you edit the **guest** user account, you should be able to see the following configuration:

archiva

[Admin] User Roles   Search for: [   ]

Username:	guest
Full Name:	Guest
Email:	

Find

Search

Browse

Manage

Reports

User Management

User Roles

Appearance

Upload Artifact

Delete Artifact

Administration

Repository Groups

Repositories

Proxy Connectors

Legacy Support

Network Proxies

Repository Scanning

Database

redback-xwork-integration-core

Redback XWork Integration Security Core

Assigned Roles:

☑ Guest

Available Roles:

☐ Registered User
☐ System Administrator
☐ User Administrator

Archiva

Available Roles:

☐ Global Repository Manager
☐ Global Repository Observer

Resource Roles:

	Repository Manager	Repository Observer
internal	☐	☑
releases	☐	☐
snapshots	☐	☑

Submit
Reset

As you can see the guest user doesn't yet have read access to the `releases` repository. In our examples, we will assume that the repository will be available to everyone that can access Archiva. So to make this consistent with the `snapshots` repository, check the **Repository Observer** box for `releases` and submit the form.

You can see for yourself how the guest account works by logging out of Archiva and clicking **Browse** on the navigation menu. The artifacts that were requested and were downloaded to our proxy repository from the previous chapters should be visible in the **Browse** page, similar to what is seen in the following screenshot:

As we work through the rest of the chapter, we will cover a few more things about access control in Archiva. Now that we are familiar with the security basics, we are ready to tackle some of the more advanced features of Archiva.

In Chapter 2, *Staying in Control with Archiva*, we configured the `internal` repository to act as a proxy cache for the remote repositories such as: `central`, `maven2-repository.dev.java.net`, and `jboss.repo`. In the next section, we will learn additional techniques for configuring our Archiva repositories.

Introducing repository groups

In Archiva 1.1, the concept of **repository groups** (also known as virtual repositories) was introduced. Taking the meaning of the term *virtual* literally, these repositories are physically non-existent repositories. A virtual repository is simply a URL which gives a single interface to a group of managed repositories.

Let's visualize this with a simple scenario. For example, we have a Maven 2 project which has dependencies on artifacts that reside in multiple repositories. In this case, we will assume that we have a nearby proxy cache configured in Archiva for each of them. (You can refer back to Hooking up Maven with Archiva from Chapter 2, *Staying in Control with Archiva*, on how to do this). Given this scenario, it would mean that we have to configure each of these repositories in our `settings.xml` (or POM), in order for us to get the needed artifacts and to be able to build our project. If these repositories are secured, we also need to configure our credentials for each. This leaves us with a long (and possibly messy) `settings.xml`. Remember, a messy configuration is an attraction for errors.

To avoid this problem, we can make use of repository groups in Archiva. We can create a repository group and configure or add multiple repositories under that group. So when an artifact request is made (for example, by Maven) using the repository group URL, the repositories underneath it will be searched until the requested artifact is found and returned to the client.

The following section teaches us how to configure repository groups and experience their strength first-hand.

Configuring and using repository groups

We shall be continuing to use the Centrepoint project from the sample for Chapter 9, *Continuum in Depth*.

Before jumping into configuration, it is good to see how it will be without the aid of repository groups. In Chapter 9, *Continuum in Depth*, we released the organization POM Apache Maven 2: Effective Implementations Book and deployed it to the releases repository in Archiva. As the Centrepoint project refers to that released version, anyone who builds that project must be able to get the organization POM from the releases repository. This is a perfect setup for using repository groups. Let's begin by wiping out our local repository again and building the Centrepoint project.

```
centrepoint$ mvn clean install
```

The build should fail with the following error:

```
[INFO] Scanning for projects...
Downloading: http://localhost:8081/archiva/repository/internal/com/
effectivemaven/effectivemaven-parent/1/effectivemaven-parent-1.pom
[INFO] ------------------------------------------------------------
[ERROR] FATAL ERROR
[INFO] ------------------------------------------------------------
[INFO] Failed to resolve artifact.
GroupId: com.effectivemaven
ArtifactId: effectivemaven-parent
Version: 1
Reason: Unable to download the artifact from any repository
  com.effectivemaven:effectivemaven-parent:pom:1
from the specified remote repositories:
  internal (http://localhost:8081/archiva/repository/internal)
```

Our organization POM cannot be found because it resides in the Archiva releases repository, and we don't have it configured in our settings.xml. The version in ../effectivemaven-parent/pom.xml is also not used because the versions now differ. To get past this problem, we must add the following configuration in the settings.xml:

```
<profiles>
  <profile>
    <id>repositories</id>
    <activation>
      <activeByDefault>true</activeByDefault>
    </activation>
    <repositories>
```

```
    <repository>
      <id>releases</id>
      <name>Archiva Managed Releases Repository</name>
      <url>
        http://localhost:8081/archiva/repository/releases
      </url>
      <releases>
        <enabled>true</enabled>
      </releases>
      <snapshots>
        <enabled>false</enabled>
      </snapshots>
    </repository>
  </repositories>
  </profile>
</profiles>
```

We already configured the `<server>` credentials for the `releases` repository in Chapter 2, *Staying in Control with Archiva*, when we tried deploying to Archiva using Maven so we no longer need to configure that.

If you try building Centrepoint again, the build will still fail. Notice that Maven didn't even seem to try looking for the artifact from the `releases` repository we added previously. This is because we have locked down Maven to use only the local mirror repository `internal`. This is the effect of the `<mirrorOf>*</mirrorOf>` configuration in our `settings.xml` which we did in Chapter 2, *Staying in Control with Archiva*. Just change it to `<mirrorOf>*,!releases</mirrorOf>` so that Maven would respect the additional repositories.

Execute the build again. This time we should be able to get a successful build.

However, for every member of the team working on the Centrepoint project, the `settings.xml` (now over 40 lines long) is needed at the minimum. As the project grows bigger, more artifacts are added. Also, if these new artifacts are located in other repositories, you would need to add this repository to your `settings.xml` and so on and so forth.

We already learned at the start of this section that in situations such as this, a repository group can make things easier for us developers. Let us see how we can create one.

Let's go back to our running Archiva instance. Click **Repository Groups**, then type `public` in the **Identifier** field on the upper right-hand corner of the page and click **Add Group**. We now have a virtual repository named **public** with the following URL: `http://localhost:8081/archiva/repository/public`.

You may change the name of the repository group to a more appropriate one if the repositories are not really for public consumption.

To add managed repositories under the group, just select the repository you would like to add from the list under the created group and click **Add Repository**. Add the `releases` and `internal` repositories (this order is used so that requests for the organization's artifacts are never made on external proxied repositories). Note that we don't want to add the `snapshots` repository to the group as that might change the behavior of the repository. One example of this is when dealing with version ranges. You might end up getting a snapshot version instead of a released version.

Now, with this configuration, we are telling Archiva that if an artifact request is made on the repository group **public**, it should look for the artifact in these two repositories (based on the order they are listed) and return the first matching artifact it sees.

 You can change the ordering of the repositories to be searched by moving a repository up or down the repository group configuration via the **Up** and **Down** icons.

After configuration, the page should look similar to the following:

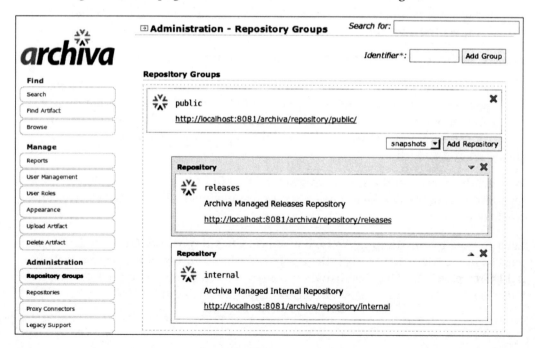

Now that we have a repository group that we can use, let's configure it in our
`settings.xml`. Remove the profile we added previously, and adjust the mirror
section as follows:

```
<mirrors>
  <mirror>
    <id>public</id>
    <url>http://localhost:8081/archiva/repository/public</url>
    <mirrorOf>*</mirrorOf>
  </mirror>
</mirrors>
```

Notice how much shorter and simpler our `settings.xml` is now.

Group credentials

The guest user has access to all of the repositories in the group so we
don't need a corresponding `<server>` for the mirror. However, if read
access control applies to any repositories in the group, make sure to add
a `<server>` for the ID of the mirror (not the underlying repositories
that are no longer visible to Maven). The existing `<server>` definitions
continue to be used for deployment, as deployment cannot be done to
a group.

Let's try building Centrepoint again, but this time with a clean local repository,
using the new `settings.xml`. We should be able to see both `com.effectivemaven:`
`effectivemaven-parent:pom:1` and the other dependencies from the central
repository being retrieved from our `public` repository group, ending with a
successful build as follows:

```
[INFO] Scanning for projects...
Downloading: http://localhost:8081/archiva/repository/public//com/
effectivemaven/effectivemaven-parent/1/effectivemaven-parent-1.pom
1K downloaded
[INFO] Reactor build order:
...
[INFO] ------------------------------------------------------------
[INFO] Building Centrepoint
[INFO]    task-segment: [clean, install]
[INFO] ------------------------------------------------------------
Downloading: http://localhost:8081/archiva/repository/public//org/apache/
maven/plugins/maven-clean-plugin/2.2/maven-clean-plugin-2.2.pom
3K downloaded
Downloading: http://localhost:8081/archiva/repository/public//org/apache/
maven/plugins/maven-plugins/10/maven-plugins-10.pom
```

What else can we do with repository groups? Consider, for example, that we added new dependencies to our Centrepoint project and these dependencies are projects being worked on by another team within the company. Let's say the other team have their own deployment repository (separate from ours) managed by Archiva as well. We no longer have need to make any changes in our `settings.xml` (or POM). The repository just needs to be added in the **public** repository group and the appropriate permissions assigned to the Centrepoint project developers' accounts.

Configuration is much simpler now and is concentrated in Archiva itself. Developers and team members won't have to configure their `settings.xml` each time a new repository is needed.

RSS feeds—discovering new artifacts in your repository

RSS has become the de facto standard with regard to news feeds and updates on the web. The Archiva community has seen how the project can take advantage of this current trend by providing RSS feeds for new artifacts in the repository. Projects that use or depend on specific libraries would be able to know when a new release is available or when there is a new build. This is especially useful when a project is dependent on a fix that would be available in the next release or in the next build.

 A **Repository Observer** role is required at least in order to subscribe to a feed in Archiva.

There are two levels of RSS feeds available in Archiva: **repository level** and **artifact level**. In the following sections, we will be using Thunderbird's RSS feed reader for demonstration purposes. You can get Thunderbird from `http://www.mozillamessaging.com/en-US/thunderbird/` and can set it up using the installation guides at `http://www.mozillamessaging.com/en-US/support/`. You can also use other RSS feed readers such as Google Reader. If access to your repositories require authentication, your feed reader must support authentication. If security is lenient, you can just disable authentication for read operations to your repository by granting the guest account the **Repository Observer** role.

Repository level feeds

Repository level feeds notify subscribed users of new artifacts found in
the repository. To subscribe to a repository level feed, first go to `http://`
`localhost:8081/archiva/admin/repositories.action` (**Repositories** page).

Unfortunately, at the time of writing, only system administrators are able to access
this page so you must log in to Archiva using the `admin` account we created in
Chapter 2, *Staying in Control with Archiva*, if you have not already done that.

From this page, you can right-click on the RSS feed icon on the upper righthand
corner of repository `snapshots` configuration and copy the link location.

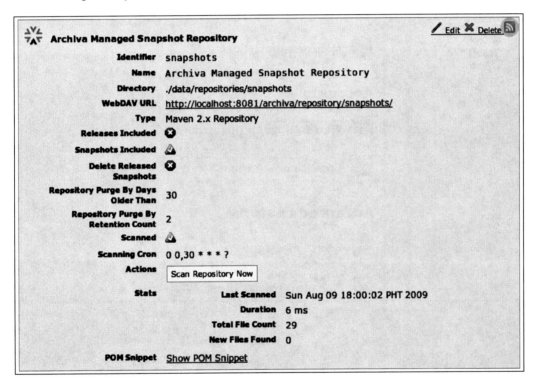

If you have not created an account for your RSS feeds in Thunderbird, go to
File | New | Account... in the top menu. Select **RSS News & Blogs** then click **Next**.
Use the default **Account Name "News & Blogs"**, click the **Next** button then **Finish**.
A folder with the same name as the **Account Name** should appear on the left pane,
similar to the one in the following screenshot:

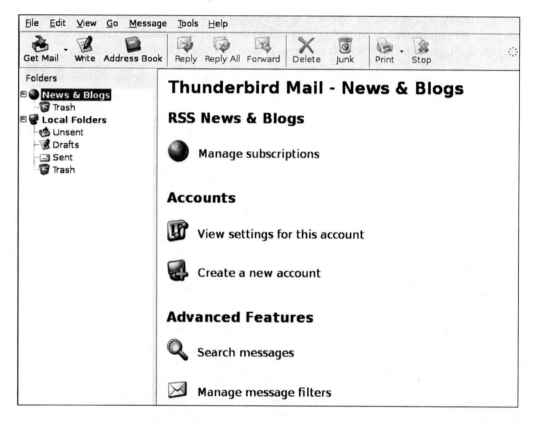

Under the **RSS News & Blogs** link seen in the previous screenshot, click **Manage subscriptions**. Add a new RSS subscription for the snapshots repository by pasting the URL we copied in step two into the **Feed URL** field.

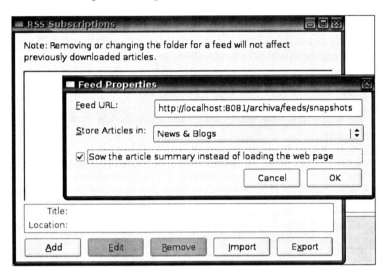

The feed subscription to the snapshots repository should immediately appear under the **News & Blogs** folder. Clicking on the feed should yield something similar to the following:

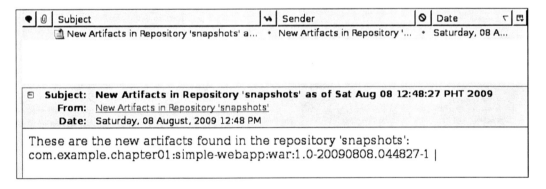

Notice that the feed in the previous screenshot shows the subject line **New Artifacts in Repository 'snapshots' as of Sat Aug 08 12:48:27 PHT 2009**. The date corresponds to the date and time of an execution of the repository scan. It is during this scanning when new artifacts in the repository are discovered. When the reader updates or checks for new feeds, Archiva gets all the new artifacts found (if there are any) during each execution of the repository scanner and sends them back as multiple entries to the feed reader.

Artifact level feeds

In contrast to repository level feeds, artifact level feeds notify subscribed users of new versions of a specific artifact deployed or discovered in the repository. You can use this if you want finer grained notifications or if you are interested only in a specific artifact. This is useful when you're waiting for certain project dependencies to be released as it can provide you immediate notification once the release is available in the repository. You can also use this to be notified of newly deployed builds for purposes such as QA testing or simply for development.

Now, let's say we want to know when there are new builds of the Centrepoint distribution available.

This time we start by logging in to Archiva and going to the **Browse** page.

Click on the group **com.effectivemaven.centrepoint** to view the artifacts under the group. You should see the different Centrepoint projects listed, each with a corresponding RSS feed icon beside it:

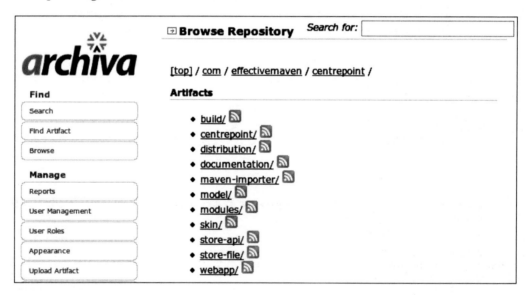

Again we can right-click the RSS feed icon next to **distribution** and copy the link location.

Finally, we go back to Thunderbird and add it as a new feed under **News & Blogs**, the same way we added the feed for the snapshots repository earlier. Check that the feed URL you copied is: http://localhost:8081/archiva/feeds/com. effectivemaven.centrepoint/distribution. The artifact path in the URL distinguishes this feed from the repository feed.

After the feed is added in Thunderbird, clicking on the feed should display text identical to the following:

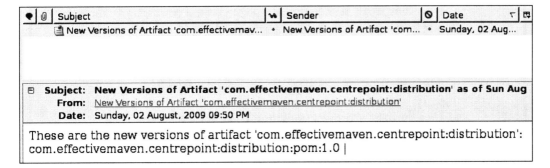

Similar to the behavior of repository level feeds, when the reader updates or checks for new feeds, information about newly found versions of the artifact in the Archiva repositories will be sent back to the feed reader.

Let's try deploying a new snapshot of `Centrepoint Distribution`. Go to your local checkout of Centrepoint and execute the following from the command-line:

```
centrepoint$ mvn clean deploy
```

After the project is deployed, go back to Thunderbird and force it to update the feed for `Centrepoint Distribution`. You should see a new entry appear in its corresponding folder.

So far, with Archiva, all we have been talking about is the end-user functionality like deploying and discovering new artifacts in the repositories. The next sections discuss the other side of the spectrum—the administrator functionality.

Deleting artifacts in your repository

Sometimes the need for deleting artifacts from the repository arises. For example, if an artifact was deployed by accident to the repository or the artifact has already been released but an old snapshot version is still available. In Archiva, there are different ways of deleting artifacts from the repository—through WebDAV, via the web application, through the scheduled repository purging, or by directly deleting it in the file system.

It is not recommended that artifacts be deleted directly from the file system. Not only does it require access to the server itself, it is also prone to error. Artifacts that should not be deleted could be deleted by mistake. In case you still want to directly delete an artifact from the file system, all files related to the artifact such as *metadata files* and *checksums* must also be deleted. The repository must be scanned as well in order to update the metadata files. This can be done by clicking the **Scan Repository Now** button of the repository configuration in the **Repositories** page. The database scanning also needs to be explicitly executed to immediately remove the deleted artifact from the database.

One of the advantages of using the **Delete Artifact** form in the web application is that you do not need to have direct access to the server. All you need is the required Archiva permissions, which come with the **Repository Manager** role (without the permissions **Delete Artifact** will not be visible in the navigation menu). Another advantage is that the repository scanning no longer needs to be explicitly executed as Archiva already executes the repository and database scanning consumers to update the index and the database for you.

Now, let's try deleting an old artifact from one of the repositories. You may recall how in Chapter 9, *Continuum in Depth,* when we went through Continuum's release process that we released Centrepoint 1.0. If you go to `http://localhost:8081/archiva/repository/snapshots/com/effectivemaven/centrepoint/centrepoint`, the old `1.0-SNAPSHOT` version of the project still exists. We will remove this artifact from the repository using the delete artifact web form.

First, click **Delete Artifact** from the navigation menu and then fill in the form as follows:

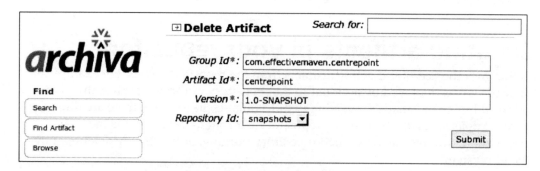

Click the **Submit** button. After the artifact has been deleted, you should see the confirmation message **Artifact 'com.effectivemaven.centrepoint:centrepoint:1.0-SNAPSHOT' was successfully deleted from repository 'snapshots'**. If you browse the repository at `http://localhost:8081/archiva/repository/snapshots`, the related artifacts such as the POM, `maven-metadata.xml`, and the checksums were also deleted.

To delete artifacts through WebDAV, just open the repository using a WebDAV client and delete the artifact like in a regular file system. As for the scheduled repository purging, we will discuss this in the following sections.

We have tackled the subjects of repository groups, RSS feeds, and deleting artifacts in the repository. This chapter would never be complete without covering repository maintenance. The succeeding sections will be all about that.

The Archiva reports

Archiva generates two types of reports. These are the *repository statistics*, providing information such as statistical data of a repository's content and the *repository health* report, which makes us aware of any problems in the repository such as artifacts that have invalid POM files. Both accept different criteria for customizing the generated output as seen in the following screenshot:

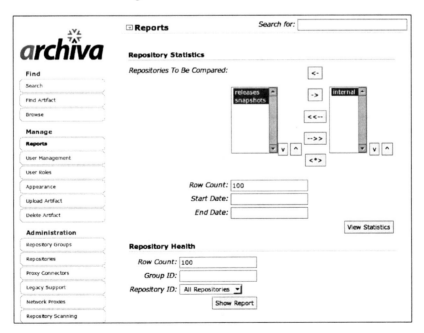

Now, let's discuss the configuration for each report.

Repository statistics

This report provides statistical repository information such as the total number of artifacts in the repository, its total size, the number of plugins in the repository, and the likes based on a given repository scan execution time. This report can be used for analyzing the current content of your repositories, and tracking its growth, usage, and evolution over time. The report can be constrained by the given **Start Date** and **End Date**. If no **Start Date** and **End Date** are provided, all statistics right from the start up to the current date will be included in the report (to a maximum of the number of rows given in the **Row Count**).

For the **Repository Statistics**, we can also configure the **Repositories To Be Compared**. If only one repository is selected in **Repositories To Be Compared**, the generated report will contain details of a single repository. The following is a sample report where only one repository is selected:

⊡ **Statistics Report**   *Search for:*

◀◀ **1** ▶▶

Export to CSV

⊡ **Statistics for Repository 'internal'**

Date of Scan	Total File Count	Total Size	Artifact Count	Group Count	Project Count	Plugins	Archetypes	Jars	Wars	Deployments	Downloads
Mon Aug 10 23:00:02 PHT 2009	4083	25821233	664	63	204	23	0	161	0	0	0
Mon Aug 10 22:00:33 PHT 2009	4083	25821233	664	63	204	23	0	161	0	0	0
Mon Aug 10 18:00:03 PHT 2009	4083	25821233	664	63	204	23	0	161	0	0	0
Mon Aug 10 17:00:01 PHT 2009	4083	25821233	664	63	204	23	0	161	0	0	0
Mon Aug 10 16:00:02 PHT 2009	4083	25821233	664	63	204	23	0	161	0	0	0
Mon Aug 10 15:00:02 PHT 2009	4083	25821233	664	63	204	23	0	161	0	0	0
Mon Aug 10 14:00:01 PHT 2009	4083	25821233	664	63	204	23	0	161	0	0	0
Mon Aug 10 13:00:01 PHT 2009	4083	25821233	664	63	204	23	0	161	0	0	0
Mon Aug 10 12:00:01 PHT 2009	4083	25821233	664	63	204	23	0	161	0	0	0

Let's run through the contents of the sample **Repository Statistics** report given previously for repository `internal`. The **Total File Count** pertains to the total number of files in the repository during each execution of the repository scan. The **Total Size**, on the other hand, is the size (in bytes) of the repository at that time. The number of unique groups and artifact names are broken down in the report as well as the number of plugins, archetypes, JAR, and WAR files.

 The last two columns — number of deployments and artifact requests — are not yet implemented but will be fixed in the future releases.

On the other hand, if more than one repository is selected in the **Repositories To Be Compared**, the generated report would contain a comparison of the latest statistics of the repositories based on the specified **End Date**. This is useful for tracking which repositories are the most utilized. For example, if different development groups host their own repositories, the comparison can show which groups are using the most space. Look at the following screenshot for a sample comparison report to see the difference from the previous one:

⊞ **Statistics Report**   *Search for:*

◀◀ **1** ▶▶

Export to CSV

⊟ **Latest Statistics Comparison Report**

Repository	Total File Count	Total Size	Artifact Count	Group Count	Project Count	Plugins	Archetypes	Jars	Wars	Deployments	Downloads
internal	4083	25821233	664	63	204	23	0	161	0	0	0
releases	155	15870075	22	2	12	0	0	6	1	0	0
snapshots	37	35231	2	1	1	0	0	0	1	0	0

To allow you to view this report outside of the web application, the report can be exported as a CSV file by clicking on the **Export to CSV** link. You should be able to open the exported file as an Excel spreadsheet.

Repository health

One of the secrets behind a successful and reproducible build is a clean and healthy repository. Corrupt metadata or an invalid or missing POM file are the usual causes for a build to break. To prevent this from happening, we must ensure that the repositories we are getting our artifacts from are in good health.

Archiva provides a way of doing this through the Repository Health report and its built-in utilities for updating metadata and fixing checksums. The **Repository Health** report provides a detailed list of artifacts in the repository that are found to be defective. It gives a starting point for correcting any problems and can be used when diagnosing build errors with a particular artifact.

For example, a common reason for an artifact being defective is when the version of the artifact specified in the POM is different from the actual version in its filename. This could easily happen when using `deploy:deploy-file` (or even using the Archiva web upload form) as the actual filename used for the uploaded artifact is determined based on the supplied parameters. It is a possibility that the included POM in the upload has different coordinates from the provided parameters. These defects are discovered during Archiva's database scan, when the actual POM file is read and added to the database. We can narrow down the report by providing a specific **Group ID** and/or a **Repository ID** which will be used for querying defective artifacts that match these criteria. If you try querying for the report using the default configuration, you should be able to see a generated report similar to the following one, which shows a defective POM in repository **internal**.

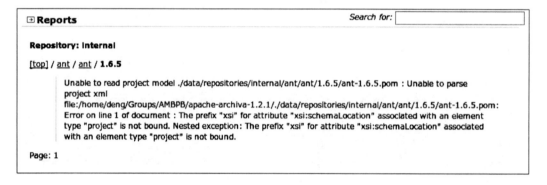

To repair such an error, you can manually fix the POM in the Archiva repository by updating it in the file system. If the defect is caused by a transfer error when the artifact was proxied, you can delete the artifact (including the metadata and checksums) then force Archiva to retrieve it again by requesting it.

A word of caution though—*making these changes could affect the reproducibility of a dependent project's build*. For example, it is possible that the actual artifact in the central repository is the defective one. If you fixed the artifact in your `internal` Archiva repository, project builds that go through the local proxy may get a successful build. However, the project is built directly off central and the build fails because the dependency artifact is defective.

That summarizes monitoring the health of our repositories. The next section discusses the built-in Archiva utilities which in one way or another clean up and repair broken artifacts and metadata in the repositories.

The Archiva consumers

We've talked a little about consumers in Chapter 2, *Staying in Control with Archiva*. In this section, we'll go into the details about what they really are.

What is a consumer?

A **consumer** is a plugin-like component in Archiva. When repositories are scanned or changes to the repository are made, they are able to process the change to keep the rest of the system up to date and perform any other necessary operations. Some examples of these operations are—indexing, repository clean up, adding of artifact information to the database, and fixing metadata.

There are basically two types of consumers in Archiva. These are the **repository consumers** and the **database consumers**. The former are attached to the repository scanning and are executed on each artifact processed from the file system. On the other hand, the latter are executed on each artifact in the database when the database scanning is triggered. The list of available repository consumers is displayed at the bottom section of the **Repository Scanning** page, while the database consumers are listed in the **Database Scanning** page. Administrators can enable and disable the consumers to be executed in these respective pages.

Archiva's maintenance-savvy consumers

The consumers that we'll be tackling in this section are those that do maintenance work. We will only cover the four major consumers concerned with this kind of task: the `repository-purge`, `metadata-updater`, `create-missing-checksums`, and `database-cleanup` consumers.

Purging outdated snapshots

The main purpose of the `repository-purge` consumer is cleansing the repositories of old snapshot artifacts. It can be configured to clean up the repository based on two criteria: **by the age of a snapshot artifact** and **by retention count**. You will have noticed these configuration options on the repository configuration pages—enabling this consumer will put them into action. If the former criteria are used, the last modified date of the artifact is checked to see if it is older by that number of days from the current date, and if so, then the artifact will be deleted. Otherwise, if the latter criteria are used, we can be rest assured that there will always be the given number of artifacts retained for each snapshot version of an artifact and any older artifacts will be deleted.

You can also use the criteria together. If we set the **Repository Purge By Days Older Than** to 100 and the **Repository Purge By Retention Count** to **2**, then there will always be two artifacts for each snapshot version retained in the repository. The rest of the artifacts for that snapshot version will be deleted, if and only if their last modified date is older than 100 days from the current date.

If we want to specifically use the by retention count criteria, we need to set the **Repository Purge By Days Older Than** to zero. For example, if we set the **Repository Purge By Retention Count** to one and the **Repository Purge By Days Older Than** to zero, then for every snapshot version there will always be one artifact (the most recently deployed) retained and the rest of the artifacts for that snapshot version will be deleted regardless of its age.

Let's try out purging by retention count. We will be using our Centrepoint project again for this demonstration. First, we need to deploy a few snapshot builds of the projects which we will be purging later on.

From the sample code we were working with earlier, deploy the project to the snapshots repository at least twice:

centrepoint$ mvn deploy

If we look at the Centrepoint distribution in `http://localhost:8081/archiva/ repository/snapshots/com/effectivemaven/centrepoint/distribution/ 1.1-SNAPSHOT/`, we should see something similar to what is shown in the following:

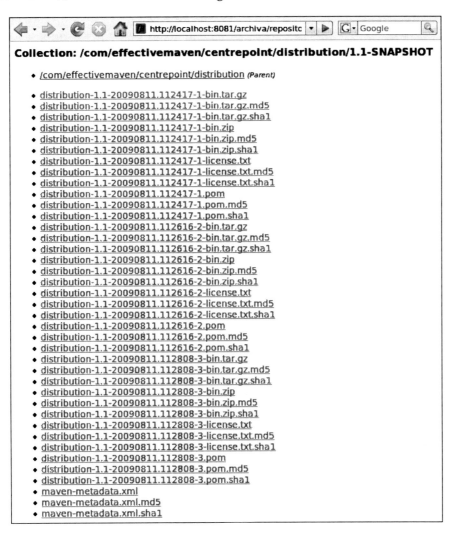

The repository purging is not enabled by default in Archiva. To turn it on, go to the **Repository Scanning** tab and select it from the checklist at the bottom of the screen, then press **Update Consumers**. Due to a bug in Archiva 1.2.1, you may need to restart the server for this to take effect.

The next step is to configure the repository purge by retention count. Edit the **snapshots** repository configuration and set **Repository Purge By Days Older Than** to zero (0) to disable that criteria. Retain the **Repository Purge By Retention Count** to two (2). Save the changes then execute the repository scanning by clicking the **Scan Repository Now** button. After the repository scan finishes its execution, refresh `http://localhost:8081/archiva/repository/snapshots/com/effectivemaven/centrepoint/distribution/1.1-SNAPSHOT/`. This time, you should only see the last two builds (the artifacts with `-2` and `-3` as build numbers) as we told the `repository-purge` consumer we only want to retain two builds of each snapshot version of an artifact for the `snapshots` repository.

Now, going back to the screenshot of the **snapshots** repository configuration earlier, notice the **Delete Released Snapshots** checkbox near the bottom. This field is also another configuration for the `repository-purge` consumer. When it is enabled, if a released version for a given snapshot is found (in any Archiva managed repository), all of the snapshots will be removed. We will again use the Centrepoint artifacts as examples here. In the earlier section — Deleting artifacts in your repository — we only removed `com.effectivemaven.centrepoint:centrepoint:pom:1.0-SNAPSHOT`. Browsing to `http://localhost:8081/archiva/repository/snapshots/com/effectivemaven/centrepoint/` shows us that the other Centrepoint `1.0-SNAPSHOT` artifacts are still in the `snapshots` repository even though `1.0` has already been released. We will use the **Delete Released Snapshots** feature to automatically remove these old snapshot artifacts.

Now, edit the `snapshots` repository configuration and tick the **Delete Released Snapshots** checkbox, then save the changes. As done earlier, execute the repository scanner. After a while, if we check the `snapshots` repository again we will notice that the old `1.0-SNAPSHOT` Centrepoint artifacts are now gone.

Correcting Maven metadata

The `metadata-updater` consumer is used specifically for updating and fixing the `maven-metadata.xml` files in the repository. This is very useful in cases when artifacts are deleted from the file system and the metadata files weren't updated. When this consumer is executed during the repository scan, artifact metadata files are updated and fixed based on the actual versions of an artifact that is physically present in the file system.

Correcting metadata only affects reproducibility if ranges or automatic plugin versioning are used. In those cases, reproducibility is likely to be affected over time anyway as pointed out in Chapter 7, *Maven Best Practices*. For this reason, it is usually a good idea to enable this consumer on your repositories.

Creating missing checksums

The `create-missing-checksums` consumer is simply for generating checksum files, both MD5 and SHA-1, for artifacts with missing checksum files. It also fixes incorrect checksums that it finds during repository scanning.

This can be useful if you have a number of problems with incorrect checksums, or if you want them to be auto-corrected on deployment. However, caution is needed. If it is possible that the checksum was actually correct and the *artifact* has been modified, this will remove the ability to detect it (which is a more serious problem!).

Database cleanup consumers

There are three consumers that perform internal Archiva clean up: `not-present-remove-db-artifact`, `not-present-remove-db-project` and `not-present-remove-indexed`. These three are used for cleaning up the database of artifact and POM information, and cleaning up the index of artifacts that have been removed or no longer present in the file system, respectively. After these consumers are executed, deleted artifacts should no longer appear in the web application **Browse** and **Search**.

If you find that you receive stale information in the web interface, ensure these consumers are enabled and re-scan the repositories.

Summary

In this chapter, we have learned about the different roles and permissions in Archiva. We've also learned about repository groups and a couple of techniques on how to configure them.

Other features provided by Archiva such as RSS feeds and artifact deletion were covered, while the last parts of the chapter were dedicated to maintenance. We'll learn more about enterprise needs of Archiva in Chapter 12, *Maven, Archiva and Continuum in the Enterprise*, but next we will cover another important team topic — Archetypes.

11
Archetypes

Throughout the previous chapters of the book, we have been using a few of the Maven archetypes, such as the Quickstart archetype and the Webapp archetype, to construct our sample project Centrepoint. In this chapter, we will cover archetypes in more detail. We will see how useful these little things are and learn how each of them works. We will also learn about custom archetypes and even write our own archetype as an exercise.

What are Maven archetypes?

Wikipedia defines an **archetype** as follows:

> *An archetype is an original model of a person, ideal example, or a prototype after which others are copied, patterned, or emulated.*

This definition is also applicable to Maven's concept of archetypes. A Maven archetype is simply a template of a Maven project.

Recalling what we have learned in the earlier chapters, we know that a Maven project has a specific directory structure. There are different directories for sources, tests, resource files, and more. Depending on what we need, we have to create some (or all) of these directories by hand. A Maven archetype makes this easier for us. It creates the directory structure and default files for us in just one command.

However, even though Maven projects are usually consistent, they are not always the same. Each type of package contains a different set of content. For example, a full J2EE project uses a different directory structure for its source and configuration files from a simple web application. To make things easier (and quicker) for us, a Maven archetype is available for different types of packages. These archetypes have different structures, configuration files, and default POM configuration depending on what type it is. Some of the available archetypes are for creating Maven plugins, J2EE projects, web applications, AppFuse projects, and more. We will learn about them in the succeeding sections.

Benefits of Maven archetypes

As the archetypes conform to Maven's standard directory layout, they also implement best practices. One good example of this is the Maven Quickstart Archetype which, when used, creates both the source and test directories suggesting to users that they write unit tests. A default main class with a corresponding test class is included in the generated project to illustrate the right location to place the source files.

A few years ago, I conducted Maven 2 training for a group of instructors at one of the smaller schools here in Manila. While I was discussing the standard directory layout that Maven implements, one of the participants made fun of how deep the directory structure was. We hadn't gotten to the demo/hands-on part yet so the participants hadn't actually seen Maven in action. I just couldn't resist it, so I opened the terminal in my laptop and showed them how I can create that directory layout I've been droning on with just one command. That simple Maven show off did the trick for them.

What the participant made fun of was actually true. Maven has a deep directory structure, but aside from the obvious time savings in creating it automatically, being able to create an error-free and consistent structure is one of the reasons why the Maven archetypes were born.

Generating projects

The Archetype plugin makes it possible for Maven to create Maven projects from a template. Let's start with the most popular goal of the plugin which is archetype:generate.

From archetype:create to archetype:generate

In the previous releases of the Maven Archetype plugin, Maven projects were created from archetypes using the archetype:create goal. When using the archetype:create goal, you needed to know and provide all of the information about the archetype plus the values you want to use on the command line. For example:

```
mvn archetype:create -DgroupId=com.effectivemaven.chapter11 \
    -DartifactId=sample-app -Dversion=1.0-SNAPSHOT \
    -DpackageName=com.effectivemaven.chapter11.sample \
    -DarchetypeArtifactId=maven-archetype-webapp
```

It's easy to know this if we're using an archetype we created, but what if we're not? We have to hunt through the documentation to find all the available Maven archetypes (unless we've memorized all of them).

Now with the `archetype:generate` goal, we don't need to know any of this information upfront (though we can still supply it on the command line if we like). It's way more convenient as the default Maven archetypes configured for `archetype:generate` consists of 46 (yes, 46!) archetypes. That's a lot, I must say. Also, we don't have to dig around for the list of available archetypes somewhere because it's already provided for us. By this point we are already familiar with how `archetype:generate` works from previous examples in the book. Later in the chapter, we will learn how to customize the catalog that determines the list of archetypes that appears when the goal is run.

Using archetypes within multi-module projects

Change is a constant thing in software development. We start with a simple application and that simple application becomes larger as the project progresses. In Maven terms—as we add more features, we add more modules. Thus, our simple Maven project now becomes a complex multi-module project.

As we have already seen in Chapter 3, *Building an Application Using Maven*, we can make use of archetypes for creating multi-module projects. Let's recall what we have learned from that chapter:

- To construct a multi-module project, always start with a parent POM first.
- For each module you want to add, execute `archetype:generate` just inside the directory where your parent POM resides. The `generate` mojo allows you to define the type of module you want to add, be it a web app module, a documentation module, a regular module, or even a custom one.
- The generated module automatically references the existing POM where the module was created as its immediate parent. On the other end, the generated module is automatically configured as a new `<module>` in the existing POM.

You may be curious why there is no generic archetype for multi-module projects. It is simply easier and far more flexible to just execute the Archetype plugin each time you need to add a new module. For example, what if your project is composed of different types of modules like in the case of the Centrepoint project (which has a web app module and a documentation module) from the previous chapters? Another scenario to consider is nested modules. You can't always determine at the beginning of the project how many modules (and sub-modules) the project will eventually have.

Common archetypes

When we tried out the `archetype:generate` mojo in Chapter 3, *Building an Application Using Maven*, a list of archetypes were shown to us. Aside from those we've already used, there were a number of other standard Maven project types available. Additionally, you may have noticed that some of them are framework and application-specific. As some frameworks or applications require a specific directory structure or format, archetypes conforming to these requirements and at the same time with Maven's, have been created.

Here, we will look at examples of both and how they can be used to generate a project of that type.

Maven site archetype

We already covered the simple site archetype in Chapter 3, *Building an Application Using Maven*, but there is also a more complete skeleton—the `maven-archetype-site`. This site contains examples of several documentation formats as well as documentation in different languages. To generate a site using this archetype, just execute the command:

```
$ mvn archetype:generate \
        -DarchetypeArtifactId=maven-archetype-site
```

You can also run the command without the parameter and select the desired archetype from the list.

The generated site should have the following directory structure:

```
|-- pom.xml
`-- src
    `-- site
        |-- apt
        |   |-- format.apt
        |   `-- index.apt
        |-- fml
        |   `-- faq.fml
        |-- fr
        |   |-- apt
        |   |   |-- format.apt
        |   |   `-- index.apt
        |   |-- fml
        |   |   `-- faq.fml
        |   `-- xdoc
        |       `-- xdoc.xml
        |
```

```
|-- site.xml
|-- site_fr.xml
`-- xdoc
    `-- xdoc.xml
```

The generated site's directory structure shows that you can set up any type of project (even non-code projects). They don't have to contain a `src/main/java` directory.

Looking at the generated site's `pom.xml`, a `<distributionManagement>` section is already present. This URL should be replaced by the URL where you will be deploying your project's web site. Notice also that the `maven-site-plugin` is configured for English and French localization. The corresponding files and directories for the French localization are the `site_fr.xml` and `fr/` directory. The localization is already in place to help users to get started in the right way. Archetypes can be used as examples to learn from as well as project starting points.

Maven Mojo (plugin) archetype

For creating Maven 2 plugins, a Mojo archetype is also available.

```
$ mvn archetype:generate \
        -DarchetypeArtifactId=maven-archetype-mojo
```

Using this archetype to generate a project, the following directory structure will be created:

```
|-- pom.xml
`-- src
    `-- main
        `-- java
            `-- com
                `-- effectivemaven
                    `-- chapter11
                        `-- mojo
                            `-- MyMojo.java
```

Here, a default mojo called `MyMojo` is created by default. If you take a look at its source code, you would see that it already extends `AbstractMojo` (from the dependency `maven-plugin-api`), which is a requirement for Maven plugins. Notice that the mojo also has the `@goal` and `@phase` annotations denoting the command that will be used to execute it and the phase in the Maven life cycle where it will be bound by default, respectively. The default configuration gives you a hint of the things you need to configure when developing Maven plugins.

As you can see, archetypes can be used to create projects for very specific purposes as a refinement of the standard Java module (the code within them need not be a trivial template).

For more details about plugin development, visit `http://maven.` `apache.org/guides/introduction/introduction-to-` `plugins.html`.

Maven simple J2EE archetype

A widely used platform in developing enterprise Java applications is the Java EE platform. In Java EE, components are divided into different layers. There's the web layer, application/business layer, and the persistence layer. Having multiple layers makes it a good candidate for using Maven to standardize its directory structure. To help you with this, a Maven archetype called `maven-archetype-j2ee-simple` is at your disposal.

```
$ mvn archetype:generate \
        -DarchetypeArtifactId=maven-archetype-j2ee-simple
```

Executing the `generate` mojo using this archetype results in the creation of the following directory structure and configuration files:

```
|-- ear
|   `-- pom.xml
|-- ejbs
|   |-- pom.xml
|   `-- src
|       `-- main
|           `-- resources
|               `-- META-INF
|                   `-- ejb-jar.xml
|-- pom.xml
|-- primary-source
|   `-- pom.xml
|-- projects
|   |-- logging
|   |   `-- pom.xml
|   `-- pom.xml
|-- servlets
|   |-- pom.xml
|   `-- servlet
|       |-- pom.xml
|       `-- src
|           `-- main
|               `-- webapp
```

```
|                               |-- WEB-INF
|                               |    `-- web.xml
|                               `-- index.jsp
`-- src
    `-- main
        `-- resources
```

This is actually a multi-module archetype, but it is strictly specific for J2EE applications, as we can see from the module names and the default configuration files. So as you can see, it is possible to create multi-module archetypes where it makes sense.

The `ear` module is where the J2EE project is assembled. If we take a look at the `ear/pom.xml`, we will see the Maven Ear plugin configured. This plugin is the one that packages the project into an ear file.

The `ejbs/` directory is where the **EJBs** (**Enterprise Java Beans**) are placed. By default, the `maven-ejb-plugin` that will be used for packaging the EJBs is already configured in the `pom.xml`. The latest release of the plugin (2.2) assumes the version used of EJB is 2.1 — that's why an `ejb-jar.xml` deployment descriptor (which is no longer mandatory for EJB 3.0) is also created. This can be overridden by setting the appropriate version in the plugin configuration.

The `primary-source/` directory should contain the core projects or modules of the J2EE application while the `projects/` directory must contain the sub-projects or components used by the core modules. A `logging/` component is also created by default in the `projects/` directory. Looking at the `pom.xml` in `primary-source/`, the logging component is already configured as a dependency.

As for the web-specific components (web layer), these should be placed in the `servlets/` directory. The standard directory path for web applications, including a default web descriptor (`web.xml`) and an `index.jsp`, is also ready for the `servlet/` sub-directory.

And last but not the least, we have the root `pom.xml`. There are several things already configured in the root POM — `maven-site-plugin`, `dependencyManagement`, and `distributionManagement`. Notice that the `maven-site-plugin` and the dependencies are configured inside the `pluginManagement` and `dependencyManagement` respectively:

```xml
<build>
  <pluginManagement>
    <plugins>
      <plugin>
        <groupId>org.apache.maven.plugins</groupId>
        <artifactId>maven-site-plugin</artifactId>
```

```
      <configuration>
        <unzipCommand>/usr/bin/unzip -o > err.txt</unzipCommand>
      </configuration>
      </plugin>
    </plugins>
  </pluginManagement>
</build>
<dependencyManagement>
  <dependencies>
    <dependency>
      <groupId>root.project.projects</groupId>
      <artifactId>logging</artifactId>
      <version>1.0</version>
    </dependency>
    <dependency>
      <groupId>root.project</groupId>
      <artifactId>primary-source</artifactId>
      <version>1.0</version>
    </dependency>
    <dependency>
      <groupId>root.project.servlets</groupId>
      <artifactId>servlet</artifactId>
      <version>1.0</version>
      <type>war</type>
    </dependency>
    <dependency>
      <groupId>root.project</groupId>
      <artifactId>ejbs</artifactId>
      <version>1.0</version>
      <type>ejb</type>
    </dependency>
  </dependencies>
</dependencyManagement>
<distributionManagement>
  <site>
    <id>site</id>
    <name>project website</name>
    <url>scp://local.company.com/websites/project.company.com/</url>
  </site>
</distributionManagement>
```

The reason behind this is inheritance. As we've seen in previous chapters, shared configuration is best in the parent POM so it can be inherited and duplication is avoided.

Analyzing the generated directory structure again demonstrates how Maven enforces best practices. It keeps the whole project/application modularized right from the start, making its components easier to modify, more readable, and less coupled.

If we check the POM files in each of the generated modules given previously, we will see that there are already a couple of J2EE/EJB-specific configurations in them—from the building of EJBs up to the bundling of the components into an ear file. This ensures that the project build goes through the required processes and generates the necessary files for J2EE projects.

The AppFuse Spring archetype

AppFuse is an open source project whose main goal is to make building web applications easier and more efficient, by providing a project skeleton depending on the framework stack you want to use for your project. One of its means for providing a project skeleton is through Maven archetypes. As of this writing, there are nine AppFuse archetypes available:

- JSF Basic archetype
- Spring MVC Basic archetype
- Struts 2 Basic archetype
- Tapestry Basic archetype
- AppFuse Core archetype
- JSF Modular archetype
- Spring MVC Modular archetype
- Struts 2 Modular archetype
- Tapestry Modular archetype

In this chapter, we will only cover one of the most commonly used among them, which is the AppFuse Spring MVC Basic archetype. This archetype is specifically for creating a web application using the Hibernate, Spring, and Spring MVC stack.

For more details about AppFuse, see http://appfuse.org/display/APF/Home.

Executing the `generate` mojo and using the `appfuse-basic-spring` archetype should result in the following directory structure and configuration files being created:

```
|-- README.txt
|-- pom.xml
`-- src
    |-- main
    |   |-- java
    |   |   `-- com
    |   |       `-- effectivemaven
    |   |           `-- chapter11
    |   |               `-- App.java
    |   |-- resources
    |   |   |-- ApplicationResources.properties
    |   |   |-- ApplicationResources_de.properties
    |   |   |-- ApplicationResources_en.properties
    |   |   |-- ApplicationResources_es.properties
    |   |   |-- ApplicationResources_fr.properties
    |   |   |-- ApplicationResources_it.properties
    |   |   |-- ApplicationResources_ko.properties
    |   |   |-- ApplicationResources_nl.properties
    |   |   |-- ApplicationResources_no.properties
    |   |   |-- ApplicationResources_pt.properties
    |   |   |-- ApplicationResources_pt_BR.properties
    |   |   |-- ApplicationResources_tr.properties
    |   |   |-- ApplicationResources_zh.properties
    |   |   |-- ApplicationResources_zh_CN.properties
    |   |   |-- ApplicationResources_zh_TW.properties
    |   |   |-- META-INF
    |   |   |   `-- persistence.xml
    |   |   |-- applicationContext-resources.xml
    |   |   |-- default-data.xml
    |   |   |-- ehcache.xml
    |   |   |-- hibernate.cfg.xml
    |   |   |-- jdbc.properties
    |   |   |-- log4j.xml
    |   |   |-- mail.properties
    |   |   `-- sql-map-config.xml
    |   `-- webapp
    |       |-- WEB-INF
    |       |   |-- applicationContext-validation.xml
    |       |   |-- applicationContext.xml
```

```
|         |        |-- dispatcher-servlet.xml
|         |        |-- menu-config.xml
|         |        |-- urlrewrite.xml
|         |        |-- validation.xml
|         |        |-- validator-rules-custom.xml
|         |        |-- validator-rules.xml
|         |        `-- web.xml
|         `-- common
|                  `-- menu.jsp
|-- site
|     `-- site.xml
`-- test
    |-- java
    |     `-- com
    |            `-- example
    |                   `-- chapter11
    |                          `-- AppTest.java
    `-- resources
           |-- config.xml
           |-- login.xml
           |-- sample-data.xml
           `-- web-tests.xml
```

We now see from this archetype that it is possible to build complex template projects from the same archetype mechanics.

The required Hibernate and core Spring configuration files are created in `src/main/resources` as they deal with the backend side of the web application. As for the Spring MVC configuration files, they are created and placed in `src/main/webapp/WEB-INF/` as they contain configuration for the frontend. Different directories have also been created for the unit tests and the documentation. This layout enforces the implementation of a standard layout by defining a separation among the components of the web application. If you take a look at the generated POM, you will see that a lot has already been configured, making the project ready for use. There's configuration for the database, for the IDEs, for running the application in Jetty, for running database unit tests, and even for integration testing.

Other examples

Aside from the archetypes we covered in the previous sections, there are also other framework-specific archetypes that are listed in the archetype catalog file in the remote repository (`http://repo1.maven.org/maven2`). Unfortunately, we will not be covering them in this book, but you will see that many of the same benefits we've seen above can apply to these other project types.

We've listed below some of them which might be helpful if you're starting a project with a specific framework already in mind:

- **Spring-OSGi archetype**: Archetype for creating a Spring-OSGi bundle that is ready for use. Details on how to use this archetype can be obtained from: http://www.springsource.org/node/361

- **AppFuse archetypes**: The archetypes for each framework stack are provided by AppFuse. We covered one of them in the previous section. To see how the other archetypes behave, visit http://appfuse.org/display/APF/AppFuse+QuickStart

- **Groovy archetypes**: The archetypes for creating projects written in Groovy. More details about them are available at http://groovy.codehaus.org/GMaven+-+Building+Groovy+Projects

- **MyFaces archetypes**: The archetypes for creating Apache MyFaces projects such as portlet-enabled webapps and webapps that use MyFaces Trinidad. More details about them can be obtained from http://myfaces.apache.org/build-tools/archetypes/index.html

- **Camel archetypes**: The archetypes used for creating Apache Camel projects configured to be used with other applications or languages such as ActiveMQ, Java, and Scala. To get more details about these archetypes, visit http://camel.apache.org/camel-maven-archetypes.html

Writing a new archetype

Aside from the archetypes included by default, we can also create our own custom archetype. In this section, we will learn how to do that.

An archetype consists of the following files:

- The archetype descriptor (archetype.xml): This is where the specific files for the Maven directories are configured. For example, if we want App.java to be in the source directory, then this is where we specify that.

- The archetype's pom.xml: Each archetype is also treated like a regular Maven project. In fact, they are just a JAR with resources in a special place.

- The template directory structure: This will be copied into the generated project (remember the src/main/java/... directory layout created by the Maven Quickstart Archetype earlier).

- The default pom.xml: It is included with the template directory structure and this will be the pom.xml to be used (or rather placed) in the generated project.

Creating our own custom archetype involves a couple of steps. We will be returning to the Centrepoint project we've been using throughout the book and creating a plugin archetype for the project.

Creating an archetype from a skeleton

When creating an archetype for the first time, it is certainly possible to create it by hand. However, if the content is non-trivial or contains a lot of files, the Archetype plugin offers an easier way to create the proper archetype files from an existing project by using the `create-from-project` goal.

To create our archetype, we will use the provided `plugin-skeleton` project included with this chapter. This directory has been created as a fully-functional plugin from which we can generate the archetype templates.

From the command-line, go to the root directory of the `plugin-skeleton` and execute:

```
plugin-skeleton$ mvn archetype:create-from-project
```

You should see the archetype being generated. The build output should be similar to the following:

```
[INFO] ------------------------------------------------------------
[INFO] Preparing archetype:create-from-project
[INFO] ------------------------------------------------------------
[INFO] Building My Centrepoint Plugin
[INFO] ------------------------------------------------------------
[INFO] No goals needed for project - skipping
[INFO] Setting property: classpath.resource.loader.class => 'org.
codehaus.plexus.velocity.ContextClassLoaderResourceLoader'.
[INFO] Setting property: velocimacro.messages.on => 'false'.
[INFO] Setting property: resource.loader => 'classpath'.
[INFO] Setting property: resource.manager.logwhenfound => 'false'.
[INFO] [archetype:create-from-project {execution: default-cli}]
[INFO] Setting default groupId: com.effectivemaven.centrepoint
[INFO] Setting default artifactId: centrepoint-plugin
[INFO] Setting default version: 1.0-SNAPSHOT
[INFO] Setting default package: com.effectivemaven.centrepoint.plugins
[INFO] Archetype created in target/generated-sources/archetype
```

As you can see, the archetype has been created in the `target/generated-sources/archetype` directory, ready for use. As this is a temporary location, we will move it permanently into the Centrepoint project so that it can be built and distributed for general use.

We will create a directory named `plugin-archetype` in the `centrepoint` directory of the sample code (at the same level as the `documentation` module). To do this, we copy the generated archetype from above `plugin-skeleton/target/generated-sources/archetype` to `centrepoint/plugin-archetype`.

Now, we need to incorporate it into the Centrepoint project, in the same way as we did for new modules in Chapter 3, *Building an Application Using Maven*. After you've finished copying the archetype, edit `plugin-archetype/pom.xml` and add a reference to the Centrepoint parent:

```
<parent>
  <groupId>com.effectivemaven.centrepoint</groupId>
  <artifactId>centrepoint</artifactId>
  <version>1.1-SNAPSHOT</version>
</parent>
```

 In case you didn't release Centrepoint from the previous chapter, you can continue to rebuild the project and still use `1.0-SNAPSHOT` version.

We can again remove the `<groupId>` and `<version>` elements which are already inherited from the declared parent. Next, let's update the `<artifactId>` to match the convention other modules have used and make it match the module's directory name:

```
<artifactId>plugin-archetype</artifactId>
```

Also, let's improve the name to make it more appropriate and more descriptive. Change the `<name>` value to:

```
<name>Centrepoint Plugin Archetype</name>
```

Finally, add the module to the top-most POM so that it will be included when we build Centrepoint:

```
<modules>
    ...
    <module>plugin-archetype</module>
</modules>
```

Going back to `plugin-archetype/pom.xml`, notice that it has a different `<packaging>` from what we have encountered so far in the previous chapters. The `maven-archetype` packaging is a new feature that is introduced in the 2.0 version of the Archetype plugin to easily distinguish regular artifacts from archetypes and to enhance the lifecycle. Using this type of packaging requires `org.apache.maven.archetype:archetype-packaging` component to be included — that's why it was already declared as a build `<extension>` in the POM.

To be able to use the plugin archetype, we need to install it in our local repository first. Execute the following command from `centrepoint/plugin-archetype` directory:

```
plugin-archetype$ mvn clean install
```

In the build output log after installing the `plugin-archetype`, notice that there were several archetype goals executed during the build:

```
[INFO] [clean:clean]
[INFO] [resources:resources]
[INFO] [archetype:jar]
[INFO] [archetype:add-archetype-metadata]
[INFO] [archetype:integration-test]
[INFO] [install:install]
[INFO] Installing /path/to/centrepoint/plugin-archetype/target/plugin-
archetype-1.1-SNAPSHOT.jar to /path/to/.m2/repository/com/effectivemaven/
centrepoint/plugin-archetype/1.1-SNAPSHOT/plugin-archetype-1.1-SNAPSHOT.jar
[INFO] [archetype:update-local-catalog]
[INFO] -----------------------------------------------------------
[INFO] BUILD SUCCESSFUL
[INFO] -----------------------------------------------------------
```

The first one was the `archetype:jar` goal, which packages the archetype into a JAR file. As it is simply a bundle of the template files and directories, it does not have a `MANIFEST.MF` file included, unlike a regular artifact JAR.

The second goal executed was `archetype:add-archetype-metadata`. What this goal does is it *attaches* the archetype artifact's metadata to the generated artifact, so that it will be installed or deployed into the repository. This ensures that the latest version in the repository metadata is up-to-date.

The third goal was the `archetype:integration-test`, which is already self-descriptive. It executes the integration tests (if there are some) for the archetype. Finally, there was `archetype:update-local-catalog` where the archetype catalog file in the local repository is also updated to reflect the newly available archetype. We will learn about the catalog file later on.

Using the custom archetype

Now, let's use our Centrepoint plugin archetype to create a sample plugin. If you released the project in previous chapters, obtain the latest distribution of our Centrepoint application from `http://localhost:8081/archiva/` `repository/releases/com/effectivemaven/centrepoint/distribution/1.0/` `distribution-1.0-bin.zip`. You can also build the sources from trunk and use the generated distribution from the `centrepoint/distribution/target` directory.

Unpack the distribution. Now, start the Centrepoint application by executing the following command from the `bin/` directory:

```
centrepoint-1.0/bin$ ./centrepoint console
```

Access the application from the browser by navigating to `http://localhost:8080/` `centrepoint`. Now, let's add the Centrepoint project itself to the application by providing the following values:

Information about the latest version of the project that is available in our local repository will be displayed after importing the project. If you take a look at the project information page, notice that the right hand side is bare. Now, let's say we want to add a links panel to that empty space to make it easier to navigate the web application. Our Centrepoint application is actually designed to be pluggable. You can add panels to the right-hand side of the project information page using plugins.

Stop Centrepoint first by executing *Ctrl+C* in the console. Now, let's start creating our links panel by first creating the plugin skeleton from the plugin archetype, by running the following in an empty directory:

```
$ mvn archetype:generate -DarchetypeCatalog=local
```

The choices will be fewer than we've seen in the past:

```
1: local -> plugin-archetype (Centrepoint is a basic but useful
application that sets up a dashboard of project information from Maven,
Archiva, and Continuum).
```

The Archetype plugin makes use of a special file called the **archetype catalog** (`archetype-catalog.xml`) for determining the archetypes in a repository. When the `generate` mojo executes, it looks for this file to get the list of archetypes or to check if the specified archetype is in the repository. You can use `-DarchetypeCatalog` parameter to specify the repository/repositories to check for the catalog file(s) like what we did in the command previously. We can also set multiple locations for the catalog file, delimited by a comma (,). There are five options for specifying each catalog, namely:

- `internal` (catalog file included with the Archetype plugin).
- `local` (specifies the local repository path, which is `<USER.HOME>/.m2/`).
- `remote` (specifies the central repository `http://repo1.maven.org/maven2`).
- A specific path for a catalog file in the local file system (denoted by `file://PATH/TO/CATALOG/FILE`).
- A URL specifying the path to a catalog file in a remote location (denoted by `http://URLPATH/TO/CATALOG/FILE`).

In our case, as our archetype is locally available, we locked down the Archetype plugin to only look at the `local` catalog file for the archetype we specified.

Since the 2.0-alpha-5 release of the Archetype plugin, the default value for the `archetypeCatalog` parameter was changed from `internal,local` to `remote,local`. This implies that if no value is explicitly configured, the plugin will get the catalog files from the central repository and your local Maven 2 repository. Otherwise, if no catalog files were retrieved from the specified locations, the `internal` catalog file will be used.

Going back to our Centrepoint plugin, provide the following input parameters when prompted:

```
groupId : com.effectivemaven.centrepoint.plugins
artifactId : my-sample-plugin
version : 1.0-SNAPSHOT
package : com.effectivemaven.centrepoint
```

We will only use the skeleton plugin for demonstration purposes. After our sample plugin has been created, package it into a JAR file by executing the following:

```
my-sample-plugin$ mvn package
```

Finally, copy the generated JAR file from `target/my-sample-plugin-1.0-SNAPSHOT.jar` to the `webapps/centrepoint/WEB-INF/lib` of the Centrepoint distribution which we ran earlier.

Start the Centrepoint application again in `console` mode. Once the application is running, navigate to `http://localhost:8080/centrepoint` in your browser. This time, when you access the Centrepoint project information page, you should see a **Links** panel on the righthand side of the page (similar to what we have below) in place of the previous empty space:

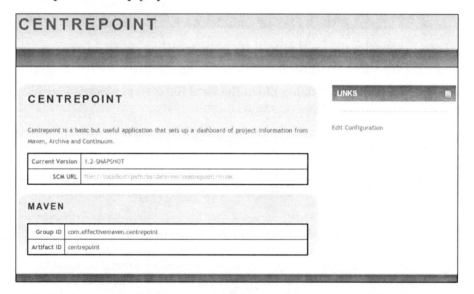

To add a link, click **Edit Configuration**. Set `http://www.effectivemaven.com` to link to the project's site then click **Update**. A link to the project web site with the name **My Link** under the **Links** panel should appear.

We will repeat the same process in the next chapter to create plugins for Archiva and Continuum.

Managing catalogs

In the previous section, we've learned about the archetype catalog file and what it's for. Now, we will see how this file is generated and kept in sync with the actual archetypes in the repository.

To generate an archetype catalog file for a repository, we can make use of the
`crawl` mojo of the Archetype plugin. This goal searches a repository in the local file
system for available archetypes and generates a catalog file listing all the archetypes
it found.

Let's crawl our Archiva repository `internal` which is conveniently in our local file
system. From the command line, execute:

```
$ mvn archetype:crawl -Drepository=/path/to/apache-archiva-1.2.1/data/
repositories/internal
```

You should see the artifacts in our `internal` repository listed in the command line,
similar to the output below.

```
[INFO] [archetype:crawl]
repository /path/to/apache-archiva-1.2.1/data/repositories/internal
catalogFile null
[INFO] Scanning /path/to/apache-archiva-1.2.1/data/repositories/internal/
cglib/cglib-nodep/2.1_3/cglib-nodep-2.1_3.jar
[INFO] Scanning /path/to/apache-archiva-1.2.1/data/repositories/internal/
javax/servlet/servlet-api/2.4/servlet-api-2.4.jar
[INFO] Scanning /path/to/apache-archiva-1.2.1/data/repositories/internal/
ant/ant/1.6.5/ant-1.6.5.jar
[INFO] Scanning /path/to/apache-archiva-1.2.1/data/repositories/internal/
ant/ant-launcher/1.6.5/ant-launcher-1.6.5.jar
[INFO] Scanning /path/to/apache-archiva-1.2.1/data/repositories/internal/
plexus/plexus-utils/1.0.3/plexus-utils-1.0.3.jar
[INFO] Scanning /path/to/apache-archiva-1.2.1/data/repositories/internal/
commons-lang/commons-lang/2.3/commons-lang-2.3.jar
[INFO] Scanning /path/to/apache-archiva-1.2.1/data/repositories/internal/
commons-lang/commons-lang/2.1/commons-lang-2.1.jar
[INFO] ---------------------------------------------------------
[INFO] BUILD SUCCESSFUL
[INFO] ---------------------------------------------------------
```

An `archetype-catalog.xml` file should have been created in the root directory of
the `internal` repository. It should contain the archetypes found, including their
basic information, similar to what we have here:

```
<?xml version="1.0" encoding="UTF-8"?>
<archetype-catalog>
  <archetypes>
    <archetype>
      <groupId>org.apache.maven.archetypes</groupId>
```

```
      <artifactId>maven-archetype-webapp</artifactId>
      <version>1.0</version>
      <description>webapp</description>
    </archetype>
    <archetype>
      <groupId>org.apache.maven.archetypes</groupId>
      <artifactId>maven-archetype-site-simple</artifactId>
      <version>1.0</version>
      <description>plugin</description>
    </archetype>
    <archetype>
      <groupId>org.apache.maven.archetypes</groupId>
      <artifactId>maven-archetype-quickstart</artifactId>
      <version>1.0</version>
      <description>quickstart</description>
    </archetype>
  </archetypes>
</archetype-catalog>
```

Having this lookup file makes it possible for the Archetype plugin to list all of the available archetypes in the repository.

To explicitly update the catalog file with the artifacts information as it is installed into the local repository, the Archetype plugin provides the `update-local-catalog` goal. We actually saw this executed earlier when we installed our `plugin-archetype` to the local repository. In that case, it added the `plugin-archetype` in the local archetype catalog.

Summary

Archetypes are not only helpful in creating projects, they also provide an easy way for implementing best practices. They provide us with a convenient way of creating and conforming to Maven's standard directory layout and configuration.

In the next chapter, which is the last chapter of this book, we will go back to Archiva and Continuum and learn how to effectively configure both applications in the enterprise environment.

12
Maven, Archiva, and Continuum in the Enterprise

This chapter covers enterprise-specific setup and configuration of Archiva and Continuum. The first half of the chapter tackles security configuration and setup while the other half is centered on integrating the two with other applications in the enterprise.

In the security section, we will learn about Redback, which is the security system used by both Archiva and Continuum. We'll also do a quick run through of how to configure it with other existing security systems—specifically with LDAP.

Also, in the integration section, we will explore how Archiva and Continuum can be used with other applications.

Configuring security

Security is one of the most important and critical areas in an enterprise. Access to sensitive information should be restricted to a limited number of people. Some companies also require central security systems (such as LDAP, single sign-on, and so on), so that they can be integrated with the applications they use.

This section is concerned with configuring security for Archiva and Continuum in line with these points.

In the previous chapters, we learned that these two applications use Redback for their security, but we haven't really dug deeper into how Redback is integrated with them.

A brief look at Redback

Redback is a **RBAC (role-based access control)** security framework that can be easily integrated in an application. It is divided into three major components, namely: authentication, authorization, and user management. Apart from this, it also has support for different frameworks to allow seamless integration with an application. As of the current version, Redback can be integrated with Struts 2 applications, and can use databases or LDAP to authenticate users.

> Archiva and Continuum were previously using Webwork but both migrated to Struts 2. James William Dumay (who also worked on Archiva's migration to Struts 2 and developed the Atlassian XMLRPC Binder which we will see later on) migrated Redback to align with these two applications.

By default, Redback comes with four built-in roles: **System Administrator**, **User Administrator**, **Registered User**, and **Guest**. The first two roles are specific to administrative tasks while the last two are on the opposite end—these are the roles with the least amount of rights or control over the application.

The **User Administrator** role grants the user the permissions necessary to manage the users of the application. Users with this role can create a new user, update a user's information, grant and remove a user's roles, and delete a user. On the other hand, the **System Administrator** role grants all permissions or access to the application including users and role management. The **Registered User** role specifies that a user is registered through the application. Users with this role should be able to edit their own account details. The last is the **Guest** role, which simply grants the guest user access to the application.

Apart from the built-in roles, it also comes with two default users: **admin** and **guest**. Neither of these users can be deleted. User **admin** is the default **System Administrator**, which will be created when the application starts up (if there's no user database detected). On the other hand, the **guest** user is the default user whom we can assign specific roles which we want to allow to be accessed by anyone without the need to authenticate themselves. You can refer back to the "Roles and permissions" section of Chapter 10, *Archiva in a Team*, for an example of how the guest account works.

> Redback makes use of descriptor files (called `redback.xml`) to identify the roles, operations, and permissions to be created in an application. The built-in roles and permissions we've covered previously are defined within Redback itself. For more information on how to integrate it to your application, visit `http://redback.codehaus.org/`.

By default, Redback is configured to use a database. If you look at Archiva and Continuum's Jetty configuration files (`conf/jetty.xml`) you should be able to see something similar to the following:

```
<!-- Users / Security Database -->
<New id="users" class="org.mortbay.jetty.plus.naming.Resource">
    <Arg>jdbc/users</Arg>
    <Arg>
        <New class="org.apache.derby.jdbc.EmbeddedDataSource">
            <Set name="DatabaseName"><SystemProperty name="appserver.base"
                            default=".."/>/data/databases/users</Set>
            <Set name="user">sa</Set>
            <Set name="createDatabase">create</Set>
        </New>
    </Arg>
</New>

<New id="usersShutdown"
    class="org.mortbay.jetty.plus.naming.Resource">
    <Arg>jdbc/usersShutdown</Arg>
    <Arg>
        <New class="org.apache.derby.jdbc.EmbeddedDataSource">
            <Set name="DatabaseName"><SystemProperty name="appserver.base"
                            default=".."/>/data/databases/users</Set>
            <Set name="user">sa</Set>
            <Set name="shutdownDatabase">shutdown</Set>
        </New>
    </Arg>
</New>
```

The previous configuration is specific to Redback. If `appserver.base` is the default value, it is recommended that you change the default location of the `users` database and move it out of the application's installation directory to avoid accidental deletion when upgrading. You could also choose to use a different database (such as PostgreSQL, and so on) by reconfiguring these options.

Setting up security for multiple teams in Continuum

Going back to our running Continuum instance from Chapters 8 and 9, let's create a new user for demonstration purposes. From the **Users** page, create a new user **testuser1** whose password is **pass123**. After creating the user, you should see the list of roles that can be assigned to the user:

⊞ **redback-xwork-integration-core**

Redback XWork Integration Security Core

Available Roles:

- ☐ Guest
- ☐ Registered User
- ☐ System Administrator
- ☐ User Administrator

⊞ **Continuum**

Available Roles:

- ☐ Continuum Group Project Administrator
- ☐ Continuum Group Project Developer
- ☐ Continuum Group Project User
- ☐ Continuum Manage Build Environments
- ☐ Continuum Manage Build Templates
- ☐ Continuum Manage Installations
- ☐ Continuum Manage Local Repositories
- ☐ Continuum Manage Purging
- ☐ Continuum Manage Queues
- ☐ Continuum Manage Scheduling

Resource Roles:

	Project Administrator	Project Developer	Project User
Apache Maven 2: Effective Implementations Book	☐	☐	☐
Centrepoint	☐	☐	☐
Centrepoint Selenium Tests	☐	☐	☐
Default Project Group	☐	☐	☐

As you can see, the roles are grouped into three categories. The first ones are the built-in roles from Redback, which we covered in the previous section while the last two are the user roles specific for Continuum.

Let's first take a look at the last group—the **Resource Roles**. These are the resource-level roles that are dynamically generated for each **Project Group** created in Continuum. They are also removed once the **Project Group** is deleted. For each resource, there are three types of roles generated, namely the **Project Administrator**, **Project Developer**, and **Project User**. The **Project Administrator** is the role that is necessary for performing administrative tasks for the specific project group. Users with this role can grant or modify the roles of users with `Project Administrator`, `Project Developer`, or `Project User` roles belonging to the same project group. They can also perform the operations allowed for a `Project Developer`.

Users with a **Project Developer** resource role are allowed to perform the following operations: add, edit, delete, and build a project in the group, build and release the entire project group or a project in the group, configure build definitions and notifiers for the group and for each project in the group, and view the build queues. Also, last but not the least, users with the **Project User** role are only allowed read or view-access to the project group and/or projects in the group and the build queues.

In Continuum, the main point of separation is at the project group level and it is the major reason why it is the information grouping (or resource) that was chosen for the dynamic roles.

In an enterprise, there are a large number of projects with each project having its own development team. The ideal setup with regard to multiple projects within a company is that one project is equal to one project group in Continuum, with the team lead having the `Project Administrator` role and the team members having the `Project Developer` role.

Sometimes though, a very large project can be divided into smaller development teams with each team handling one or a set of modules in the project. If the project's modules are big, the usual distribution or division of the teams is per module (in short, one development team per module). As a best practice in Continuum, project groups should match the logical development groupings. Let's see why. For example, our user **testuser1** belongs to the QA team which works on the Selenium tests for our Centrepoint project. So in the resource roles matrix, assign the user with a **Project Developer** role for **Centrepoint Selenium Tests**.

Resource Roles:

	Project Administrator	Project Developer	Project User
Apache Maven 2: Effective Implementations Book	☐	☐	☐
Centrepoint	☐	☐	☐
Centrepoint Selenium Tests	☐	☑	☐
Default Project Group	☐	☐	☐

Submit
Reset

Click the **Submit** button then log out from Continuum. Now, we will log in as user **testuser1.** Provide the credentials we set earlier. As this is our first login, we will be asked to change our password. Specify **pass1** as the new password (or select something suitable).

 The forced changing of passwords for an individual user can be disabled by an administrator by not selecting the **Force User to Change Password** checkbox in the **User Edit** page. In this case, they were forced to change their password as the account was created by the administrator with a temporary password.

After logging in and changing our password, notice that we're only able to see and access the following in Continuum:

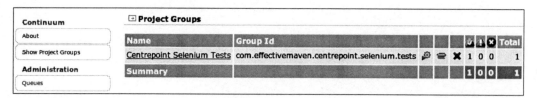

If you go to the **Centrepoint Selenium Tests Project Group Summary**, you should be able to build, release, add, edit, and delete the projects in the group, and also edit their build definitions and notifiers. Now, we know from the previous chapters that **Centrepoint Selenium Tests** is dependent on Centrepoint itself as the tests are specifically for the Centrepoint web application. Also because of this, developers of the selenium-tests module need to be able to at least see the builds for Centrepoint in some cases. For example, when they didn't get the latest snapshot of the webapp module or the tests are failing because of changes in the webapp and they want to know why. To address this need, we can grant our user testuser1 with a **Project User** role for Centrepoint.

To do this, log out from Continuum and log in as admin again. Edit the testuser1 user account and assign it the resource role **Project User** for **Centrepoint**. Save the changes you made and log out from Continuum.

Now, log in again as user testuser1. This time, we should be able to see Centrepoint in the **Project Groups** list.

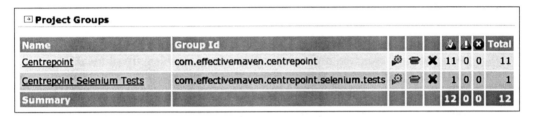

Notice that the build, release, and delete icons are disabled for the Centrepoint group. This is because we're only a user of the project group and should not be able to modify anything. If you look at Centrepoint's project group summary, you will not be able to see any of the buttons for adding, building, deleting, and releasing the group. All you will be able to do is view the project information and configuration, and the results of the builds and releases.

As you can see from the setup we did previously, we were able to keep a separation among the different development teams and at the same time exercise control over which operations can be performed by whom on what projects. That is the big advantage of having different resource-based roles.

Apart from the dynamic roles, there are ten other roles in Continuum to take note of. Most of these roles deal with administrative tasks. The first three roles in the list are equivalent to the resource roles we've discussed previously, but for all groups rather than for a specific project group only. Let's run through the rest:

- **Continuum Manage Build Environments**: Users with this role are allowed to manage (add, edit, and delete) the build environments in Continuum. This role usually comes hand-in-hand with the **Continuum Manage Installations** role.

- **Continuum Manage Build Templates**: This role allows the user to manage (add, edit, and delete) build definition templates.

- **Continuum Manage Installations**: This role allows the user to manage (add, edit, and delete) Continuum installations.

- **Continuum Manage Queues**: This role allows the user to view and cancel builds in the build queues. It can be combined with the **Continuum Group Project Administrator** to give the user control over the build queues.

- **Continuum Manage Scheduling**: This role allows the user to manage (create, update, and remove) schedules in Continuum.

- **Continuum Manage Purging**: This role allows the user to configure (create, update, execute, and remove) purging/cleaning up of local repositories and working directories in Continuum.

- **Continuum Manage Local Repositories**: Users with this role are allowed to configure (create, update, and remove) local repositories in Continuum. They can also execute purging on a local repository.

At the enterprise level where an application deals with a lot of users, it is necessary to define and categorize the operations of an application into different roles. Not only is this less confusing, it is also easier to manage.

Setting up security for multiple teams in Archiva

In Chapter 10, *Archiva in a Team*, we discussed Archiva's dynamic roles a little and learned that the basis for these roles are the *repositories*. We've also learned that it has two types of dynamic roles, namely the **Repository Manager** and the **Repository Observer**. Now, we will take a closer look at how we can best make use of them at the enterprise level when multiple teams are involved.

When dealing with multiple teams, the following setup is usually effective:

- Have one (or more) read-only local proxy cache that is accessible within the local area network only. We can create one or more managed repositories in Archiva, configure it to proxy remote repositories such as the central repositories or `java.net` and serve all artifact requests made within the network. Given this case, the `guest` account can be assigned the **Repository Observer** role for these repositories.

- Have separate snapshot and release repositories for each team, with members of the team having **Repository Manager** roles for both repositories. This can go hand-in-hand with deploying nightly builds from Continuum where in each project group has its own deployment repository.

- Grant the **Repository Observer** role to users outside the team (or the `guest` account if it is public within its network) that need access to the releases. If security is more of a concern for just some of the artifacts, you may want a separate deployment repository for the different security realm.

In certain cases, when one internal project is dependent on another internal project, we can either—configure only one repository for both projects, configure the repository containing the dependency as an additional repository in the `settings.xml`, or make use of virtual repositories (combo of local proxy cache and repository containing the dependency). The last two options are recommended as both the setups require just a **Repository Observer** role on the end of the team members who need the artifact.

When configuring Continuum to deploy nightly builds in Archiva, it is good practice to have a general user account in Archiva which Continuum would use to deploy to the repository (for example, a user account named `buildserver`). Make sure that this user has a **Repository Manager** role for the deployment repository. The credentials would need to be set in a `settings.xml` used by the local Maven installation used by Continuum. Note that this should be different for different project groups if extra security is needed, as anyone that can commit code can read this password.

Setting the repository as the level of security separation can also be a restriction. There can be instances when you only want a user to be able to access one artifact in your repository, but you can't as access control is at the repository level. While not available at the time of writing, improvements such as this will be available in future versions of Archiva.

Additional Redback configuration

For runtime configuration, Redback makes use of a properties file called `security.properties`. Archiva and Continuum have their own default `security.properties` files. In Archiva, it can be found in `apps/archiva/WEB-INF/classes/org/apache/maven/archiva/` while it can be found in `apps/continuum/WEB-INF/classes/org/apache/maven/continuum/` in the Continuum bundle. To customize the Redback configuration, you can override it with a custom one by placing it in either the `conf` directory of the bundle (if it is for one application) or in `<USER_HOME>/.m2` (if it is for both applications). Note that the latter means that a `security.properties` file in `<USER_HOME>/.m2` always takes precedence over the default one included with the application.

If Continuum and Archiva are running on the same machine using the same user account, keep in mind that if you place a `security.properties` file in `<USER_HOME>/.m2`, both applications will be using the same configuration file. There are some configurations that are application specific — these options should be kept in their respective application configuration files.

A number of things such as application configuration, LDAP configuration, email settings, and security policies can be configured in the `security.properties` file.

The defaults are quite strict, so let's try configuring Archiva's security settings. If your Archiva instance is currently running make sure that you stop it first. Go to your Archiva installation and create `conf/security.properties`.

First, we will configure a few security policies. We will set the `admin` and `archiva` user accounts from being locked:

```
security.policy.unlockable.accounts=admin
security.policy.unlockable.accounts=archiva
```

This is useful for automated and built-in accounts where they can get locked by repeated bad attempts very easily and need to be kept available.

Let's say we also want to prevent passwords from expiring so users will not have to keep changing them and worry about keeping track of their old passwords. To do this, we need to add the following configuration:

```
security.policy.password.expiration.enabled=false
```

Now, let's enforce a few password rules in Archiva. We will require all passwords to be alphanumeric and must have a minimum length of five characters. Add the following to put these restrictions in place:

```
security.policy.password.rule.alphanumeric.enabled=true
security.policy.password.rule.characterlength.minimum=5
```

We will also customize the contents of the validation mail sent by Redback for users who register in Archiva. To change the subject heading of the email and the name of who sent the email, just add this configuration:

```
email.from.name=Archiva
```

After adding the previous configuration, save the `security.properties` file and start Archiva. To verify that the policies we have set in place are implemented, go to Archiva and register as a new user. Once you've validated your account, try providing a password that contains only alphabet characters or a password with less than five alphanumeric characters. Neither should be accepted by the application.

You can also add the same security configuration for your Continuum instance (in `conf/security.properties`). Just make sure that you change the validation mail settings from Archiva to Continuum.

For a complete list of the properties that can be configured, see `http://redback.codehaus.org/configuration.html`. The values shown in the page are the default Redback configuration.

Using LDAP

Earlier, we learned that Redback can be integrated with LDAP. Configuring this used to be a bit challenging to do, but thanks to Emmanuel Venisse (who is also the current PMC Chair of Apache Continuum), it's now very easy to do. In this section, we will go through the steps on how to set this up.

 LDAP support in Redback is currently read-only, meaning you cannot add, edit, or delete users from within the application, only directly on the LDAP backend.

To configure LDAP in Archiva or Continuum, you need to edit the `application.xml` (located in `apps/[APPLICATION]/WEB-INF/classes/META-INF/plexus/`) and the `security.properties` used.

In the `application.xml`, you need to uncomment the following configuration:

```
<component>
  <role>org.codehaus.plexus.redback.common.ldap.connection.
                  LdapConnectionFactory</role>
  <role-hint>configurable</role-hint>
  <implementation>org.codehaus.plexus.redback.common.ldap.connection.
                  ConfigurableLdapConnectionFactory</implementation>
  <requirements>
   <requirement>
    <role>
     org.codehaus.plexus.redback.configuration.UserConfiguration
    </role>
   </requirement>
  </requirements>
</component>
```

This component is the one that manages Redback's connection to the LDAP server. Now, in order for this to be used, you need to set a few configuration options in the `security.properties` file. First, you need to tell Redback that you will be using LDAP by setting this:

```
user.manager.impl=ldap
ldap.bind.authenticator.enabled=true
redback.default.admin=admin
security.policy.password.expiration.enabled=false
```

Then, you need to provide the connection parameters that will be used by Redback's LDAP connection factory:

```
ldap.config.hostname=ldap.hostname
ldap.config.port=389
ldap.config.base.dn=o=com
ldap.config.context.factory=com.sun.jndi.ldap.LdapCtxFactory
ldap.config.bind.dn=uid=username,o=com
ldap.config.password=passw0rd
```

The first two properties correspond to the host name and the port of the LDAP server to connect to. The third property — `ldap.config.base.dn` — is the baseDn (the Distinguished Name) of the LDAP system at which to start the search. The fourth property — `ldap.config.context.factory` — corresponds to the context factory for LDAP connections. On the other hand, the last two properties specify the core user and its password that will be used for authenticating to the LDAP server. This user must be able to perform the necessary searches in the directory structure.

Going back to the `application.xml`, you also need to uncomment this section which is needed for mapping attributes in the LDAP server to user information in Redback:

```
<component>
  <role>org.codehaus.plexus.redback.common.ldap.UserMapper</role>
  <role-hint>ldap</role-hint>
  <implementation>
   org.codehaus.plexus.redback.common.ldap.LdapUserMapper
  </implementation>
  <configuration>
   <email-attribute>email</email-attribute>
   <full-name-attribute>givenName</full-name-attribute>
   <password-attribute>userPassword</password-attribute>
   <user-id-attribute>cn</user-id-attribute>
   <user-base-dn>o=com</user-base-dn>
   <user-object-class>inetOrgPerson</user-object-class>
  </configuration>
  <requirements>
   <requirement>
    <role>
     org.codehaus.plexus.redback.configuration.UserConfiguration
    </role>
   </requirement>
  </requirements>
</component>
```

You can also set the configuration parameters highlighted previously in the `security.properties` file. Again, if you're constantly upgrading your application, it would be better if you move them out of the `application.xml` to the properties file. To do that, remove the `<configuration>` section from the previous component configuration, then set the following in the `security.properties` file instead:

```
ldap.config.mapper.attribute.email=mail
ldap.config.mapper.attribute.fullname=givenName
ldap.config.mapper.attribute.password=userPassword
ldap.config.mapper.attribute.user.id=cn
ldap.config.mapper.attribute.user.base.dn=o=com
ldap.config.mapper.attribute.user.object.class=inetOrgPerson
```

The first four properties correspond to the attribute names that contain the email address, name, password, and user ID details of a user in the LDAP system. On the other hand, the `ldap.config.mapper.attribute.user.base.dn` specifies the subtree which will be searched for the users. Last, but not the least, is the `ldap.config.mapper.attribute.user.object.class` property. This property signifies the `objectClass` used in the LDAP server for identifying users.

With the previous configuration, you should be able to use LDAP in Archiva or Continuum.

You can further improve the performance when looking up users in LDAP by uncommenting this in the `application.xml`:

```
<component>
   <role>org.codehaus.plexus.redback.users.UserManager</role>
   <role-hint>cached</role-hint>
   <implementation>org.codehaus.plexus.redback.users.cached.
                             CachedUserManager</implementation>
   <description>CachedUserManager</description>
   <requirements>
    <requirement>
     <role>org.codehaus.plexus.redback.users.UserManager</role>
     <role-hint>ldap</role-hint>
     <field-name>userImpl</field-name>
    </requirement>
    <requirement>
     <role>org.codehaus.plexus.cache.Cache</role>
     <role-hint>users</role-hint>
     <field-name>usersCache</field-name>
    </requirement>
   </requirements>
</component>
```

Make sure to change this in the `security.properties` file as well:

```
user.manager.impl=cached
```

For more details about LDAP configuration in Redback, you can take a look at `http://redback.codehaus.org/integration/ldap.html`.

Interfacing with other tools in the enterprise

Archiva and Continuum can also be integrated with other tools in the enterprise. Both applications make this possible through web services. In this section, we will see how this can be done. We will create plugins for both applications and use them with our Centrepoint application.

Continuum web services

Continuum's web services feature is implemented using XML-RPC. If you recall from Chapter 9, *Continuum in Depth*, XML-RPC is also used for the distributed builds. To demonstrate how this works, we will create a Continuum plugin which will retrieve build results from Continuum and display it in our Centrepoint application.

Building the Continuum plugin

First, let's create a new directory named `plugins`. This will be a new top level tree, as it does not need to be within the Centrepoint project. As these plugins are developed independently of Centrepoint they can be versioned and released separately.

We will use the archetype we created from Chapter 11, *Archetypes*, to create our Continuum plugin.

 If you haven't followed the examples from the previous chapter, you can rebuild the source code for this chapter from the `centrepoint` directory to make the archetype available. You may also need to change the generated model dependency from `1.0` to `1.1-SNAPSHOT` if you haven't run the release examples in Chapter 9, *Continuum in Depth*.

To create the plugin, execute the following command from inside the plugins directory we created earlier:

```
plugins$ mvn archetype:generate \
          -DarchetypeGroupId=com.effectivemaven.centrepoint \
          -DarchetypeArtifactId=plugin-archetype \
          -DarchetypeVersion=1.1-SNAPSHOT
```

Provide the following input when prompted:

```
groupId : com.effectivemaven.centrepoint.plugins
artifactId : continuum-builds-plugin
version : 1.0-SNAPSHOT
package: com.effectivemaven.centrepoint.plugins.continuum
```

After the `continuum-builds-plugin` has been created, change the `<name>` and add a `<description>` in the generated POM:

```
<name>Centrepoint Plugin for Continuum Builds</name>
<description>
  Retrieve build results from a Continuum server and display
  as a panel in the Centrepoint project page.
</description>
```

Now, let's start customizing our plugin. Open the `continuum-builds-plugin` in your IDE.

> If you worked through Chapter 8, *Continuum – Ensuring the Health of your Source Code*, this might be a good time to set the plugins up in source control and add them to Continuum as well!

Once the plugin has been loaded in your IDE, rename the template classes `MyModel` and `MyModelTest` to `ContinuumModel` and `ContinuumModelTest` respectively. Rename `MyPlugin` and `MyPluginTest` as well to `ContinuumBuildsPlugin` and `ContinuumBuildsPluginTest`. You also need to update `src/main/resources/META-INF/centrepoint/plugin.properties` to reflect the new name of the plugin.

Now, in both `ContinuumModel` and `ContinuumBuildsPlugin`, and their corresponding tests, change all the references from `my-plugin` to `continuum-builds`.

We also need to change the title for our Continuum panel, so in the `ContinuumBuildsPlugin`, change the following part:

```
public String getTitle( Project project )
{
    return "Continuum Build Results";
}
```

We also need to update the test case for this change. In `ContinuumBuildsPluginTest`, update the following:

```
public void testTitle()
{
    assert "Continuum Build Results".equals(
        plugin.getTitle( null) );
    assert "Continuum Build Results".equals(
        plugin.getTitle( project ) );
}
```

We've now changed the archetype boilerplate into our basic but specific project. Let's verify that our plugin builds by executing the following in the command line:

```
continuum-builds-plugin$ mvn install
```

You should get a successful build in the end.

Now that our plugin builds, we can start tweaking it to display build results from a project in Continuum via web services. Starting with the `ContinuumModel`, change the following variable:

```
private String link;
```

to

```
private Integer projectId;
```

The `projectId` variable represents the number or ID of the project in Continuum which we will use shortly. We are using `Integer` so that it can be `null` initially. We have replaced the `link` variable as we won't be using it. Make sure that you also change its getter and setter methods. The last three methods in `ContinuumModel` also need to be changed as follows:

```
public Map<String, String> getValuesAsMap()
{
  Map<String, String> values = new HashMap<String, String>();
  values.put( "projectId", projectId != null ?
    Integer.toString( projectId ) : null );
  return values;
}

public void setValuesFromMap( Map<String, String> values )
{
  String value = values.get( "projectId" );
  this.projectId = value != null ?
    Integer.valueOf( value ) : null;
}
public List<String> getKeys()
{
  return Arrays.asList( "projectId" );
}
```

We also need to update the `ContinuumModelTest` to reflect the changes in the variable name and data type. You can refer to the sample code included with this chapter for the changes. Take note of the new method at the end which was added to check that the `Integer` type is handled:

```
@Test(expectedExceptions=NumberFormatException.class)
public void testSetMapNonIntegerValue()
{
  Map<String, String> values =
              Collections.singletonMap( "projectId", "foo" );
  model.setValuesFromMap( values );
}
```

The changes we made in the model also affect ContinuumBuildsPlugin. For now, we will just empty out the items returned until we can obtain them from Continuum:

```
public List<PanelItem> getItems( Project project )
{
  //PanelItem item = new PanelItem( "My Link",
  //getModel( project ).getLink() );
  //return Arrays.asList( item );
  return Collections.emptyList();
}
```

You can remove (or just comment out) the last three test cases in ContinuumBuildsPlugin since we changed the plugin to return an empty items list.

Now that we are done with the model changes specific to the sample application, we can construct the main part of the plugin that receives the build results, in the next section.

 There are some other potential configuration options you might like to add yourself. We could set a maximum number of results to list as another integer. If we were accessing a restricted part of Continuum we might have wanted to configure the username/password here, however we will grant guest access to the project so it is unnecessary in this example.

Using Continuum's web services

Continuum has almost all of its features available as web services. The web services are exposed by a single class called ContinuumService. To view this class' full API, visit http://continuum.apache.org/ref/1.3.3/apidocs/org/apache/maven/continuum/xmlrpc/ContinuumService.html.

Aside from the ContinuumService class, included with Continuum is a client API which is the layer that we will use to access the Continuum services. With XML-RPC, some objects are not mapped by default, but using the Continuum XML-RPC Client there's no need to transform the objects returned. Instead, we get the actual result object. (In XML-RPC, objects are returned as Map<Object, Object> or an array of objects, for example, Objects[]). The full reference of the client is available at http://continuum.apache.org/ref/1.3.3/apidocs/org/apache/maven/continuum/xmlrpc/client/ContinuumXmlRpcClient.html.

Let's start configuring our plugin to get a project's build results from Continuum. First, we must add the Continuum dependency to our plugin:

```
<dependency>
  <groupId>org.apache.continuum</groupId>
  <artifactId>continuum-xmlrpc-api</artifactId>
  <version>1.3.3</version>
</dependency>
<dependency>
  <groupId>org.apache.continuum</groupId>
  <artifactId>continuum-xmlrpc-client</artifactId>
  <version>1.3.3</version>
</dependency>
```

 You can replace the version with the newest version of Continuum you want to work with to access the newest features while retaining backward compatibility.

Now, we will replace the `getItems()` method of `ContinuumBuildsPlugin` which we commented out earlier. First, we will get the ID and URL from the configuration by adding the following code in the method. If you look at the sample code included with the chapter, you can see that we also added some error checks so that the panel shows an appropriate message if they are not present:

```
int projectId = getModel( project ).getProjectId();
String ciManagementUrl = project.getCiManagementUrl();
```

Now, let's get down to business. In order to get the project's build results, we need to connect to Continuum:

```
List<BuildResultSummary> results;
ContinuumXmlRpcClient client;

try
{
  URL serviceURL = new URL( ciManagementUrl + "/xmlrpc" );
  client = new ContinuumXmlRpcClient( serviceURL );
  results = client.getBuildResultsForProject( projectId );
}
catch ( Exception e )
{
  logger.warning( "Error reading build results: " + e.getMessage() );
  return errorMessage( "Unable to retrieve results: check application
                        logs for details" );
}
```

Looking at the code we added previously, you will see that we created the client and had it connect to /xmlrpc under Continuum. Note that we did not pass in the username and password as we will be using guest accessible functions. Next, we made a call to the ContinuumXmlRpcClient to get the build results for the given project identifier.

We now have a series of results that summarize the details.

From the API of the Continuum client, we knew that getting the build results returns a list of BuildResultSummary objects. The BuildResultSummary contains build information such as the build definition used, the state of the build, the build trigger, the start time and end time of the build, and so on. We will get the data that our plugin will be displaying on the project dashboard in the Centrepoint application from these results. We will construct a message like this on success:

```
2009-08-09 18:08:30 - #7 (0m11s)
```

That is, the (date build started, build number, and durationtime taken), or on failure:

```
2009-08-09 18:07:59 - Failed
```

To do this, we will loop through the build results and construct our message format:

```
String resultBaseUrl = ciManagementUrl +
    "/buildResult.action?projectId=" + projectId;
List<PanelItem> items = new ArrayList<PanelItem>();
for ( BuildResultSummary result : results )
{
  String title = new SimpleDateFormat( "yyyy-MM-dd HH:mm:ss" ).
              format( result.getStartTime() ) + " - ";

  String status = client.getProjectStatusAsString( result.getState() );
  if ( result.isSuccess() || "OK".equals( status ) )
  {
    String time = new SimpleDateFormat( "m'm'ss's'" ).format( result.
                getEndTime() - result.getStartTime() );
    title += "#" + result.getBuildNumber() + " (" + time + ")";
  }
  else
  {
    title += status;
  }
  String url = resultBaseUrl + "&buildId=" + result.getId();
  PanelItem item = new PanelItem( title, url );
  items.add( item );
}
return items;
```

Starting at the fourth line from the bottom in the previous code, we constructed a link to the build result then added it as an item in the panel list which we will be returned by the method. You can refer to the sample code for the full source of this method.

 This particular example application does no caching of the items so the request will be done on every execution. You may wish to cache the Continuum results for a period of time to avoid hitting the Continuum server with too many requests in a similar situation.

Now, we're almost ready to test it out!

 A good practice would be to write a unit test for this new method. For simplicity we haven't done so in the example code, but you'd be able to by injecting a mock implementation of the XML-RPC client for testing purposes.

Before we can use this in Centrepoint, there is one more thing that we need to do. Our deployment process is to copy the plugin JAR into Centrepoint's `WEB-INF/lib` directory. But we added dependencies, so these classes won't work on their own. One alternative would be to add all the other JARs as well. But we learned in Chapter 6, *Useful Maven Plugins*, that we can use the Shade plugin to make it easier. Add the following in the `<build>` section of our plugin's POM:

```
<plugins>
  <plugin>
   <groupId>org.apache.maven.plugins</groupId>
   <artifactId>maven-shade-plugin</artifactId>
   <version>1.2</version>
   <executions>
    <execution>
     <phase>package</phase>
     <goals>
      <goal>shade</goal>
     </goals>
     <configuration>
      <artifactSet>
       <excludes>
        <exclude>com.effectivemaven.centrepoint:model</exclude>
       </excludes>
      </artifactSet>
     </configuration>
    </execution>
   </executions>
  </plugin>
</plugins>
```

What we are doing here is shading all of the dependencies except for the Centrepoint model (as we need to use the one from the Centrepoint web application)

 To ensure that the plugin has less chance of conflicting with others, in a bigger system we should probably use the relocation feature to make the dependencies self-contained. Of course, a more sophisticated plugin system using something like OSGi could also dynamically load the dependencies and ensure classloaders don't clash.

Now, let's build our plugin by executing this in the command-line:

```
continuum-builds-plugin$ mvn package
```

After the plugin has been packaged, copy `target/continuum-builds-plugin-1.0-SNAPSHOT.jar` into `centrepoint-1.0/webapps/centrepoint/WEB-INF/lib`. Start Centrepoint using `./bin/centrepoint console`, then go to `http://localhost:8080/centrepoint`.

You will need to make sure that your Continuum instance from Chapter 8 and 9 is running. If you haven't set it up, you might like to skim Chapter 8 at this point.

Before we add the Centrepoint project to our dashboard, we need to make sure it knows where to find Continuum.

Go to the `centrepoint` directory in your local checkout from the previous chapter. It should have a version of `1.1-SNAPSHOT`, and at present it has a parent of `effectivemaven-parent` version 1. We should upgrade its parent to `2-SNAPSHOT`.

Now, in the `effectivemaven-parent` directory, the POM should already have the version `2-SNAPSHOT` from when we released it in Chapter 9, *Continuum in Depth*. We can now add the `<ciManagement>` information for the team:

```xml
<ciManagement>
  <system>continuum</system>
  <url>http://localhost:8082/continuum</url>
</ciManagement>
```

Install both POMs into the local repository for Centrepoint to find:

```
effectivemaven-parent$ mvn install
centrepoint$ mvn -N install
```

 The -N option builds the parent POM only, and does not process the modules. We have used it here for performance reasons.

Now, we can add our project to our dashboard. Go to `http://localhost:8080/` `centrepoint/project/add-maven` and fill in the form with `com.effectivemaven.` `centrepoint` as the **Group ID** and `centrepoint` as the **Artifact ID**, then click **Import**. This will take you to the project page with information about the project.

 If you have to re-add the project to change any information from the local repository, such as adding the `<ciManagement>` element, you will need to restart the server first as the underlying Maven libraries will cache the POM information that was loaded the first time.

Notice that there is a panel on the right side of the screen for Continuum. Initially it will say that there is no Continuum project configured. You can edit the configuration and provide the ID of the Continuum project. In our case, we will show the build results of the **Centrepoint Distribution**. To determine its project ID in Continuum, go to the **Project Group Summary** page of Centrepoint in Continuum then click **Centrepoint Distribution**. You should see the project ID from the requested URL in the navigation bar (for example, `/continuum/projectView.` `action?projectId=11`).

Now that you know the Continuum project ID of Centrepoint Distribution, go back to the Centerpoint application and set it in the configuration as follows:

CENTREPOINT

projectId	11
Update	

When returning to the project page, you will see an error in the panel. From the logs, you should see the following:

```
INFO: Connecting to http://localhost:8082/continuum/xmlrpc for
project 11

Aug 23, 2009 4:27:40 PM com.effectivemaven.centrepoint.plugins.
continuum.ContinuumBuildsPlugin getItems
WARNING: Error reading build results: Failed to invoke method
getBuildResultsForProject in class org.apache.maven.continuum.xmlrpc.
server.ContinuumServiceImpl: You're not authorized to execute this
action.
```

In case you get a different error, there might be another problem with Continuum. For example, a WARNING: Error reading build results: Failed to read servers response: Connection refused means Continuum is not running on the specified URL.

To resolve this error, go back to Continuum and grant the guest user the **Project User** role for Centrepoint. After doing this, return to the Centrepoint application again and refresh the page. You should be able to see the build results listed, similar to what we have here:

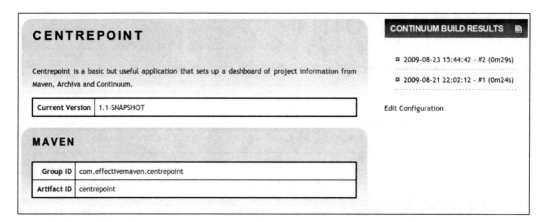

And that is how easy it is to use Continuum's web services. Aside from the work in assembling the Centrepoint structure, just a few lines were needed to retrieve the information from Continuum itself.

In the previous exercise , we only used one of the many methods exposed by Continuum. Some of the methods that you may want to take note of are the methods for adding and building projects in Continuum, retrieving individual project information and build results, and for canceling project builds.

Archiva web services

Web services were introduced to Archiva in version 1.2. Similarly, what we did with the Continuum plugin in the previous section, we will create an Archiva plugin to demonstrate how web services work.

Building the Archiva plugin

First, let's extract common configuration into a parent POM for the Archiva and Continuum plugins. Create a `plugins-parent` directory and add a POM with the following information:

```
<project xmlns="http://maven.apache.org/POM/4.0.0"
         xmlns:xsi="http://www.w3.org/2001/XMLSchema-instance"
         xsi:schemaLocation="http://maven.apache.org/POM/4.0.0
                    http://maven.apache.org/maven-v4_0_0.xsd">
  <modelVersion>4.0.0</modelVersion>
  <parent>
    <groupId>com.effectivemaven</groupId>
    <artifactId>effectivemaven-parent</artifactId>
    <version>1</version>
    <relativePath>
      ../../effectivemaven-parent/pom.xml
    </relativePath>
  </parent>
  <groupId>com.effectivemaven.centrepoint.plugins</groupId>
  <artifactId>plugins-parent</artifactId>
  <version>1-SNAPSHOT</version>
  <packaging>pom</packaging>
  <dependencies>
    <dependency>
      <groupId>com.effectivemaven.centrepoint</groupId>
      <artifactId>model</artifactId>
      <version>1.0</version>
    </dependency>
    <dependency>
      <groupId>org.testng</groupId>
      <artifactId>testng</artifactId>
      <version>5.8</version>
      <classifier>jdk15</classifier>
      <scope>test</scope>
    </dependency>
  </dependencies>
</project>
```

The Shade plugin was not moved up, for reasons we will see shortly. As we're referencing the `effectivemaven-parent` POM, the `plugins-parent` will inherit some of its information. Due to this, all of the above and the compiler settings can be removed from the Continuum plugin POM once the parent is added. The Continuum plugin's POM should look like the following after the changes are made:

```
...
<modelVersion>4.0.0</modelVersion>
<parent>
  <groupId>com.effectivemaven.centrepoint.plugins</groupId>
  <artifactId>plugins-parent</artifactId>
  <version>1-SNAPSHOT</version>
  <relativePath>../plugins-parent/pom.xml</relativePath>
</parent>
<artifactId>continuum-builds-plugin</artifactId>
<version>1.0-SNAPSHOT</version>
<name>Centrepoint Plugin for Continuum Builds</name>
<description>
Retrieve build results from a Continuum server and display
as a panel in the Centrepoint project page.
</description>
<dependencies>
  <dependency>
    <groupId>org.apache.continuum</groupId>
    <artifactId>continuum-xmlrpc-api</artifactId>
    <version>1.3.3</version>
  </dependency>
  <dependency>
    <groupId>org.apache.continuum</groupId>
    <artifactId>continuum-xmlrpc-client</artifactId>
    <version>1.3.3</version>
  </dependency>
</dependencies>
<build>
  <plugins>
    <plugin>
      <groupId>org.apache.maven.plugins</groupId>
      <artifactId>maven-shade-plugin</artifactId>
      <version>1.2</version>
      <executions>
        <execution>
          <phase>package</phase>
          <goals>
            <goal>shade</goal>
```

```
          </goals>
          <configuration>
            <artifactSet>
              <excludes>
                <exclude>
                  com.effectivemaven.centrepoint:model
                </exclude>
              </excludes>
            </artifactSet>
          </configuration>
        </execution>
      </executions>
    </plugin>
  </plugins>
</build>
...
```

Now, to create our Archiva plugin, execute the following from inside the `plugins/` directory:

```
plugins$ mvn archetype:generate \
          -DarchetypeGroupId=com.effectivemaven.centrepoint \
          -DarchetypeArtifactId=plugin-archetype \
          -DarchetypeVersion=1.1-SNAPSHOT
```

Provide the following input parameters when prompted:

```
group Id : com.effectivemaven.centrepoint.plugins

artifactId : archiva-search-plugin

version : 1.0-SNAPSHOT

package: com.effectivemaven.centrepoint.plugins.archiva
```

Similar to what we did with the Continuum plugin, we will also make a few modifications. First, let's set the parent as we did previously, then remove the inherited Compiler plugin configuration and Centrepoint Model and TestNG dependencies. We will also update the `<name>` in the POM and add a `<description>`:

```
<name>Centrepoint Plugin for Archiva Search</name>
<description>
Retrieve search results from an Archiva server and display
as a panel in the Centrepoint project page.
</description>
```

Now we can remove the generated model created by the archetype as this plugin won't need any configuration. Remove MyModel and MyModelTest from the generated plugin.

Because we removed the model, we also need to update the plugin. You can open the Archiva plugin in your IDE to start making the changes. First, remove the ConfigurablePanel<MyModel> interface from MyPlugin. Then, remove getModel() and getId() methods from MyPlugin. You also need to modify the getItems() method. For now, we can just empty out the items returned until we can obtain them from XMLRPC:

```
public List<PanelItem> getItems( Project project )
{
  //PanelItem item = new PanelItem( "My Link",
  //getModel( project ).getLink() );
  //return Arrays.asList( item );
  return Collections.emptyList();
}
```

We will also comment out for now the affected test cases in MyPluginTest.

Next, we will rename rename MyPlugin and MyPluginTest to ArchivaSearchPlugin and ArchivaSearchPluginTest respectively. We also need to update src/main/resources/META-INF/centrepoint/plugin.properties to reflect the new plugin name.

Finally, in the plugin (and the corresponding test case), change the title on the panel as follows:

```
public String getTitle( Project project )
{
  return "Archiva Search Results";
}
```

Let's see if our plugin builds:

archiva-search-plugin$ mvn install

You should get a successful build afterwards.

Using Archiva's web services

Archiva exposes two types of services: the *administration service* and the *search service*. As the name implies, the administration service is for administrative tasks such as executing a repository scan, retrieving Archiva repositories, and enabling and disabling consumers. On the other hand, the search service provides methods for searching artifacts in the Archiva repositories. The IAM project (a Maven integration plugin for Eclipse) uses this service to provide artifact search from Archiva repositories in Eclipse. You can refer to the latest API to see all the exposed methods `http://archiva.apache.org/ref/1.2.1/apidocs/org/apache/archiva/web/ xmlrpc/api/package-summary.html`.

In our exercise, we will only be interfacing with the `SearchService`. Now, let's start configuring our plugin. The first step is again to add the dependencies.

```
<dependencies>
  <dependency>
    <groupId>org.apache.archiva</groupId>
    <artifactId>archiva-xmlrpc-api</artifactId>
    <version>1.2.1</version>
  </dependency>
  <dependency>
    <groupId>com.atlassian.xmlrpc</groupId>
    <artifactId>atlassian-xmlrpc-binder</artifactId>
    <version>0.9</version>
  </dependency>
</dependencies>
```

As you may notice, this is a bit different from Continuum's. Instead of a custom client for interfacing with the actual service, we use Atlassian's XMLRPC Binder. It binds and converts the object types returned by the web services so we don't need to do any conversion on our end.

Now going back to our plugin, add the following in the `getItems()` method:

```
MavenCoordinates coordinates =
(MavenCoordinates) project.getExtensionModel( "maven" );
```

We will use the Maven coordinates of the project to search for it in Archiva. Again, we get the URL from the project:

```
String repositoryUrl = project.getRepositoryUrl();
```

This is parsed to remove the repository ID so that we can determine what the
/xmlrpc URL should be. In this case, the Service URL is constructed using the
Atlassian Binder library:

```
Binder binder = new DefaultBinder();
URL serviceUrl = new URL( archivaUrl + "/xmlrpc" );
ConnectionInfo connect = new ConnectionInfo();
connect.setUsername( "guest" );
connect.setPassword( "" );
SearchService searchService = binder.bind( SearchService.class,
                             serviceUrl, connect );
```

Now, we are going to use the getArtifactVersions() method to get all available
versions in the repository:

```
artifacts = searchService.getArtifactVersions
(coordinates.getGroupId(), coordinates.getArtifactId());
```

Similar to what we did in the Continuum plugin, we will create the results by
iterating through the returned search results by the web service and add it to our
panel list:

```
String browseUrl = archivaUrl + "/browse/" +
  coordinates.getGroupId() + "/" +
  coordinates.getArtifactId() + "/";
List<PanelItem> items = new ArrayList<PanelItem>();
for ( Artifact artifact : artifacts )
{
  PanelItem item = new PanelItem(artifact.getVersion(),
    browseUrl + artifact.getVersion());
  items.add(item);
}
```

You can refer to the final plugin code included with this chapter to view the
full source.

We're now getting ready to build our plugin but first, we need to add the Shade
configuration again. Unfortunately, the Archiva libraries drag a number of
implementation dependencies. Some clash with those from the Centrepoint web
application, so we also need to exclude them from shading. Add the following
configuration in the POM:

```
<build>
  <plugins>
   <plugin>
     <groupId>org.apache.maven.plugins</groupId>
     <artifactId>maven-shade-plugin</artifactId>
```

```
<version>1.2</version>
<executions>
 <execution>
  <phase>package</phase>
  <goals>
   <goal>shade</goal>
  </goals>
  <configuration>
   <artifactSet>
    <excludes>
     <exclude>
      com.effectivemaven.centrepoint:model
     </exclude>
     <!--
       Exclude conflicts with the Centrepoint libraries
     -->
     <exclude>
      org.codehaus.plexus:plexus-component-api
     </exclude>
     <exclude>org.apache.maven:maven-model</exclude>
     <exclude>xerces:xerces</exclude>
     <exclude>xerces:xercesImpl</exclude>
     <exclude>xerces:xmlParserAPIs</exclude>
    </excludes>
   </artifactSet>
  </configuration>
 </execution>
</executions>
</plugin>
</plugins>
</build>
```

Now, let's build our project. Execute the following from the command-line:

```
archiva-search-plugin$ mvn package
```

Once the build finishes, copy `target/archiva-search-plugin-1.0-SNAPSHOT.jar` into `centrepoint-1.0/webapps/centrepoint/WEB-INF/lib`. Start Centrepoint again by executing `./bin/centrepoint console` then go to `http://localhost:8080/centrepoint`. Make sure that your Archiva instance from Chapter 2 or 10 is running and that there are deployments of Centrepoint in it.

If you go back to the Centrepoint project page, you will see the Archiva panel on the right-hand side. It has an error though, and if you take a look at the logs, you should see the following:

```
WARNING: Error retrieving results from: http://localhost:8081/archiva:
Could not execute RPC method getArtifactVersions
java.lang.RuntimeException: Could not execute RPC method
getArtifactVersions
at com.atlassian.xmlrpc.RPCCallMethodInterceptor.invoke(RPCCallMethodI
nterceptor.java:74)
...
Caused by: org.apache.xmlrpc.XmlRpcException: Password expired.
...
```

It turns out that there is a bug in Archiva 1.2.1 that rejects the guest password because it is set to force change on startup. A workaround for this is to log in to the Archiva UI with the guest username and no password. When prompted to change the password, just enter the new password and confirmation (anything will work).

With this change in place, return to Centrepoint and refresh the page—you should now see the versions appear!

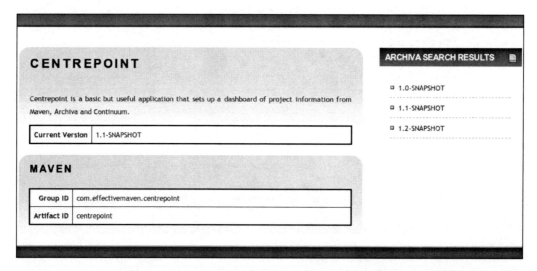

Aside from retrieving versions of an artifact, it is also possible to do a quick search (like the one from the Archiva UI) via web services. Another similar feature from the UI is searching for an artifact using checksums (like in **Find Artifact**). The same rule applies with regard to permissions, only those repositories which a user has access to will be included in the search.

As for the administration service, you can retrieve and enable/disable the database and repository consumers, execute a repository or database scan, delete an artifact from a repository and retrieve all Archiva repositories. Of course, you must have the necessary permissions in order to execute them.

Summary

We got to know more about Redback in this chapter. We were able to see how to take advantage of Redback's dynamic roles in configuring security for both Archiva and Continuum.

In the latter part of the chapter, we saw how we can integrate Archiva and Continuum with other tools through web services.

A Troubleshooting Maven

Maven's strengths can also be its weaknesses. With so much functionality provided by plugins, when something goes wrong it can be hard to tell exactly what is at fault. Here we will look at some common scenarios and learn how to investigate an issue when it occurs.

These may not be solutions, or the ideal behavior for Maven to exhibit in many cases, but it should give you the tools necessary to track down the cause of a problem before investing too many hours into it.

Examining Maven output

If an error occurs that seems unfamiliar, the first step is to examine the output of the build.

This can be as simple as looking for the last goal executed. In the event that the error message is not clear enough, we will at least know what Maven was running at the time it occurred, and can jump to the plugin web site for information on the possible cause, or at least configuration options that will alter the behavior or output of the plugin (such as the verbosity level) to help troubleshoot.

However, often the error is not that simple, and finding the cause in a large amount of output is difficult. Two steps can be taken to make this part easier.

Firstly, you can scan the output for the **[WARN]** or **[ERROR]** prefix. While not always used, anything logged at this level by a Maven plugin may indicate a problem. If you prefer not to scan the output, you can also run Maven with the `-q` option. This is an extremely quiet mode of operation, logging only warnings, errors, and messages output directly to the system by plugins.

A more reasonable measure you can take in advance is to reduce the amount of output during the build. This has a number of side benefits, such as reducing the size of build results in a continuous integration server, but more importantly helps you see what is really happening in the build. A key offender in the area of build output can be unit tests. As they often do their own logging or produce their own output, this may appear during the build rather than just receiving the test summary.

However, Surefire has a configuration option to remedy this by channeling all of the output into a separate file for each test. It can be configured like this:

```
<plugin>
  <groupId>org.apache.maven.plugins</groupId>
  <artifactId>maven-surefire-plugin</artifactId>
  <version>2.4.3</version>
  <configuration>
    <redirectTestOutputToFile>true</redirectTestOutputToFile>
  </configuration>
</plugin>
```

As simple as this step seems, it can be of great benefit in maintaining your build without any loss of information.

> Of course, another option that gives greater control is to avoid the use of the System.out and System.err streams in your test cases, and to configure the logging system used by your code to be as silent as possible, or to write to a file directly.

A final note on Maven output: **don't be misled**. There are some plugins and even internals of Maven that will report a **[WARN]** or even **[ERROR]** message where the behavior is actually correct but it is trying to communicate something that may only potentially be a problem, or is actually a programming fault. Review each message carefully to see if it is the cause of a problem rather than assuming that it is by the label.

Using debug mode

Often, rather than focusing on a piece of output to find an error, you will need more information than is presented by default for successful debugging. Maven offers two levels of extra information.

The first is the -e option. This simply reports the Java exception that caused Maven to fail when a build error occurs. Intended more for developers troubleshooting bugs in their plugins, it can be of benefit to all in certain circumstances. By examining the stack trace, you have two extra courses of action:

- Review the *nested exceptions* (by looking for the **Caused by** text) for a potential cause that was not originally reported by Maven. This can occur when a plugin does not carry along important information from an original exception. For example, a download may fail due to a particular HTTP error code, but that may only be reported at two or three levels of exceptions deep.
- If the plugin is open source, you can use the stack trace to examine the source code of the plugin and try to understand the actual problem. Obviously, this would be a last resort!

The stack trace will also be helpful to developers that might later need to fix a bug that caused the problem you are experiencing, so this option is helpful to capture when reporting the issue.

The second option is the kitchen sink alternative, referred to as **debug output**, which is the -X option. This outputs everything logged anywhere in Maven, and unfortunately there is no middle-of-the-road alternative. It will contain information on the parameters passed to plugins, class paths used to execute Java code, command line parameters for external tools, information about dependency resolution, and much, much more. You should almost certainly capture the output to a file to examine the failure afterwards.

Confirming the expected models

The assembly of the actual project model used for the Maven build can be a reasonably complex process through inheritance and the application of profiles and management sections of the POM. For this reason, it can be useful to examine exactly what model Maven is attempting to use to see if there is an error in the content.

The Help plugin can be of assistance here. In addition to the goals outlined in Chapter 1, *Maven in a Nutshell*, three goals are particularly geared towards troubleshooting.

The first is the effective-pom goal:

```
$ mvn help:effective-pom
```

The output of this goal is very straightforward. It consists of a full listing of the POM file as Maven resolves it. This will have populated fields that have been inherited; including defaults, as well as adjusting paths to the location you are running the build from, and so on.

Its counterpart for your settings files is the `effective-settings` goal:

```
$ mvn help:effective-settings
```

Again, this will display the complete settings model being used by Maven, collapsing the one located in the Maven installation with the one stored in the home directory.

Settings caution

Occasionally, your Maven settings will contain sensitive information such as passwords in plain text. While these may be stored in a relatively secure location on your hard drive, executing the above goal will output them to the screen. In particular, do not blindly copy that output into a bug report or mailing list post while you are investigating a problem! Maven 2.1.0 and above have the capability to mask those passwords to avoid such issues.

Analyzing dependencies

Problems are often much more subtle than a direct error in the build, however, and dependencies can be a major cause. Because Maven resolves transitive dependencies, it is common to be using dependencies, or versions, that you may not have expected. Similar types of problems you are likely to see are:

- Incorrect versions of dependencies being used
- Duplicated dependencies (for example, if an artifact changes to a new group ID in a more recent version, both versions will appear in the dependency tree)
- Missing dependencies
- Unwanted dependencies
- Incorrect dependency scopes leading to incorrect classpaths for certain goals

As illustrated in Chapter 1, *Maven in a Nutshell*, the Enforcer plugin can be used as preventative medicine against some of these problems.

One of the most useful tools you will be able to use in evaluating these problems is the `dependency:tree` goal. Here is the output from the sample web application used in Chapter 1, *Maven in a Nutshell*:

```
[INFO] [dependency:tree]
[INFO] com.effectivemaven.chapter01:simple-webapp:war:1.0-SNAPSHOT
[INFO] +- org.slf4j:slf4j-api:jar:1.5.0:compile
[INFO] +- org.slf4j:slf4j-simple:jar:1.5.0:runtime
[INFO] \- org.testng:testng:jar:jdk15:5.8:test
[INFO]    \- junit:junit:jar:3.8.1:test
```

As you can see, we did not introduce many transitive dependencies, though it may have been surprising to see that we are still using JUnit as a part of TestNG!

Much like the earlier `effective-pom` goal, the tree above will illustrate exactly what dependencies Maven ends up using in the build. This information is also shown in debug mode, though it contains a lot more of the decision points and other interspersed debug output that can make it much harder to read.

The remedies for dependency problems vary—you may use the dependency management section to enforce a particular version, the exclusions section of the dependency declaration to prune a particular dependency from the tree, or alter the repository metadata of another project to ensure it is correct in future. These alternatives are also discussed in Chapter 7, *Maven Best Practices*.

One final issue is worth special attention here. Maven constructs its dependency tree by reading the POM file for an associated dependency and drawing the transitive dependencies from that. If Maven fails to resolve the POM due to a missing file or other download problem, the build will still continue (as it is historically valid, though now considered deprecated, to have a project without a POM). In this case, the project will be considered to have no dependencies, even though they may have been expected. If this occurs, Maven will display a prominent warning message early in the build.

Download problems

Getting into trouble downloading artifacts for the build or dependencies of the project can be a common issue in Maven builds as well. The following are some tips for alleviating these issues.

If you have an outright connection issue, the debug output described earlier may contain the exception that occurred, even if the build happened to continue. It is worth taking the URL that Maven was attempting to download from and checking that you can access it from a browser to rule out any external factors.

 You might be inclined to use the command line application `wget` on GNU-based systems. This may give you a false failure, however, as applications that are capable of scraping content are banned from the central repository from time to time to prevent bandwidth abuse.

You may notice a problem in these situations where a repository has been "blacklisted":

```
[INFO] Repository 'central' will be blacklisted
```

This is often misinterpreted as meaning that the repository will never be used again—but this is not the case. It is actually only blacklisted during the same build to avoid repeatedly trying to use a repository that cannot be reached or may have timed out, for the speed of the build. The decision is not remembered across builds and the repository will be used again on the next run.

If you operate in a constrained network environment, you should also check your proxy settings or server username and password for the repository in question (the `help:effective-settings` goal described above can be of assistance here).

If the download itself seems to succeed but the **resolution** process fails with an artifact not being found, then you may have a problem with corrupted local metadata. While the cases where this occurs have been reduced, there have been some situations that can lead to this in particular:

- Running offline or where network connections will regularly fail, causing Maven to permanently assume an artifact cannot be found

- Running in an environment where incorrect content is deliberately returned. A classic example is the Wi-Fi in the airport lounge that throws up a perfectly valid HTML login page on every single request, getting into the local repository metadata and artifacts if checksums are not being enforced (as shown in Chapter 7, *Maven Best Practices*)

- Running with an incorrect clock time that can cause update checks to stop running in the future as the files never appear out of date

While it is possible to prune out corrupted metadata selectively, it can be very tedious. The most comprehensive solution is to delete the content from the local repository entirely—and while this is technically harmless, it is not recommended, as it will cause the need to download a large portion of the internet again on subsequent runs!

For this reason, it is highly recommended to install a repository manager in a local network, or even on your own machine. This can run with a low footprint and can act as your personal proxy to all other remote repositories with a clean set of artifacts and metadata. With this in place, it is possible to delete your local repository at any time without having to worry about the cost of downloading the artifacts again on subsequent builds. It can also reduce the number of potential download problems you will experience and give you more control over how to handle issues with metadata and checksums, for example.

B

Recent Maven Features

Maven 2.0 has been the predominant version available over the last 4 years. Recently, however, some new versions have introduced features that may not yet be widely used. This appendix provides a summary of the new features and a manual on how to use them if you are a new Maven user, or are mainly familiar with prior versions of Maven.

Server password encryption

Password encryption has been available since Maven 2.1.0. At present, it is only capable of masking server passwords in `settings.xml`.

With this solution, you must still protect access to a file in your home directory to prevent users being able to find out your password. However, it offers several enhancements:

- Not storing the password in plain text avoids accidental exposure (on the screen or by pasting the file)
- Someone must access both the master key and the settings file to obtain the passwords
- The master key can be stored in a more secure location (for example, a USB thumb drive or a personal mounted network drive)

This offers a reasonable level of security for your server passwords while still allowing them to be used without regular keyboard entry.

 Passwords might still be captured when the servers are used for artifact downloads and uploads. Make sure you use a secure channel such as HTTPS or SSH for repository access.

To use the feature, let us review what we learned in Chapter 2, *Staying in Control with Archiva*, where we used it to mask the Archiva repository credentials.

The first thing that we need to do is to generate an encrypted password by executing the following command:

```
$ mvn --encrypt-master-password abc123
```

Copy and paste the result in your ~/.m2/security-settings.xml as follows:

```
<settingsSecurity>
  <master>
    {JZi5su5v5boHBztoneIMgVyniJesHwvmXNHjFk6jo30=}
  </master>
</settingsSecurity>
```

Encrypt our Archiva repository password:

```
$ mvn --encrypt-password pass123
```

Copy and paste the result to the ~/.m2/settings.xml file as follows:

```
...
<server>
  <id>snapshots</id>
  <username>archiva</username>
  <password>
    {mTjtmOvhBxEHjiAzHStjYvmdi+KMIs/8Wz6/3LdUwIo=}
  </password>
</server>
<server>
  <id>releases</id>
  <username>archiva</username>
  <password>
    {mTjtmOvhBxEHjiAzHStjYvmdi+KMIs/8Wz6/3LdUwIo=}
  </password>
</server>
...
```

The configuration is now complete and will be used on repository requests with the given repository ID.

Finally, if you would like to secure the ~/.m2/security-settings.xml file on another drive, you can move it to the new location and replace the file contents with the following pointing to the new secure location:

```
<settingsSecurity>
  <relocation>
    /Volumes/secure/settings-security.xml
  </relocation>
</settingsSecurity>
```

More details on password security in Maven are covered in `http://maven.apache.org/guides/mini/guide-encryption.html`

Reactor project selection

Maven 2.1.0 introduced additional command line options for defining a subset of the modules to build in a multi-module project. These choices can make regularly building a part of a project much more efficient during development.

We will look at these examples in the context of the final application structure that we built in Chapter 3, *Building an Application Using Maven*. Refer to the sample code for that chapter to try these for yourself.

Resuming a failed build

The first mode of operation is when we want to resume a previous build. This is most helpful when a build fails after some time in the middle of the list of modules, where we fix the issue and then wish to continue from the same point, knowing that any previously built modules are not affected.

Consider the reactor build order for Centrepoint when all default modules are built:

```
[INFO] Reactor build order:
[INFO]    Centrepoint
[INFO]    Centrepoint Documentation Skin
[INFO]    Centrepoint Java Modules
[INFO]    Centrepoint Data Model
[INFO]    Centrepoint Data Store API
[INFO]    Centrepoint Maven Project Importer
[INFO]    Centrepoint Data Store (Flat file)
[INFO]    Centrepoint Web Application
[INFO]    Centrepoint Documentation
[INFO]    Centrepoint Distribution
```

Now, let us say we encounter a broken test in the **Maven Project Importer** module. Rather than building all of the modules again, we can continue from the same point:

```
centrepoint$ mvn -rf modules/maven-importer install
```

The `-rf` argument (which is short-hand for the argument `--resume-from`), specifies a *single directory of the module to continue building from*. The order used in the next build will match the previous execution, as we can see:

```
[INFO] Reactor build order:
[INFO]    Centrepoint Maven Project Importer
[INFO]    Centrepoint Data Store (Flat file)
[INFO]    Centrepoint Web Application
[INFO]    Centrepoint Documentation
[INFO]    Centrepoint Distribution
```

This option can also be used for building a subset of the modules when you know the others have not been affected during development. However, there is a better set of options. These do not require building all of the modules in the existing order if they are unaffected.

Building a subset of modules

The other mode of operation available allows the direct specification of the module(s) to build, and corresponding type of dependencies to include.

This is achieved using the `-pl` argument (or alternatively, `--projects`) followed by a comma-delimited list of directories of the modules to build.

> You can also use the `groupId:artifactId` syntax instead of a directory to define a module to build (which also works in the `--resume-from` argument). However, this is typically going to be longer to type!

For example, to build just the `model` and `documentation` modules, you can run the following command:

```
centrepoint$ mvn -pl modules/model,documentation install
```

As you can see, only those modules are built:

```
[INFO] Reactor build order:
[INFO]    Centrepoint Data Model
[INFO]    Centrepoint Documentation
```

However, this is rarely the complete build that you would want to run. Changing the model potentially affects the testing of the modules that depend on it such as the data store, and even more importantly, the web application and distribution need to be rebuilt to include the updated library.

To ensure that these modules are included, we can add the -amd (or --also-make-dependents) argument to Maven:

```
centrepoint$ mvn -amd -pl modules/model,documentation install
```

As you can see, all of the modules described above that depend on the model are now included in the reactor build:

```
[INFO] Reactor build order:
[INFO]    Centrepoint Data Model
[INFO]    Centrepoint Data Store API
[INFO]    Centrepoint Maven Project Importer
[INFO]    Centrepoint Data Store (Flat file)
[INFO]    Centrepoint Web Application
[INFO]    Centrepoint Documentation
[INFO]    Centrepoint Distribution
```

This argument is quite helpful in consistently building a subset of the application when one or more modules have been changed and not everything is needed again. In this example, we have just skipped the parent modules and skin, but if we were building a module with fewer dependencies then the list would be much shorter.

 If we were to remove the documentation from the project list in this command, it would not be built, as it has no dependency (direct or indirect) on the model.

Now, consider the opposite use case. Let us say that we had just checked out the project and wanted to build the Maven Project Importer library. That depends on some other libraries, but we do not want to build the web application and distribution that are later in the chain.

For this purpose, we have the -am (or --also-make) argument. When added to the project list argument, it will add to the reactor any modules that are required to build the requested projects.

To illustrate the example stated above, run the following command:

```
centrepoint$ mvn -am -pl modules/maven-importer install
```

As you can see, the parent projects and dependencies of the importer module are built, but no other modules are:

```
[INFO]      Centrepoint
[INFO]      Centrepoint Java Modules
[INFO]      Centrepoint Data Model
[INFO]      Centrepoint Data Store API
[INFO]      Centrepoint Maven Project Importer
```

A final note: the `-am` and `-amd` options can also be used together to include the dependencies in *both directions* in the reactor build. Consider the following command:

```
centrepoint$ mvn -am -amd -pl modules/maven-importer install
```

When this is executed, the union of the above two lists of modules are included:

```
[INFO]      Centrepoint
[INFO]      Centrepoint Java Modules
[INFO]      Centrepoint Data Model
[INFO]      Centrepoint Data Store API
[INFO]      Centrepoint Maven Project Importer
[INFO]      Centrepoint Data Store (Flat file)
[INFO]      Centrepoint Web Application
[INFO]      Centrepoint Distribution
```

Modules that are unrelated to the importer module such as the documentation and skin are not built in this scenario.

The Reactor plugin

For those using versions earlier than Maven 2.1.0, the above functionality is available through the Reactor plugin. As you'll see below, the plugin also offers an additional goal (`reactor:make-scm-changes`) that is not available above and which will still be of use to users of Maven 2.1.0 and above.

A complete reference to the plugin can also be found at `http://maven.apache.org/plugins/maven-reactor-plugin/`.

While the plugin can still be used in newer releases of Maven, it has some drawbacks in comparison to its command line counterpart:

- It is slower as it has to run Maven to find the modules to build, then run a new Maven instance with the restricted number of modules
- Longer syntax to type
- The ordering used for resumed builds can sometimes be different to the one used originally

Let us take a look at the examples from above and how they would be applied using the Reactor plugin.

The corresponding goal to resume a failed build is `reactor:resume`, passing a `from` parameter that specifies the directory of the module to resume from. Our example above for the `-rf` argument would instead be run using:

```
centrepoint$ mvn reactor:resume -Dfrom=modules/maven-importer
```

As you can see, this is a considerably longer command to type than the example presented earlier if it is available!

We should note that as we are running a goal from Maven, we can't select the goals to run as we did with the command line version. To address this, all of the goals in the Reactor plugin support passing in the `goals` argument, which defaults to `install`. For example, to resume using the `clean deploy` goals instead, use the following:

```
centrepoint$ mvn reactor:resume -Dfrom=modules/maven-importer \
            -Dgoals="clean deploy"
```

There is no direct goal that represents the `-pl` option from the command line on its own, but rather two goals `reactor:make-dependents` and `reactor:make` that represent the two alternative switches `-amd` and `-am` respectively. To supply the projects that would be specified by the `-pl` argument, both goals take the argument `-Dmake.folders`.

Therefore, we have the following example corresponding to that of `-amd` above which will build the model and documentation modules and everything that depends on them:

```
centrepoint$ mvn reactor:make-dependents \
            -Dmake.folders=modules/model,documentation
```

Likewise, there is the following corresponding to the `-am` argument that builds the importer and everything that it depends on:

```
centrepoint$ mvn reactor:make \
            -Dmake.folders=modules/maven-importer
```

There is no corresponding command available to build both lists simultaneously as was possible with the combination of the `-am` and `-amd` arguments shown previously.

Building modules with local changes

The additional goal that exists in the Reactor plugin, but not the command line, is the `reactor:make-scm-changes` goal. The purpose of this goal is straightforward – to rebuild all modules that have had some local changes that are not committed.

The goal is simply run as:

```
centrepoint$ mvn reactor:make-scm-changes
```

To determine what to build, the plugin uses the Maven SCM library to run a status check, much like the Release plugin does before proceeding with a release. These are then collapsed into the list of modules affected, which form the project list to build. The build then continues with these modules, and any modules that depend on them.

 At present, changes to the POM in the directory where the goal is run are not detected. If this is the case, assuming all modules use that POM as the parent, then you can simply run `mvn install` to get the same behavior!

As with the previous goals, it is possible to customize the goals that are run using the `goals` command line parameter. The default is to run `install`.

Reconfiguring default life cycle goals

One of the most interesting features that has appeared in Maven 2.2.0 and above is the ability to add configuration specifically to the goal execution supplied by default lifecycle bindings.

Previously, you could only do this at the plugin level, for example:

```
<plugin>
  <groupId>org.apache.maven.plugins</groupId>
  <artifactId>maven-surefire-plugin</artifactId>
  <version>2.4.3</version>
  <configuration>
    <excludes>
      <exclude>**/selenium/**</exclude>
    </excludes>
  </configuration>
</plugin>
```

There are two problems with this:

1. It may not be appropriate for **all** goals in the plugin to take this configuration. This is a common problem with the Compiler plugin, where you may want different parameters for the `compile` and `testCompile` goals (such as the JDK level—a problem well known by TestNG users developing on JDK 1.4!)

2. You can't erase configuration through inheritance—so as the example above shows, you are stuck with those `excludes` even if you define a new goal to run a second set of tests

Consider the addition of the following to the above:

```
<profile>
  <id>selenium</id>
  <build>
    <plugins>
      <plugin>
        <groupId>org.apache.maven.plugins</groupId>
        <artifactId>maven-surefire-plugin</artifactId>
        <executions>
          <execution>
            <id>selenium-tests</id>
            <configuration>
              <includes>
                <include>**/selenium/**</include>
              </includes>
            </configuration>
            <goals>
              <goal>test</goal>
            </goals>
          </execution>
        </executions>
      </plugin>
    </plugins>
  </build>
</profile>
```

This will do nothing, as only the Selenium tests are to be run (`includes`), but all Selenium tests are disabled (by inheritance of `excludes`).

This leads to a convoluted combination of turning off the default binding and re-adding it with its configuration, as a modification to the first sample:

```
<plugin>
  <groupId>org.apache.maven.plugins</groupId>
  <artifactId>maven-surefire-plugin</artifactId>
  <version>2.4.3</version>
  <configuration>
    <skip>true</skip>
  </configuration>
  <executions>
    <execution>
      <id>unit-tests</id>
      <configuration>
        <skip>false</skip>
        <excludes>
          <exclude>**/selenium/**</exclude>
        </excludes>
      </configuration>
      <goals>
        <goal>test</goal>
      </goals>
    </execution>
  </executions>
</plugin>
```

The `skip` flag also needed to be added to the Selenium profile.

 This example is also discussed in the section Running integration tests using naming patterns in Chapter 4, *Application Testing with Maven*.

Maven 2.2.0 added a simple solution for this problem. All of the executions in the default lifecycle are assigned IDs of the form `default-phase`. Because Maven's inheritance merges executions with identical IDs, you can assign configuration directly to the built in goal and no others.

This means that the previous section can be reduced to be closer to the original, like so:

```
<plugin>
  <groupId>org.apache.maven.plugins</groupId>
  <artifactId>maven-surefire-plugin</artifactId>
  <version>2.4.3</version>
  <executions>
    <execution>
      <id>default-test</id>
      <configuration>
        <excludes>
          <exclude>**/selenium/**</exclude>
        </excludes>
      </configuration>
    </execution>
  </executions>
</plugin>
```

The goals are not necessary in the execution, as they were already given in the default binding.

This results in a more intuitive pattern for setting up multiple test executions (a common occurrence with profiles and integration tests), as well as use cases such as configuring the Compiler plugin's main and test compilation goals separately.

However, there is one more thing to watch out for. Taking advantage of this will mean the build is no longer compatible with earlier versions of Maven. To make sure you are not caught out, you should add the Enforcer plugin somewhere in the build:

```
<plugin>
  <groupId>org.apache.maven.plugins</groupId>
  <artifactId>maven-enforcer-plugin</artifactId>
  <version>1.0-beta-1</version>
  <executions>
    <execution>
      <id>enforce</id>
      <goals>
        <goal>enforce</goal>
      </goals>
      <configuration>
        <rules>
          <requireMavenVersion>[2.2.0,)</requireMavenVersion>
        </rules>
      </configuration>
    </execution>
  </executions>
</plugin>
```

In addition to changing the defaults, you can also now supply configuration that is targeted at command line invocations (without affecting the main build). More information on all of these can be found at `http://maven.apache.org/guides/mini/guide-default-execution-ids.html`.

Parallel artifact resolution

By default, Maven 2.1.0 and above will download up to five artifacts at a time. There is no need to add any additional configuration to enable this new feature.

At present, it will only download artifacts from different groups simultaneously. This limit was made to prevent potential sequencing issues. This may be enhanced in a later version of Maven, however at present it limits the possible performance gains by raising the number of parallel downloads. The main gains will be when there are a number of large artifacts to download, or when the local repository is regularly cleaned.

 Even with a repository manager very close by caching artifacts, parallel downloads can improve performance in retrieving the artifacts with a clean repository.

It is possible to change the number of active download threads, which is useful if you wish to try to add a minimal amount more performance, or if you need to limit the resources used by the Maven process.

To change the size of the thread pool, start Maven using `-Dmaven.artifact.threads`. For example, to only download single artifacts at a time:

```
$ mvn -Dmaven.artifact.threads=1 clean install
```

You may wish to set this option permanently, in which case you can use the `MAVEN_OPTS` environment variable. For example:

```
$ export MAVEN_OPTS=-Dmaven.artifact.threads=3
```

Such an option may be considered within your build server. In Continuum, this can be added to a build definition via an installation environment variable. See *Installations* in Chapter 8, *Continuum: Ensuring the Health of your Source Code* for an example of configuring `MAVEN_OPTS` in Continuum.

C

Migrating Archiva and Continuum Data

Databases are important components in both Archiva and Continuum. These are where the data used within the applications is stored and kept track of. Due to this, it is important to know how to configure and migrate them.

Using a different database

Archiva and Continuum both use embedded Derby databases for storing project and artifact information. Most companies have a standard tool set or infrastructure for the applications that they use. One good example of this is the database server. They may require all databases used within the applications in the company to be MySQL or PostgreSQL, or some other database server.

To use a different database for these applications, all you have to do is to change a few configuration options.

 If you are deploying the WAR to your own application server instead of using the standalone bundle, refer to its documentation for how to configure database drivers and JNDI connections.

First, you need to copy the database driver to the `lib/` directory of the installation. Make sure that the driver can be accessed by the application. Next, you need to update the JNDI resources for the database configuration in `conf/jetty.xml`. In the following example, we are assuming that we are using a MySQL database instead:

```
<New id="archiva" class="org.mortbay.jetty.plus.naming.Resource">
  <Arg>jdbc/archiva</Arg>
  <Arg>
    <New class="org.apache.commons.dbcp.BasicDataSource">
```

```
            <Set name="driverClassName">com.mysql.jdbc.Driver</Set>
            <Set name="url">jdbc:mysql://[database_host]:3306/
                                                    [db_name]</Set>
            <Set name="username">username</Set>
            <Set name="password">passw0rd</Set>
        </New>
      </Arg>
    </New>
```

Make sure that the database already exists and the user account you've specified has the correct permissions to read and write to the database.

You can also follow the same steps above for changing the users database.

Database backup and migrating between versions

As new features, additional fixes and new releases come, the need to upgrade an application to a more recent version becomes imminent. This holds true for both Archiva and Continuum. Looking at the history of these two projects, they both have come a long way already. A lot has changed since their very first releases.

One of the usual problems when upgrading an application is data migration. Since both applications have their own databases, they also face the same problem when upgrading.

Migrating Continuum

Project information, build configuration, build results, release results — these are just a few of the things that Continuum keeps track of in its database. Since we're dealing with history, we can't just wipe out the database and start anew.

It's a good thing that Continuum includes a database migration tool for each release. For our demonstration, we will assume that we are upgrading from 1.2.3 to 1.3.3 and we'll only be migrating just the Continuum database. The first thing that we need to do is get the database migration tool for the respective releases. Just a caution though, the 1.2.3 database migration tool has some problems so a 1.2.3.1 version of the tool was released to address this. We can get these tools at:

```
http://repo1.maven.org/maven2/org/apache/continuum/data-management-
cli/1.2.3.1/data-management-cli-1.2.3.1-app.jar
```

```
http://repo1.maven.org/maven2/org/apache/continuum/data-management-
cli/1.3.3/data-management-cli-1.3.3-app.jar
```

To perform the actual migration, you need to stop the running Continuum 1.2.3 instance first. Then to back up the old database, execute the following from the command line:

```
java -Xmx512m -jar [PATH/TO/1.2.3.1_DB_MIGRATION_TOOL]/data-management-
cli-1.2.3.1-app.jar -buildsJdbcUrl jdbc:derby:[PATH/TO/1.2.3_DB]/data/
databases/continuum -mode EXPORT -directory backups
```

Once the backup action has finished executing and the old database has been backed up, unpack the 1.3.3 binaries and start the instance. This is necessary in order to create the new database schema. Once it has successfully started, shut it down.

Now from the command line, execute the following:

```
java -Xmx512m -jar [PATH/TO/1.3.3_DB_MIGRATION_TOOL]/data-management-
cli-1.3.1-app.jar -buildsJdbcUrl jdbc:derby:[PATH/TO/1.3.3_DB]/data/
databases/continuum -mode IMPORT -directory [PATH/TO/1.2.3_BACKUP]/
backups
```

Manually update the next sequence of the IDs of the tables in the database. Set the next sequence to the highest ID value incremented by one. After doing this, start up the 1.3.3 Continuum instance.

You can use Liquibase (http://www.liquibase.org/) to verify if the database schema is correct after migration.

If you want to retain your old Continuum configuration, just copy the continuum.xml file (in conf/) of the old Continuum instance to the new one.

Migrating Archiva

It is fairly easy to upgrade Archiva compared to Continuum, since the repositories are in the local filesystem and the database and index can be easily re-created.

We will be upgrading Archiva from 1.1.4 to 1.2.1 for this demonstration. Assuming that we're not overly concerned with re-creating the Archiva database and we just want to retain the existing users, upgrading is as simple as follows.

Since the index format changed in Archiva 1.2 and 1.2.1, you need to re-create the index when upgrading from an older version of Archiva.

First, stop the running 1.1.4 instance then unpack the 1.2.1 binaries. Copy the users database from the 1.1.4 instance (found in `data/databases/` if using the default configuration) to the `data/databases/` directory of the unpacked 1.2.1 binaries. You also need to copy the Archiva configuration file so you won't have to configure everything again. Just overwrite the `archiva.xml` file in the `conf/` directory of the new installation with the one from the old Archiva instance.

Now, delete the index of each repository configured in the `archiva.xml` file. The default location is in the `[REPOSITORY_ROOT_DIRECTORY]/.index`, otherwise check the `<indexDir>` of the repository set in the configuration file.

Start the 1.2.1 instance. Execute the repository scanning for each repository and then the database scanning afterwards. Both are optional though since these tasks are scheduled. Do this only if you want your index and database to be immediately populated.

In cases when you want to retain the Archiva database, you need to execute the command below for each repository. Archiva only processes artifacts for indexing and database updates if and only if the artifact has been modified after the last repository scan. As the database is already populated, Archiva will no longer process the artifacts in the repositories when the scanning executes and our index will not be created.

```
repositories$ find [REPOSITORY_DIRECTORY_NAME] | xargs touch
```

Index

E

EJBs 355
ejbs/ directory 355
EMMA
  about 118, 119, 147
  blockRate 155
  classRate 155
  lineRate 155
  methodRate 155
Enterprise Java Beans. *See* EJBs
example application
  developer's site, constructing 144-147
  developer's site, default property value
    addition 146
  developer's site, deploying 146
  developer's site, protocols used 146
  developer's site, site:run goal 145
  developer's site, site:stage goal 145
  reviewing 144
Exec plugin
  adding, to build life cycle 214, 215
  goals, exec:exec 213
  goals, exec:java 213, 214
  purpose 213
  running 215, 216
expected models, confirming
  effective-pom goal 405
  Help plugin 405

F

Find Artifact 59
FindBugs
  about 174
  configuring 176
fork mode
  about 119
  configuring 111
functional testing
  about 124
  ways 109

G

generatePom parameter 66
getItems() method 387
GMaven project 212
goals 17
groupId:artifactId syntax 412

H

hard coding
  about 241, 242
  best practices 241

I

installations 280, 281
installing
  Archiva 40
  Continuum 257
  Maven 7, 8
integration testing
  about 109
  altering, coverage measurement 141
  altering, profiles used 138-140
  altering, TestNG parameters used 140
  running, naming patterns used 125-127
  separate module, using 134-137
integration testing, running
  application, deploying to container 131, 132
  naming patterns used 125-127
  Selenium RC server, operating 130
  Selenium tests, running 128, 129
  test grouping simplification, TestNG used
    133

J

Javadoc 147, 162
Java Service Wrapper. *See* JSW
JAXB 209
jetty
  run command:about 132

best practices 222-225
repository groups
 configuring 328, 329
 configuring, in settings.xml 331
 managed repositories, adding 330
 scenario 327
 use 327
 using 329, 332
repository health, report
 about 342
 monitoring 342
repository level, RSS feeds
 about 333
 account, creating 334, 335
 subscriptions 335
repository manager
 about 37, 38
 Archiva, installing 40
repository statistics, report
 configuring 340, 341
 using 340
reproducibility
 about 249
 Enforcer plugin, ensuring 250-252
 ensuring 249
 hindering, sources 249
 prerequisite 249
retro-translation
 using 244
role based access control. *See* **Redback**
roles
 managing 324-327
roles, types
 global repository manager 323
 global repository observer 324
 guest 324
 registered user 324
 repository manager 324
 repository observer 324
 system administrator 323
 user administrator 323
RPC 311
RSS feeds
 artifact level 336
 repository level 333
 types 332
 use 332

S

sample project
 about 67, 68
 application, assembling 93
 basic report, creating 80
 data store (flat files) 153
 documentation module, adding 85
 maven-importer 68
 model 68
 multi-module build, setting up 68
 non-code modules, preparing for 82
 Organization POM, creating 76
 store-api 68
 store-file 68
 webapp 68
Scanning Cron field 44
schedule
 about 270
 setting 272
Script Maven Plugin 213
security configuration
 for Archiva multiple teams 376, 377
 for Continuum multiple teams 372-376
 LDAP, configuring in Archiva 379, 381
 LDAP, configuring in Continuum 379, 381
 other enterprise tools, interfacing with 382
 Redback 370
 Redback configuration, adding 378, 379
settings.xml, Maven configuration file
 <mirrorOf> tag 52
 <mirrors> section 52
 <url> 52
 asterisk (*) value 52
 external:* 52
 internal 52
sever password, encrypting
 enhancements 409
 steps 410
Shade plugin
 adding, to file 200
 createDependencyReducedPom
     configuration option , enabling 202
 dependencies 199, 200
 example 197, 198
 purpose 196
 relocations feature, using 201

Thank you for buying
Apache Maven 2
Effective Implementation

Packt Open Source Project Royalties

When we sell a book written on an Open Source project, we pay a royalty directly to that project. Therefore by purchasing Apache Maven 2 Effective Implementation, Packt will have given some of the money received to the Apache Maven project.

In the long term, we see ourselves and you—customers and readers of our books—as part of the Open Source ecosystem, providing sustainable revenue for the projects we publish on. Our aim at Packt is to establish publishing royalties as an essential part of the service and support a business model that sustains Open Source.

If you're working with an Open Source project that you would like us to publish on, and subsequently pay royalties to, please get in touch with us.

Writing for Packt

We welcome all inquiries from people who are interested in authoring. Book proposals should be sent to author@packtpub.com. If your book idea is still at an early stage and you would like to discuss it first before writing a formal book proposal, contact us; one of our commissioning editors will get in touch with you.

We're not just looking for published authors; if you have strong technical skills but no writing experience, our experienced editors can help you develop a writing career, or simply get some additional reward for your expertise.

About Packt Publishing

Packt, pronounced 'packed', published its first book "Mastering phpMyAdmin for Effective MySQL Management" in April 2004 and subsequently continued to specialize in publishing highly focused books on specific technologies and solutions.

Our books and publications share the experiences of your fellow IT professionals in adapting and customizing today's systems, applications, and frameworks. Our solution-based books give you the knowledge and power to customize the software and technologies you're using to get the job done. Packt books are more specific and less general than the IT books you have seen in the past. Our unique business model allows us to bring you more focused information, giving you more of what you need to know, and less of what you don't.

Packt is a modern, yet unique publishing company, which focuses on producing quality, cutting-edge books for communities of developers, administrators, and newbies alike. For more information, please visit our website: www.PacktPub.com.

Apache JMeter

ISBN: 978-1-847192-95-0   Paperback: 140 pages

A practical beginner's guide to automated testing and performance measurement for your websites

1. Test your website and measure its performance

2. Master the JMeter environment and learn all its features

3. Build test plan for measuring the performance

4. Step-by-step instructions and careful explanations

Quickstart Apache Axis2

ISBN: 978-1-847192-86-8   Paperback: 180 pages

A practical guide to creating quality web services

1. Complete practical guide to Apache Axis 2

2. Using Apache Axis2 to create secure, reliable web services quickly

3. Write Axis2 modules to enhance web services' security, reliability, robustness and transaction support

4. This book covers Apache Axis2 version 1.3e

Please check **www.PacktPub.com** for information on our titles

Lightning Source UK Ltd.
Milton Keynes UK
17 December 2010

164467UK00001B/108/P